LOVE ROMA

2

MINOR TOYODA

TRANSLATED AND ADAPTED BY DAVID AND ERIKO WALSH
LETTERED BY FOLTZ DESIGN

BALLANTINE BOOKS • NEW YORK

Love Roma Volume 2 is a work of fiction. Names characters, places, and incidents are the products of the author's imagination or are used fictitiously. Any resemblance to actual events locales or persons, living or dead, is entirely coincidental.

2006 Del Rey Books Trade Paperback Edition

Published in the United States by Del Rey Books, an imprint of The Random House Publishing Group, a division of Random House, Inc,. New York.

First published in Japan in 2004 by Kodansha Ltd., Tokyo

Del Rey is a registered trademark and the Del Rey colophon is a trademark of Random House, Inc.

Library of Congress Control Number: 2005926810

ISBN 0-345-48263-8

Printed in the United States of America

www.delreymanga.com

1 2 3 4 5 6 7 8 9

Translated and adapted by David and Eriko Walsh
Lettered by Foltz Design

First Edition: February 2006

TABLE OF CONTENTS

Honorifics Explained

Throughout the Del Rey Manga books, you will find Japanese honorifics left intact in the translations. For those not familiar with how the Japanese use honorifics, and, more important, how they differ from American honorifics, we present this brief overview.

Politeness has always been a critical facet of Japanese culture. Ever since the feudal era, when Japan was a highly stratified society, use of honorifics–which can be defined as polite speech that indicates relationship or status–has played an essential role in the Japanese language. When addressing someone in Japanese, an honorific usually takes the form of a suffix attached to one's name (e.g. "Asuna-san"), as a title at the end of one's name, or in place of the name itself (e.g. "Negi-sensei" or simply "Sensei!").

Honorifics can be expressions of respect or endearment. In the context of manga and anime, honorifics give insight into the nature of the relationship between characters. Many translations into English leave out these important honorifics, and therefore distort the feel of the original Japanese. Because Japanese honorifics contain nuances that English honorifics lack, it is our policy at Del Rey not to translate them. Here, instead, is a guide to some of the honorifics you may encounter in Del Rey Manga.

-san: This is the most common honorific and is equivalent to Mr., Miss, Ms., Mrs., etc. It is the all-purpose honorific and can be used in any situation where politeness is required.

-sama: This is one level higher than -san. It is used to confer great respect.

-dono: This comes from the word tono, which means lord. It is an even higher level than -sama and confers utmost respect.

-kun: This suffix is used at the end of boys' names to express familiarity or endearment. It is also sometimes used by men among friends, or when addressing someone younger or of a lower station.

-chan: This is used to express endearment, mostly toward girls. It is also used for little boys, pets, and between lovers. It gives a sense of childish cuteness.

Bozu: This is an informal way to refer to a boy, similar to the English terms "kid" or "squirt."

Sempai/ Senpai: This title suggests that the addressee is one's senior in a group or organization. It is most often used in a school setting, where underclassmen refer to their upperclassmen as sempai. It can also be used in the workplace, such as when a newer employee addresses an employee who has seniority in the company.

Kohai: This is the opposite of -sempai, and is used toward underclassmen in school or newcomers in the workplace. It connotes that the addressee is of a lower station.

Sensei: Literally meaning "one who has come before," this title is used for teachers, doctors, or masters of any profession or art.

-[blank]: This is usually forgotten on these lists, but it's perhaps the most significant difference between Japanese and English. The lack of honorific means that the speaker has permission to address the person in a very intimate way. Usually, only family, spouses, or very close friends have this kind of license. Known as *yobisute,* it can be gratifying when someone who has earned the intimacy starts to call one by one's name without an honorific. But when that intimacy hasn't been earned, it can also be insulting.

A Note from the Author

The artist,
Minoru Toyoda

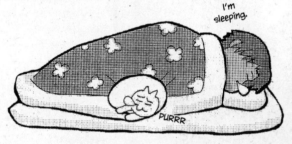

This is already volume 2.
I'm very happy about that.

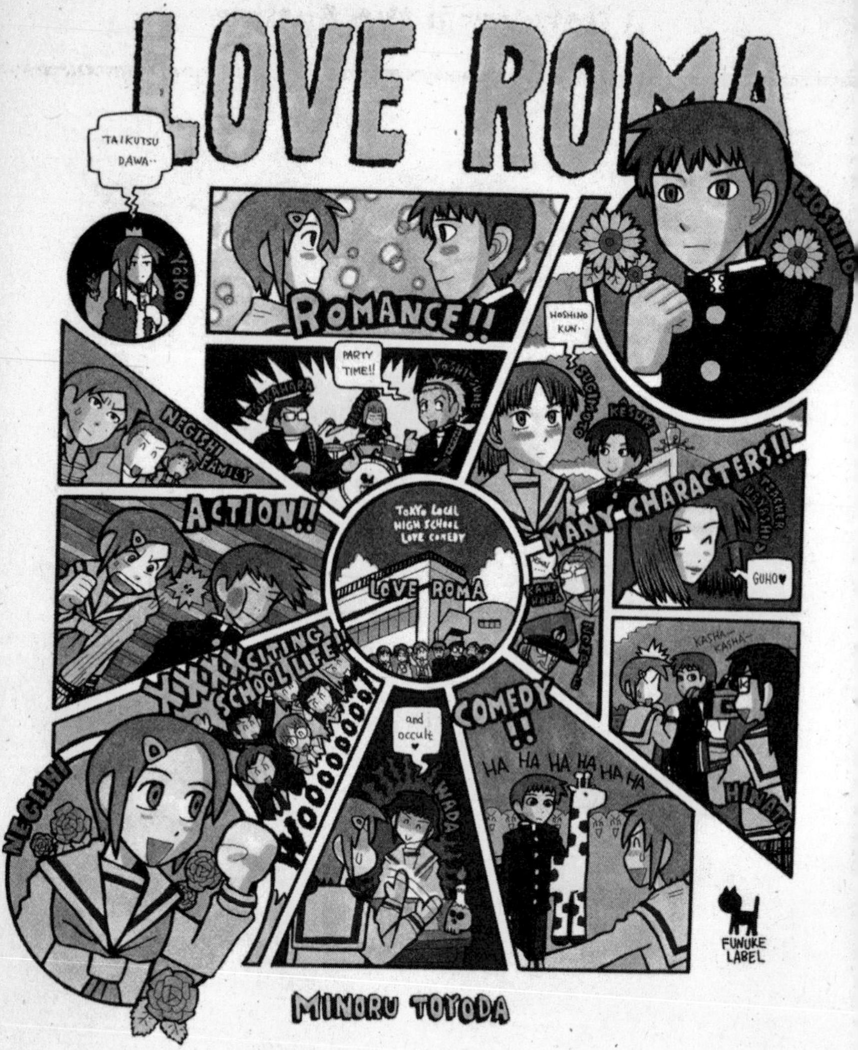
LOVE ROMA
TAIKUTSU DAWA..
YOKO
HOSHINO
ROMANCE!!
HOSHINO KUN..
PARTY TIME!!
NEGISHI FAMILY
SUGIMOTO
KESUKE
MANY CHARACTERS!!
TEACHER HAYASHI
GUHO♥
ACTION!!
TOKYO LOCAL HIGH SCHOOL LOVE COMEDY
LOVE ROMA
KASHA KASHA
XXXXCITING SCHOOL LIFE!!
COMEDY!!
and occult ♥
WADA
HA HA HA HA HA HA
HINATA
NEGISHI
FUNUKE LABEL
MINORU TOYODA

CONTENTS

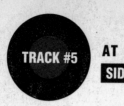

TRACK #5

AT OUR OWN PACE

SIDE A We Are Boys

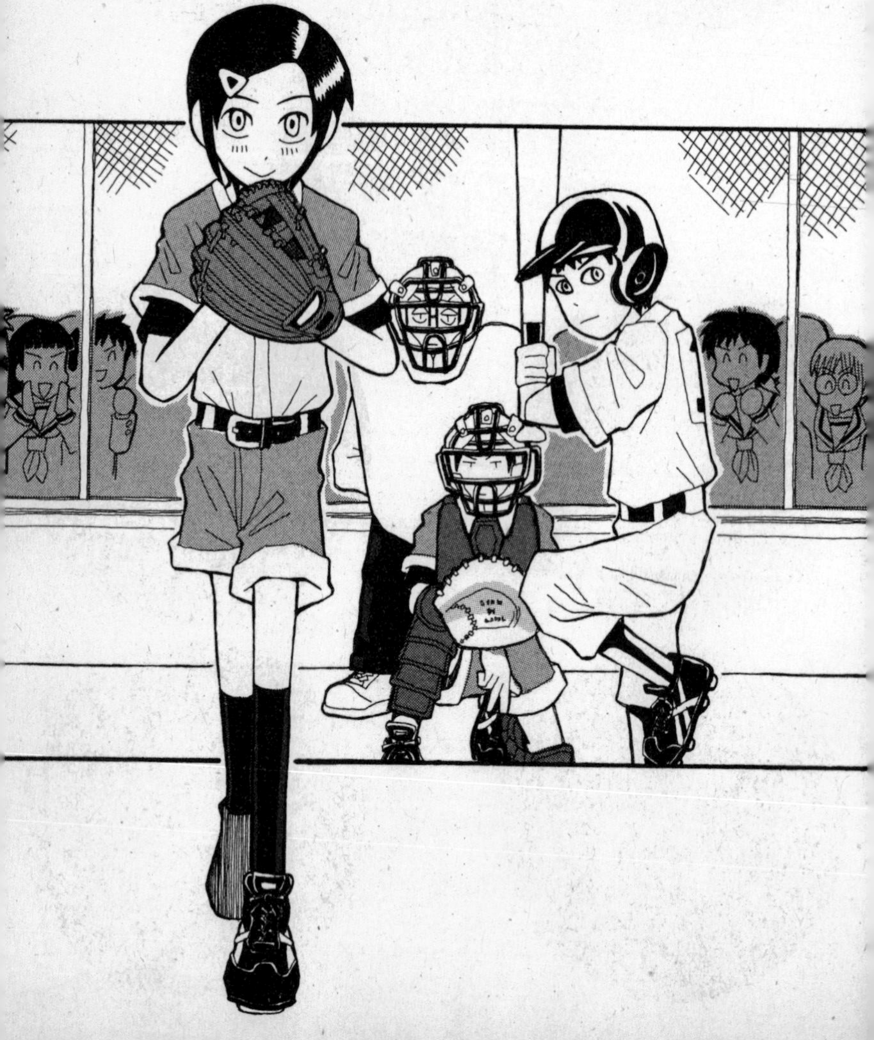

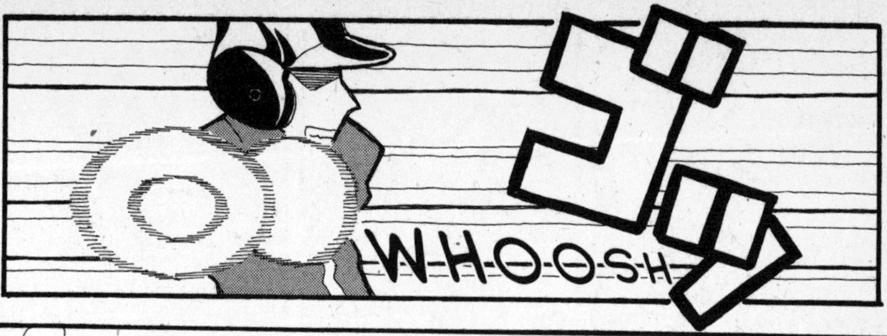
WHOOSH

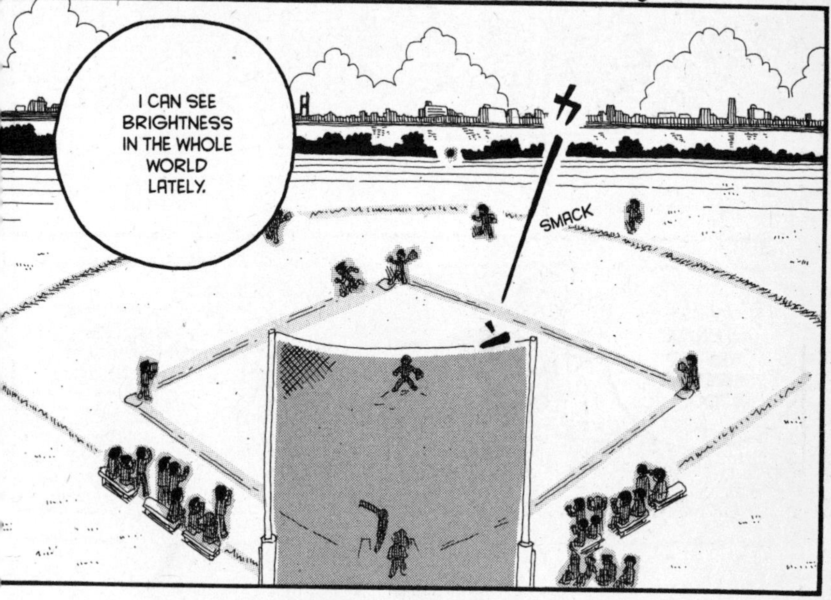
I CAN SEE BRIGHTNESS IN THE WHOLE WORLD LATELY.
SMACK

SIDE A **We Are Boys**

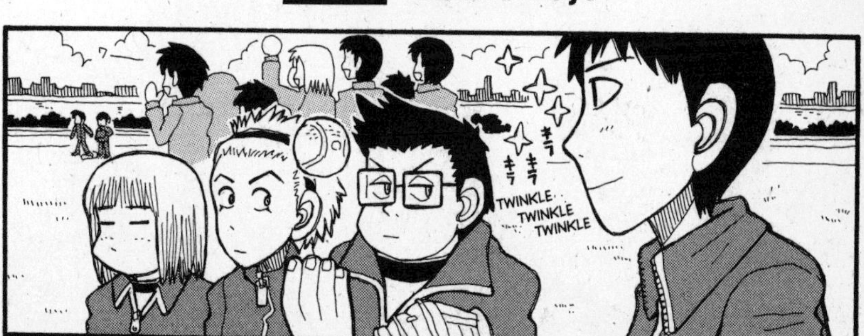
キラ
キラ
キラ
TWINKLE
TWINKLE
TWINKLE

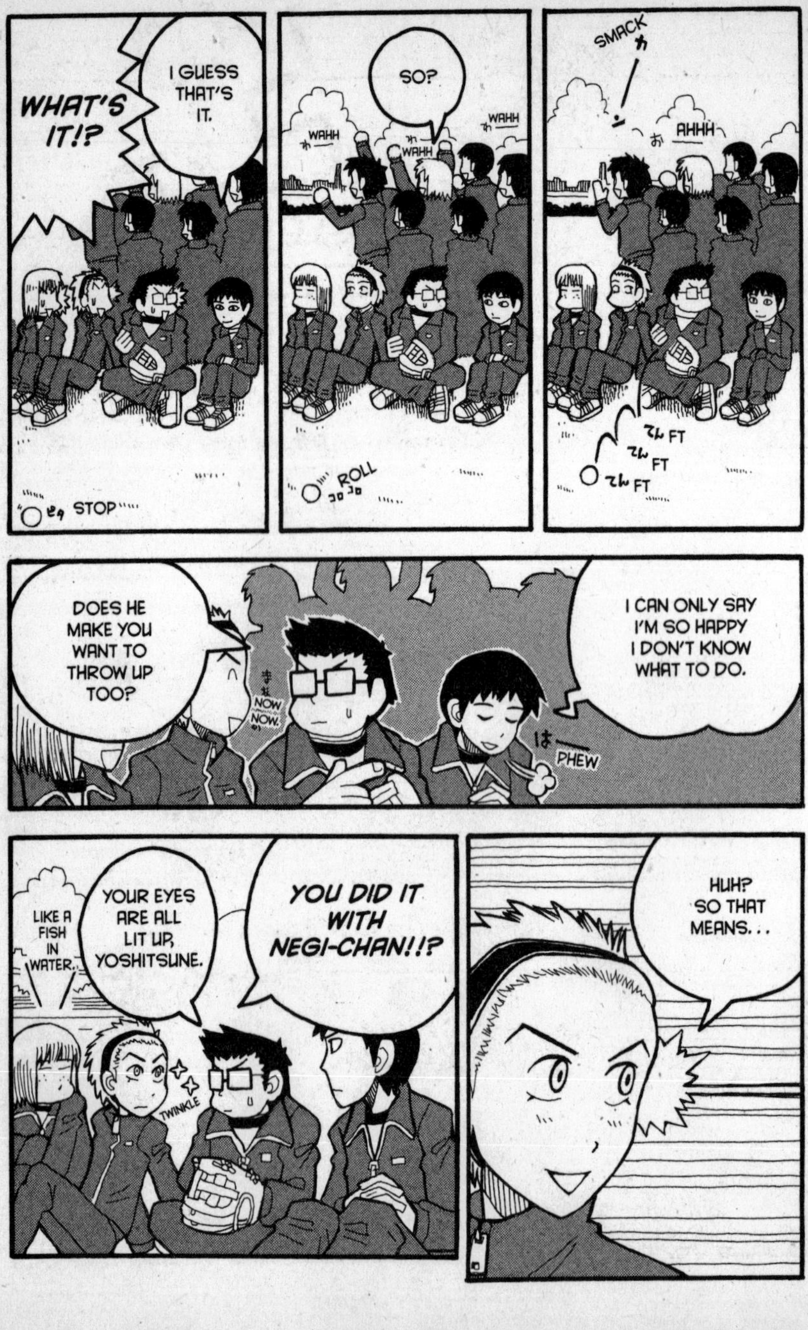
SMACK
AHHH
FT
FT
FT
SO?
WAHH
WAHH
WAHH
ROLL
I GUESS THAT'S IT.
WHAT'S IT!?
STOP
I CAN ONLY SAY I'M SO HAPPY I DON'T KNOW WHAT TO DO.
PHEW
NOW NOW.
DOES HE MAKE YOU WANT TO THROW UP TOO?
HUH? SO THAT MEANS. . .
YOU DID IT WITH NEGI-CHAN!!?
YOUR EYES ARE ALL LIT UP, YOSHITSUNE.
LIKE A FISH IN WATER.
TWINKLE

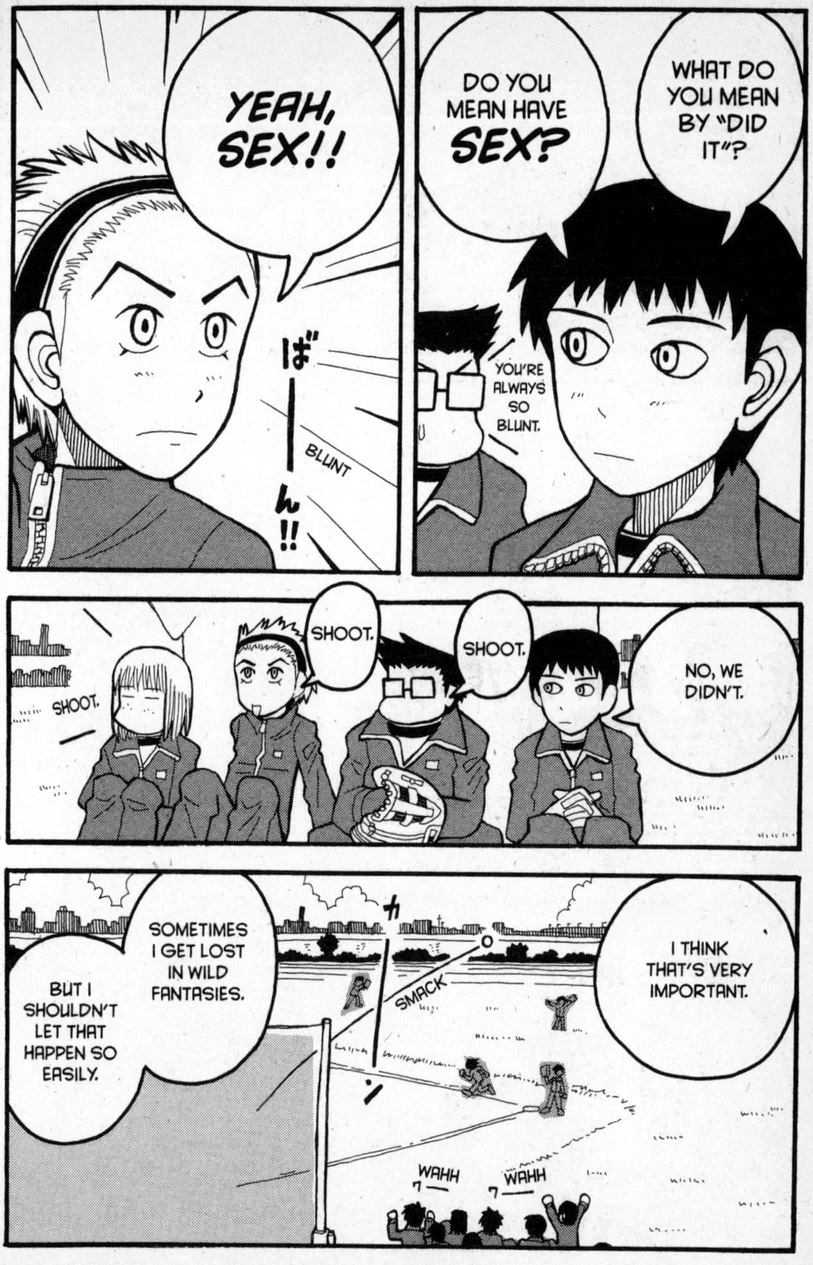
WHAT DO YOU MEAN BY "DID IT"?
DO YOU MEAN HAVE SEX?
YOU'RE ALWAYS SO BLUNT.
YEAH, SEX!!
ばーーん!!
BLUNT
NO, WE DIDN'T.
SHOOT.
SHOOT.
SHOOT.
I THINK THAT'S VERY IMPORTANT.
カ
SMACK
SOMETIMES I GET LOST IN WILD FANTASIES.
BUT I SHOULDN'T LET THAT HAPPEN SO EASILY.
WAHH
WAHH

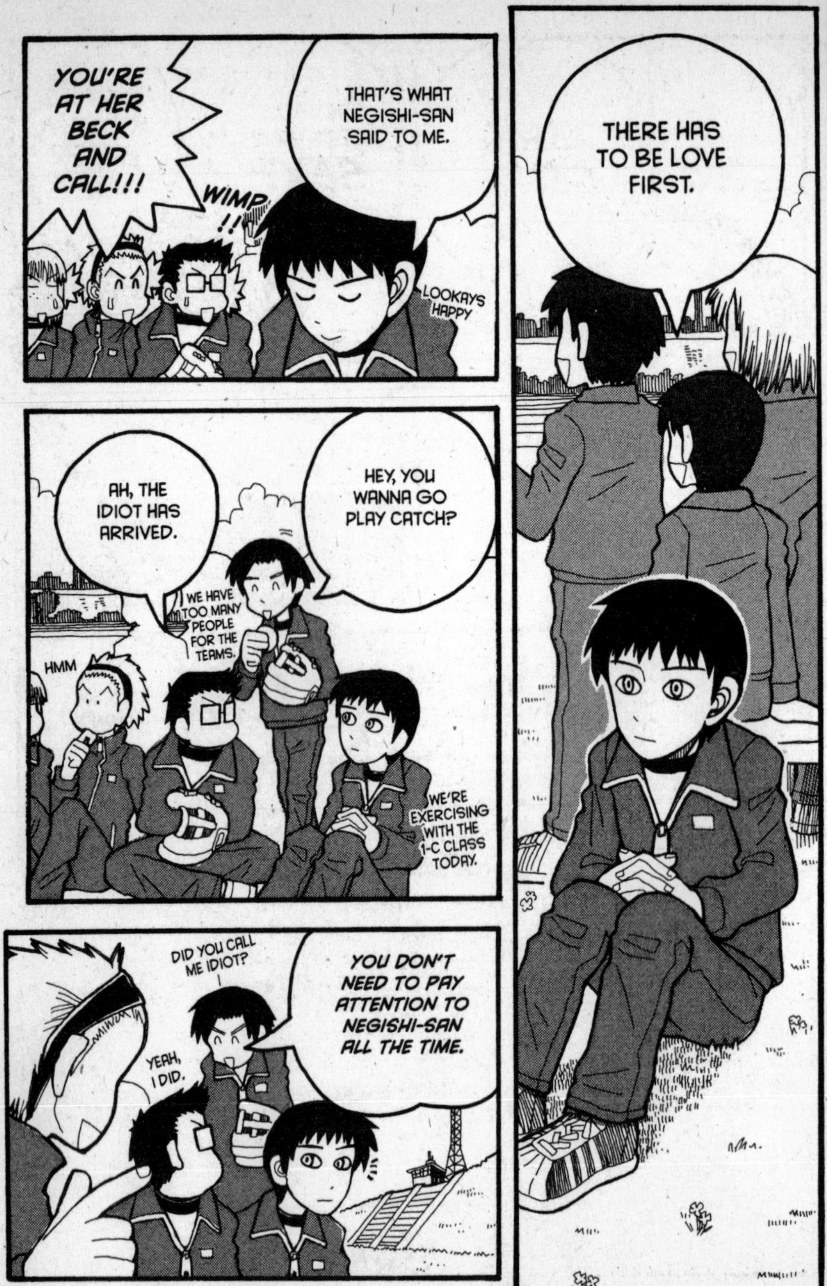
THERE HAS TO BE LOVE FIRST.
THAT'S WHAT NEGISHI-SAN SAID TO ME.
LOOKAYS HAPPY
WIMP!!
YOU'RE AT HER BECK AND CALL!!!
HEY, YOU WANNA GO PLAY CATCH?
AH, THE IDIOT HAS ARRIVED.
WE HAVE TOO MANY PEOPLE FOR THE TEAMS.
HMM
WE'RE EXERCISING WITH THE 1-C CLASS TODAY.
YOU DON'T NEED TO PAY ATTENTION TO NEGISHI-SAN ALL THE TIME.
DID YOU CALL ME IDIOT?
YEAH, I DID.

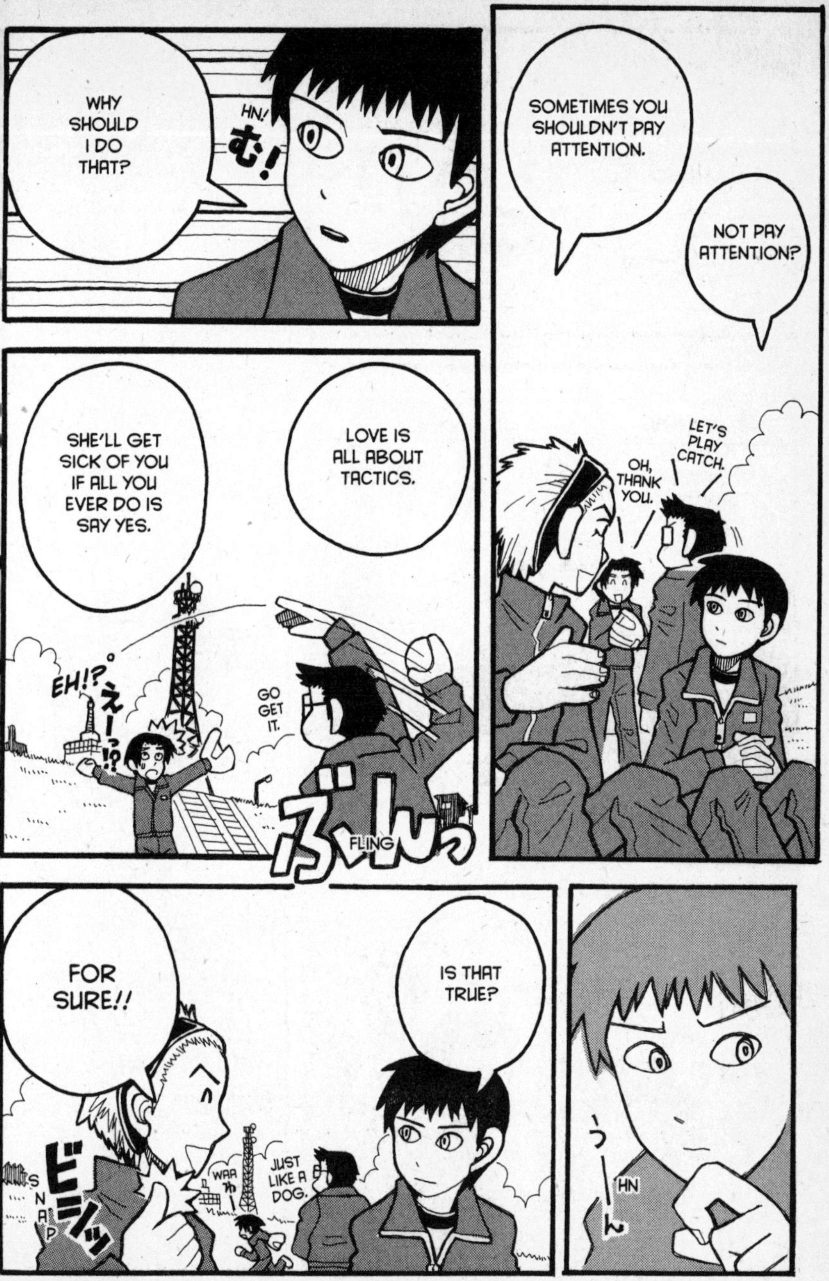

SOMETIMES YOU SHOULDN'T PAY ATTENTION.
NOT PAY ATTENTION?
LET'S PLAY CATCH.
OH, THANK YOU.
WHY SHOULD I DO THAT?
HN! む!
LOVE IS ALL ABOUT TACTICS.
SHE'LL GET SICK OF YOU IF ALL YOU EVER DO IS SAY YES.
ぶんっ FLING
GO GET IT.
EH!? えーっ!?
うーん HN
IS THAT TRUE?
FOR SURE!!
JUST LIKE A DOG.
WAA わー!
ビシッ SNAP

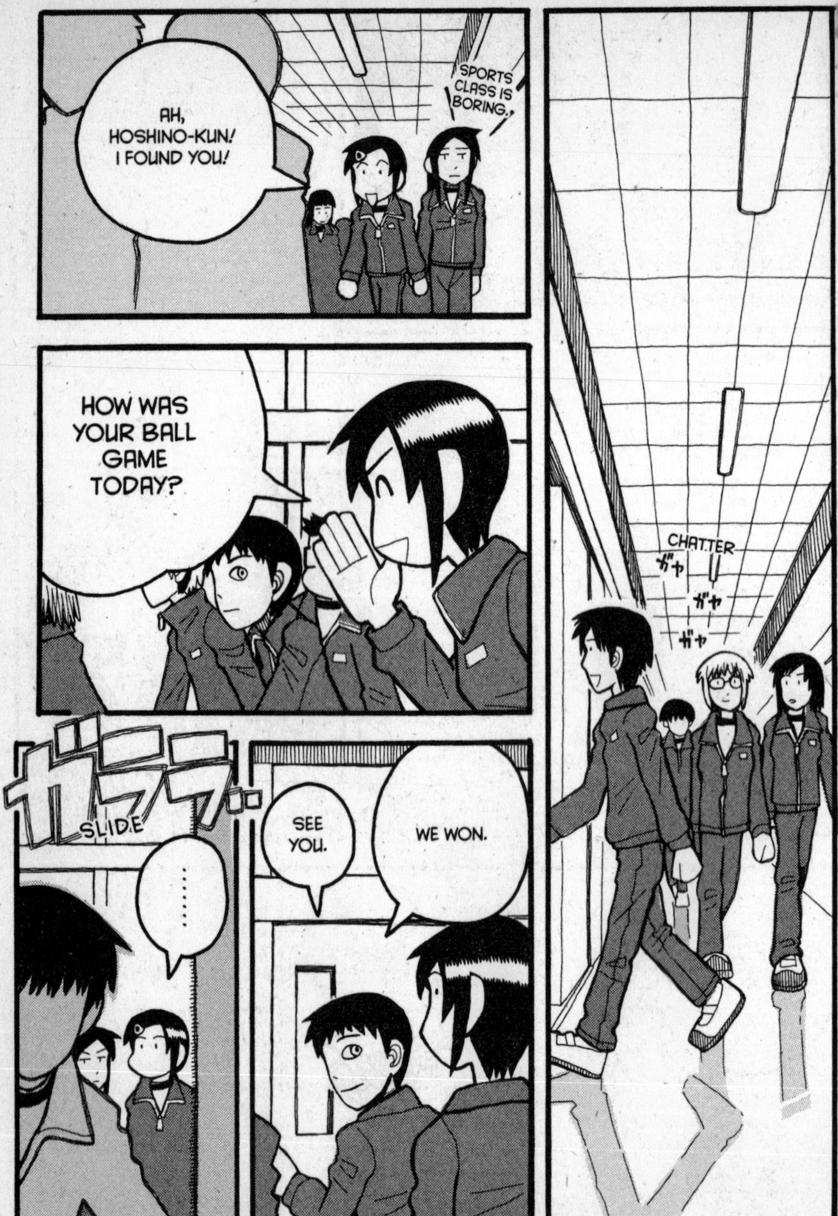
CHATTER
ガヤ
ガヤ
ガヤ
SPORTS CLASS IS BORING.
AH, HOSHINO-KUN! I FOUND YOU!
HOW WAS YOUR BALL GAME TODAY?
WE WON.
SEE YOU.
SLIDE
......

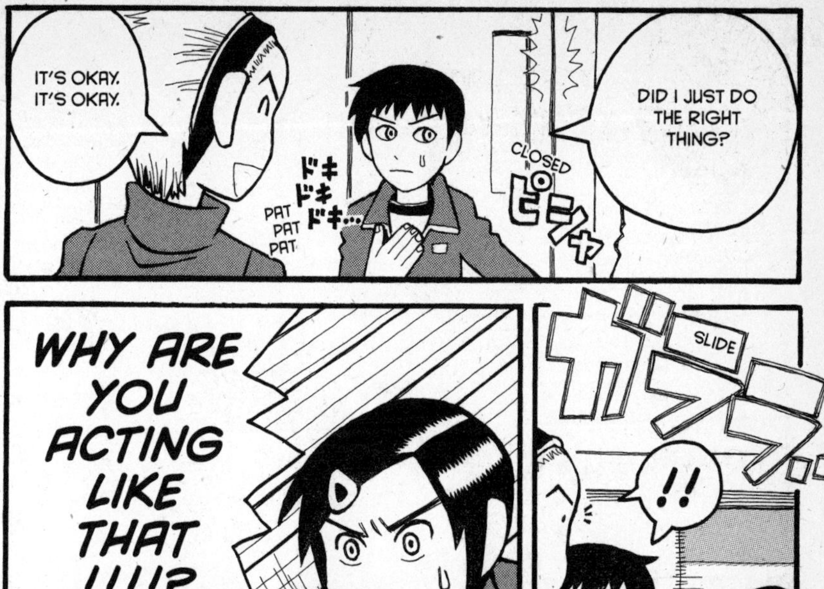
DID I JUST DO THE RIGHT THING?
CLOSED
ピシャ
ドキドキドキ…
PAT PAT PAT
IT'S OKAY. IT'S OKAY.
ガラ
SLIDE
!!
WHY ARE YOU ACTING LIKE THAT!!!!?
バキッ
SLAP

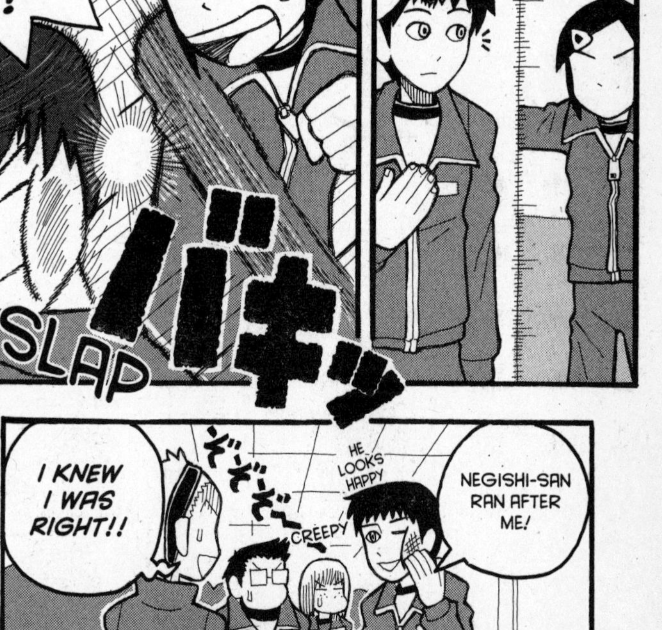
NEGISHI-SAN RAN AFTER ME!
HE LOOKS HAPPY
CREEPY
ぞぞぞ~
I KNEW I WAS RIGHT!!

SIDE A THE END.

TRACK #5
AT OUR OWN PACE
SIDE B You Are Girls

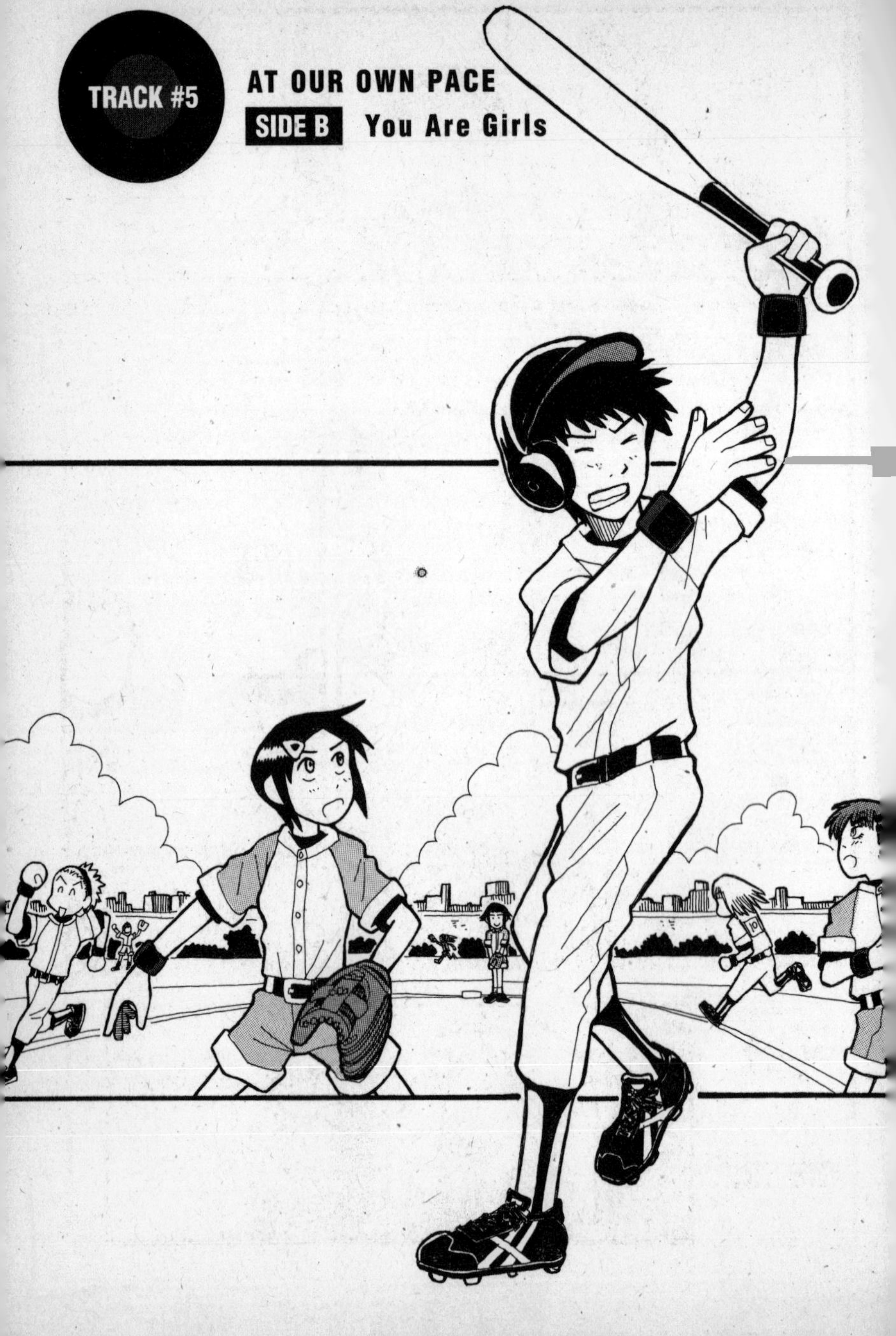

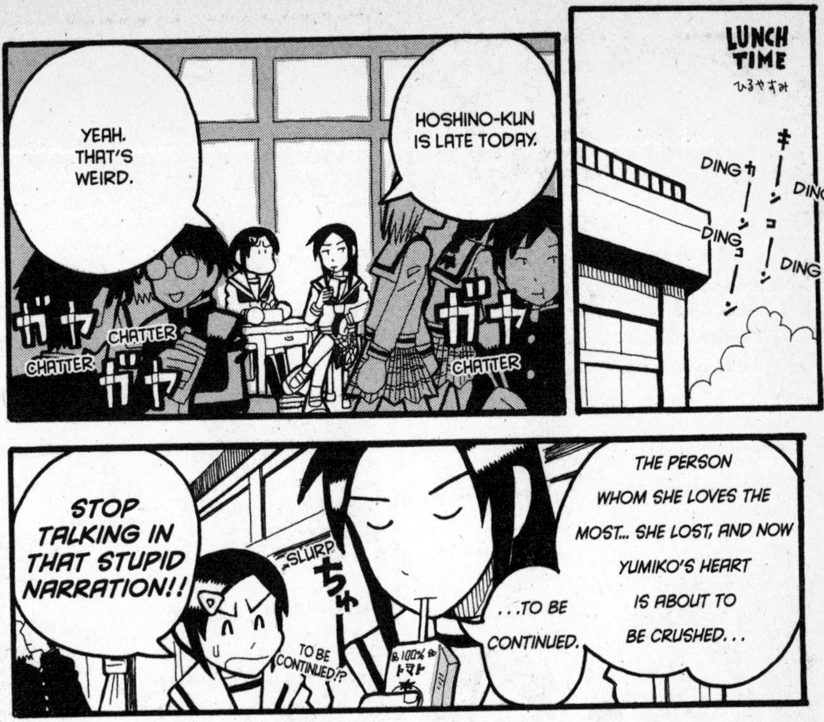
LUNCH TIME
ひるやすみ
キーンコーン
カーンコーン
DING DING DING DING
HOSHINO-KUN IS LATE TODAY.
YEAH. THAT'S WEIRD.
ガヤガヤ
CHATTER
ガヤガヤ
CHATTER
ガヤ
CHATTER
THE PERSON WHOM SHE LOVES THE MOST... SHE LOST, AND NOW YUMIKO'S HEART IS ABOUT TO BE CRUSHED...
...TO BE CONTINUED.
ちゅー
SLURP
TO BE CONTINUED!?
STOP TALKING IN THAT STUPID NARRATION!!

SIDE B You Are Girls

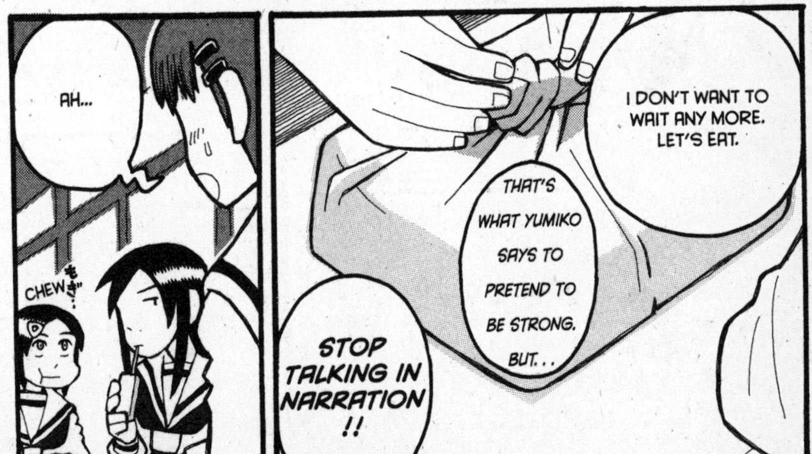
I DON'T WANT TO WAIT ANY MORE. LET'S EAT.
THAT'S WHAT YUMIKO SAYS TO PRETEND TO BE STRONG. BUT...
STOP TALKING IN NARRATION!!
AH...
もぎ
CHEW

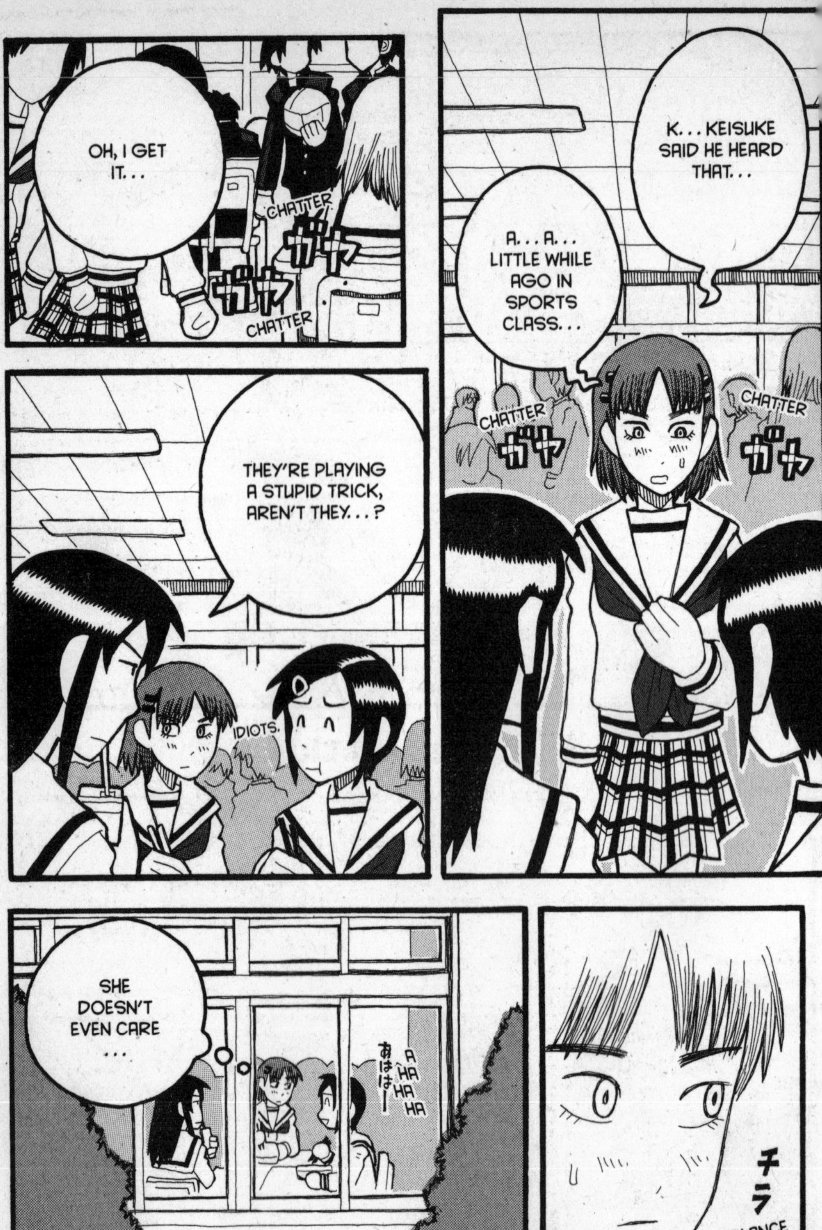
K. . . KEISUKE SAID HE HEARD THAT. . .
A. . . A. . . LITTLE WHILE AGO IN SPORTS CLASS. . .
CHATTER
ガヤ
CHATTER
ガヤ
OH, I GET IT. . .
CHATTER
ガヤ
ガヤ
CHATTER
THEY'RE PLAYING A STUPID TRICK, AREN'T THEY. . . ?
IDIOTS.
チラ
GLANCE
SHE DOESN'T EVEN CARE . . .
あはは－
A HA HA HA

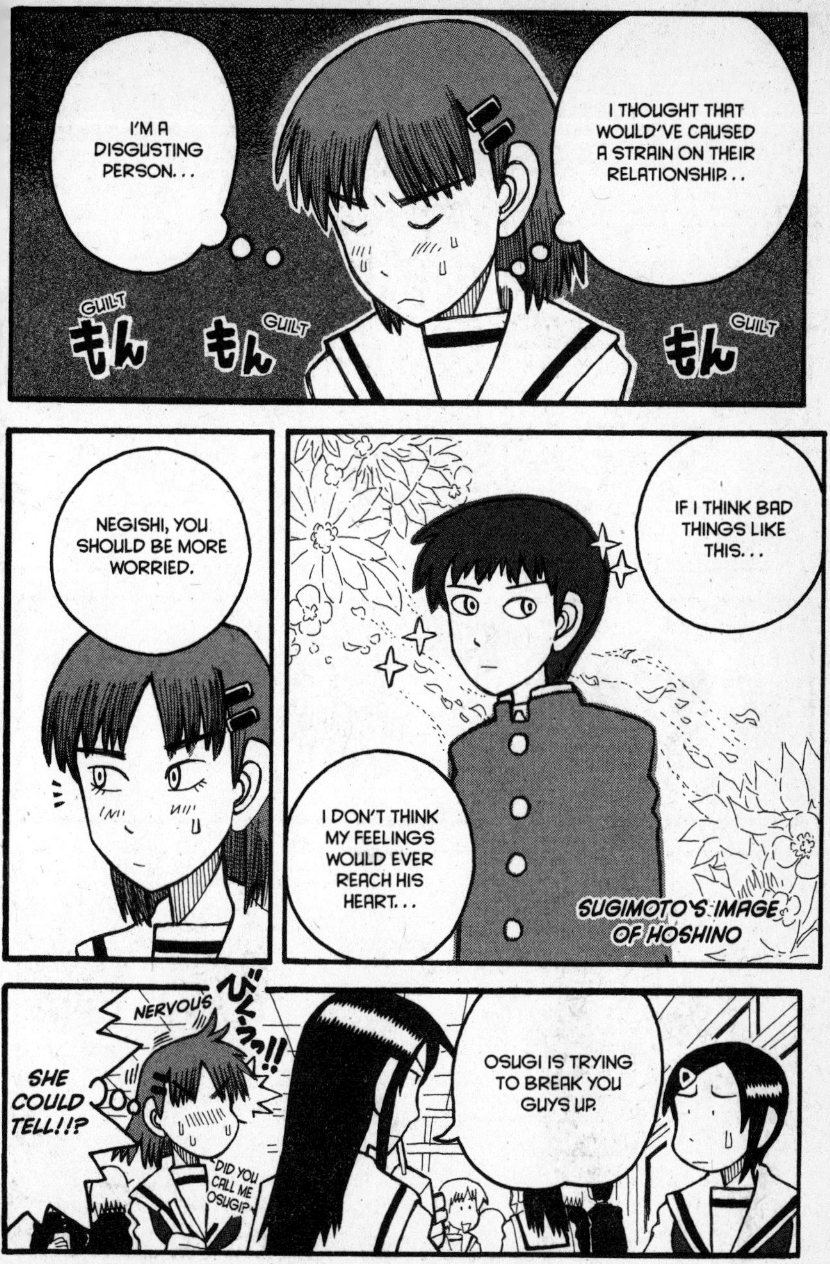
I THOUGHT THAT WOULD'VE CAUSED A STRAIN ON THEIR RELATIONSHIP...
I'M A DISGUSTING PERSON...
もん GUILT
もん GUILT
もん GUILT
IF I THINK BAD THINGS LIKE THIS...
I DON'T THINK MY FEELINGS WOULD EVER REACH HIS HEART...
SUGIMOTO'S IMAGE OF HOSHINO
NEGISHI, YOU SHOULD BE MORE WORRIED.
OSUGI IS TRYING TO BREAK YOU GUYS UP.
DID YOU CALL ME OSUGI!?
びくっっ!!
NERVOUS
SHE COULD TELL!!?

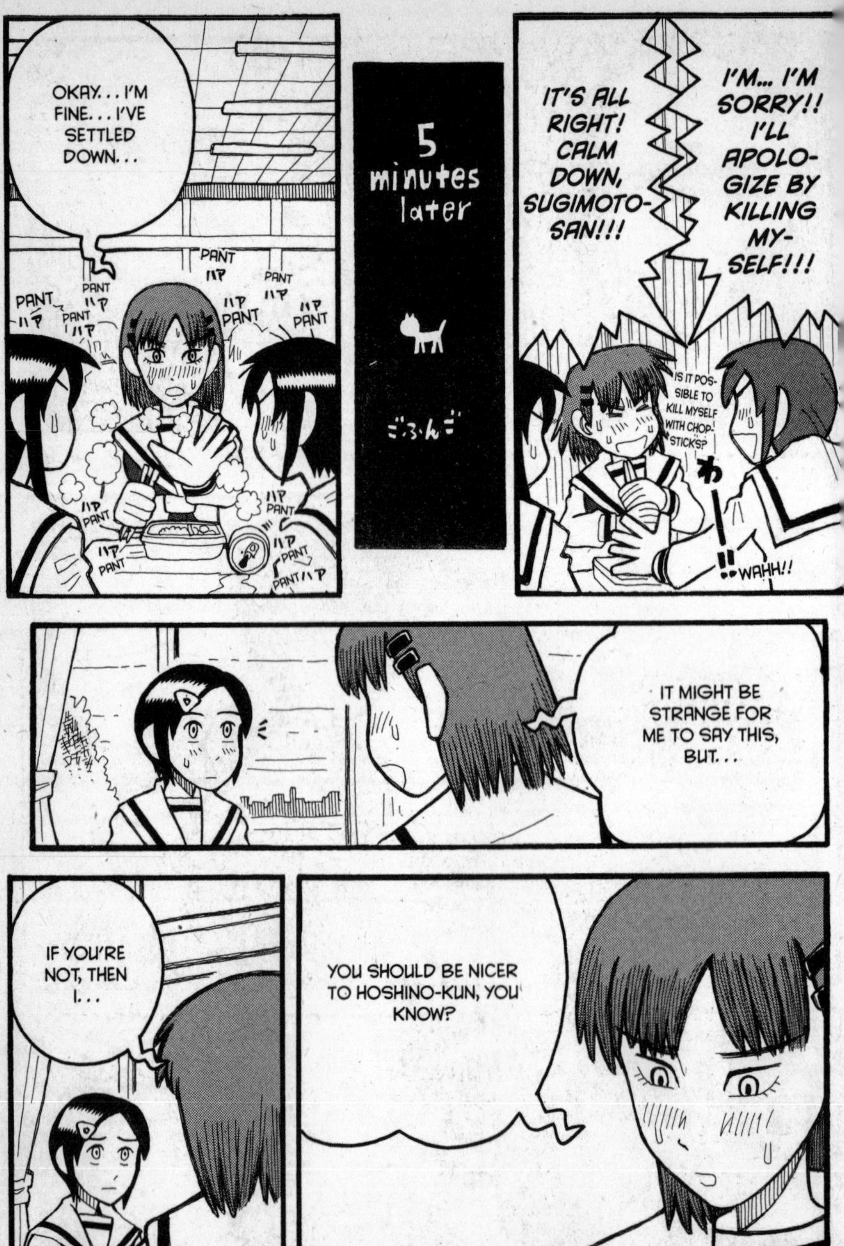
I'M... I'M SORRY!! I'LL APOLOGIZE BY KILLING MYSELF!!!
IT'S ALL RIGHT! CALM DOWN, SUGIMOTO-SAN!!!
IS IT POSSIBLE TO KILL MYSELF WITH CHOPSTICKS?
わー!!
WAHH!!
5 minutes later
OKAY... I'M FINE... I'VE SETTLED DOWN...
PANT ハア
IT MIGHT BE STRANGE FOR ME TO SAY THIS, BUT...
YOU SHOULD BE NICER TO HOSHINO-KUN, YOU KNOW?
IF YOU'RE NOT, THEN I...

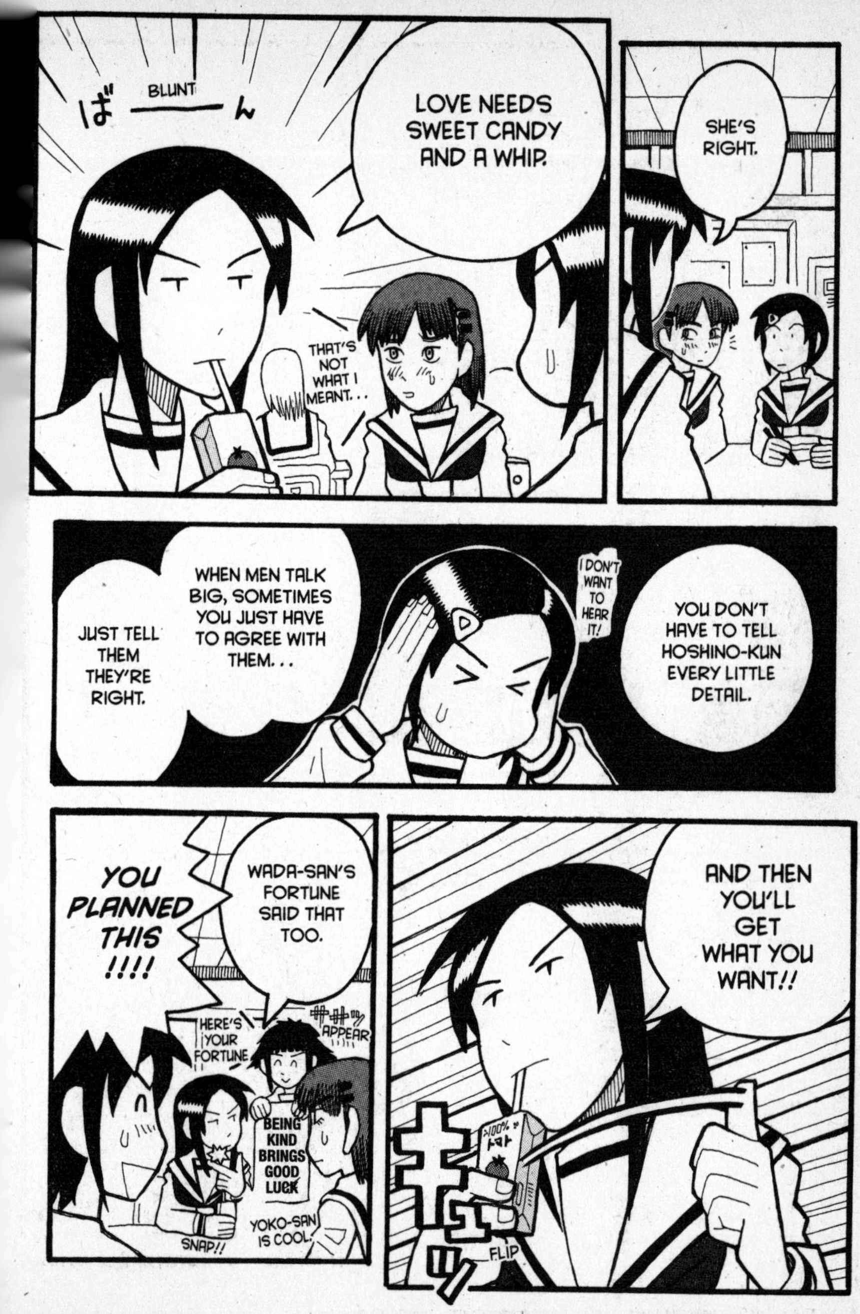
SHE'S RIGHT.
LOVE NEEDS SWEET CANDY AND A WHIP.
ばーーん
BLUNT
THAT'S NOT WHAT I MEANT. . .
YOU DON'T HAVE TO TELL HOSHINO-KUN EVERY LITTLE DETAIL.
I DON'T WANT TO HEAR IT!
WHEN MEN TALK BIG, SOMETIMES YOU JUST HAVE TO AGREE WITH THEM. . .
JUST TELL THEM THEY'RE RIGHT.
AND THEN YOU'LL GET WHAT YOU WANT!!
100% トマト
FLIP
APPEAR
WADA-SAN'S FORTUNE SAID THAT TOO.
HERE'S YOUR FORTUNE
YOU PLANNED THIS !!!!
BEING KIND BRINGS GOOD LUCK
YOKO-SAN IS COOL.
SNAP!!

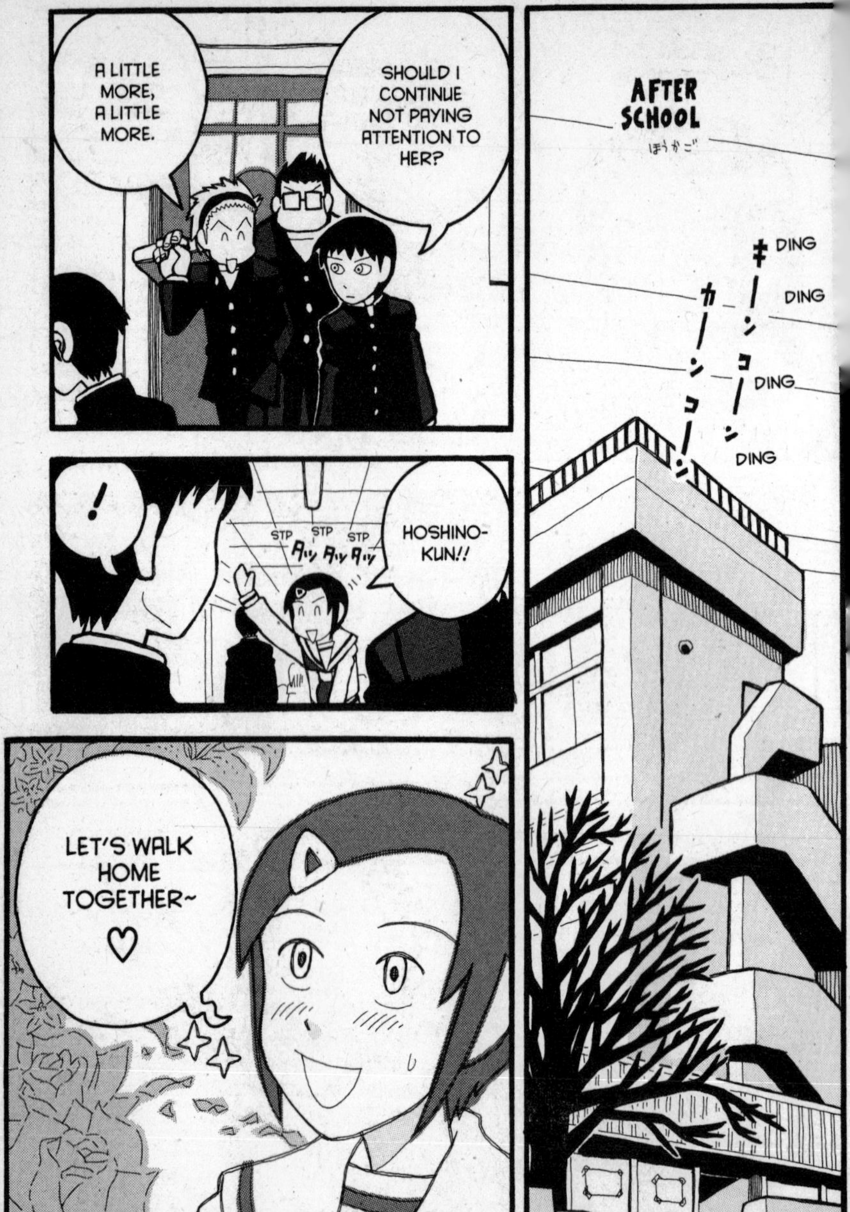
AFTER SCHOOL
ほうかご
キーンコーン
カーンコーン
DING
DING
DING
DING
SHOULD I CONTINUE NOT PAYING ATTENTION TO HER?
A LITTLE MORE, A LITTLE MORE.
HOSHINO-KUN!!
STP STP STP
タッ タッタッ
!
LET'S WALK HOME TOGETHER~ ♡

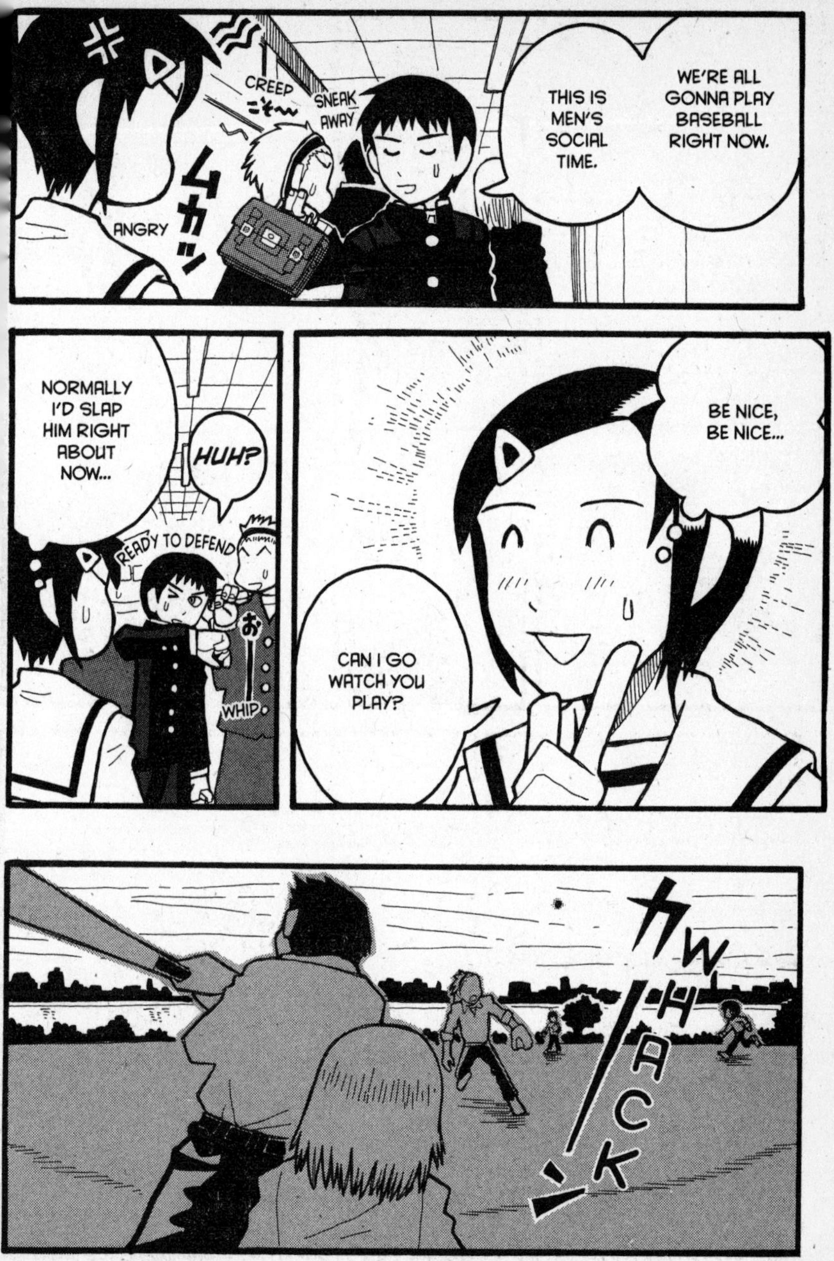
THIS IS MEN'S SOCIAL TIME.
WE'RE ALL GONNA PLAY BASEBALL RIGHT NOW.
SNEAK AWAY
CREEP
こそ～
ANGRY
ムカッ
BE NICE, BE NICE...
CAN I GO WATCH YOU PLAY?
HUH?
NORMALLY I'D SLAP HIM RIGHT ABOUT NOW...
READY TO DEFEND
お
WHIP
カ
WHACK

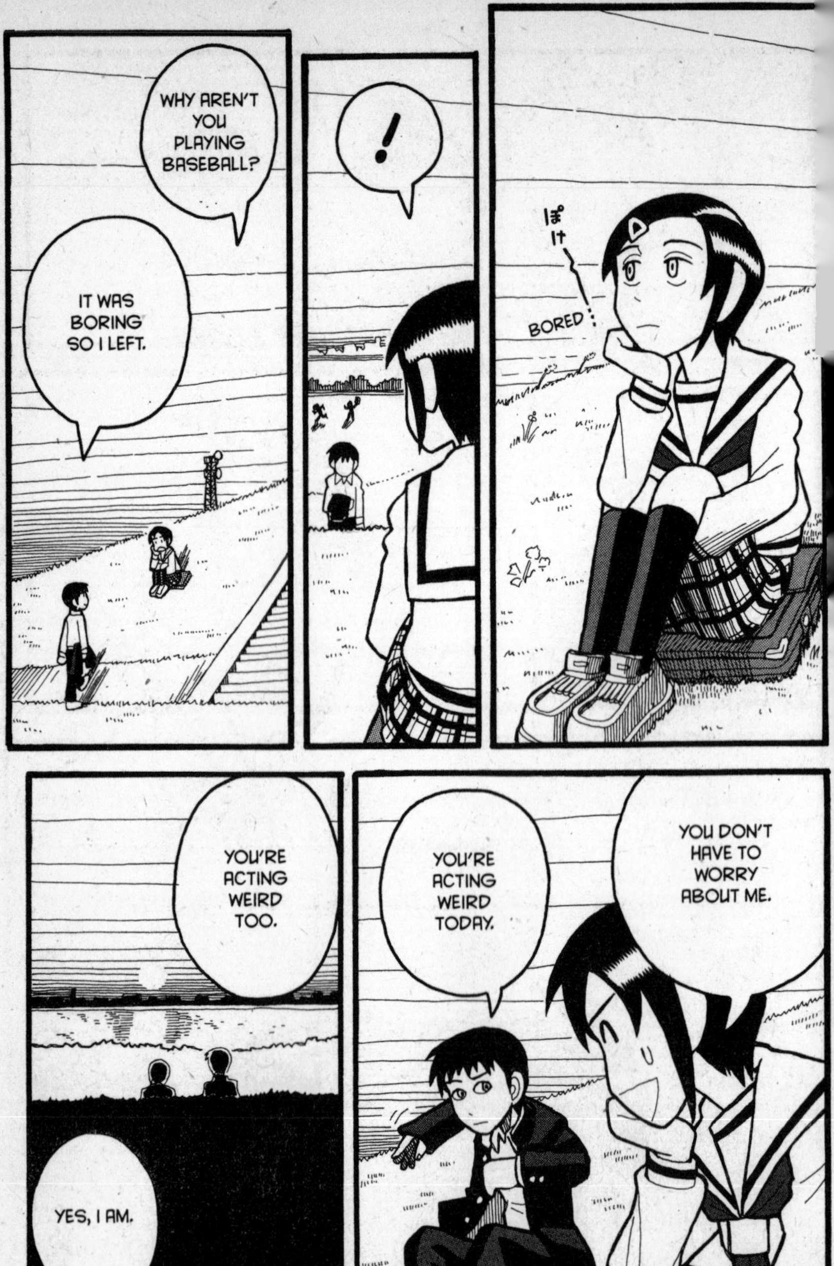
ぽけ
BORED
!
WHY AREN'T YOU PLAYING BASEBALL?
IT WAS BORING SO I LEFT.
YOU DON'T HAVE TO WORRY ABOUT ME.
YOU'RE ACTING WEIRD TODAY.
YOU'RE ACTING WEIRD TOO.
YES, I AM.

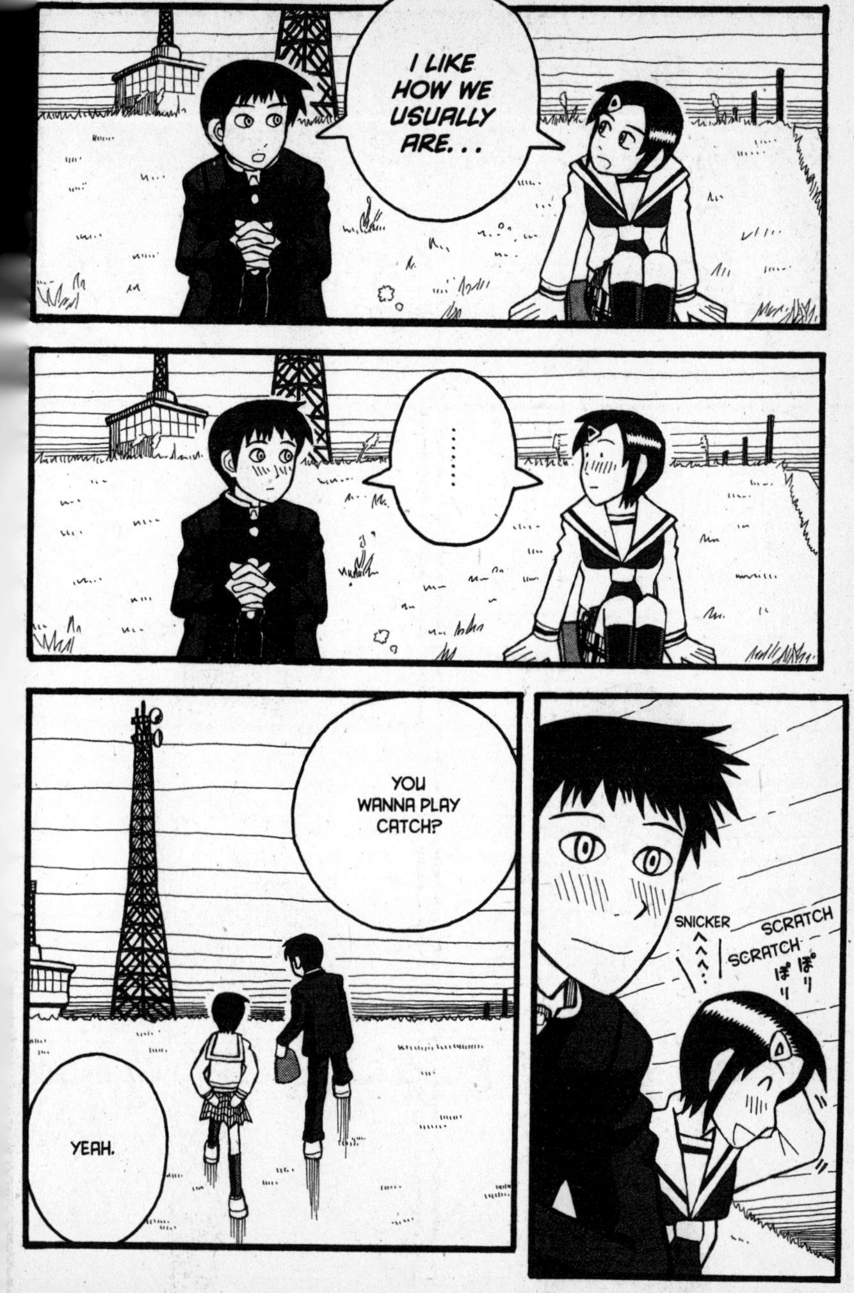
I LIKE HOW WE USUALLY ARE...
......
SNICKER
SCRATCH
SCRATCH
ぽりぽり
YOU WANNA PLAY CATCH?
YEAH.

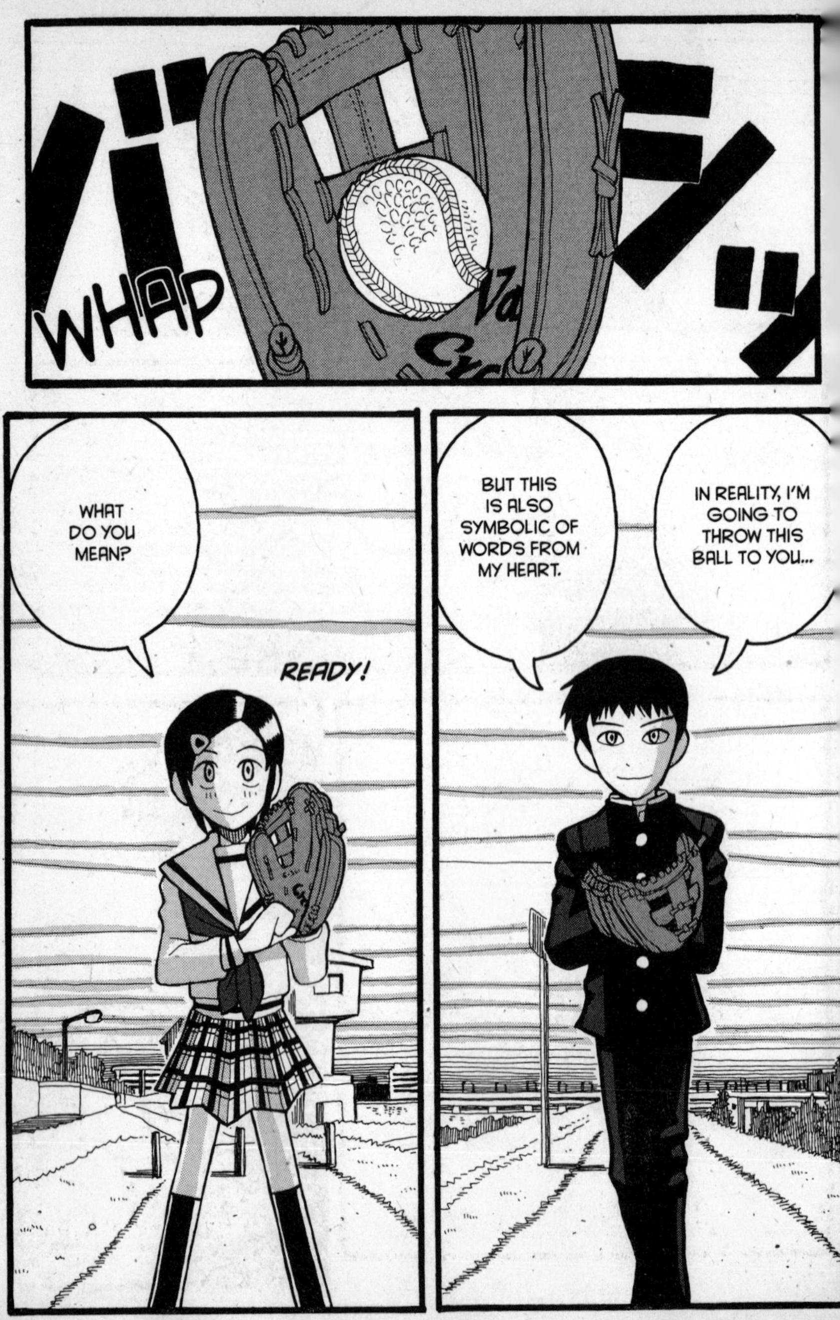
WHAP
IN REALITY, I'M GOING TO THROW THIS BALL TO YOU...
BUT THIS IS ALSO SYMBOLIC OF WORDS FROM MY HEART.
WHAT DO YOU MEAN?
READY!

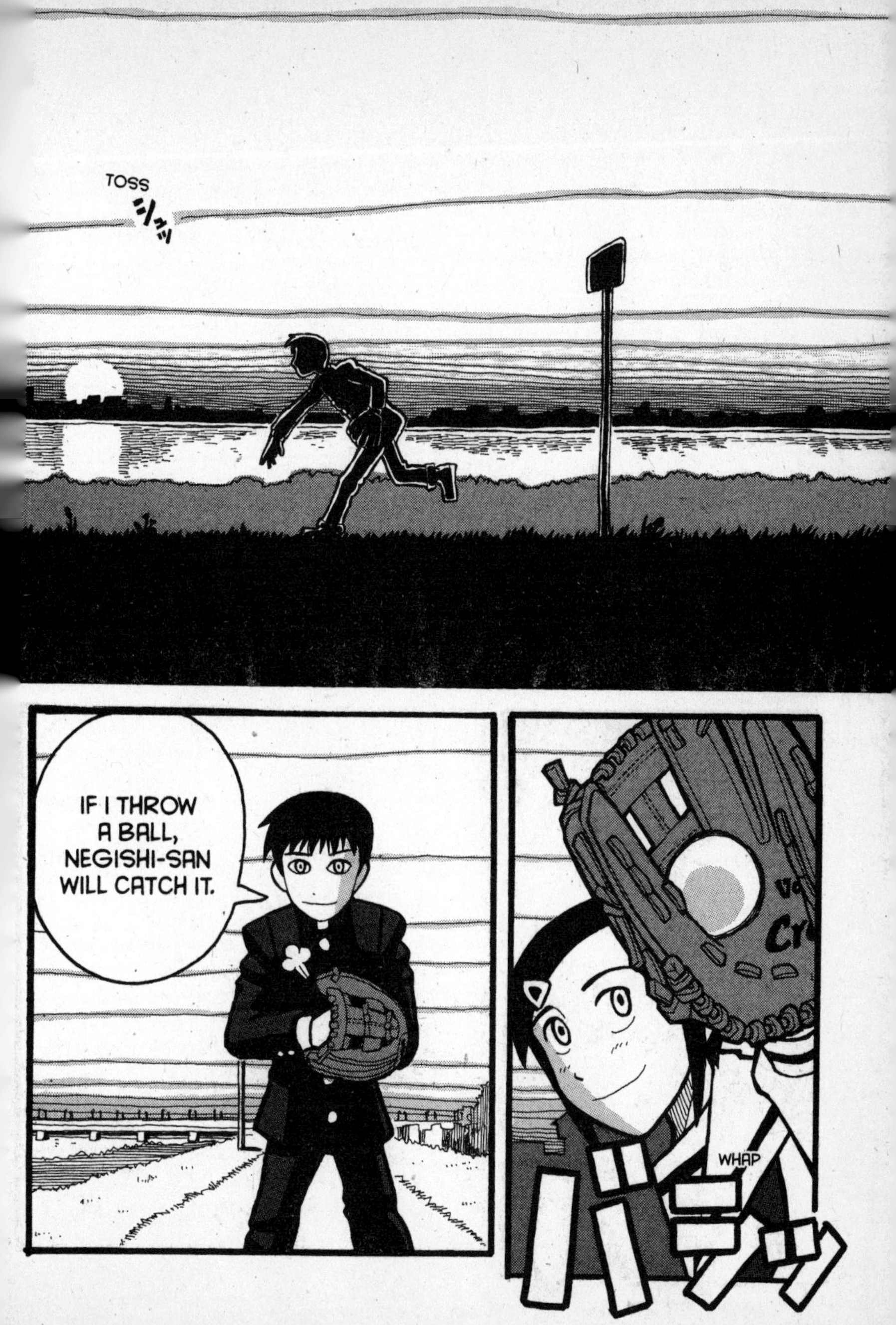
TOSS
WHAP
IF I THROW A BALL, NEGISHI-SAN WILL CATCH IT.

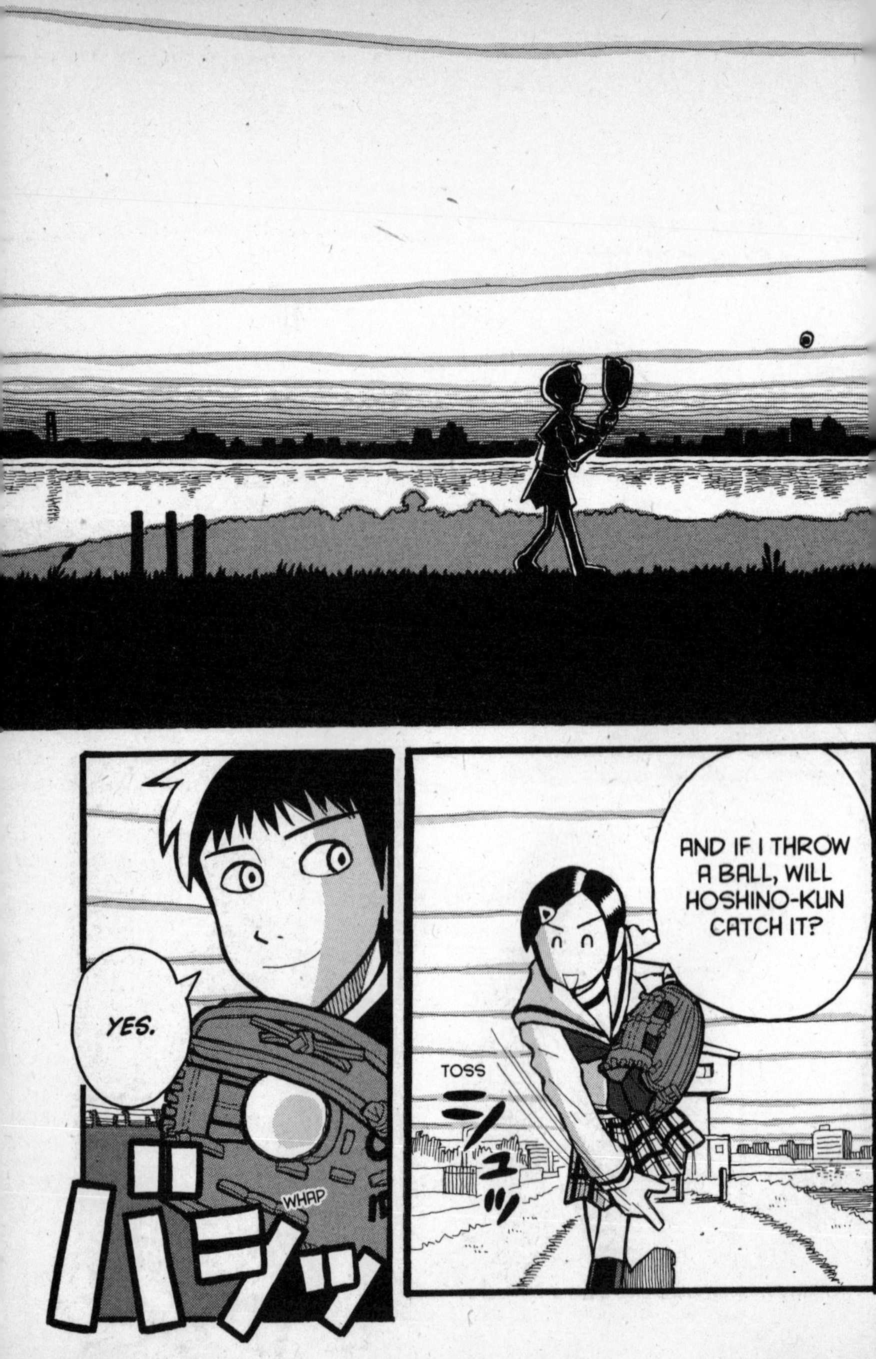
AND IF I THROW A BALL, WILL HOSHINO-KUN CATCH IT?
TOSS
YES.
WHAP

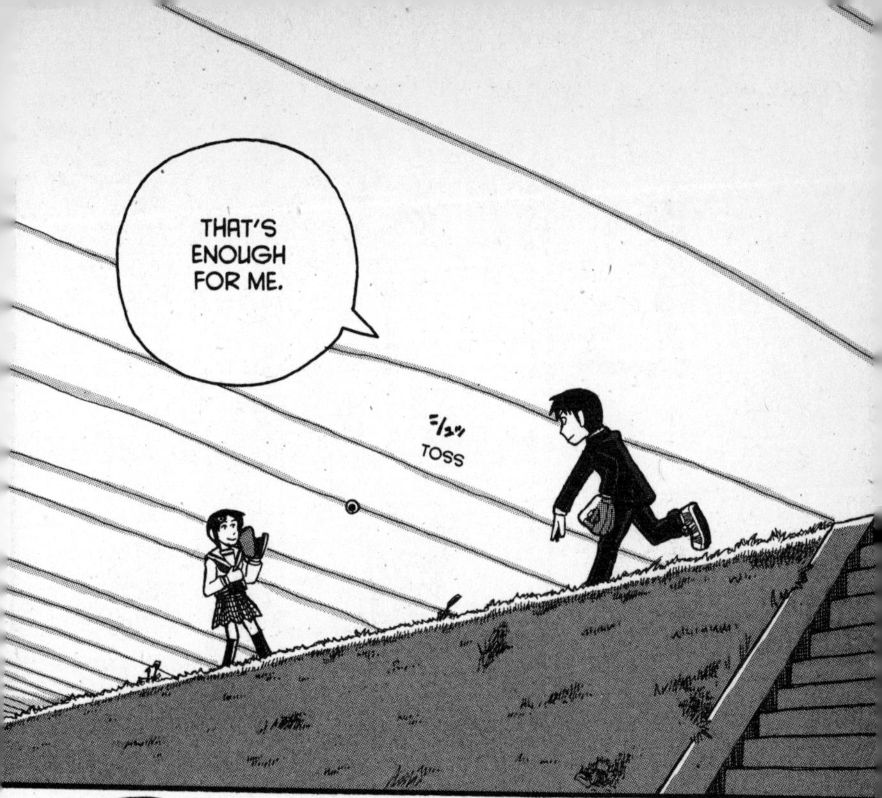
THAT'S ENOUGH FOR ME.
シュッ
TOSS

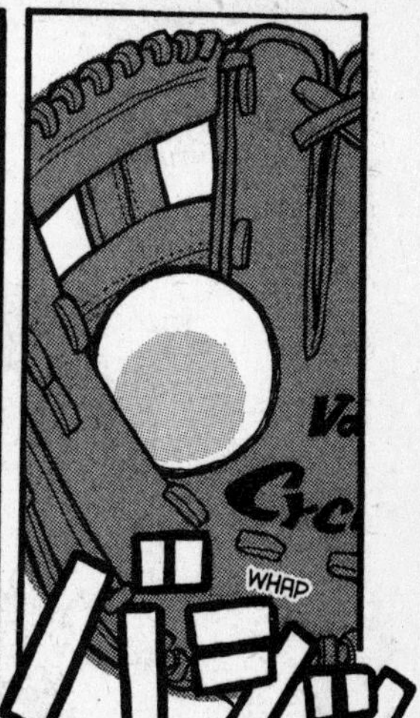
WHAP

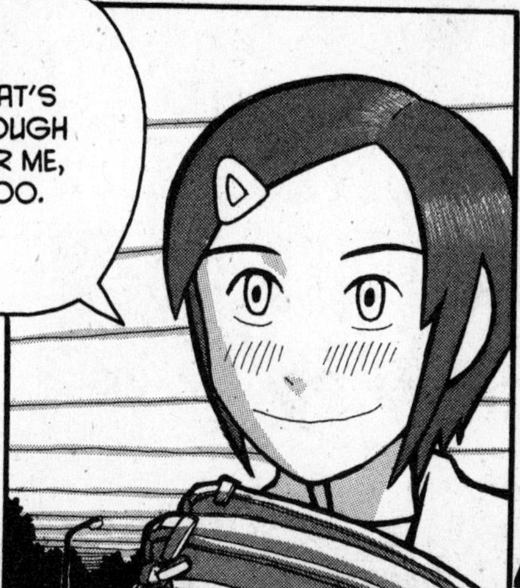
THAT'S ENOUGH FOR ME, TOO.

SIDE B THE END.

To Be Continued...

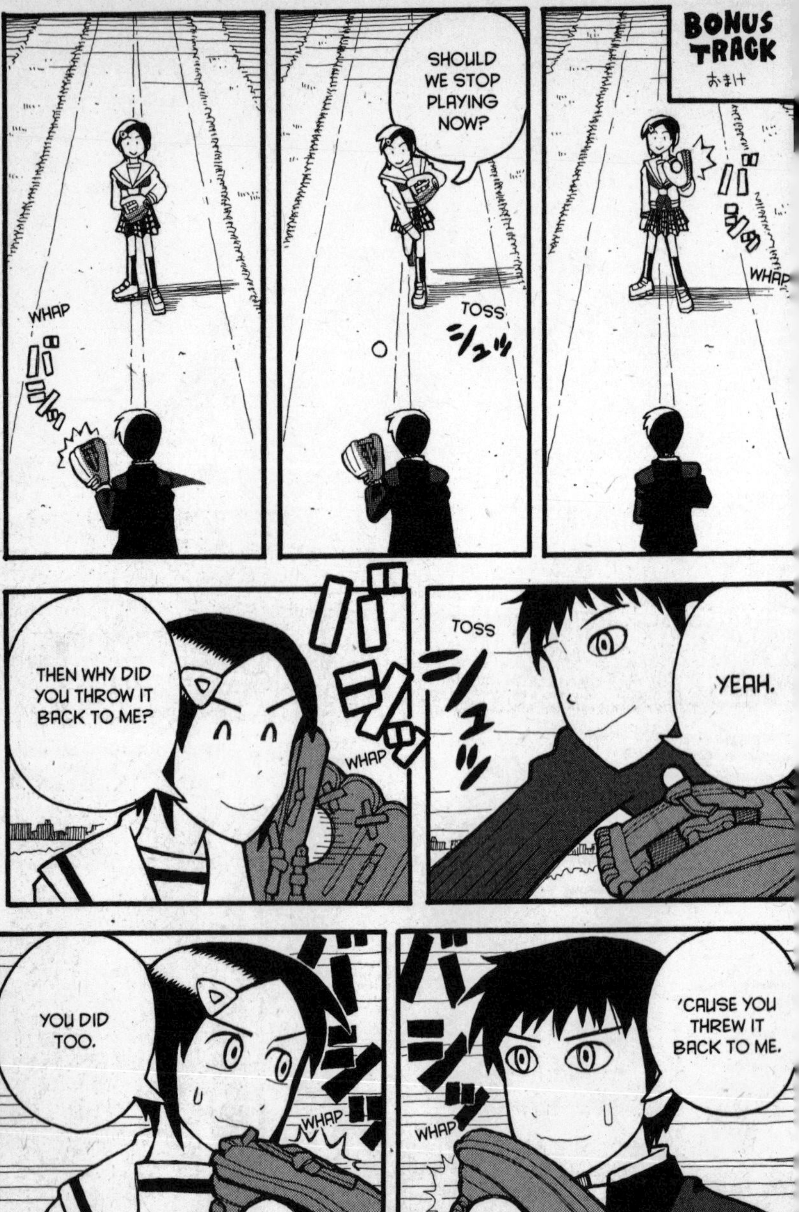
BONUS TRACK
おまけ
WHAP
SHOULD WE STOP PLAYING NOW?
TOSS
WHAP
YEAH.
TOSS
THEN WHY DID YOU THROW IT BACK TO ME?
WHAP
'CAUSE YOU THREW IT BACK TO ME.
WHAP
YOU DID TOO.
WHAP

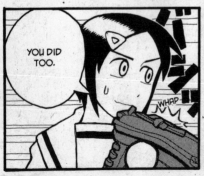

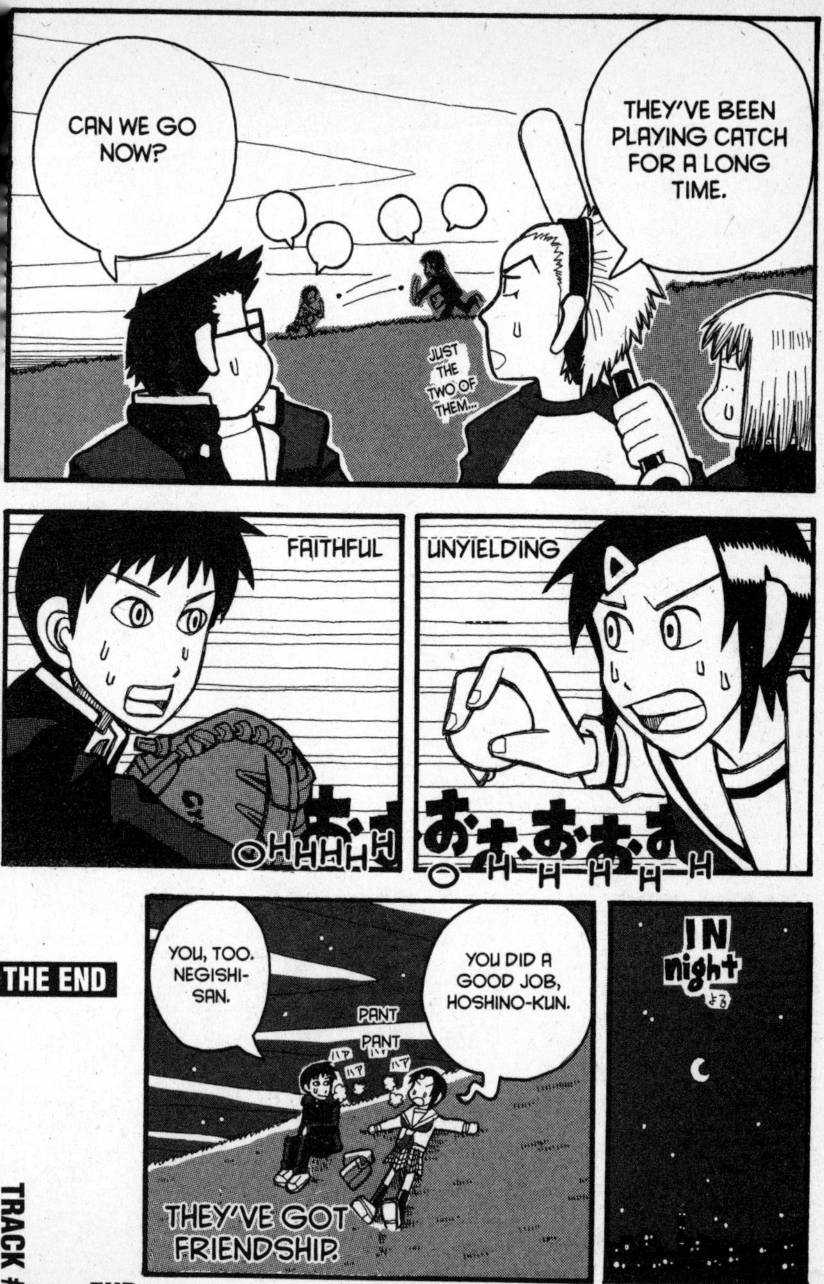
THEY'VE BEEN PLAYING CATCH FOR A LONG TIME.
JUST THE TWO OF THEM...
CAN WE GO NOW?
UNYIELDING
OHHHHHH
FAITHFUL
OHHHHH
IN night
よる
YOU DID A GOOD JOB, HOSHINO-KUN.
YOU, TOO. NEGISHI-SAN.
PANT
PANT
THEY'VE GOT FRIENDSHIP.

THE END

TRACK #5 ▶▶ END

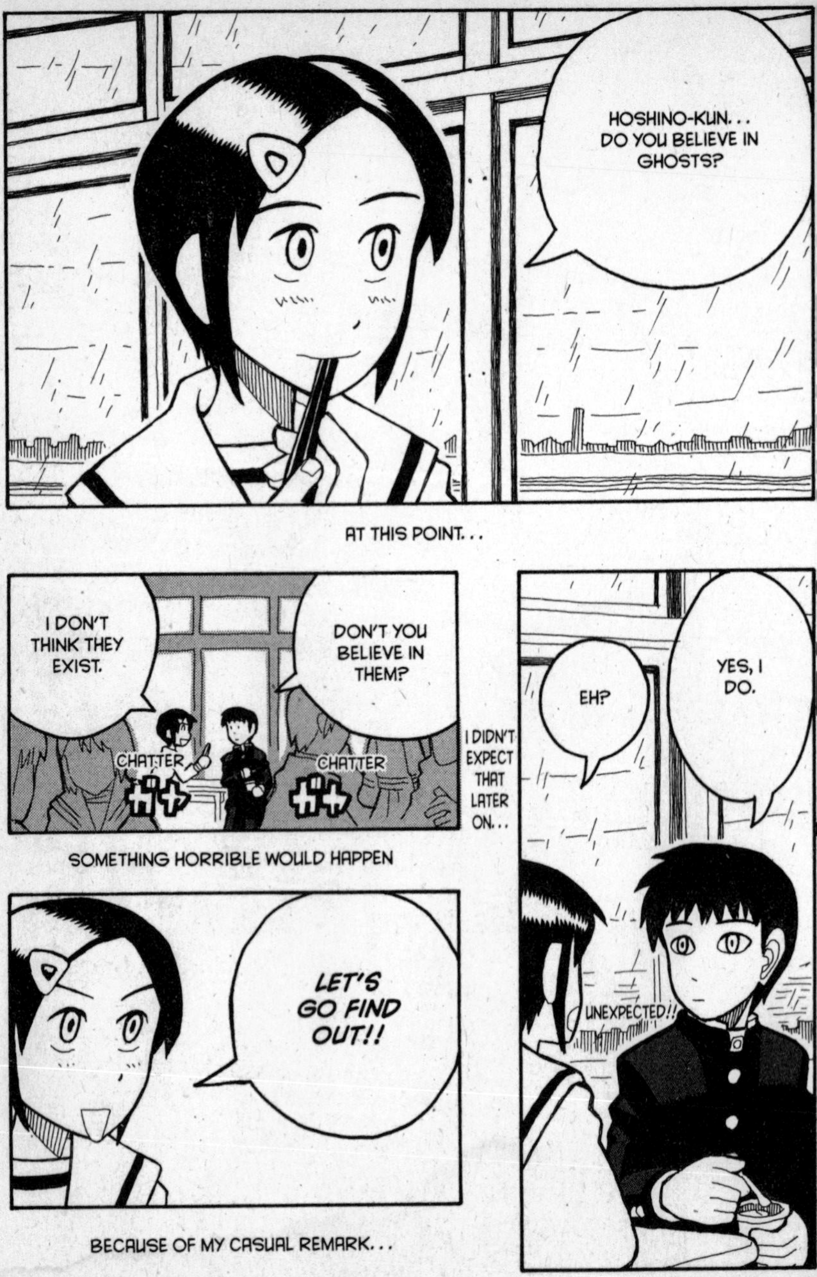
HOSHINO-KUN... DO YOU BELIEVE IN GHOSTS?
AT THIS POINT...
YES, I DO.
EH?
UNEXPECTED!!
I DIDN'T EXPECT THAT LATER ON...
DON'T YOU BELIEVE IN THEM?
I DON'T THINK THEY EXIST.
CHATTER
ガヤ
CHATTER
ガヤ
SOMETHING HORRIBLE WOULD HAPPEN
LET'S GO FIND OUT!!
BECAUSE OF MY CASUAL REMARK...

TRACK #6

GHOST STORY IN SCHOOL

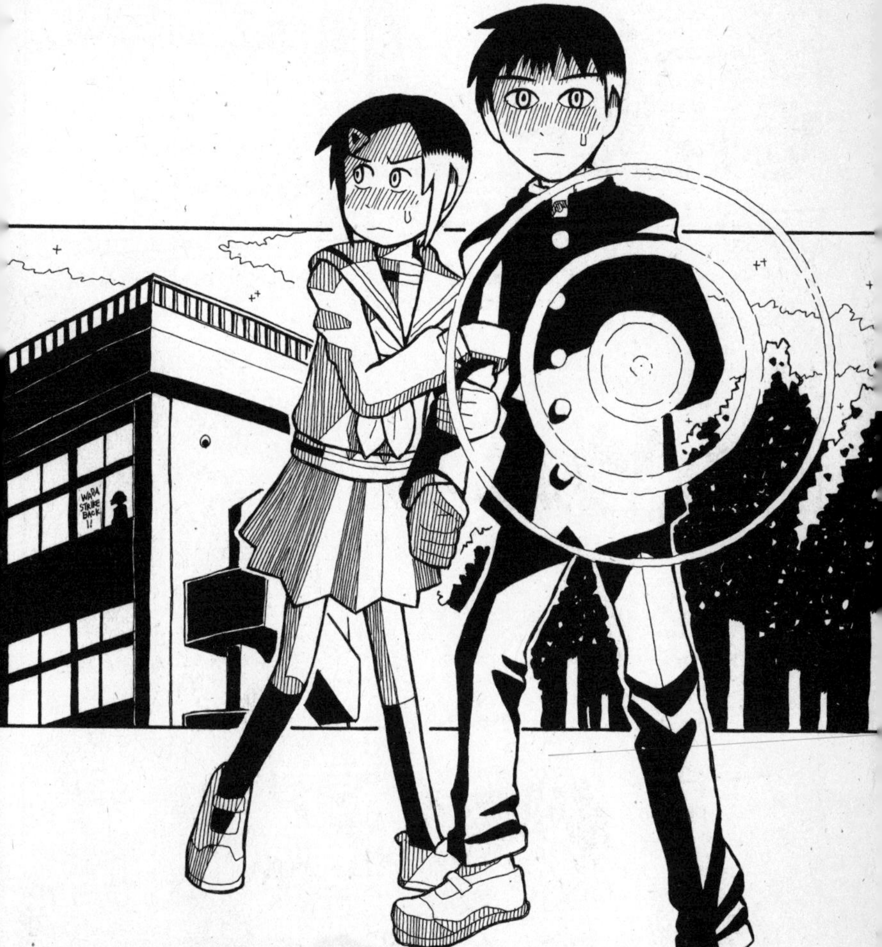
WAPA STRIKE BACK !!

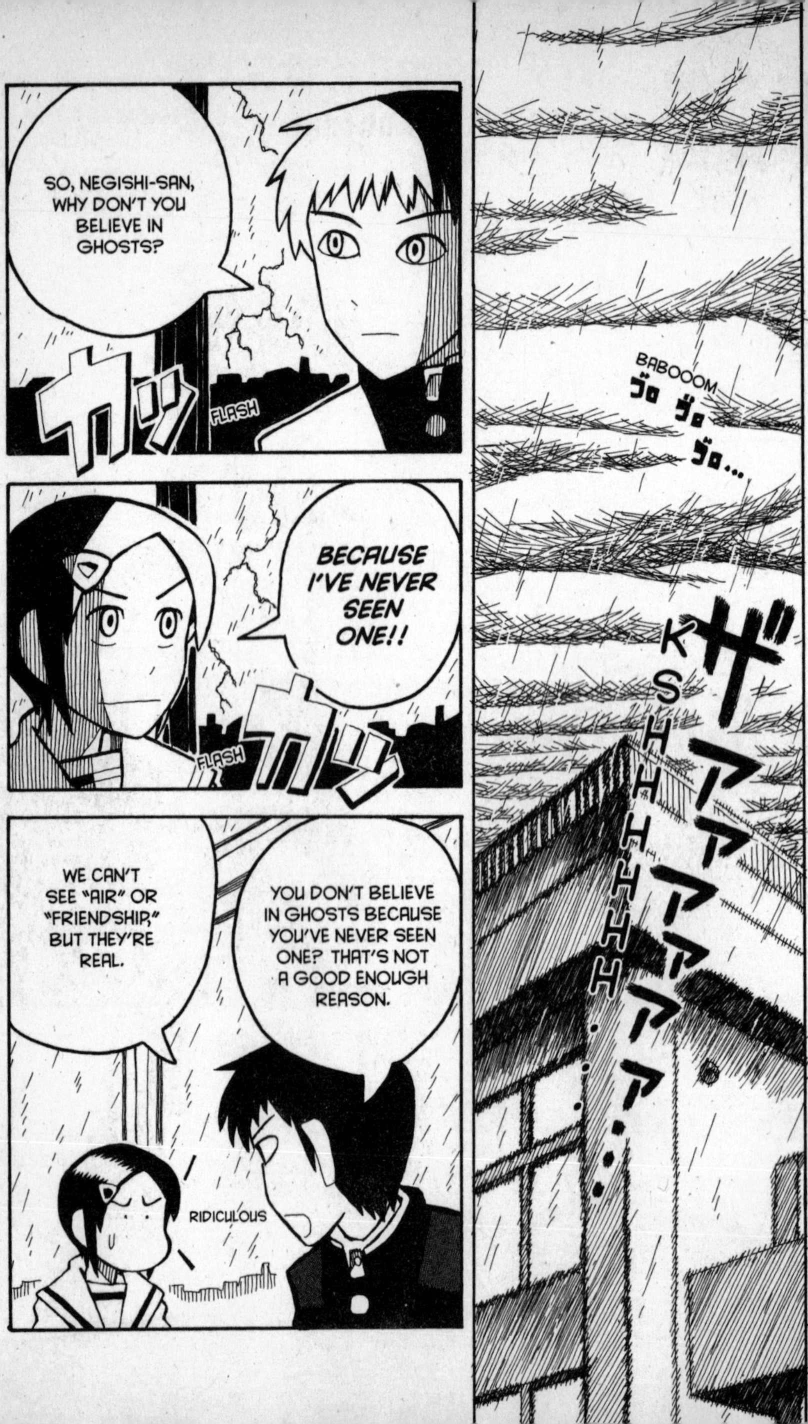
BABOOOM
ゴロ ゴロ ゴロ...
KSHHHHHHH...
ザアアアアア...
SO, NEGISHI-SAN, WHY DON'T YOU BELIEVE IN GHOSTS?
カッ
FLASH
BECAUSE I'VE NEVER SEEN ONE!!
FLASH
カッ
YOU DON'T BELIEVE IN GHOSTS BECAUSE YOU'VE NEVER SEEN ONE? THAT'S NOT A GOOD ENOUGH REASON.
WE CAN'T SEE "AIR" OR "FRIENDSHIP," BUT THEY'RE REAL.
RIDICULOUS

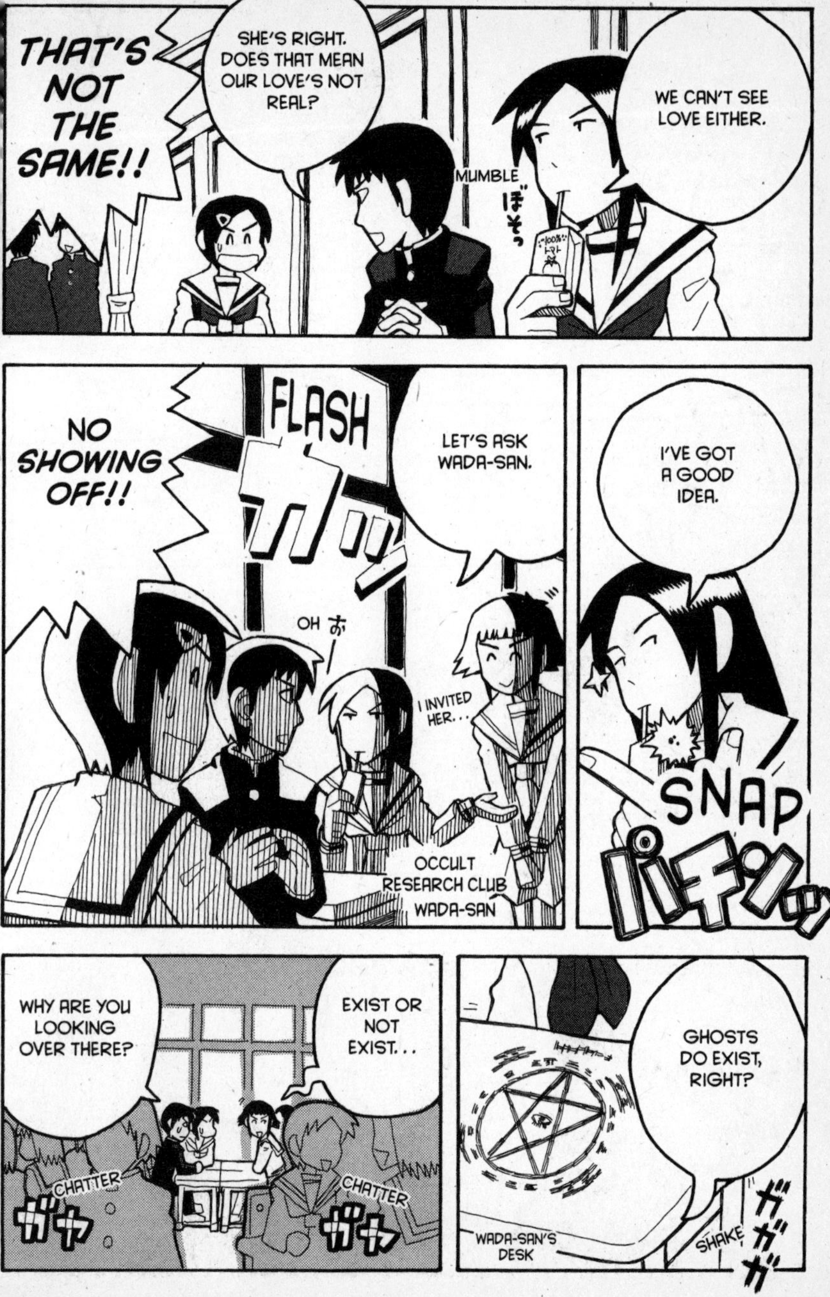
WE CAN'T SEE LOVE EITHER.
MUMBLE
ぼそっ
SHE'S RIGHT. DOES THAT MEAN OUR LOVE'S NOT REAL?
THAT'S NOT THE SAME!!
I'VE GOT A GOOD IDEA.
SNAP
パチンッ
LET'S ASK WADA-SAN.
FLASH
カッ
NO SHOWING OFF!!
OH
お
I INVITED HER...
OCCULT RESEARCH CLUB WADA-SAN
GHOSTS DO EXIST, RIGHT?
WADA-SAN'S DESK
SHAKE
ガガガ
EXIST OR NOT EXIST...
WHY ARE YOU LOOKING OVER THERE?
CHATTER
ガヤ
CHATTER
ガヤ

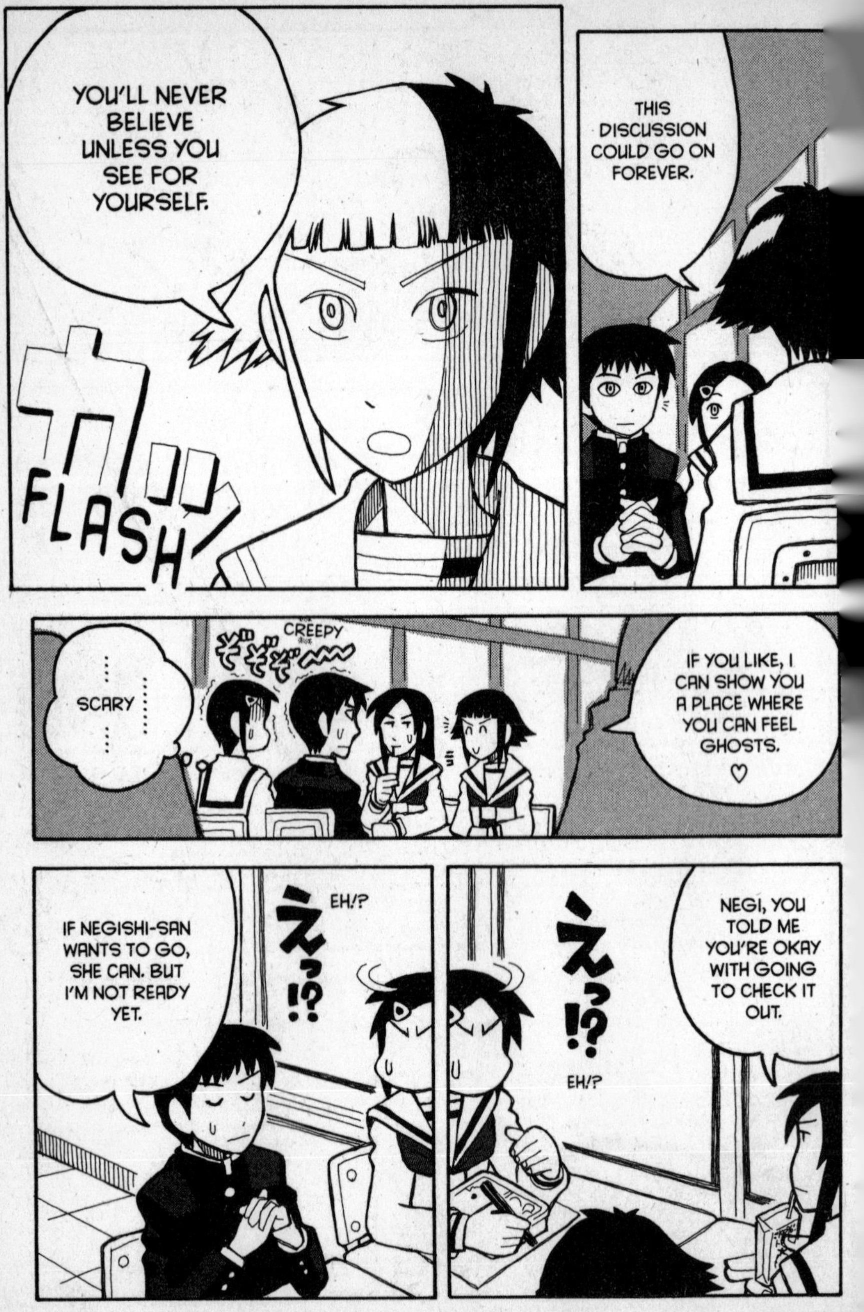
THIS DISCUSSION COULD GO ON FOREVER.
YOU'LL NEVER BELIEVE UNLESS YOU SEE FOR YOURSELF.
FLASH
IF YOU LIKE, I CAN SHOW YOU A PLACE WHERE YOU CAN FEEL GHOSTS. ♡
CREEPY
ぞぞぞ
... SCARY ... ...
NEGI, YOU TOLD ME YOU'RE OKAY WITH GOING TO CHECK IT OUT.
えっ!?
EH!?
えっ!?
EH!?
IF NEGISHI-SAN WANTS TO GO, SHE CAN. BUT I'M NOT READY YET.

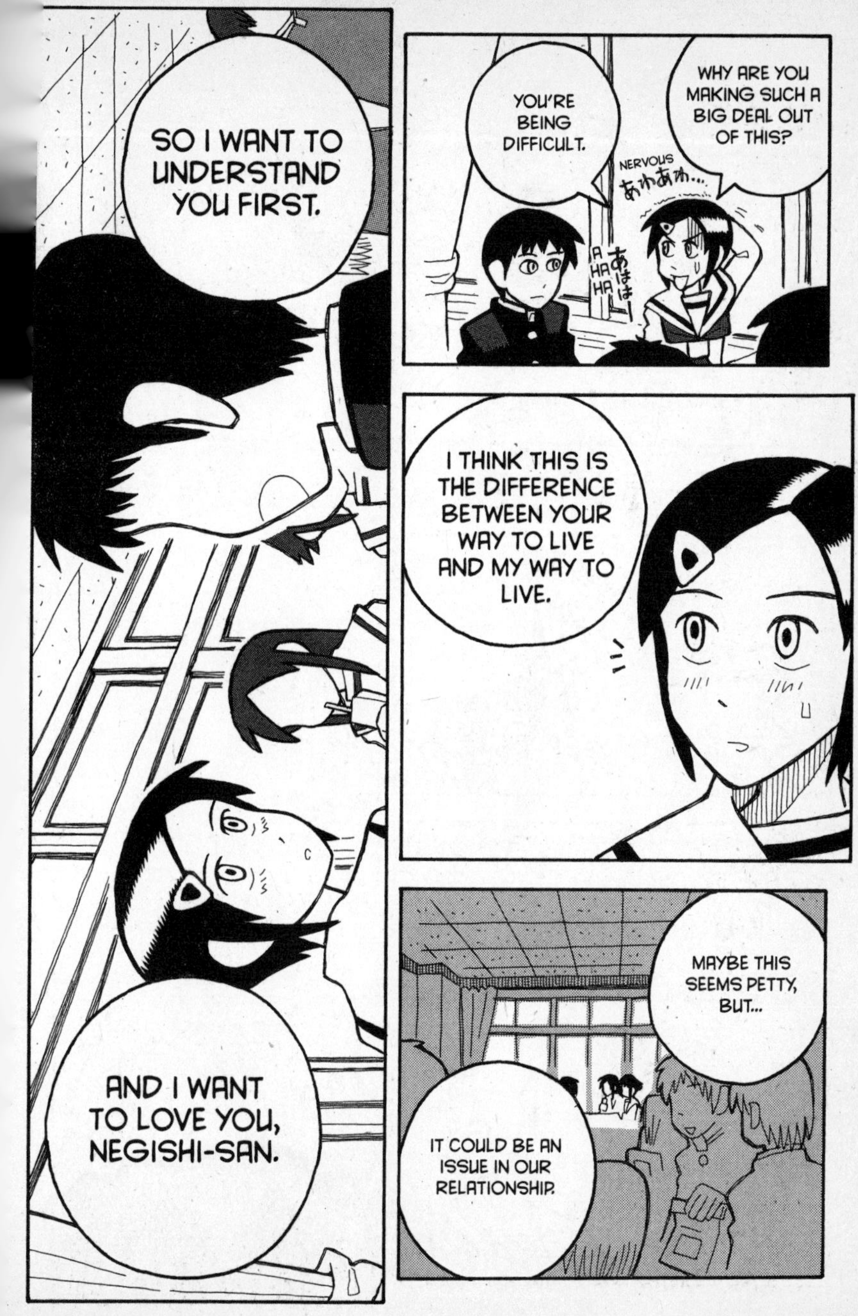
WHY ARE YOU MAKING SUCH A BIG DEAL OUT OF THIS?
NERVOUS
あわあわ...
YOU'RE BEING DIFFICULT.
あはは
A HA HA
I THINK THIS IS THE DIFFERENCE BETWEEN YOUR WAY TO LIVE AND MY WAY TO LIVE.
MAYBE THIS SEEMS PETTY, BUT...
IT COULD BE AN ISSUE IN OUR RELATIONSHIP.
SO I WANT TO UNDERSTAND YOU FIRST.
AND I WANT TO LOVE YOU, NEGISHI-SAN.

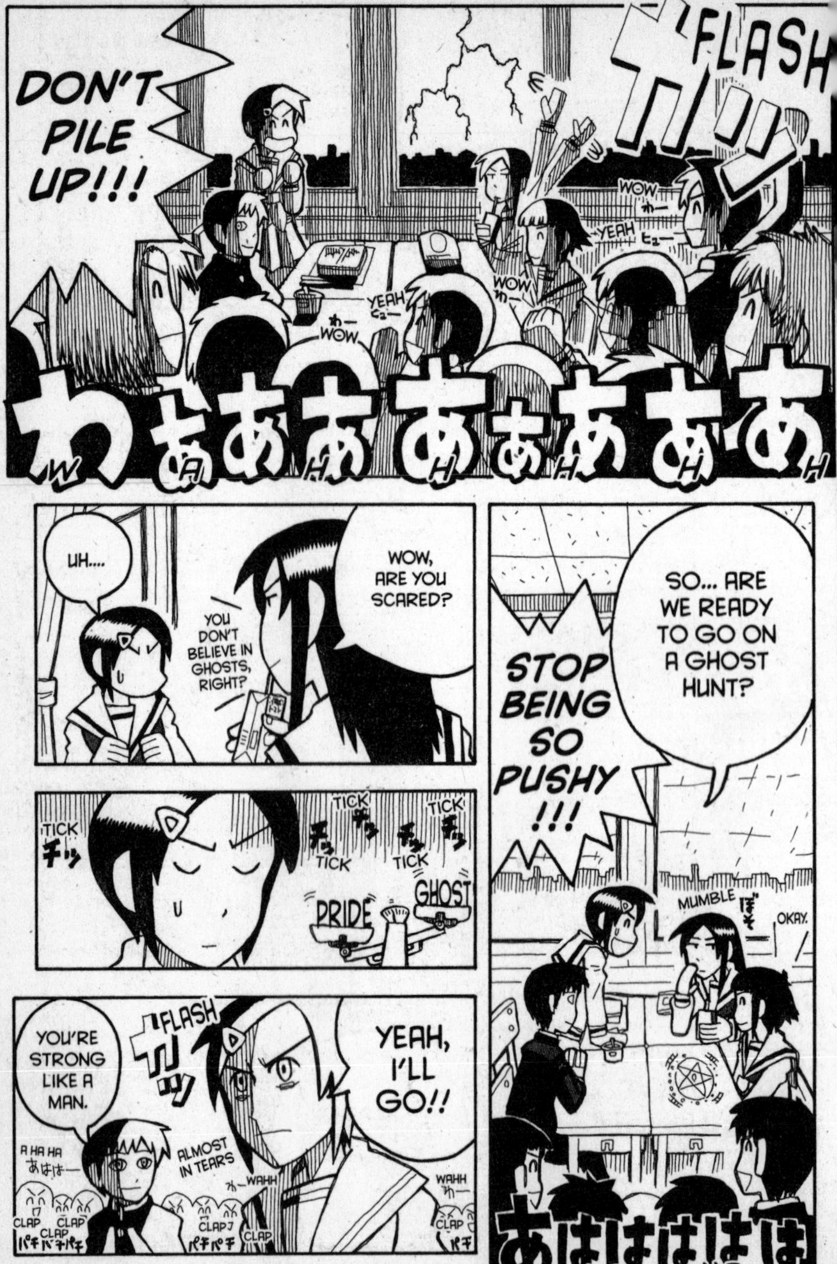
FLASH
ガッ
WOW わー
YEAH ヒュー
WOW わー
DON'T PILE UP!!!
YEAH ヒュー
わー WOW
わぁあああぁあああ
WAHHHHHHH
SO... ARE WE READY TO GO ON A GHOST HUNT?
STOP BEING SO PUSHY!!!
OKAY.
MUMBLE ぼそ
あはははは
A HA HA HA HA
WOW, ARE YOU SCARED?
YOU DON'T BELIEVE IN GHOSTS, RIGHT?
UH....
TICK チッ
TICK チッ
TICK チッ
TICK チッ
TICK チッ
GHOST
PRIDE
YEAH, I'LL GO!!
FLASH ガッ
WAHH わー
ALMOST IN TEARS
WAHH わー
YOU'RE STRONG LIKE A MAN.
A HA HA あはは
CLAP パチ
CLAP パチパチ
CLAP CLAP CLAP パチパチパチ

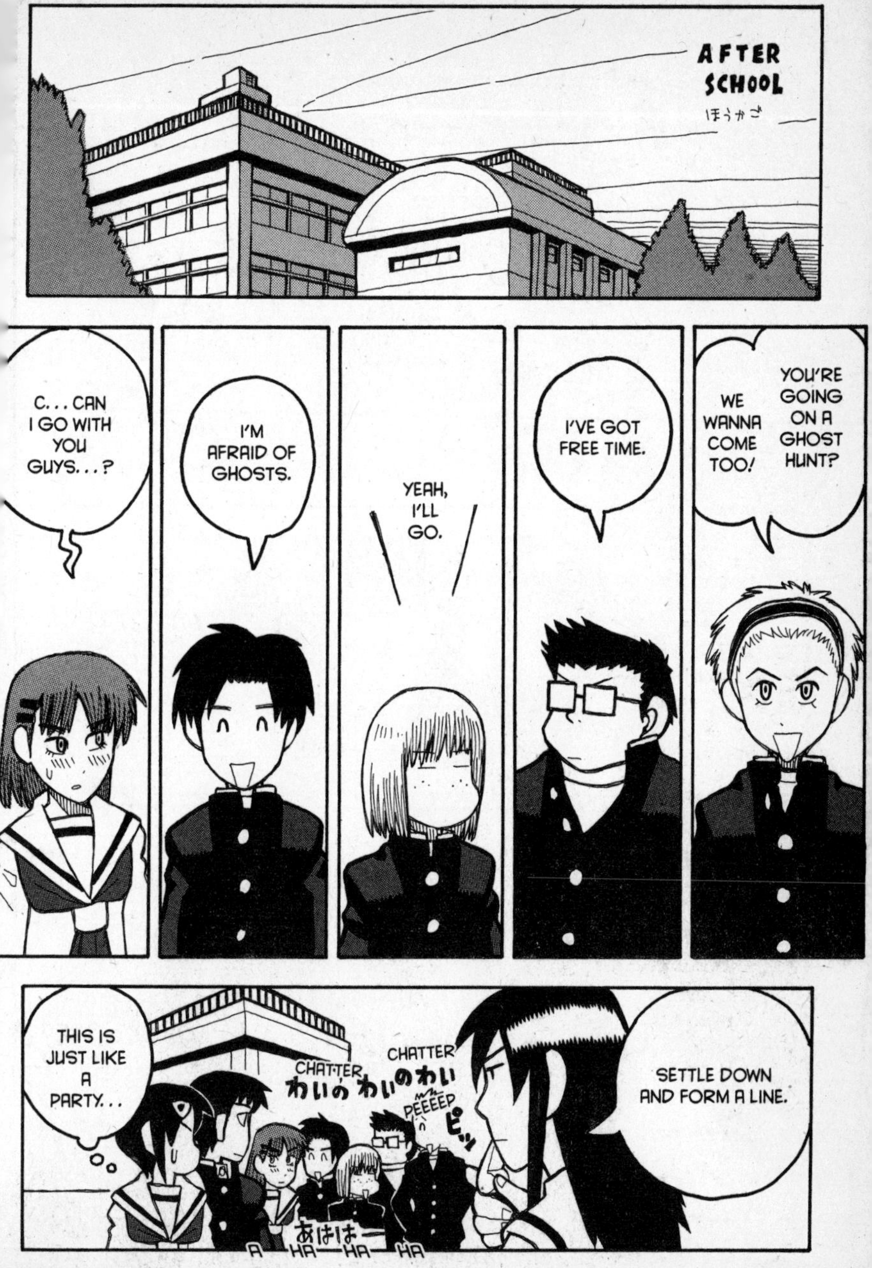
AFTER SCHOOL
ほうかご
YOU'RE GOING ON A GHOST HUNT?
WE WANNA COME TOO!
I'VE GOT FREE TIME.
YEAH, I'LL GO.
I'M AFRAID OF GHOSTS.
C... CAN I GO WITH YOU GUYS...?
SETTLE DOWN AND FORM A LINE.
ピッ
PEEEEP
CHATTER
わいのわい
CHATTER
わいのわい
あはは
A HA HA HA
THIS IS JUST LIKE A PARTY...

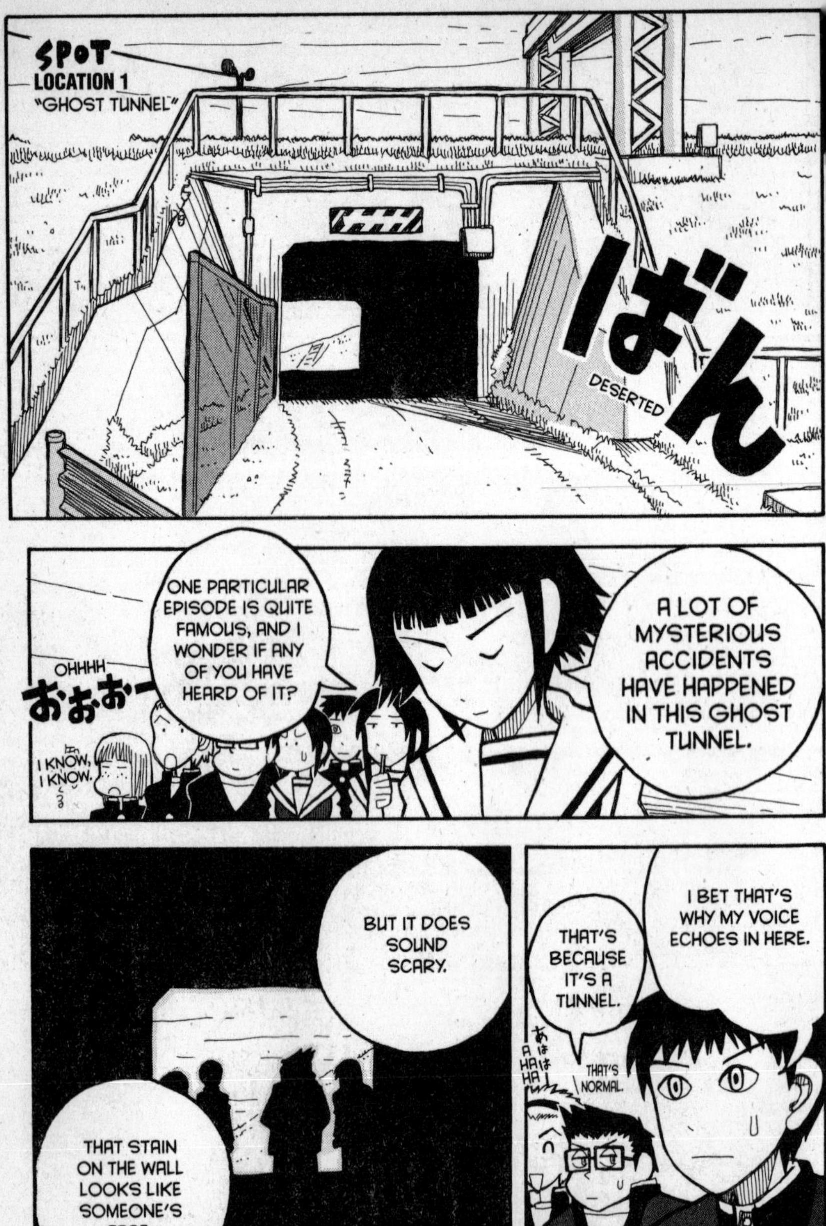
SPOT
LOCATION 1
"GHOST TUNNEL"
ばん
DESERTED
A LOT OF MYSTERIOUS ACCIDENTS HAVE HAPPENED IN THIS GHOST TUNNEL.
ONE PARTICULAR EPISODE IS QUITE FAMOUS, AND I WONDER IF ANY OF YOU HAVE HEARD OF IT?
OHHHH
おぉぉー
I KNOW, I KNOW.
I BET THAT'S WHY MY VOICE ECHOES IN HERE.
THAT'S BECAUSE IT'S A TUNNEL.
あはは
A HA HA
THAT'S NORMAL.
BUT IT DOES SOUND SCARY.
THAT STAIN ON THE WALL LOOKS LIKE SOMEONE'S FACE.

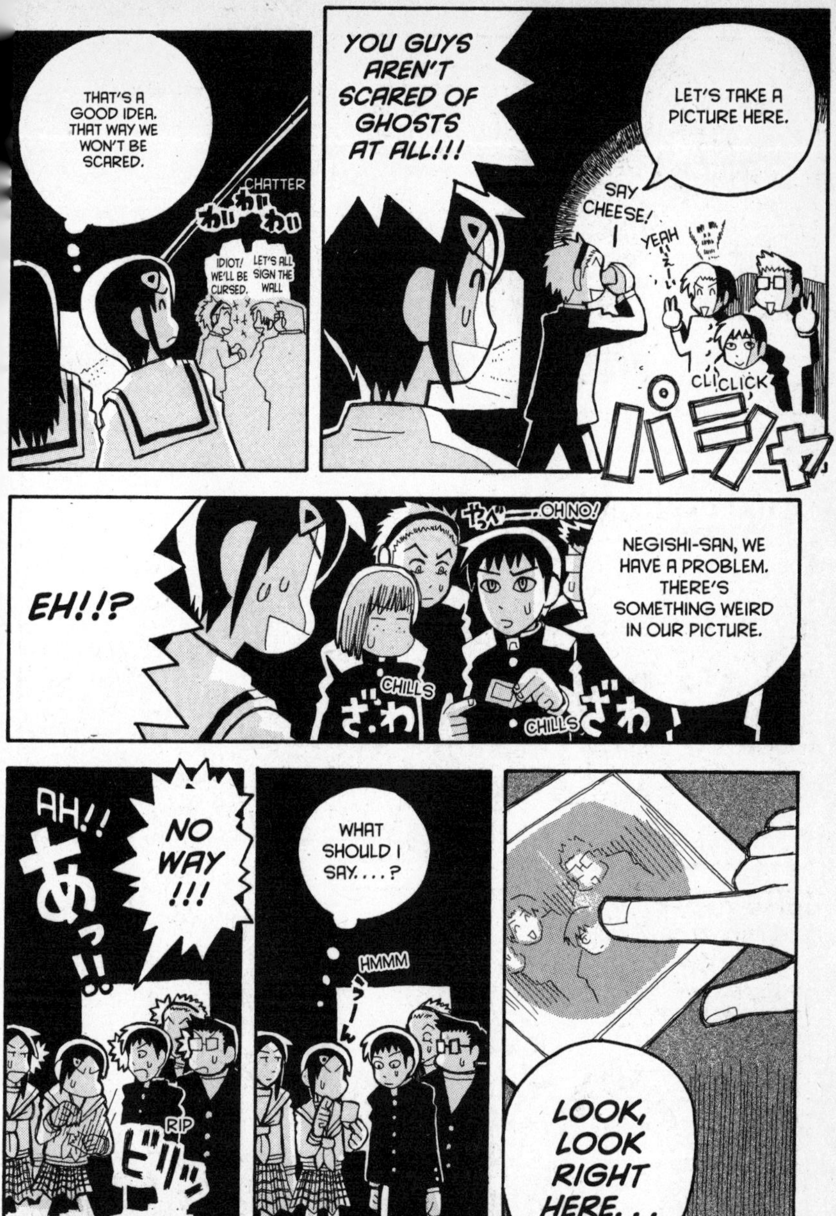
LET'S TAKE A PICTURE HERE.
SAY CHEESE!
YEAH
CLI CLICK
YOU GUYS AREN'T SCARED OF GHOSTS AT ALL!!!
THAT'S A GOOD IDEA. THAT WAY WE WON'T BE SCARED.
CHATTER
LET'S ALL SIGN THE WALL
IDIOT! WE'LL BE CURSED.
NEGISHI-SAN, WE HAVE A PROBLEM. THERE'S SOMETHING WEIRD IN OUR PICTURE.
OH NO!
CHILLS
CHILLS
EH!!?
LOOK, LOOK RIGHT HERE. . .
WHAT SHOULD I SAY. . . . ?
HMMM
NO WAY!!!
AH!!
RIP
TRYING TO FORCE IT TO GO AWAY

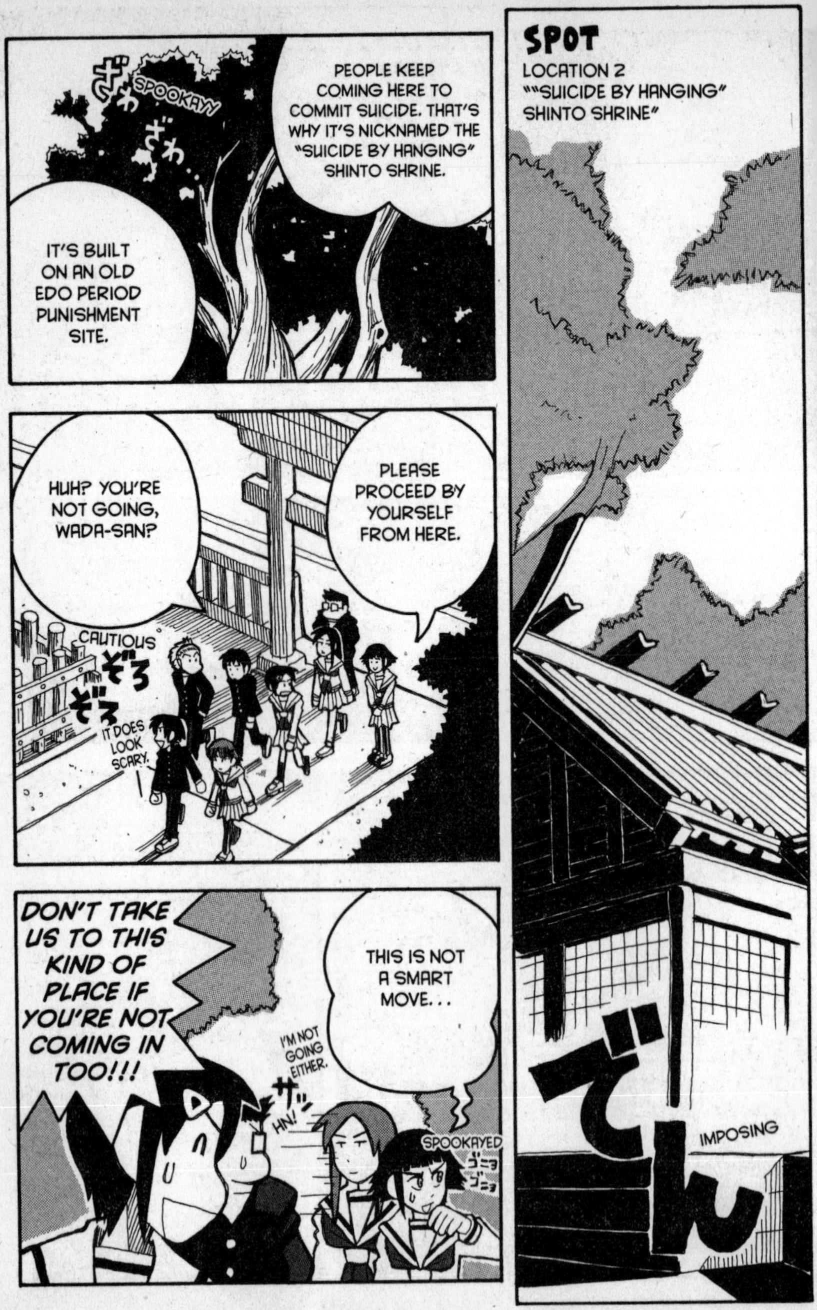
SPOT
LOCATION 2
““SUICIDE BY HANGING” SHINTO SHRINE”
でん
IMPOSING
ざわ
SPOOKAYY
ざわ...
PEOPLE KEEP COMING HERE TO COMMIT SUICIDE. THAT'S WHY IT'S NICKNAMED THE “SUICIDE BY HANGING” SHINTO SHRINE.
IT'S BUILT ON AN OLD EDO PERIOD PUNISHMENT SITE.
PLEASE PROCEED BY YOURSELF FROM HERE.
HUH? YOU'RE NOT GOING, WADA-SAN?
CAUTIOUS
ぞろぞろ
IT DOES LOOK SCARY.
THIS IS NOT A SMART MOVE...
SPOOKAYED
ゴニョゴニョ
I'M NOT GOING EITHER.
ザッ
HN!
DON'T TAKE US TO THIS KIND OF PLACE IF YOU'RE NOT COMING IN TOO!!!

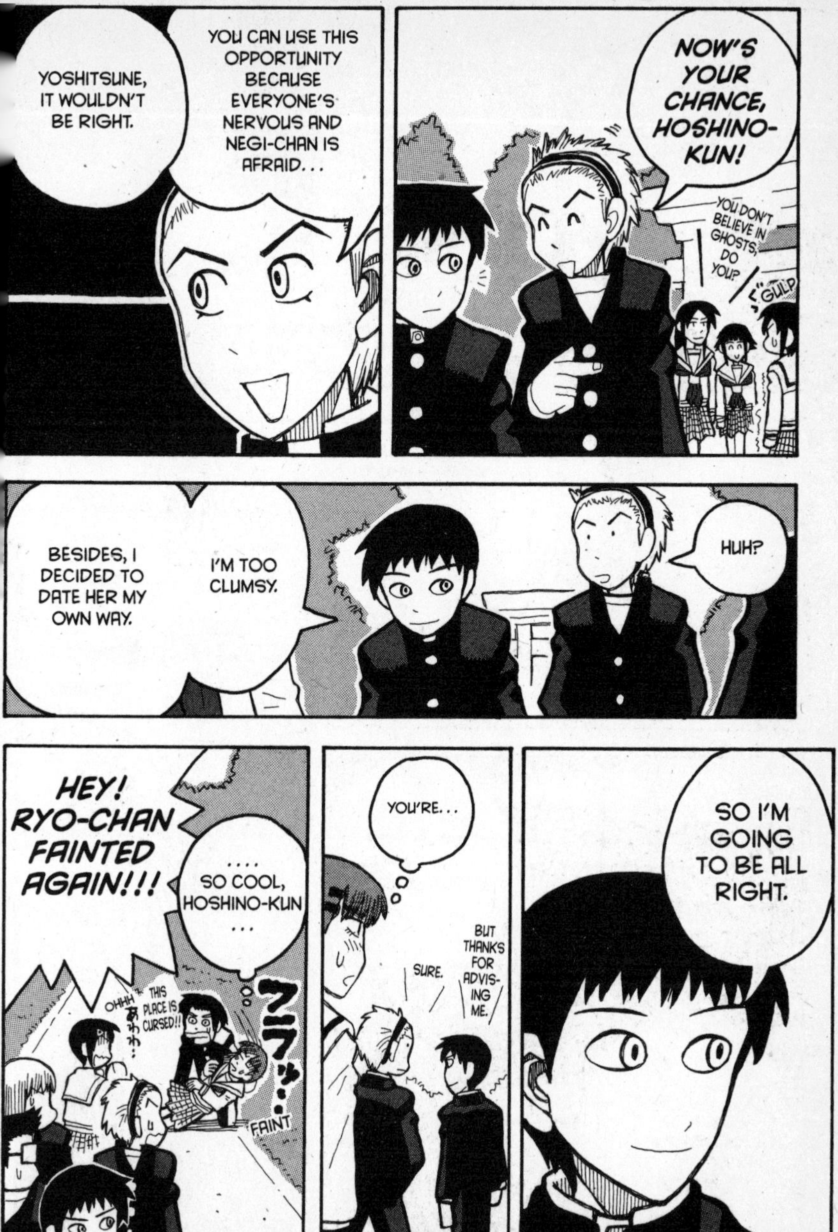
NOW'S YOUR CHANCE, HOSHINO-KUN!
YOU DON'T BELIEVE IN GHOSTS, DO YOU?
GULP
YOU CAN USE THIS OPPORTUNITY BECAUSE EVERYONE'S NERVOUS AND NEGI-CHAN IS AFRAID...
YOSHITSUNE, IT WOULDN'T BE RIGHT.
HUH?
I'M TOO CLUMSY.
BESIDES, I DECIDED TO DATE HER MY OWN WAY.
SO I'M GOING TO BE ALL RIGHT.
YOU'RE...
BUT THANKS FOR ADVISING ME.
SURE.
HEY! RYO-CHAN FAINTED AGAIN!!!
.... SO COOL, HOSHINO-KUN ...
FAINT
THIS PLACE IS CURSED!!
OHHH

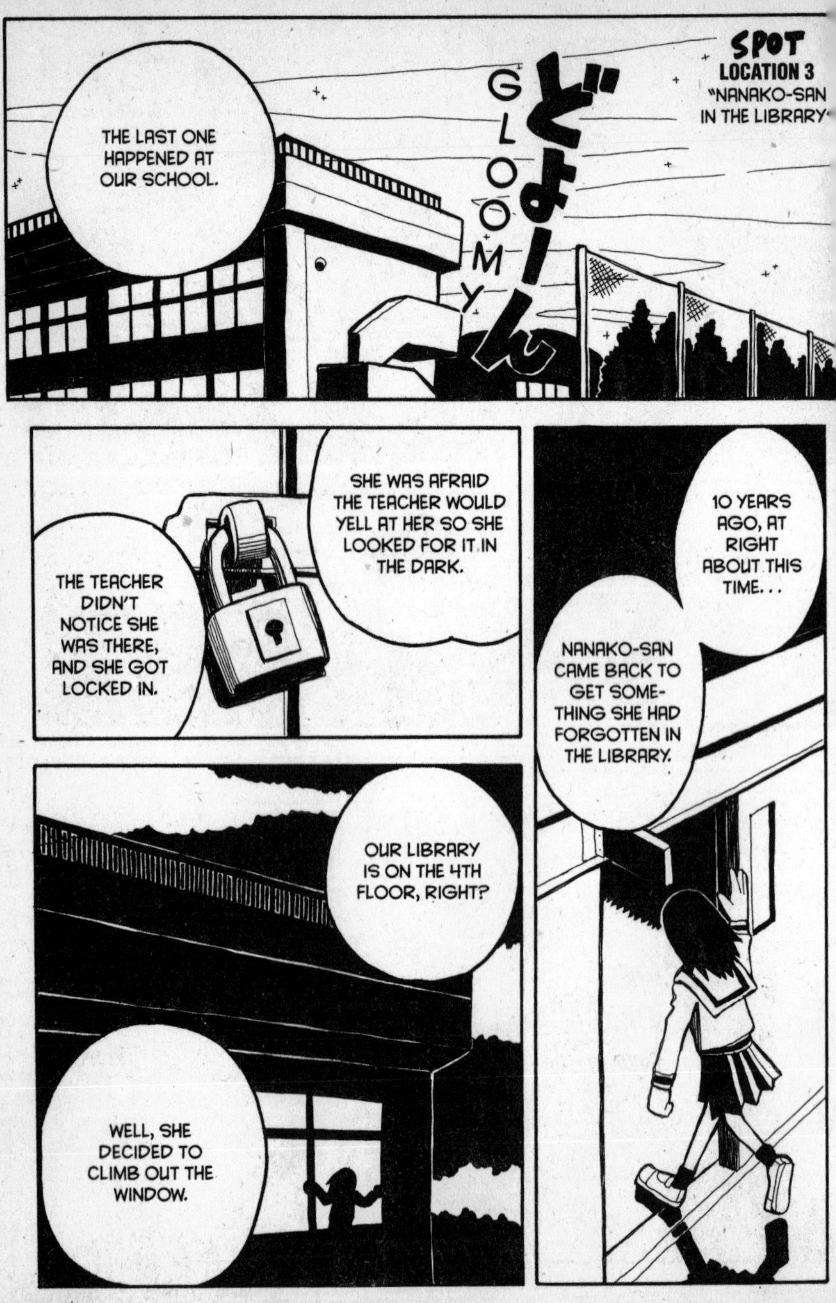
SPOT
LOCATION 3
"NANAKO-SAN IN THE LIBRARY"
どよーん
GLOOMY
THE LAST ONE HAPPENED AT OUR SCHOOL.
10 YEARS AGO, AT RIGHT ABOUT THIS TIME. . .
NANAKO-SAN CAME BACK TO GET SOME-THING SHE HAD FORGOTTEN IN THE LIBRARY.
SHE WAS AFRAID THE TEACHER WOULD YELL AT HER SO SHE LOOKED FOR IT IN THE DARK.
THE TEACHER DIDN'T NOTICE SHE WAS THERE, AND SHE GOT LOCKED IN.
OUR LIBRARY IS ON THE 4TH FLOOR, RIGHT?
WELL, SHE DECIDED TO CLIMB OUT THE WINDOW.

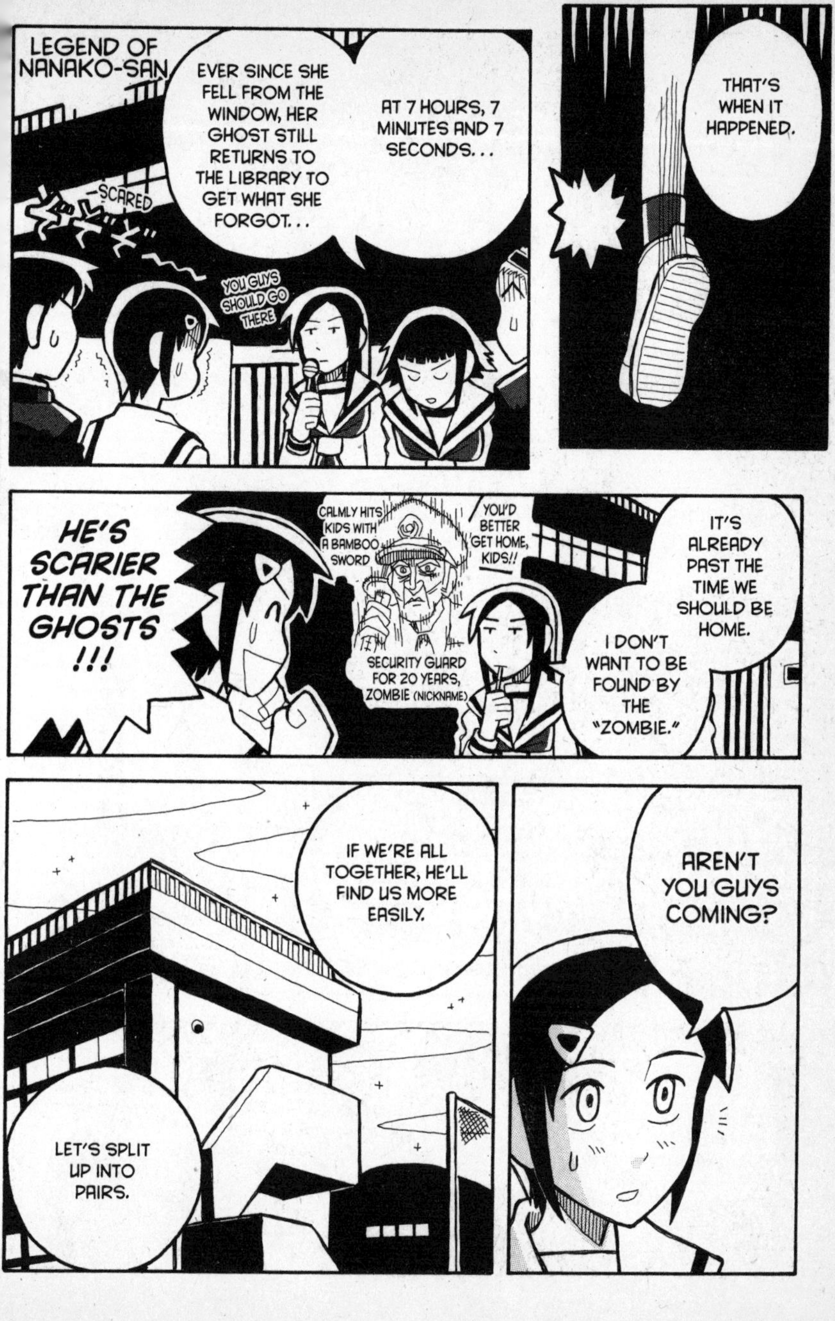
LEGEND OF NANAKO-SAN
EVER SINCE SHE FELL FROM THE WINDOW, HER GHOST STILL RETURNS TO THE LIBRARY TO GET WHAT SHE FORGOT...
AT 7 HOURS, 7 MINUTES AND 7 SECONDS...
-SCARED
YOU GUYS SHOULD GO THERE
THAT'S WHEN IT HAPPENED.
HE'S SCARIER THAN THE GHOSTS !!!
CALMLY HITS KIDS WITH A BAMBOO SWORD
YOU'D BETTER GET HOME, KIDS!!
SECURITY GUARD FOR 20 YEARS, ZOMBIE (NICKNAME)
IT'S ALREADY PAST THE TIME WE SHOULD BE HOME.
I DON'T WANT TO BE FOUND BY THE "ZOMBIE."
IF WE'RE ALL TOGETHER, HE'LL FIND US MORE EASILY.
LET'S SPLIT UP INTO PAIRS.
AREN'T YOU GUYS COMING?

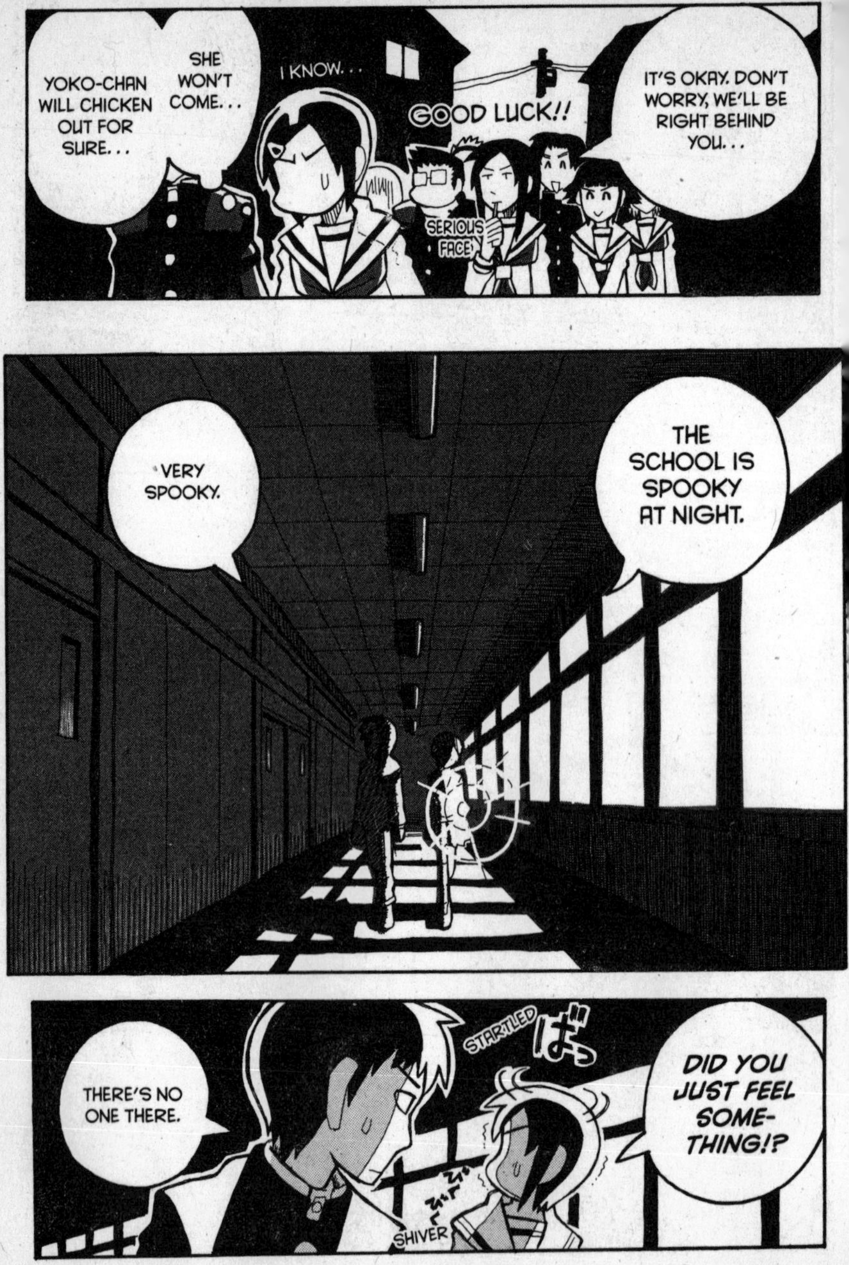
IT'S OKAY. DON'T WORRY, WE'LL BE RIGHT BEHIND YOU...
GOOD LUCK!!
SERIOUS FACE
I KNOW...
SHE WON'T COME...
YOKO-CHAN WILL CHICKEN OUT FOR SURE...
THE SCHOOL IS SPOOKY AT NIGHT.
VERY SPOOKY.
DID YOU JUST FEEL SOME-THING!?
STARTLED
ぱっ
SHIVER
THERE'S NO ONE THERE.

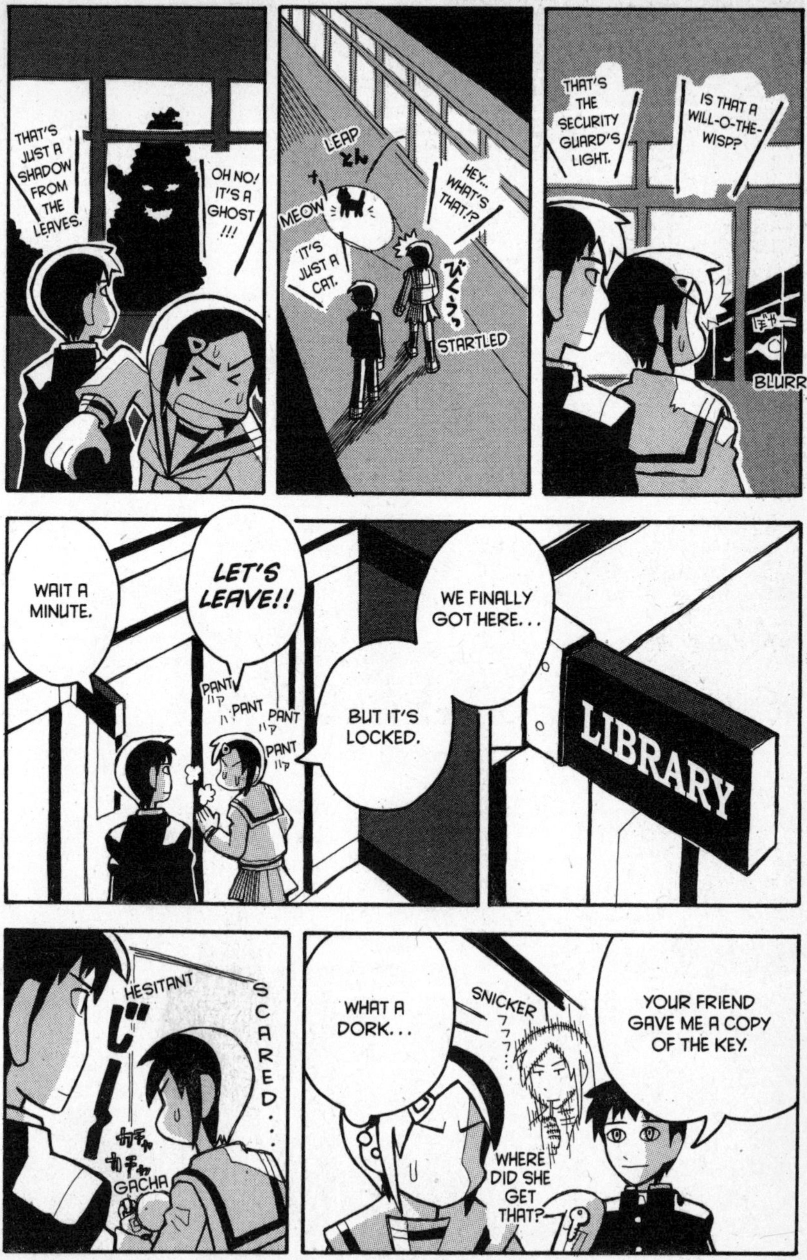
IS THAT A WILL-O-THE-WISP?
THAT'S THE SECURITY GUARD'S LIGHT.
BLURRY
HEY... WHAT'S THAT!?
STARTLED
LEAP
とん
MEOW
IT'S JUST A CAT.
OH NO! IT'S A GHOST!!!
THAT'S JUST A SHADOW FROM THE LEAVES.
WE FINALLY GOT HERE...
BUT IT'S LOCKED.
LIBRARY
LET'S LEAVE!!
PANT PANT PANT PANT
WAIT A MINUTE.
YOUR FRIEND GAVE ME A COPY OF THE KEY.
SNICKER
WHAT A DORK...
WHERE DID SHE GET THAT?
SCARED...
HESITANT
GACHA

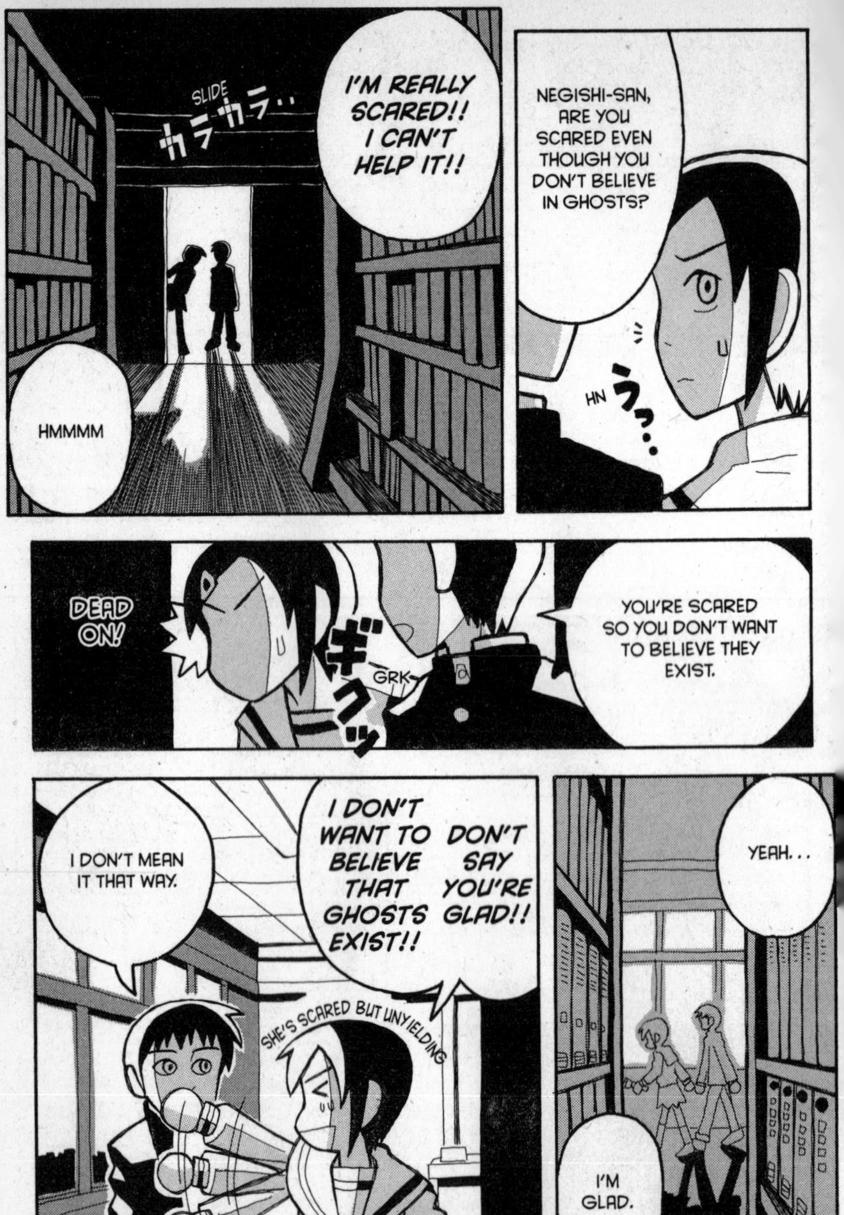
NEGISHI-SAN, ARE YOU SCARED EVEN THOUGH YOU DON'T BELIEVE IN GHOSTS?
HN うっ…
I'M REALLY SCARED!! I CAN'T HELP IT!!
SLIDE カラカラ‥
HMMMM
YOU'RE SCARED SO YOU DON'T WANT TO BELIEVE THEY EXIST.
GRK ギクッ
DEAD ON!
YEAH...
I'M GLAD.
DON'T SAY YOU'RE GLAD!!
I DON'T WANT TO BELIEVE THAT GHOSTS EXIST!!
I DON'T MEAN IT THAT WAY.
SHE'S SCARED BUT UNYIELDING

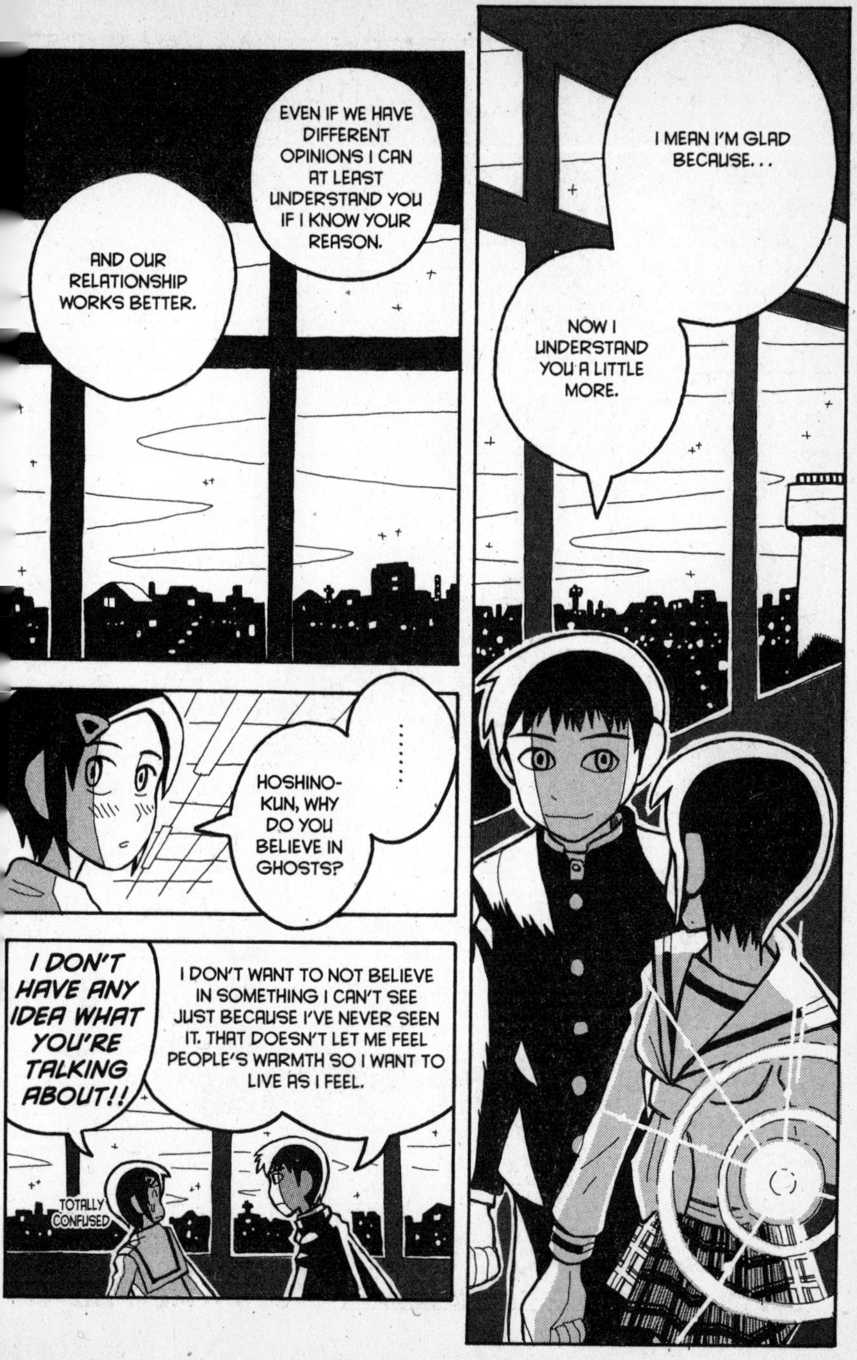
I MEAN I'M GLAD BECAUSE. . .
NOW I UNDERSTAND YOU A LITTLE MORE.
EVEN IF WE HAVE DIFFERENT OPINIONS I CAN AT LEAST UNDERSTAND YOU IF I KNOW YOUR REASON.
AND OUR RELATIONSHIP WORKS BETTER.
......
HOSHINO-KUN, WHY DO YOU BELIEVE IN GHOSTS?
I DON'T WANT TO NOT BELIEVE IN SOMETHING I CAN'T SEE JUST BECAUSE I'VE NEVER SEEN IT. THAT DOESN'T LET ME FEEL PEOPLE'S WARMTH SO I WANT TO LIVE AS I FEEL.
I DON'T HAVE ANY IDEA WHAT YOU'RE TALKING ABOUT!!
TOTALLY CONFUSED

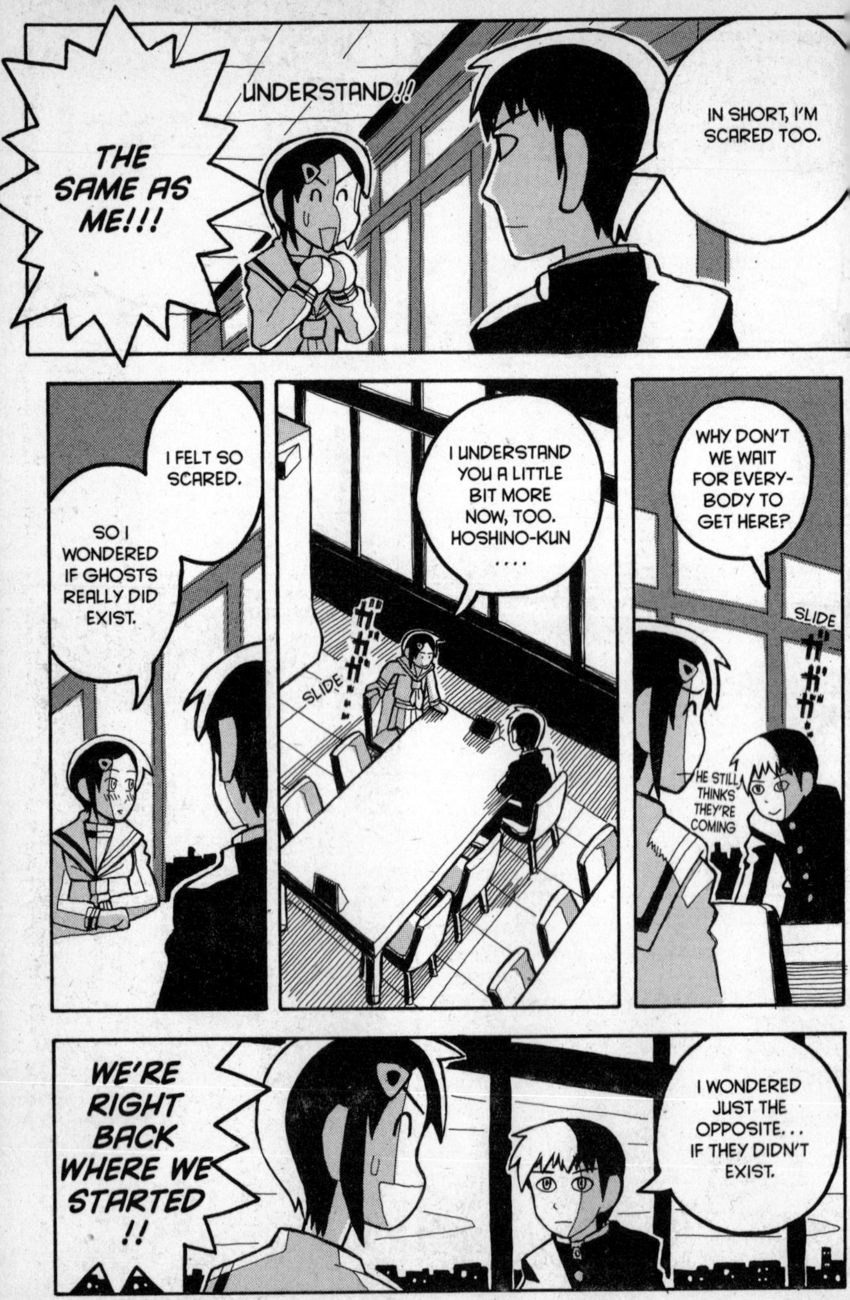
IN SHORT, I'M SCARED TOO.
UNDERSTAND!!
THE SAME AS ME!!!
WHY DON'T WE WAIT FOR EVERY-BODY TO GET HERE?
SLIDE
HE STILL THINKS THEY'RE COMING
I UNDERSTAND YOU A LITTLE BIT MORE NOW, TOO. HOSHINO-KUN . . . .
SLIDE
I FELT SO SCARED.
SO I WONDERED IF GHOSTS REALLY DID EXIST.
I WONDERED JUST THE OPPOSITE. . . IF THEY DIDN'T EXIST.
WE'RE RIGHT BACK WHERE WE STARTED !!

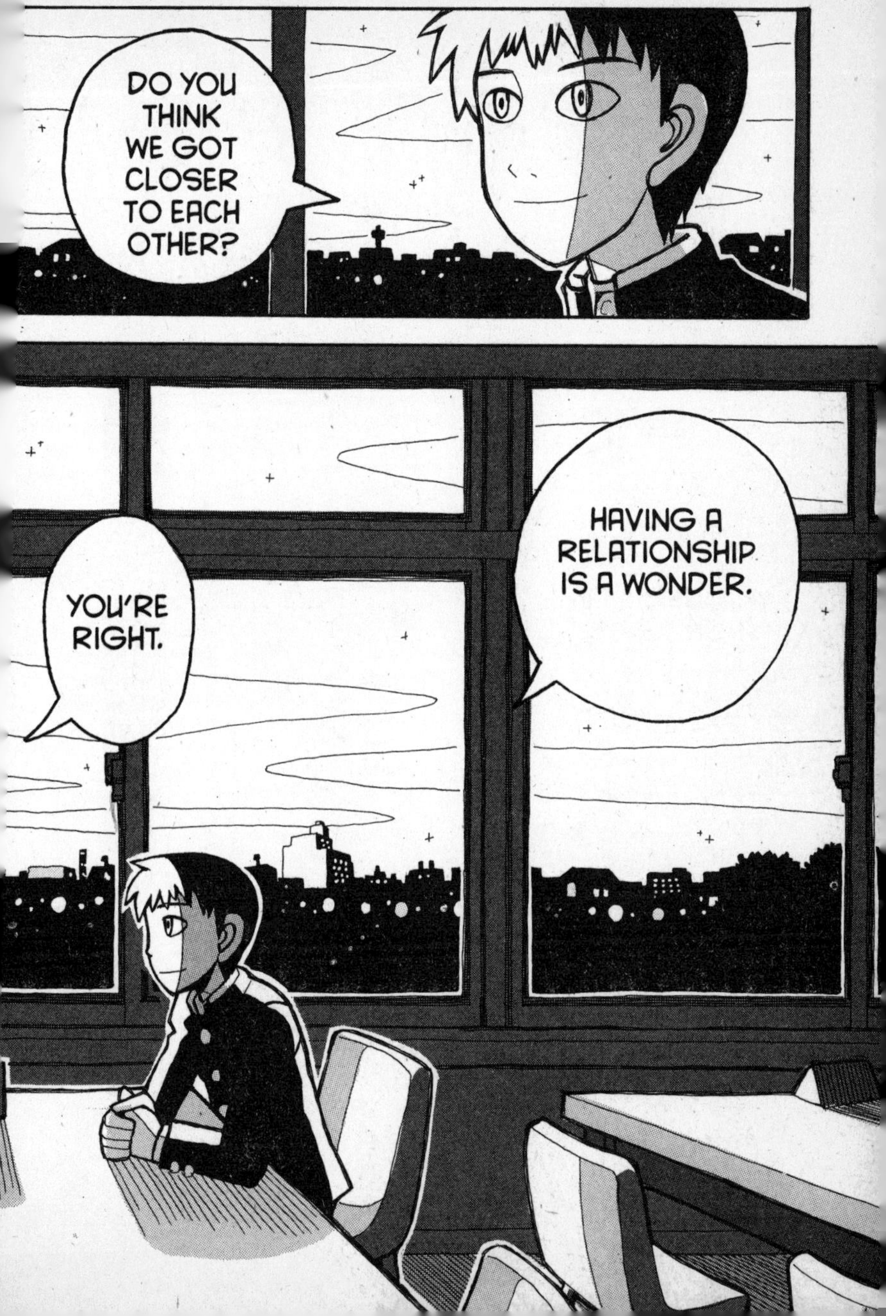
DO YOU THINK WE GOT CLOSER TO EACH OTHER?
HAVING A RELATIONSHIP IS A WONDER.
YOU'RE RIGHT.

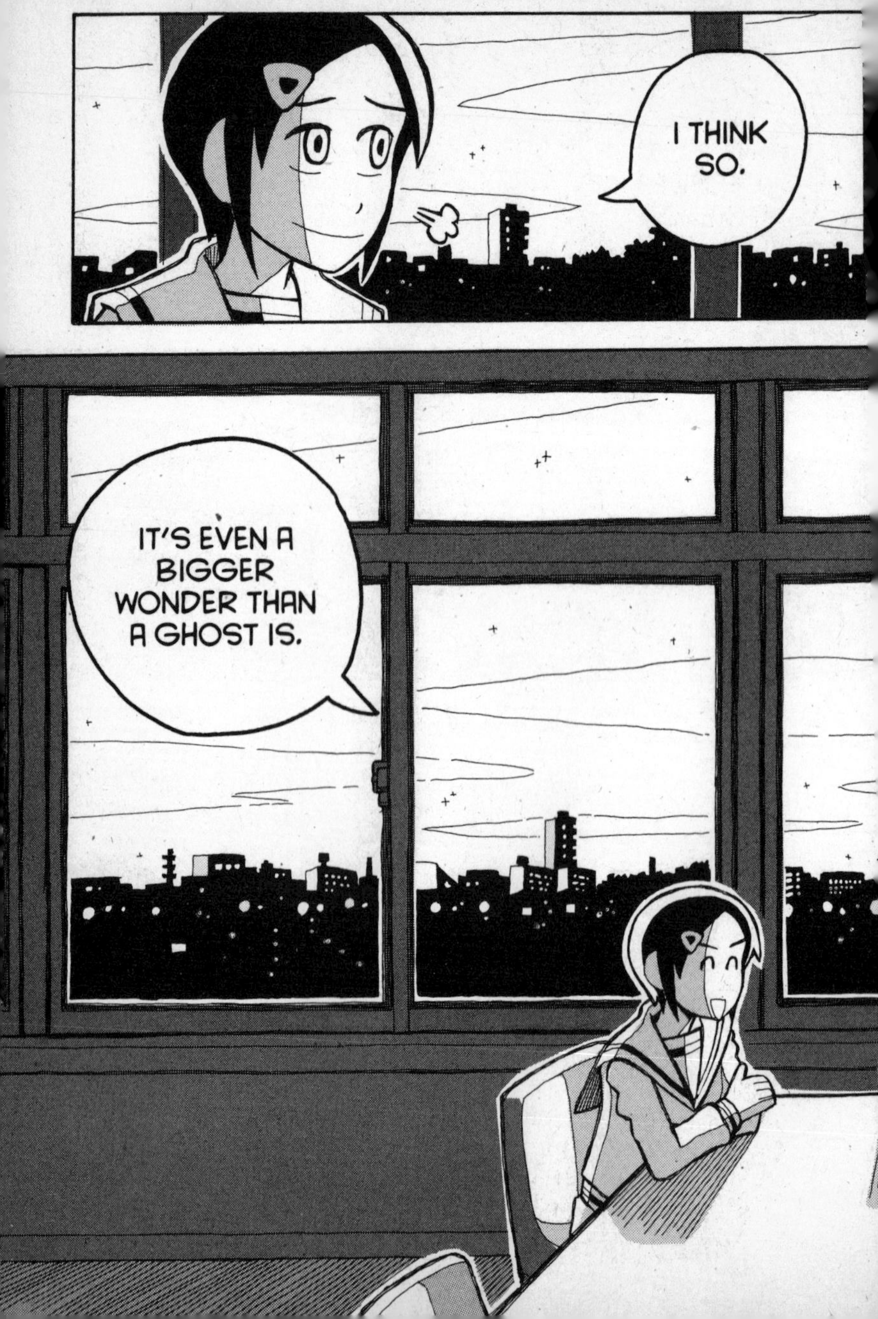
I THINK SO.
IT'S EVEN A BIGGER WONDER THAN A GHOST IS.

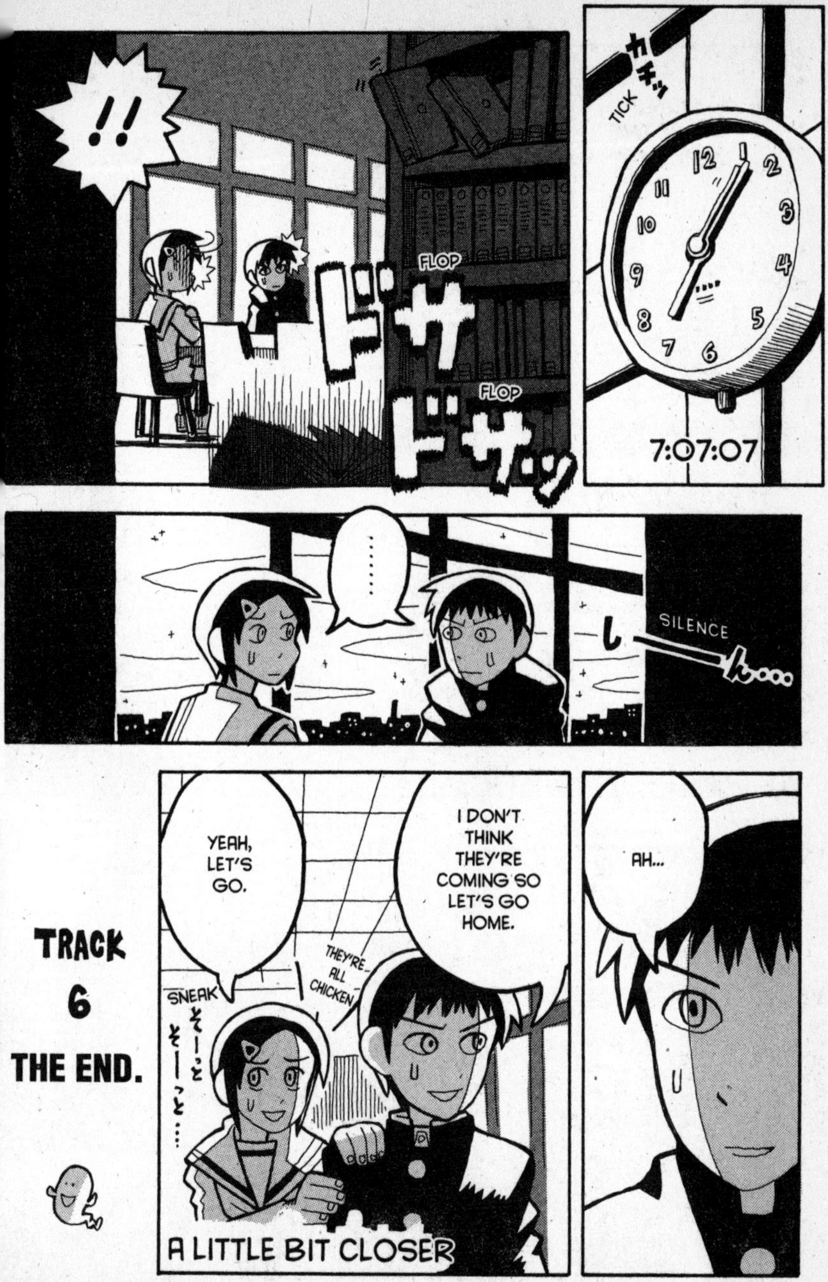

カチッ
TICK
7:07:07
!!
FLOP
ドサ
FLOP
ドサッ
……
SILENCE
しん…
AH...
I DON'T THINK THEY'RE COMING SO LET'S GO HOME.
THEY'RE ALL CHICKEN
YEAH, LET'S GO.
SNEAK
そーっと そーっと…
A LITTLE BIT CLOSER
TRACK 6 THE END.

To Be Continued...

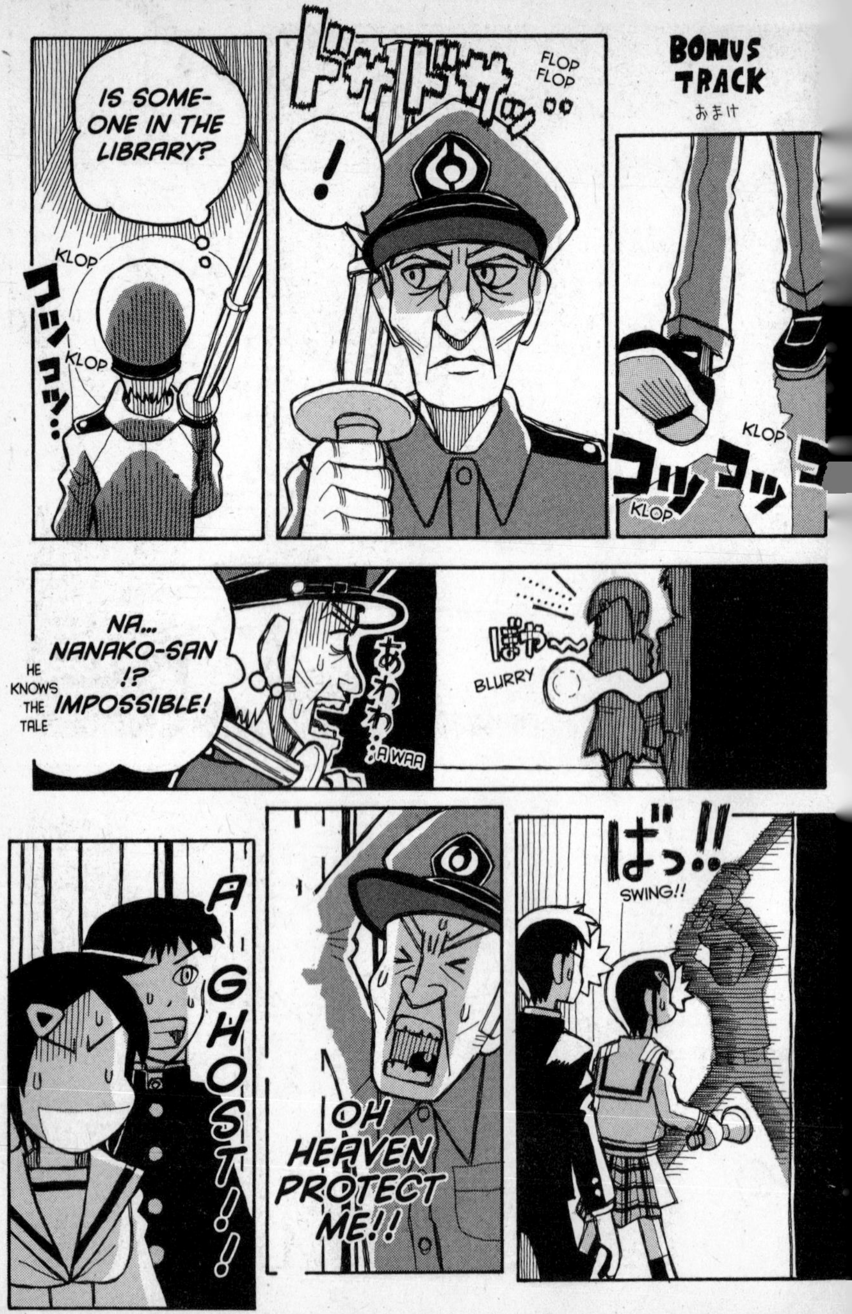
BONUS TRACK
おまけ
KLOP
コッコッコ
KLOP
ドサドサッ
FLOP FLOP
!
IS SOME-ONE IN THE LIBRARY?
KLOP
コツコツ..
KLOP
ぼや〜〜
BLURRY
NA... NANAKO-SAN !? IMPOSSIBLE!
HE KNOWS THE TALE
あわわ…
AWAA
ばっ!!
SWING!!
OH HEAVEN PROTECT ME!!
A GHOST!!!

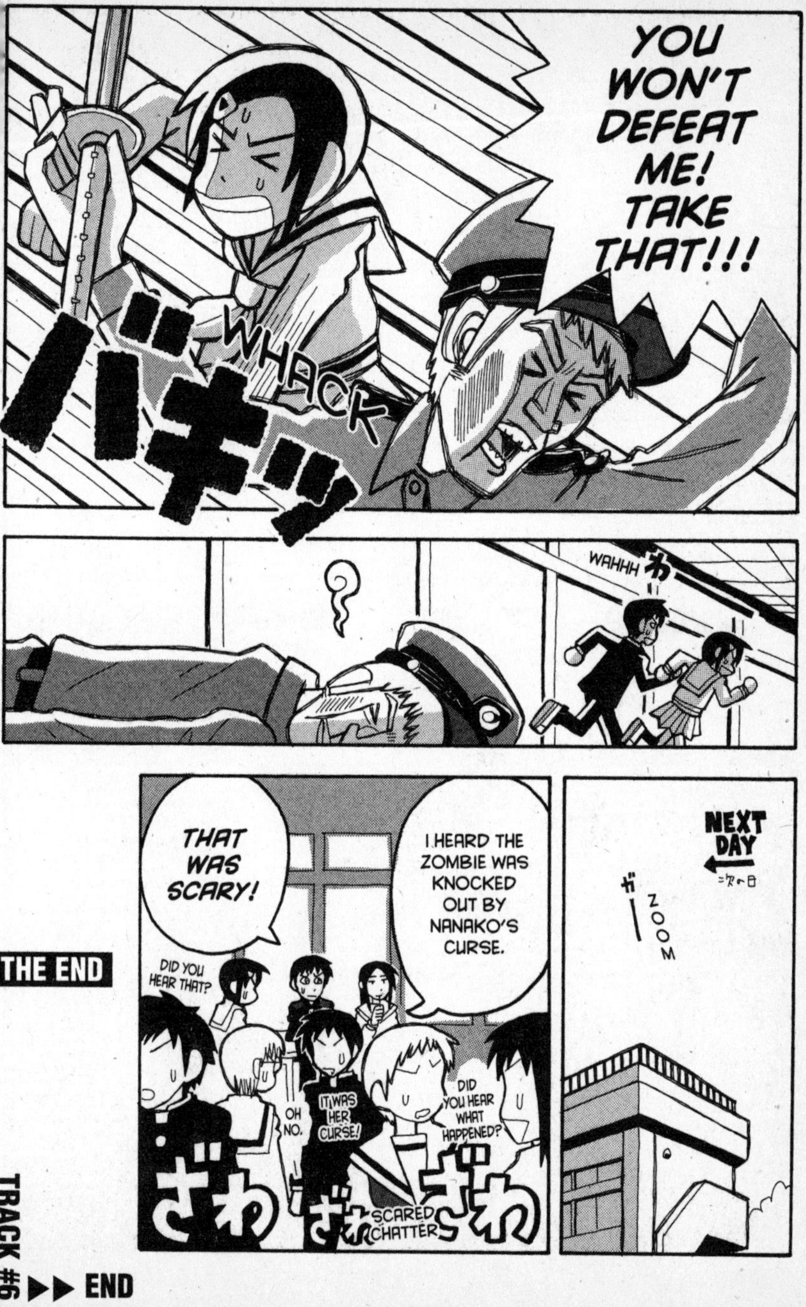
YOU WON'T DEFEAT ME! TAKE THAT!!!
バキッ
WHACK
WAHHH わー
NEXT DAY
ガー
ZOOM
I HEARD THE ZOMBIE WAS KNOCKED OUT BY NANAKO'S CURSE.
THAT WAS SCARY!
DID YOU HEAR WHAT HAPPENED?
IT WAS HER CURSE!
OH NO.
DID YOU HEAR THAT?
ざわ ざわ ざわ ざわ
SCARED CHATTER

THE END

TRACK #6 ▶▶ END

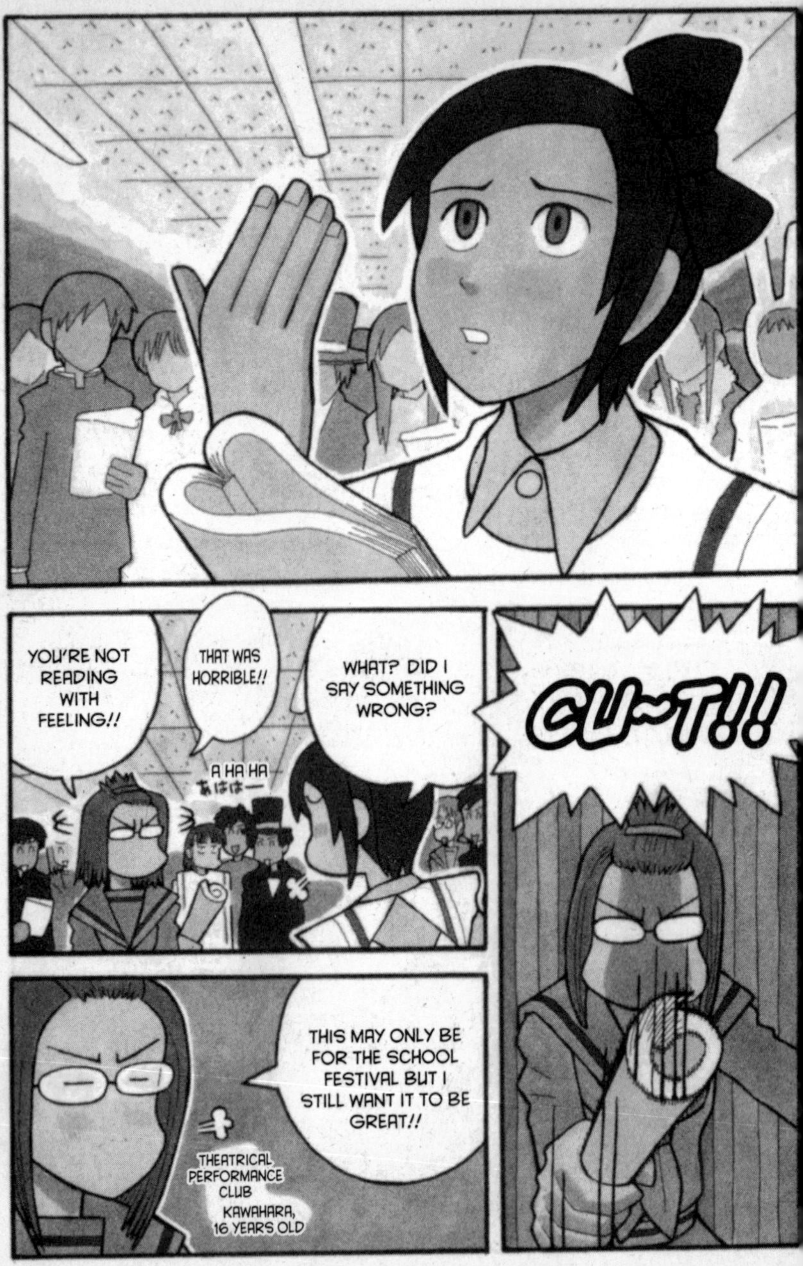
CU~T!!
WHAT? DID I SAY SOMETHING WRONG?
THAT WAS HORRIBLE!!
YOU'RE NOT READING WITH FEELING!!
A HA HA
あははー
THIS MAY ONLY BE FOR THE SCHOOL FESTIVAL BUT I STILL WANT IT TO BE GREAT!!
THEATRICAL PERFORMANCE CLUB
KAWAHARA, 16 YEARS OLD

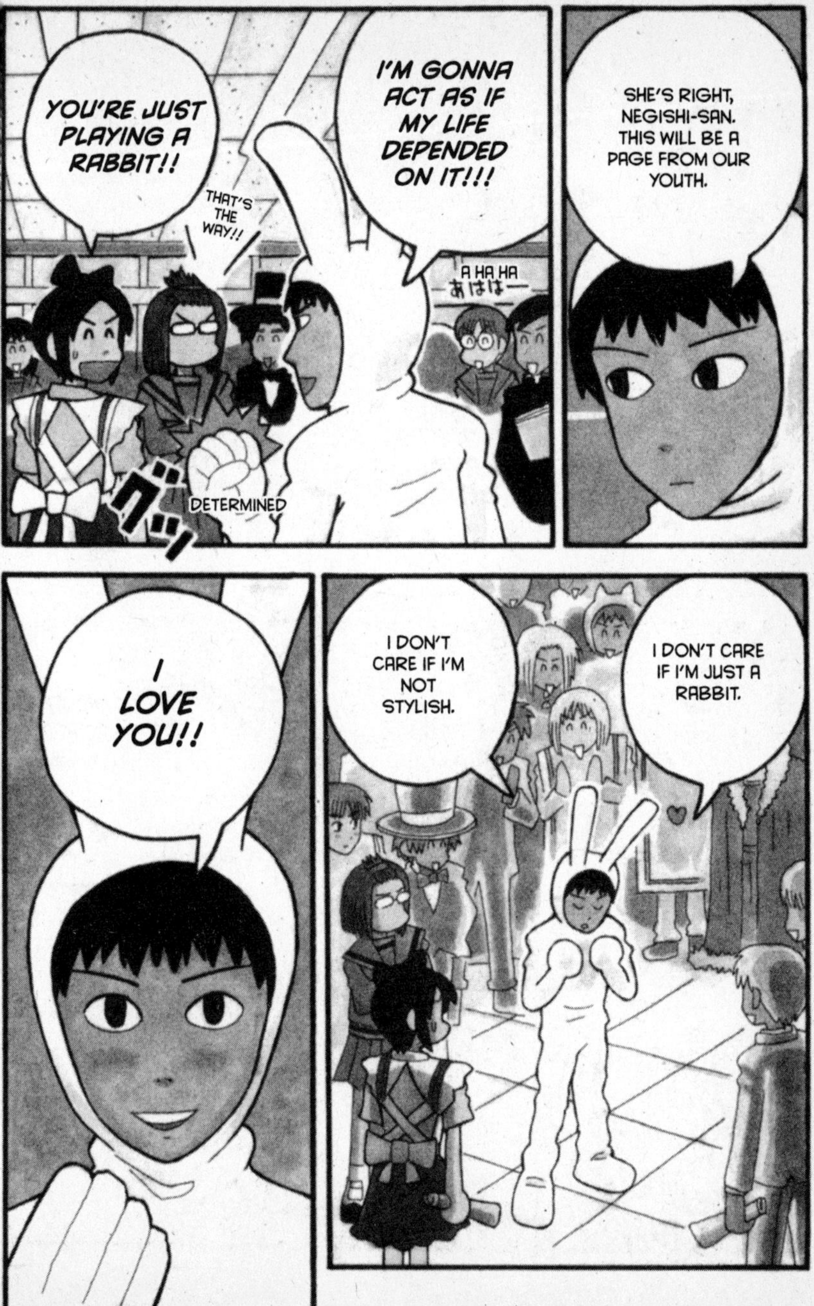
SHE'S RIGHT, NEGISHI-SAN. THIS WILL BE A PAGE FROM OUR YOUTH.
I'M GONNA ACT AS IF MY LIFE DEPENDED ON IT!!!
A HA HA
あははー
YOU'RE JUST PLAYING A RABBIT!!
THAT'S THE WAY!!
DETERMINED
グッ
I DON'T CARE IF I'M JUST A RABBIT.
I DON'T CARE IF I'M NOT STYLISH.
I LOVE YOU!!

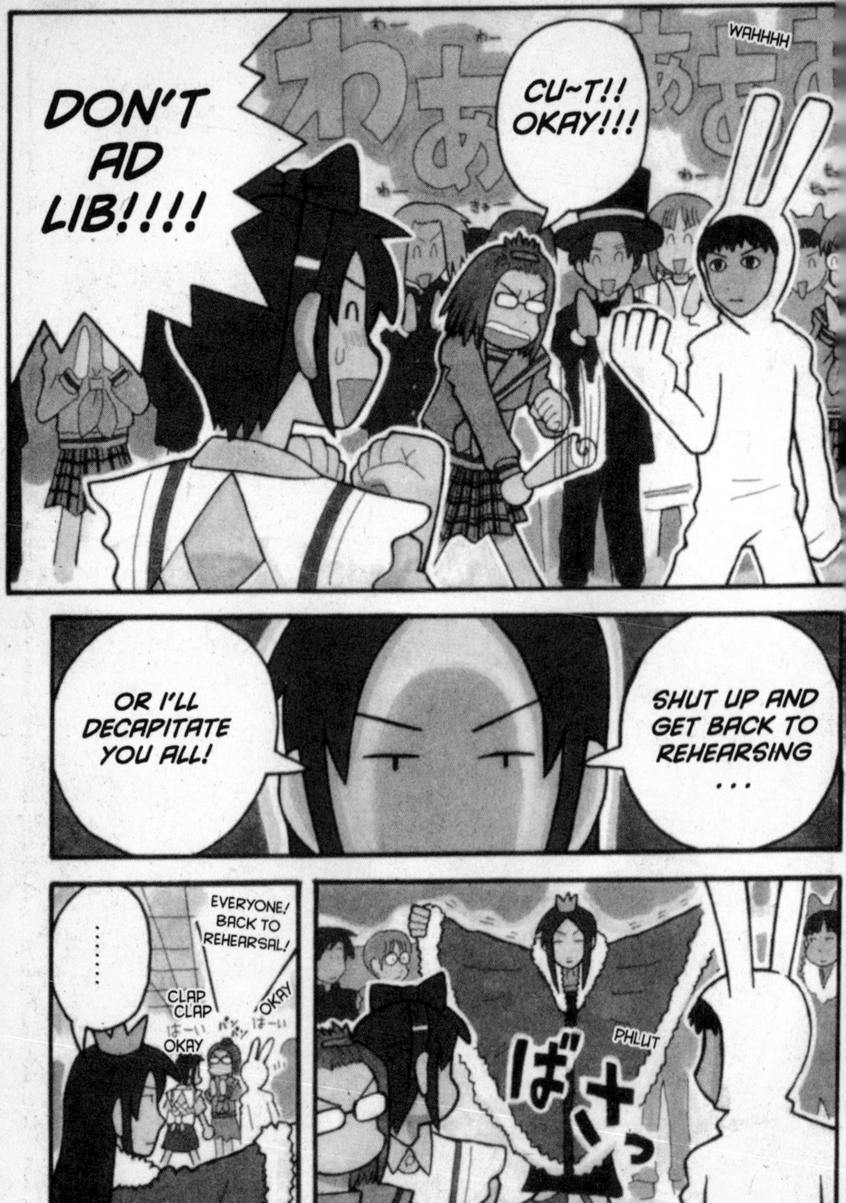
WAHHHH
CU~T!! OKAY!!!
DON'T AD LIB!!!!
SHUT UP AND GET BACK TO REHEARSING ...
OR I'LL DECAPITATE YOU ALL!
PHLUT
ばさっ
......
EVERYONE! BACK TO REHEARSAL!
OKAY
はーい
CLAP CLAP
パチパチ
OKAY
はーい

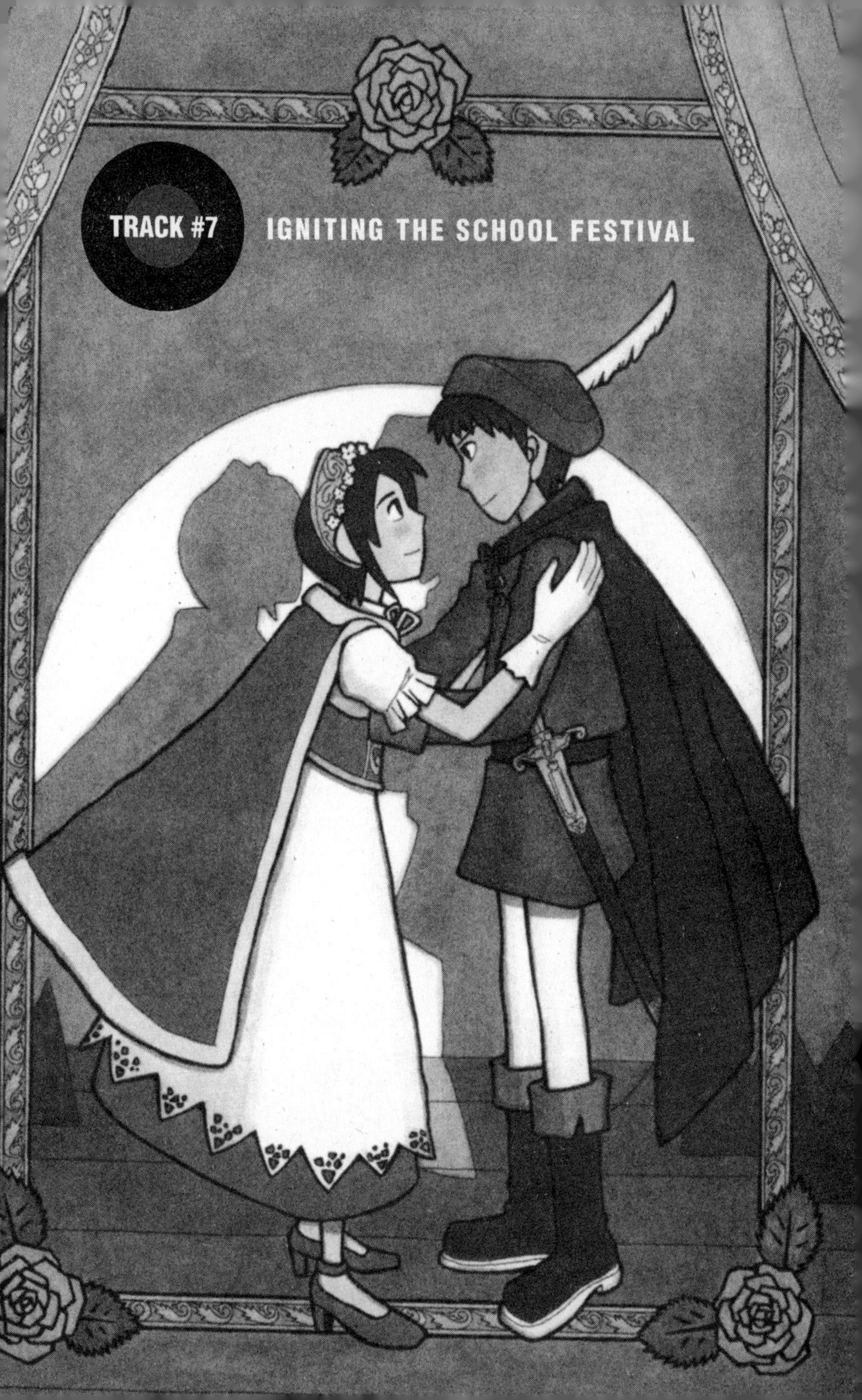
TRACK #7
IGNITING THE SCHOOL FESTIVAL

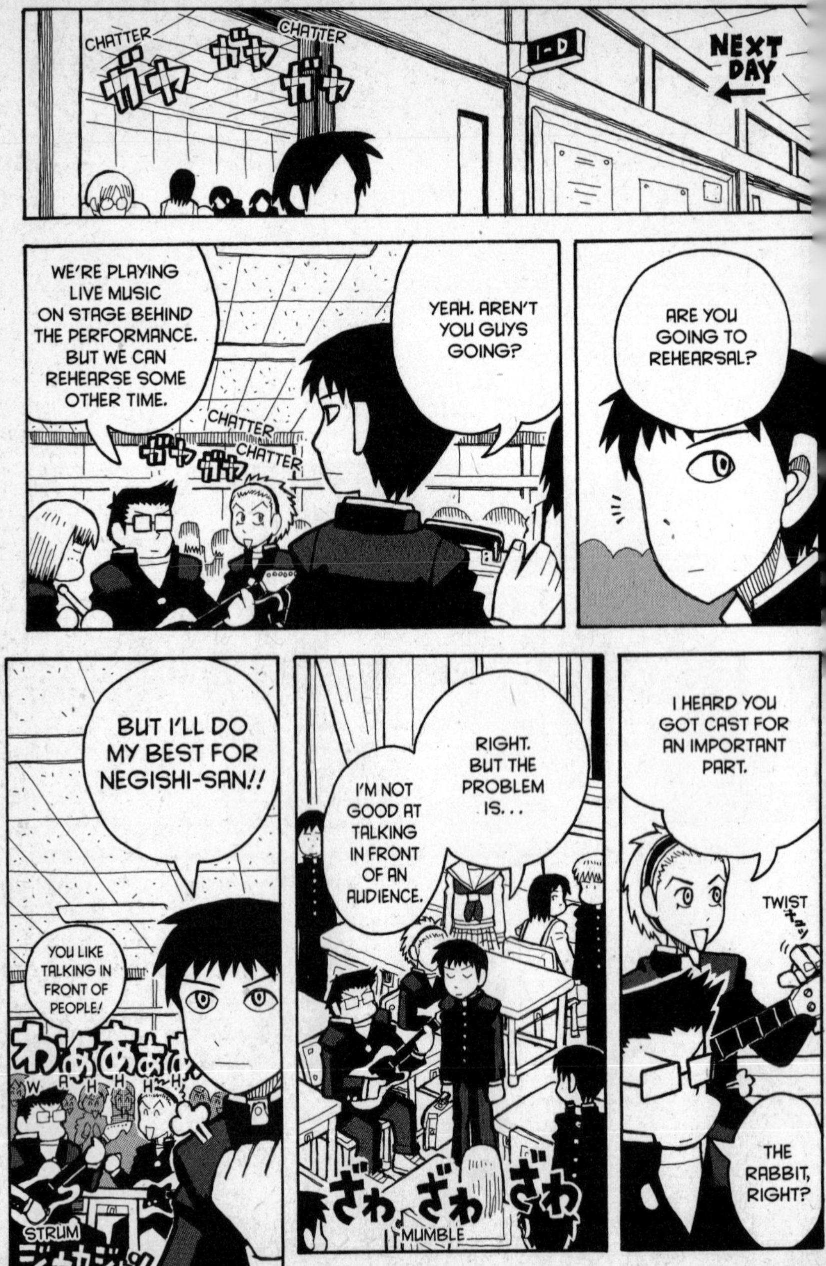
NEXT DAY
1-D
CHATTER
ガヤ
ガヤ
CHATTER
ガヤ
ARE YOU GOING TO REHEARSAL?
YEAH. AREN'T YOU GUYS GOING?
WE'RE PLAYING LIVE MUSIC ON STAGE BEHIND THE PERFORMANCE. BUT WE CAN REHEARSE SOME OTHER TIME.
CHATTER CHATTER
I HEARD YOU GOT CAST FOR AN IMPORTANT PART.
TWIST
THE RABBIT, RIGHT?
RIGHT. BUT THE PROBLEM IS. . .
I'M NOT GOOD AT TALKING IN FRONT OF AN AUDIENCE.
ざわ ざわ ざわ
MUMBLE
BUT I'LL DO MY BEST FOR NEGISHI-SAN!!
YOU LIKE TALKING IN FRONT OF PEOPLE!
WAHHH!
STRUM

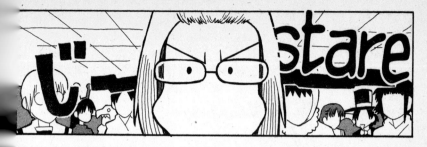

じー
stare
HEY RABBIT-SAN, WAIT UP!
YES?
EH?
WHAT'S WRONG?
IN THIS SCENE THE RABBIT IS SUPPOSED TO RUN AWAY!!
A HA HA
あはは一
IS THAT SO?
ビシッ
WHACK
A HA HA
あははは一
ARE THE RABBIT AND ALICE DATING?
DO YOU MEAN NEGI AND HOSHI-KUN?
ちう
SLURP
THEY'RE DEEPLY IN LOVE.
THAT'S INTERESTING.

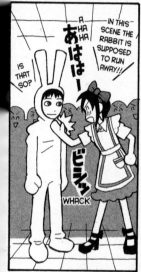

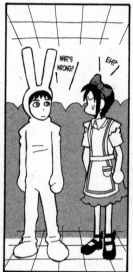

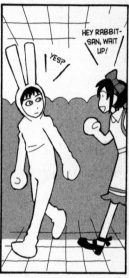

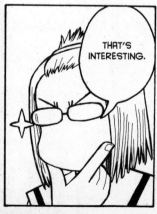

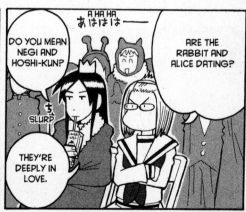

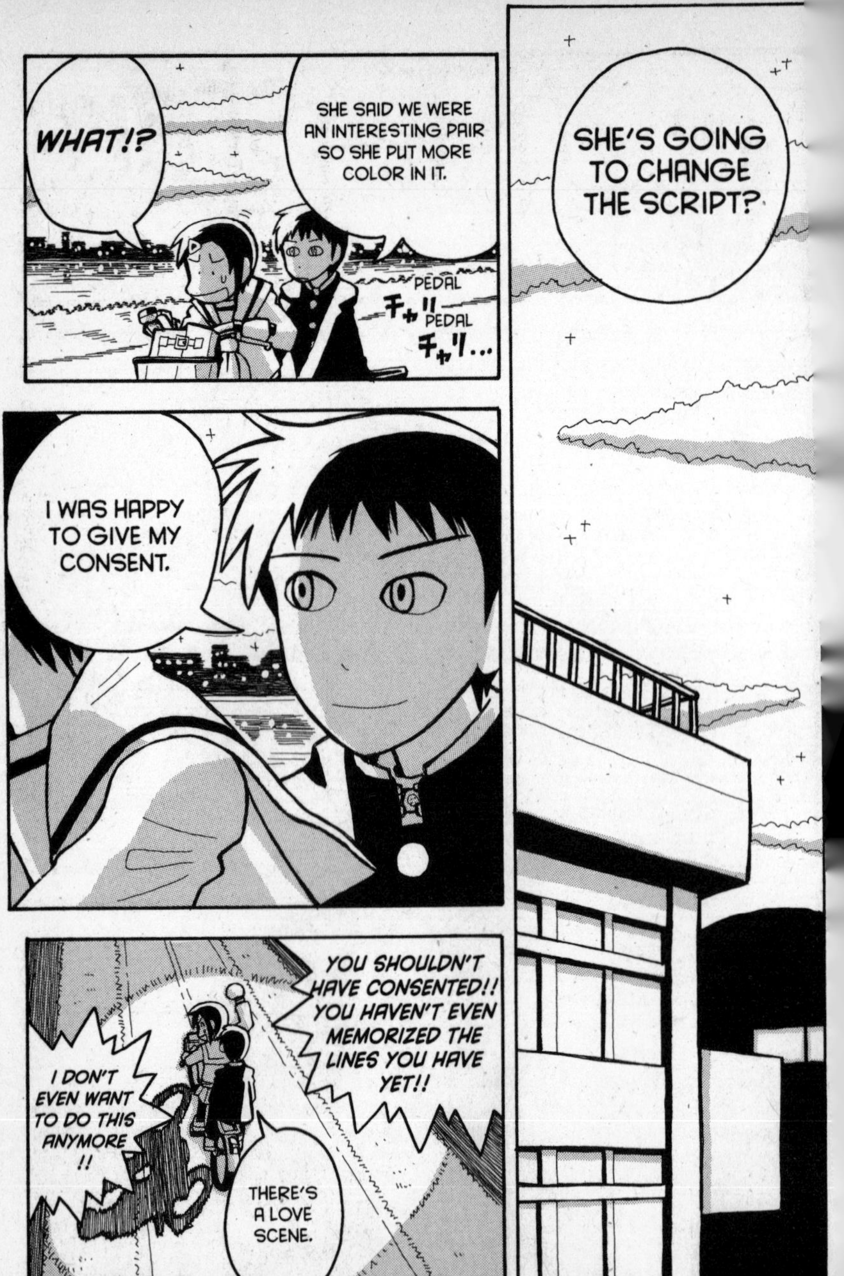
SHE'S GOING TO CHANGE THE SCRIPT?
SHE SAID WE WERE AN INTERESTING PAIR SO SHE PUT MORE COLOR IN IT.
WHAT!?
PEDAL チャリ
PEDAL チャリ...
I WAS HAPPY TO GIVE MY CONSENT.
YOU SHOULDN'T HAVE CONSENTED!! YOU HAVEN'T EVEN MEMORIZED THE LINES YOU HAVE YET!!
THERE'S A LOVE SCENE.
I DON'T EVEN WANT TO DO THIS ANYMORE !!

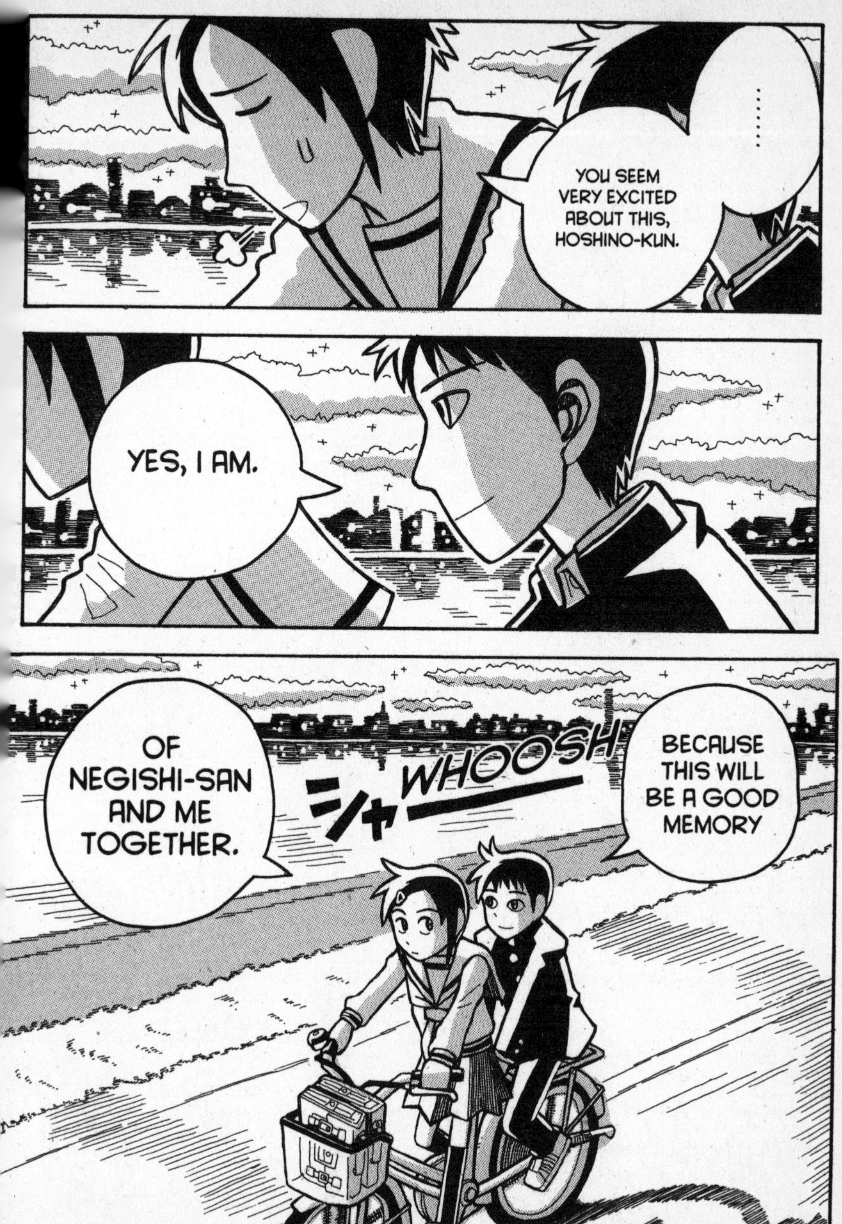
......
YOU SEEM VERY EXCITED ABOUT THIS, HOSHINO-KUN.
YES, I AM.
BECAUSE THIS WILL BE A GOOD MEMORY
シャー WHOOSH
OF NEGISHI-SAN AND ME TOGETHER.

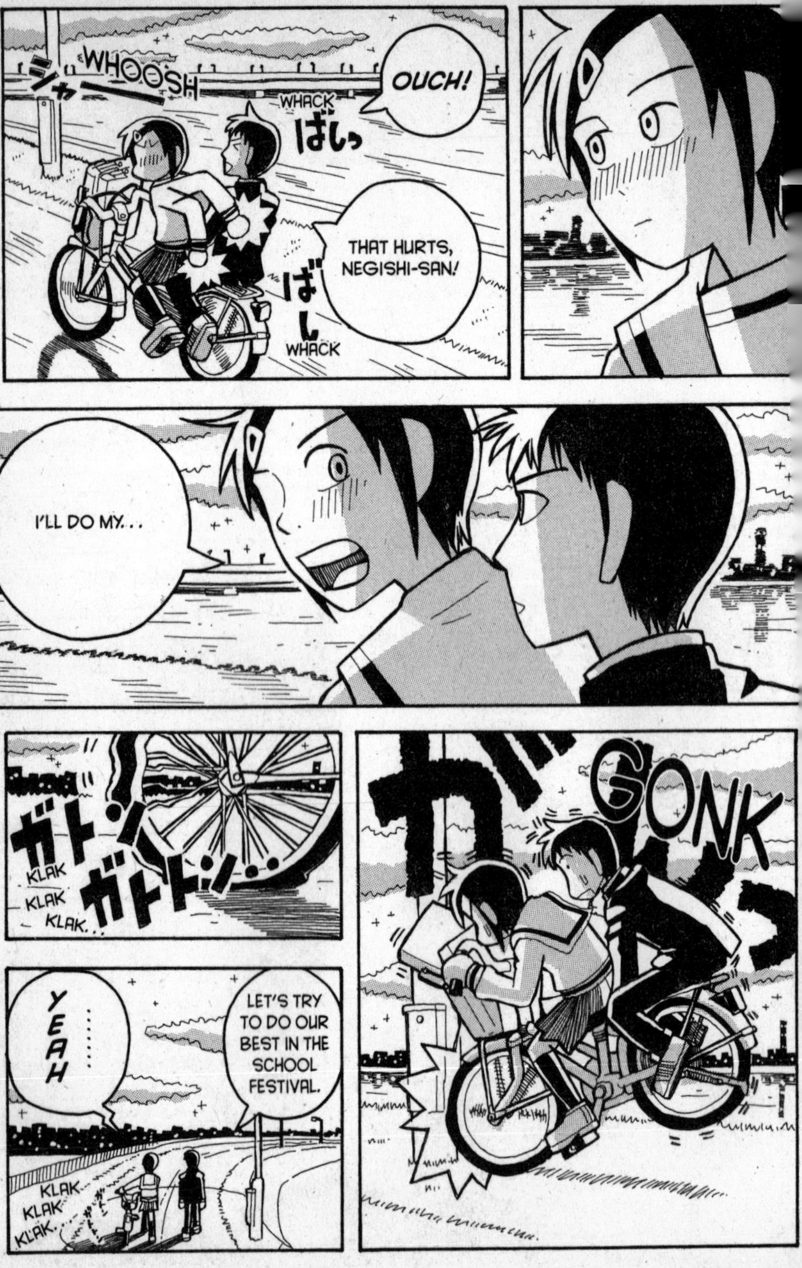
OUCH!
WHACK
ばしっ
WHOOSH
シャー
THAT HURTS, NEGISHI-SAN!
ばし
WHACK
I'LL DO MY...
GONK
ガッ
ガトッ
ガトッ
KLAK
KLAK
KLAK...
LET'S TRY TO DO OUR BEST IN THE SCHOOL FESTIVAL.
YEAH......
KLAK
KLAK
KLAK...

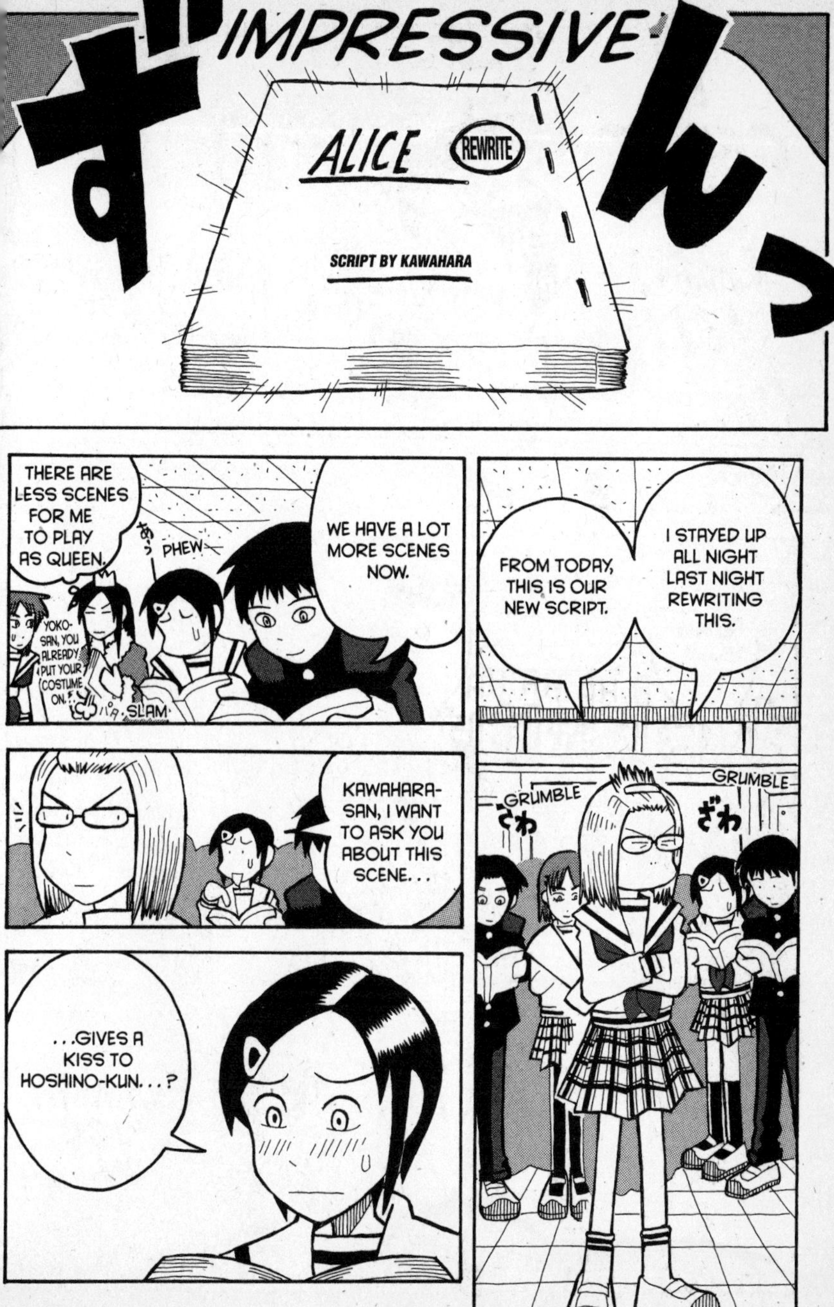

IMPRESSIVE
ずんっ
ALICE
REWRITE
SCRIPT BY KAWAHARA
I STAYED UP ALL NIGHT LAST NIGHT REWRITING THIS.
FROM TODAY, THIS IS OUR NEW SCRIPT.
WE HAVE A LOT MORE SCENES NOW.
PHEW
あっ
THERE ARE LESS SCENES FOR ME TO PLAY AS QUEEN.
YOKO-SAN, YOU ALREADY PUT YOUR COSTUME ON.
パ
SLAM
GRUMBLE
ざわ
GRUMBLE
ざわ
KAWAHARA-SAN, I WANT TO ASK YOU ABOUT THIS SCENE...
...GIVES A KISS TO HOSHINO-KUN...?

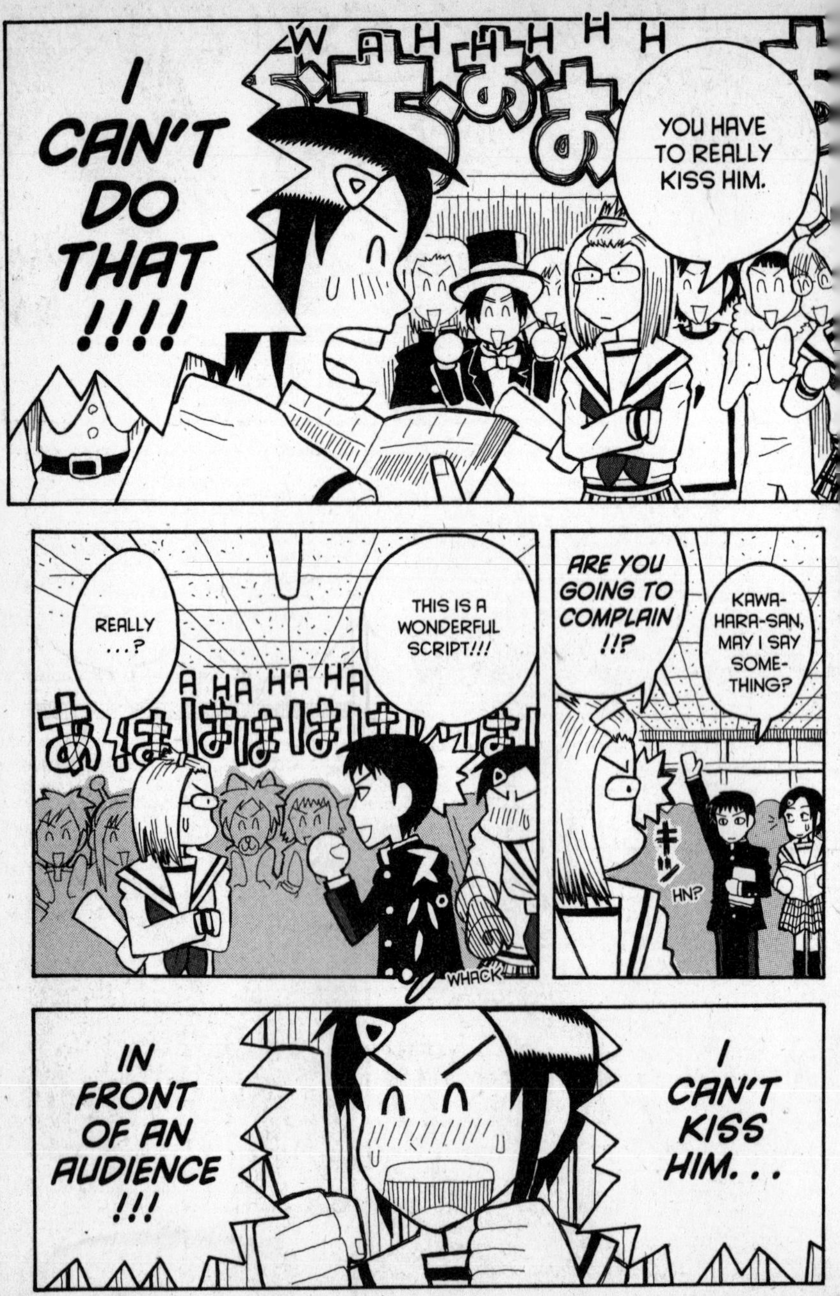

WAHHHHH
YOU HAVE TO REALLY KISS HIM.
I CAN'T DO THAT!!!!
KAWA-HARA-SAN, MAY I SAY SOME-THING?
ARE YOU GOING TO COMPLAIN!!?
HN?
THIS IS A WONDERFUL SCRIPT!!!
A HA HA HA
REALLY...?
WHACK
I CAN'T KISS HIM...
IN FRONT OF AN AUDIENCE!!!

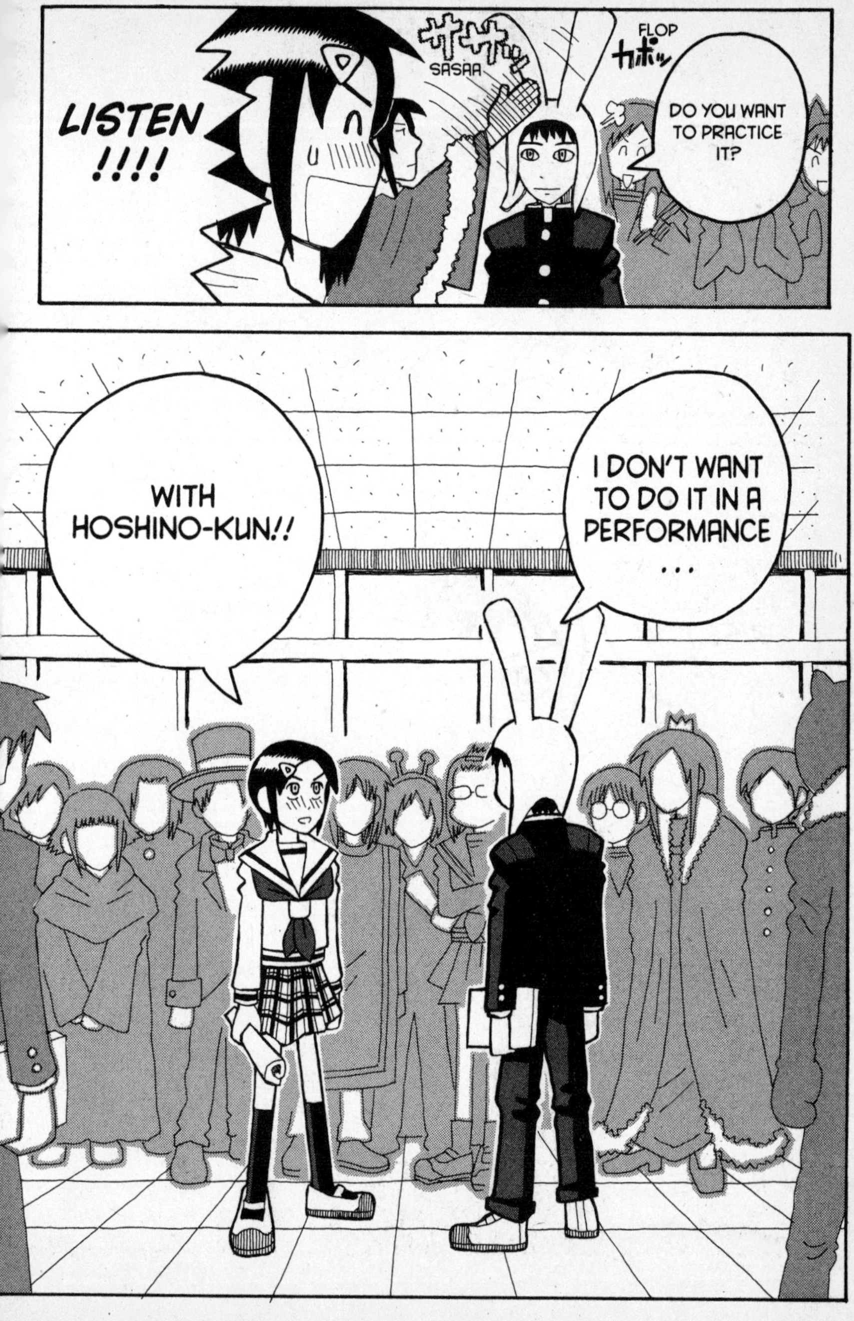

FLOP
カポッ
DO YOU WANT TO PRACTICE IT?
SASAA
LISTEN !!!!
I DON'T WANT TO DO IT IN A PERFORMANCE ...
WITH HOSHINO-KUN!!

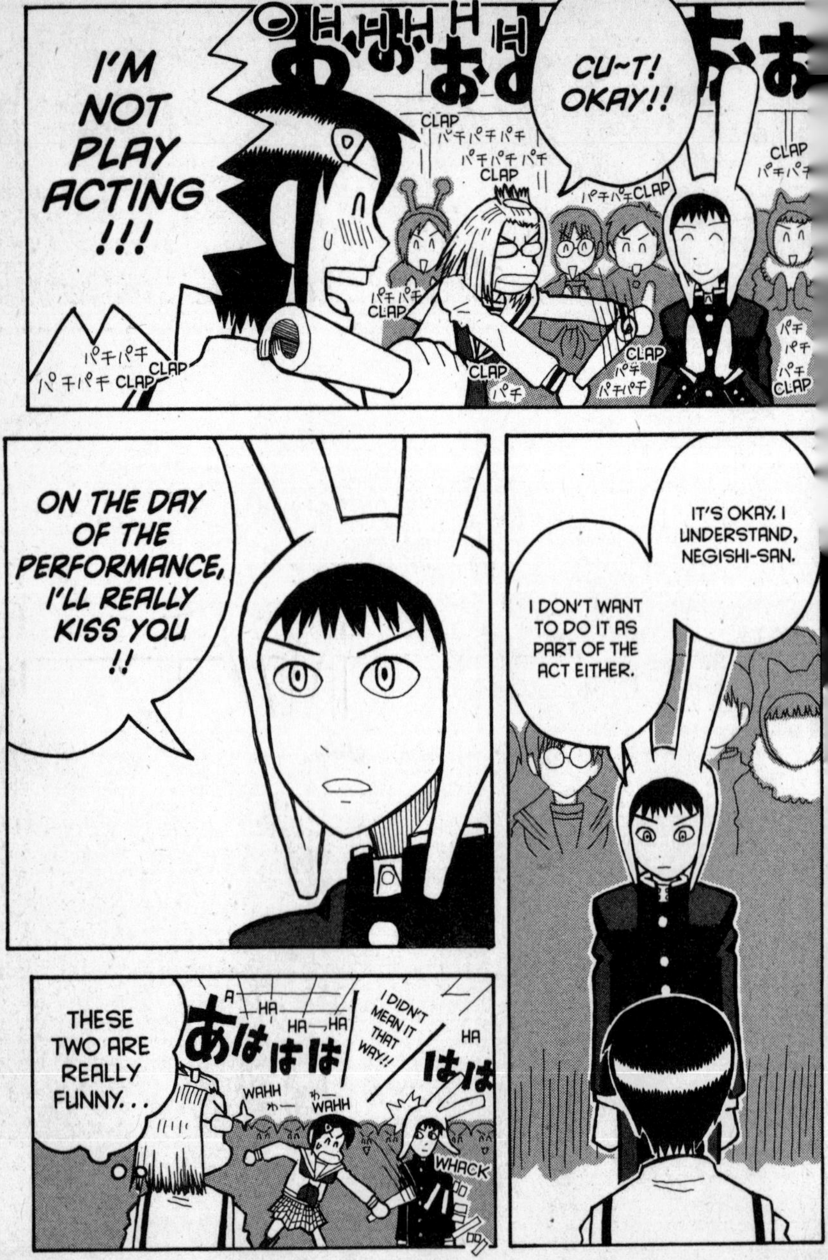
CU~T! OKAY!!
CLAP パチパチパチ
パチパチパチ CLAP
CLAP パチパチ
パチパチCLAP
HAHAHAH
I'M NOT PLAY ACTING!!!
パチパチ CLAP
CLAP パチ パチパチ
CLAP パチ
パチパチ CLAP
パチパチ パチパチ CLAP
IT'S OKAY. I UNDERSTAND, NEGISHI-SAN.
I DON'T WANT TO DO IT AS PART OF THE ACT EITHER.
ON THE DAY OF THE PERFORMANCE, I'LL REALLY KISS YOU!!
HA はは
I DIDN'T MEAN IT THAT WAY!!
A HA HA HA あははは
THESE TWO ARE REALLY FUNNY...
WAHH わー
WAHH わー
WHACK

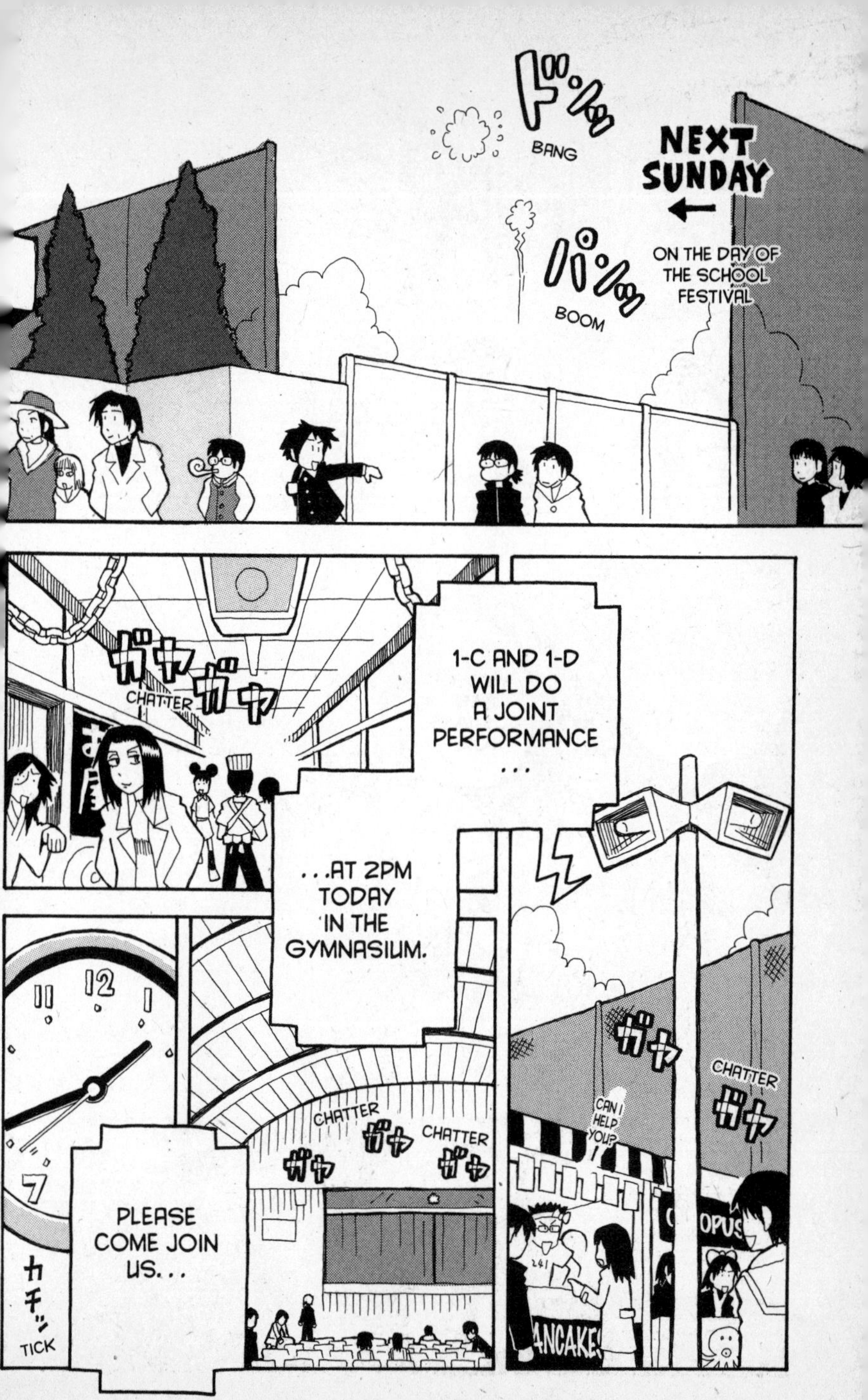

NEXT SUNDAY
ON THE DAY OF THE SCHOOL FESTIVAL
ドン
BANG
パン
BOOM
1-C AND 1-D WILL DO A JOINT PERFORMANCE . . .
. . .AT 2PM TODAY IN THE GYMNASIUM.
ガヤガヤ
CHATTER
ガヤ
CHATTER
ガヤ
CAN I HELP YOU?
OPUS
ANCAKES
CHATTER
ガヤ
CHATTER
ガヤ
ガヤ
PLEASE COME JOIN US. . .
カチッ
TICK

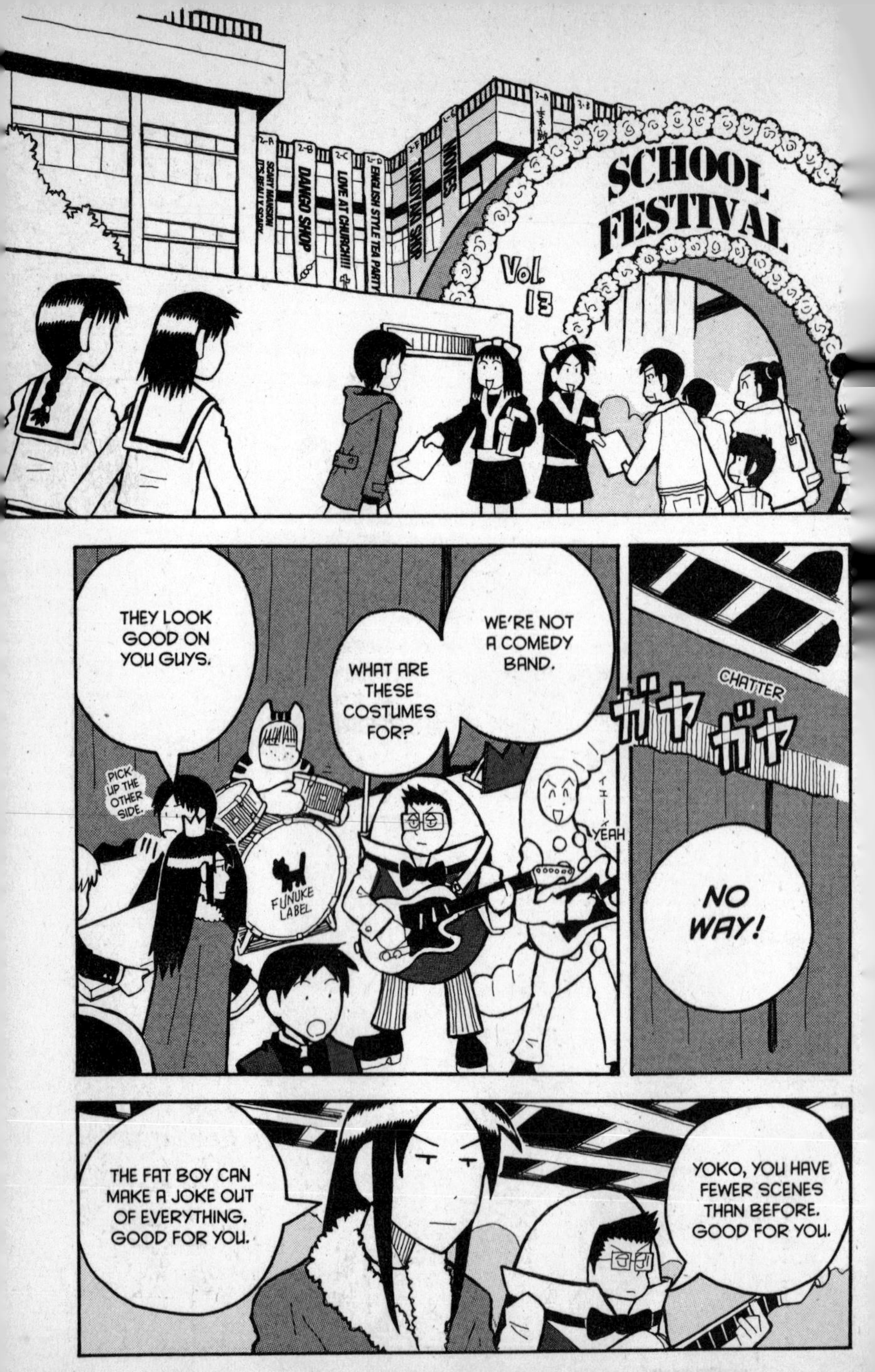
SCHOOL FESTIVAL
Vol. 13
MOVIES
TAKOYAKI SHOP
ENGLISH STYLE TEA PARTY
LOVE AT CHURCH!!!
DANGO SHOP
SCARY MANSION IT'S REALLY SCARY
CHATTER
ガヤガヤ
NO WAY!
WHAT ARE THESE COSTUMES FOR?
WE'RE NOT A COMEDY BAND.
イエー
YEAH
THEY LOOK GOOD ON YOU GUYS.
PICK UP THE OTHER SIDE.
FUNUKE LABEL
YOKO, YOU HAVE FEWER SCENES THAN BEFORE. GOOD FOR YOU.
THE FAT BOY CAN MAKE A JOKE OUT OF EVERYTHING. GOOD FOR YOU.

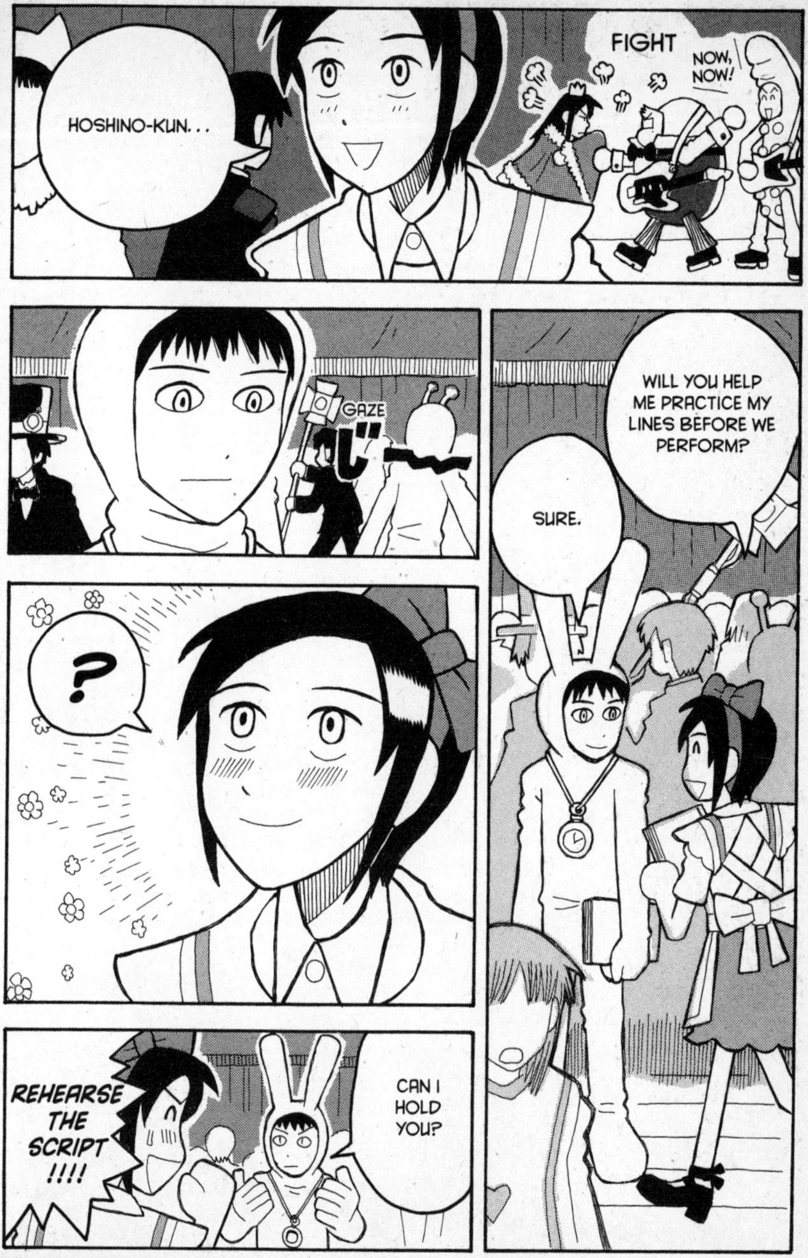
FIGHT
NOW, NOW!
HOSHINO-KUN. . .
WILL YOU HELP ME PRACTICE MY LINES BEFORE WE PERFORM?
SURE.
GAZE
?
CAN I HOLD YOU?
REHEARSE THE SCRIPT !!!!

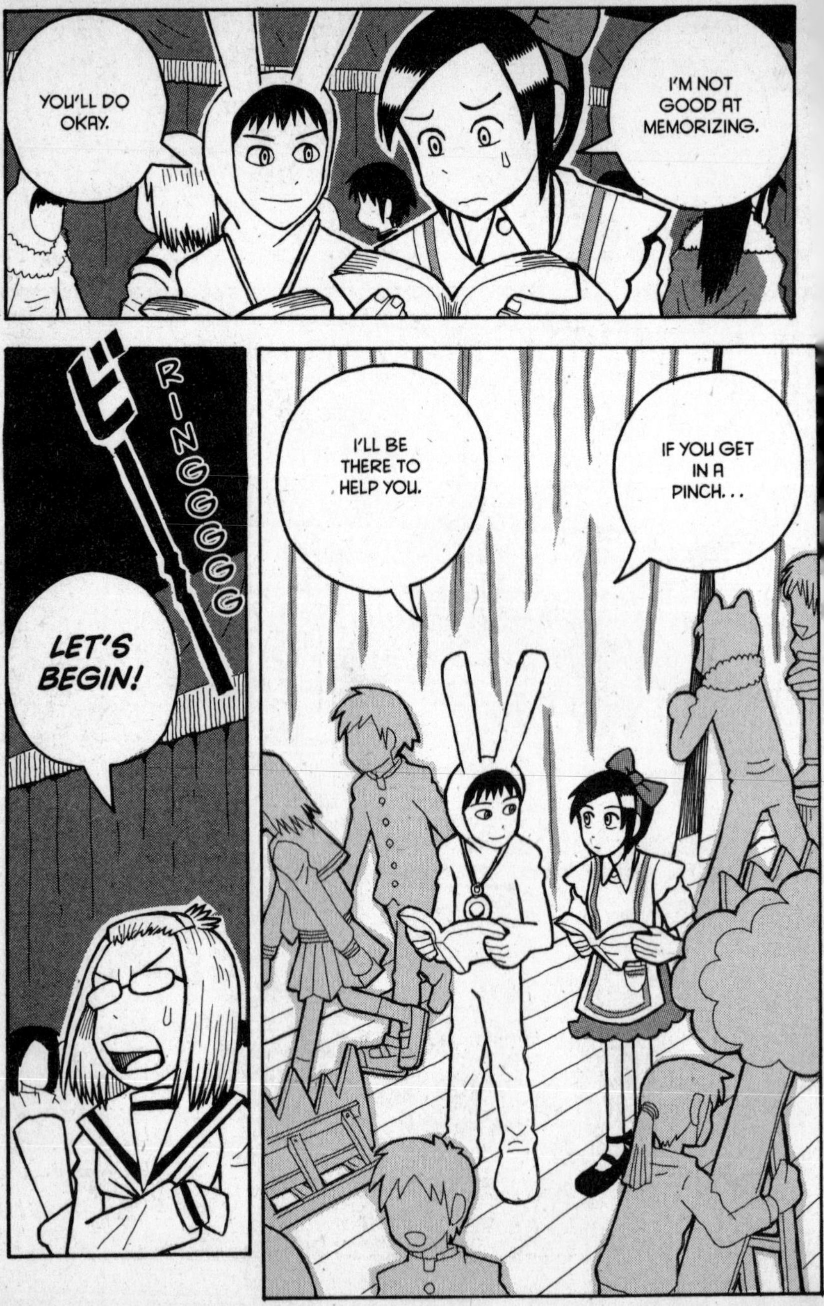
I'M NOT GOOD AT MEMORIZING.
YOU'LL DO OKAY.
IF YOU GET IN A PINCH. . .
I'LL BE THERE TO HELP YOU.
RINGGGGGGG
LET'S BEGIN!

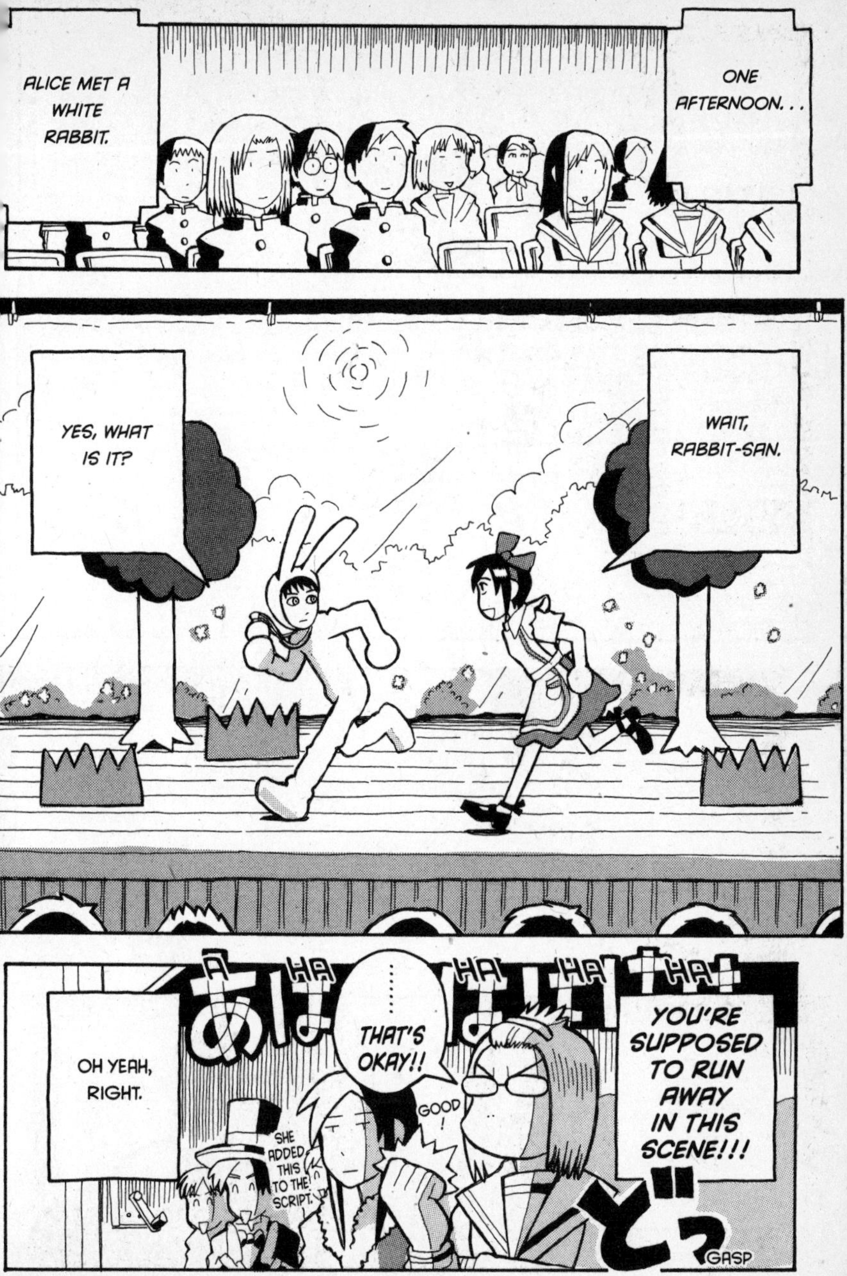
ONE AFTERNOON...
ALICE MET A WHITE RABBIT.
WAIT, RABBIT-SAN.
YES, WHAT IS IT?
A HA HA HA HA
YOU'RE SUPPOSED TO RUN AWAY IN THIS SCENE!!!
GASP
......THAT'S OKAY!!
GOOD!
SHE ADDED THIS TO THE SCRIPT.
OH YEAH, RIGHT.

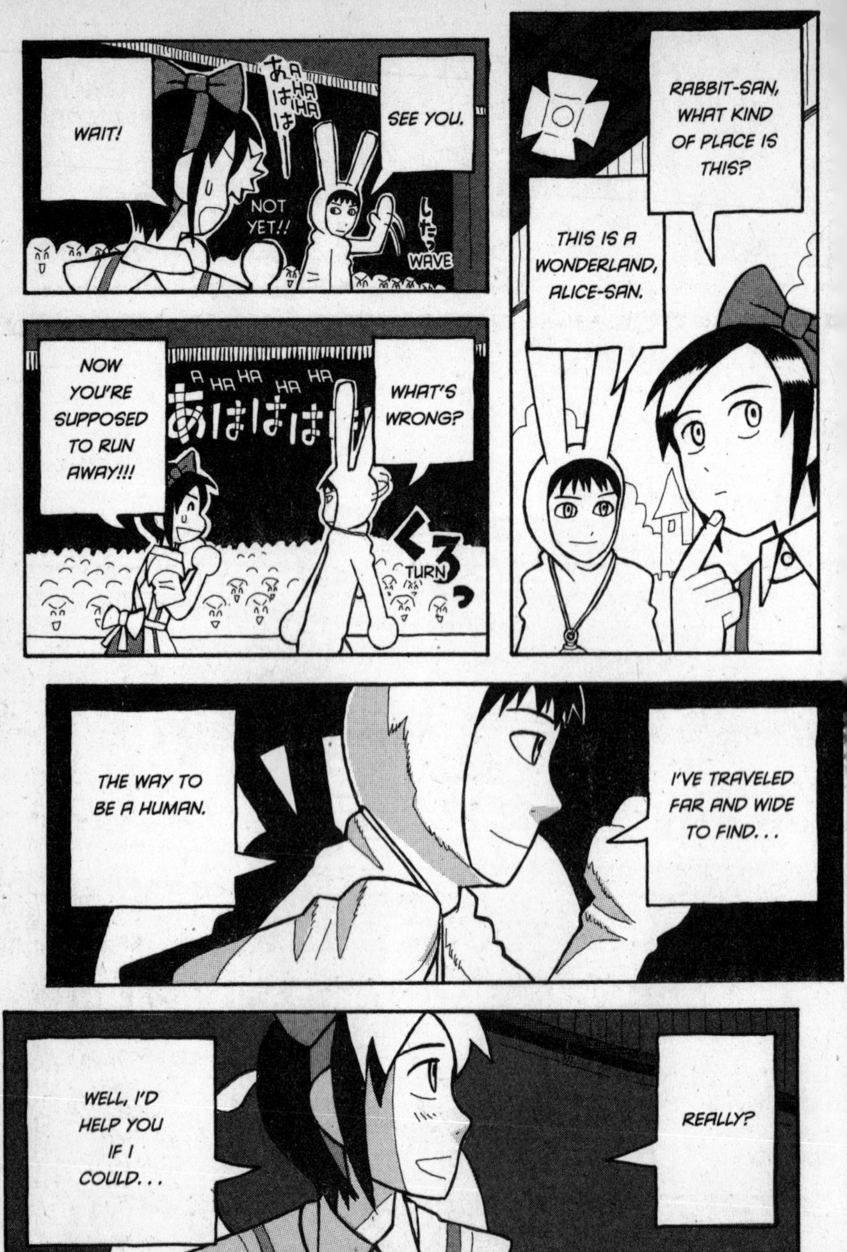
RABBIT-SAN, WHAT KIND OF PLACE IS THIS?
THIS IS A WONDERLAND, ALICE-SAN.
SEE YOU.
あははは
A HA HA
WAVE
NOT YET!!
WAIT!
WHAT'S WRONG?
TURN
あははは
A HA HA HA HA HA
NOW YOU'RE SUPPOSED TO RUN AWAY!!!
I'VE TRAVELED FAR AND WIDE TO FIND...
THE WAY TO BE A HUMAN.
REALLY?
WELL, I'D HELP YOU IF I COULD...

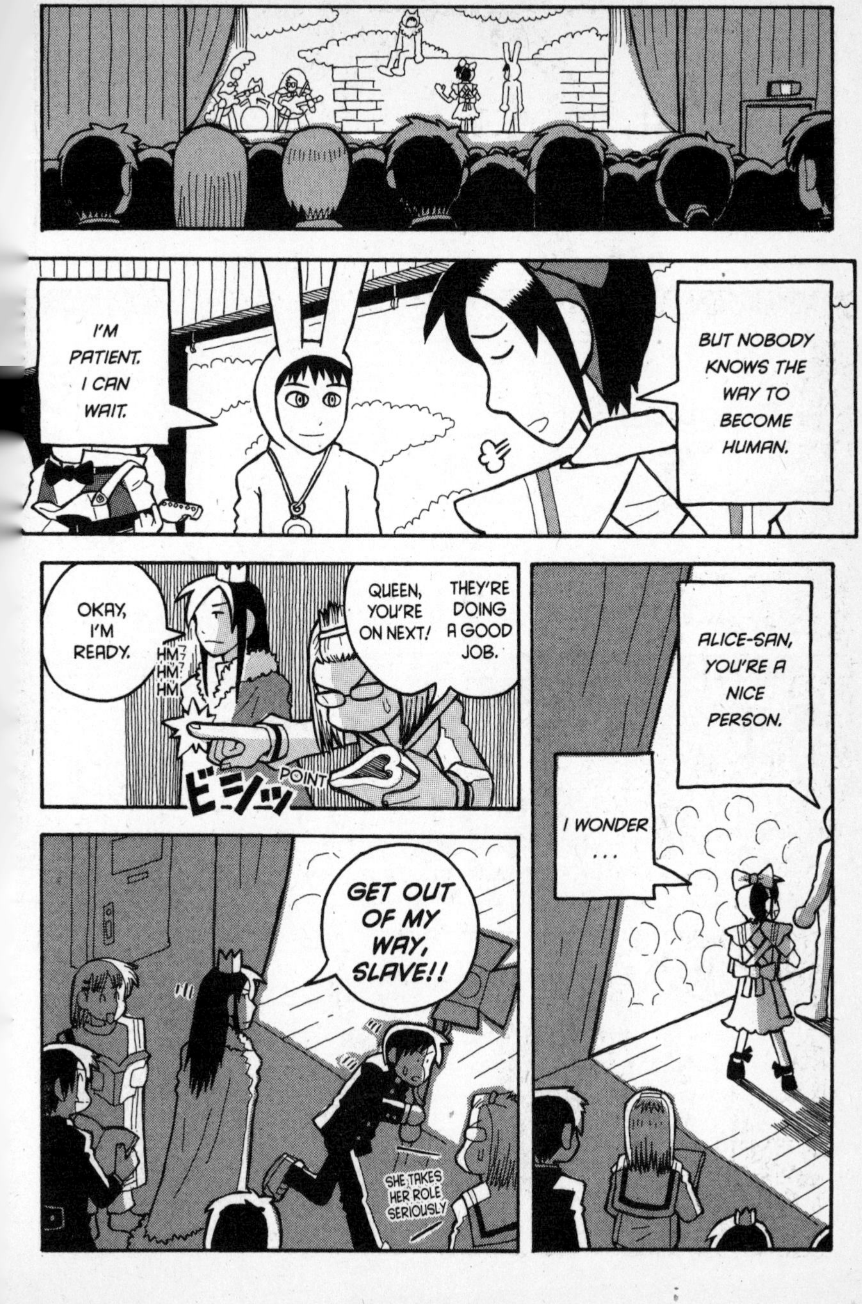
BUT NOBODY KNOWS THE WAY TO BECOME HUMAN.
I'M PATIENT. I CAN WAIT.
ALICE-SAN, YOU'RE A NICE PERSON.
I WONDER . . .
THEY'RE DOING A GOOD JOB.
QUEEN, YOU'RE ON NEXT!
OKAY, I'M READY.
HM HM HM
POINT
ビシッ
GET OUT OF MY WAY, SLAVE!!
SHE TAKES HER ROLE SERIOUSLY

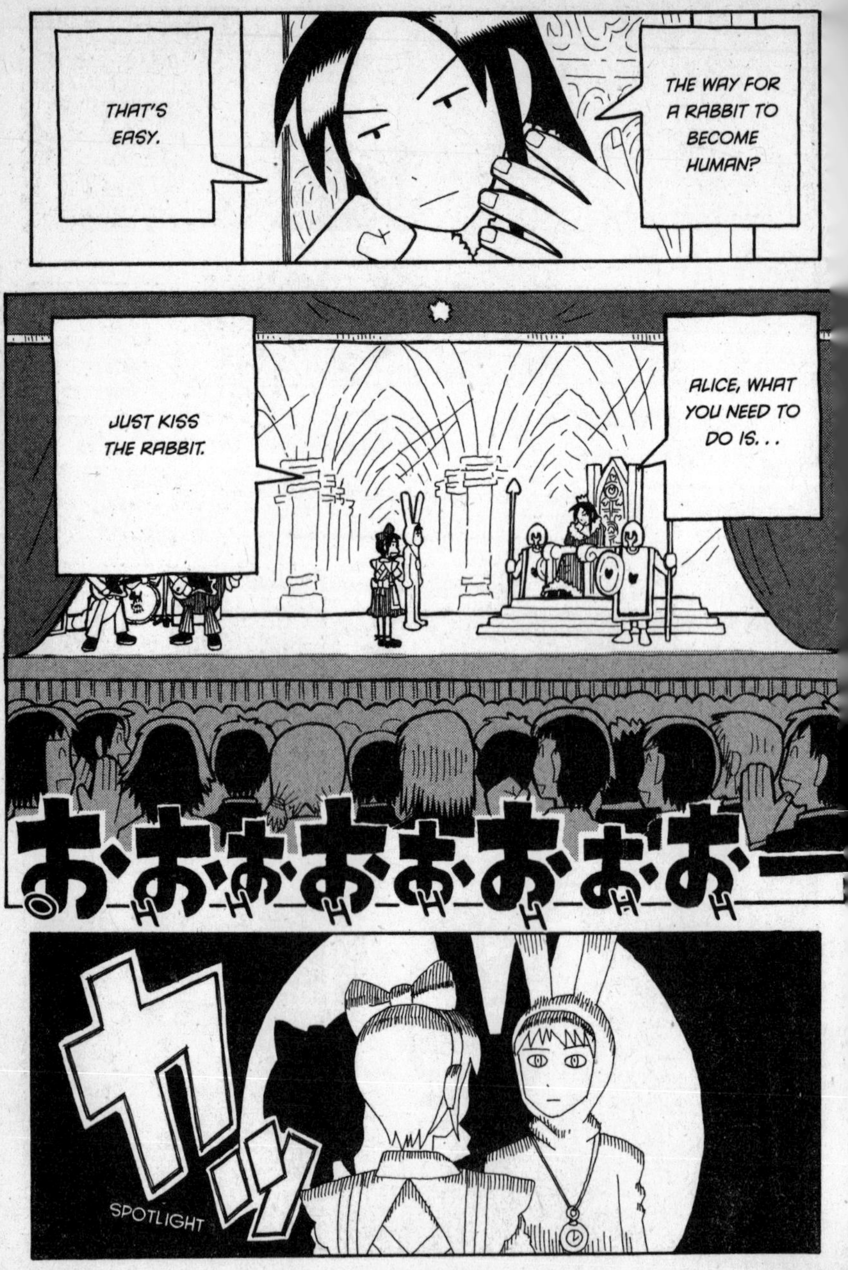
THE WAY FOR A RABBIT TO BECOME HUMAN?
THAT'S EASY.
ALICE, WHAT YOU NEED TO DO IS...
JUST KISS THE RABBIT.
おおおおおおおおー
OHHHHHHH
カッ
SPOTLIGHT

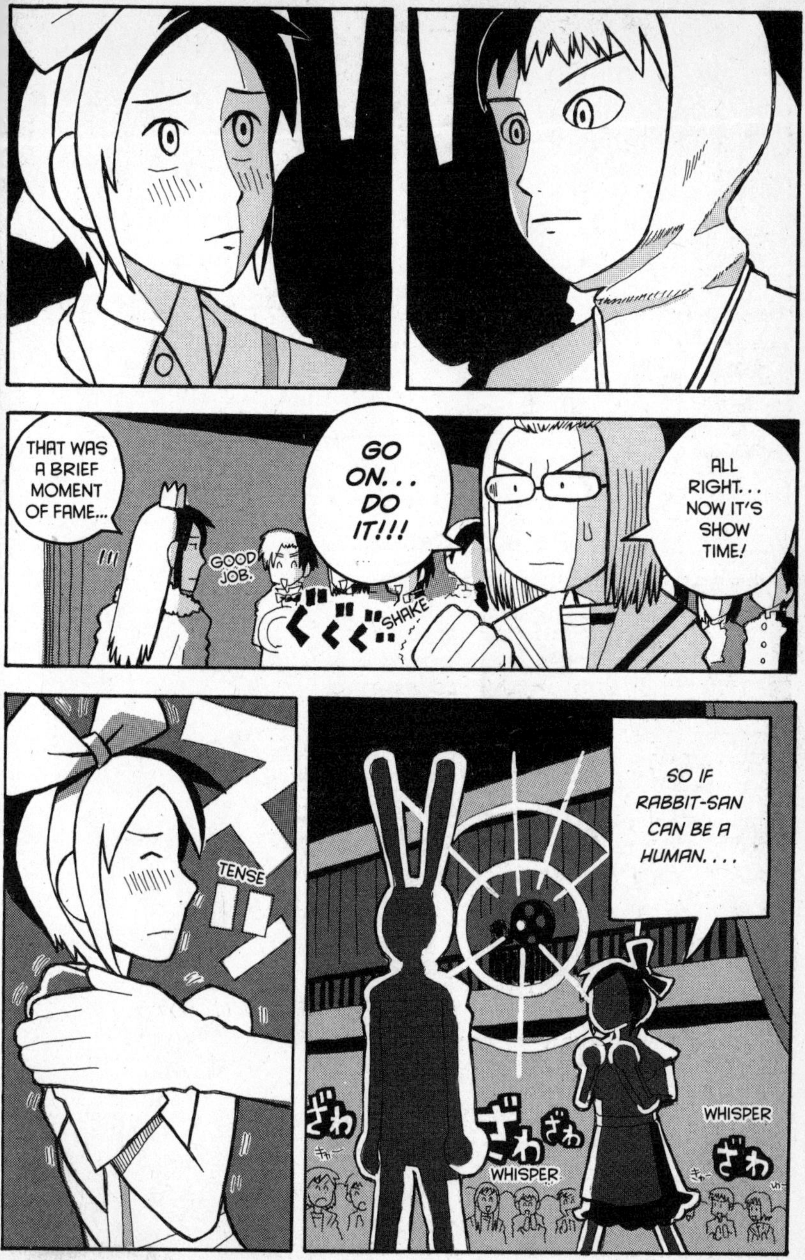
ALL RIGHT... NOW IT'S SHOW TIME!
GO ON... DO IT!!!
SHAKE
GOOD JOB.
THAT WAS A BRIEF MOMENT OF FAME...
SO IF RABBIT-SAN CAN BE A HUMAN....
WHISPER
WHISPER
TENSE

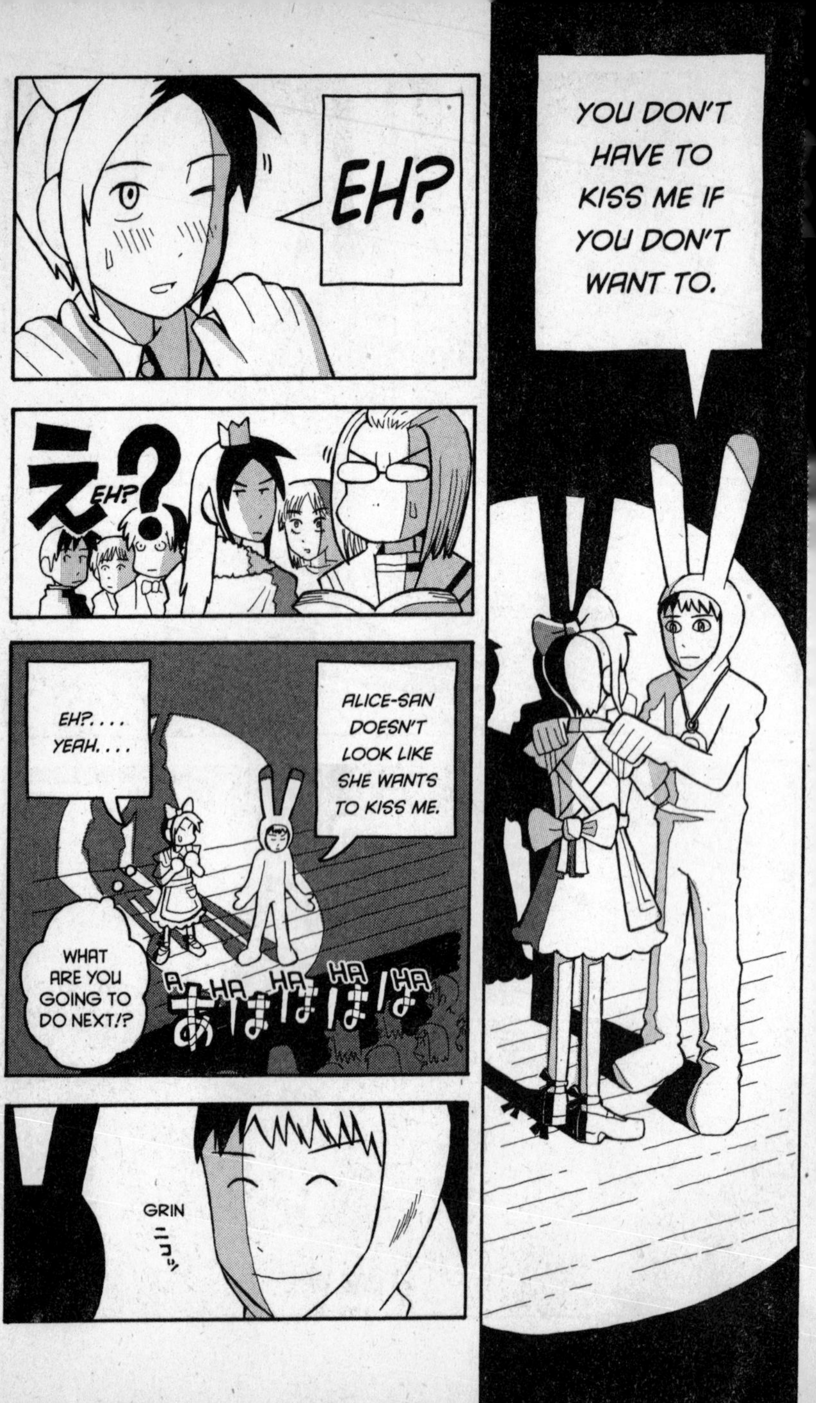
YOU DON'T HAVE TO KISS ME IF YOU DON'T WANT TO.
EH?
え?
EH?
ALICE-SAN DOESN'T LOOK LIKE SHE WANTS TO KISS ME.
EH?.... YEAH....
WHAT ARE YOU GOING TO DO NEXT!?
あはははは
A HA HA HA HA
GRIN
ニコッ

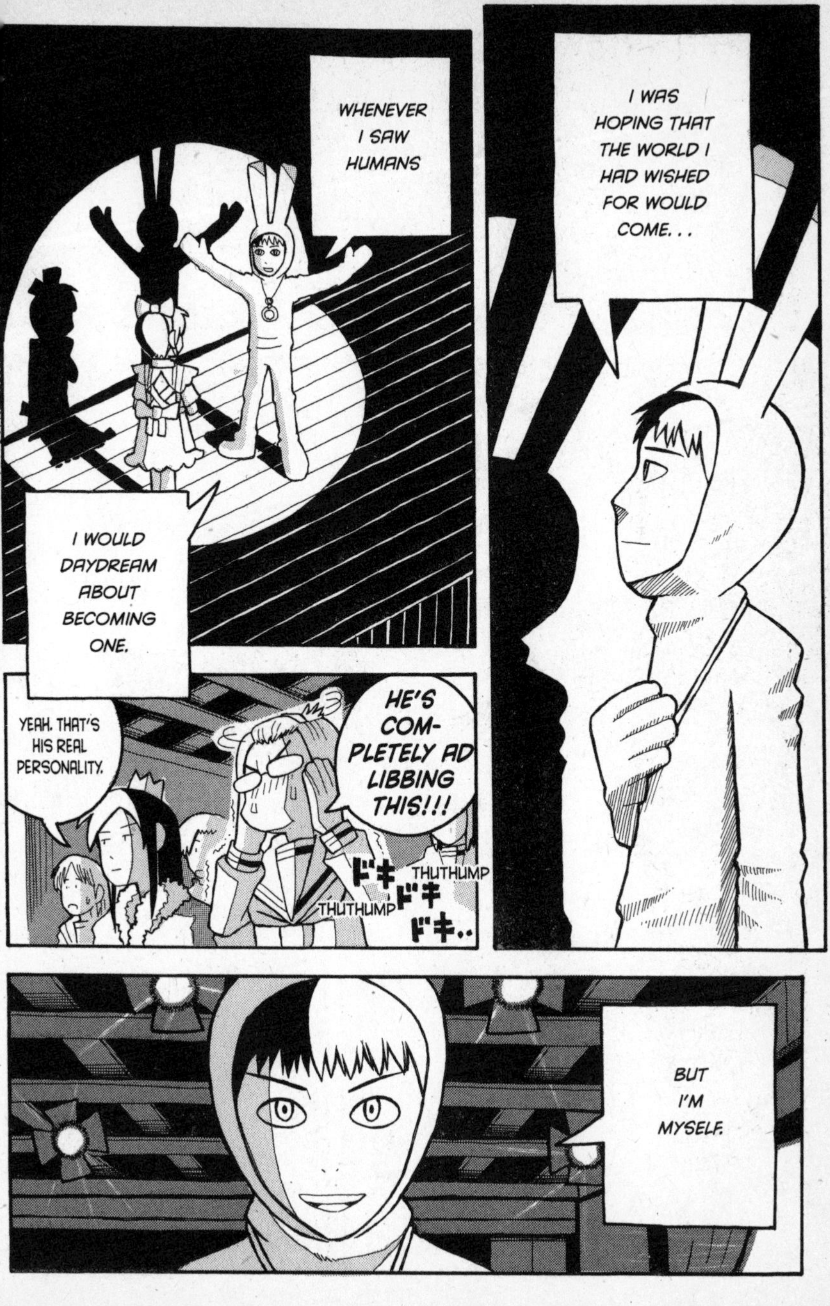
I WAS HOPING THAT THE WORLD I HAD WISHED FOR WOULD COME. . .
WHENEVER I SAW HUMANS
I WOULD DAYDREAM ABOUT BECOMING ONE.
HE'S COMPLETELY AD LIBBING THIS!!!
YEAH. THAT'S HIS REAL PERSONALITY.
ドキ THUTHUMP
ドキ THUTHUMP
ドキ..
BUT I'M MYSELF.

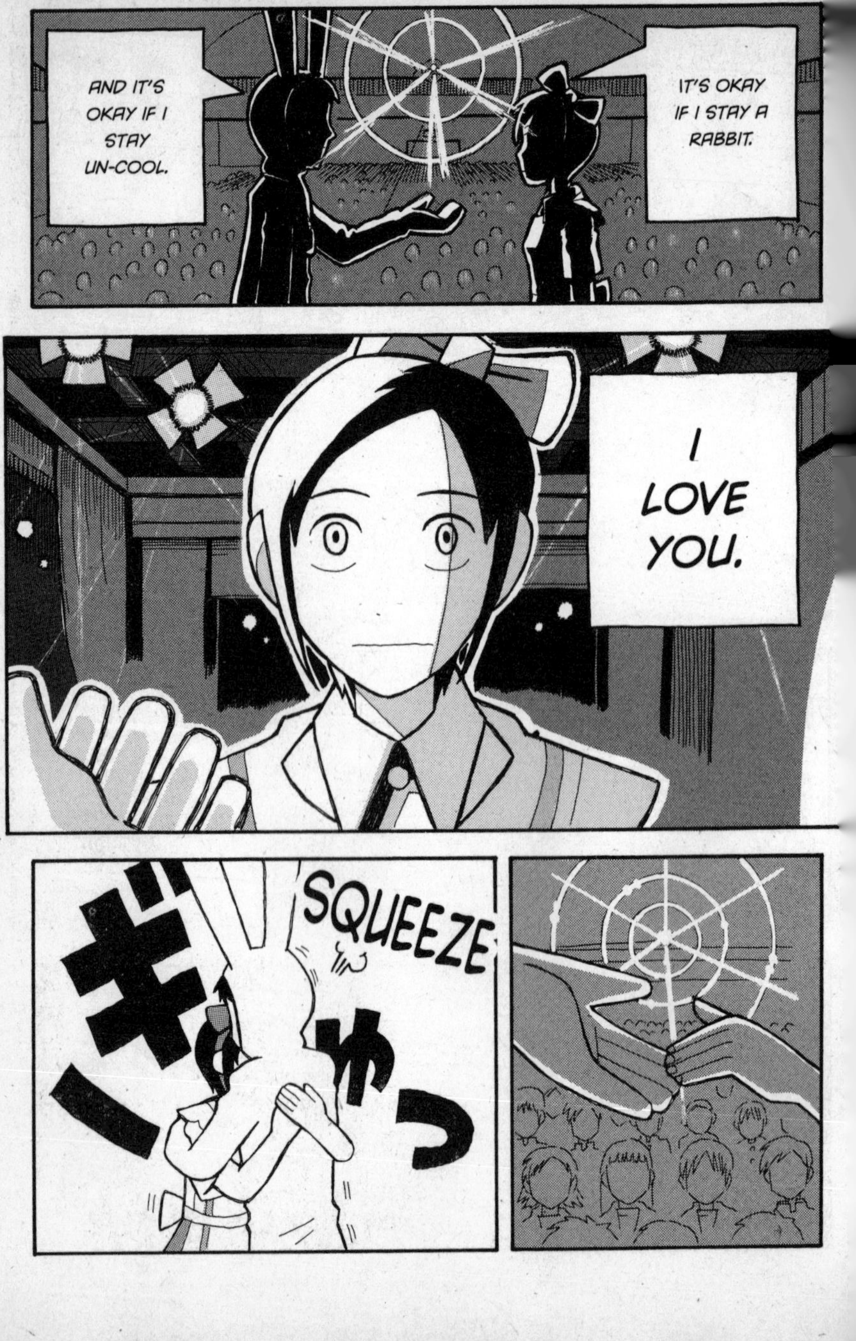
IT'S OKAY IF I STAY A RABBIT.
AND IT'S OKAY IF I STAY UN-COOL.
I LOVE YOU.
SQUEEZE

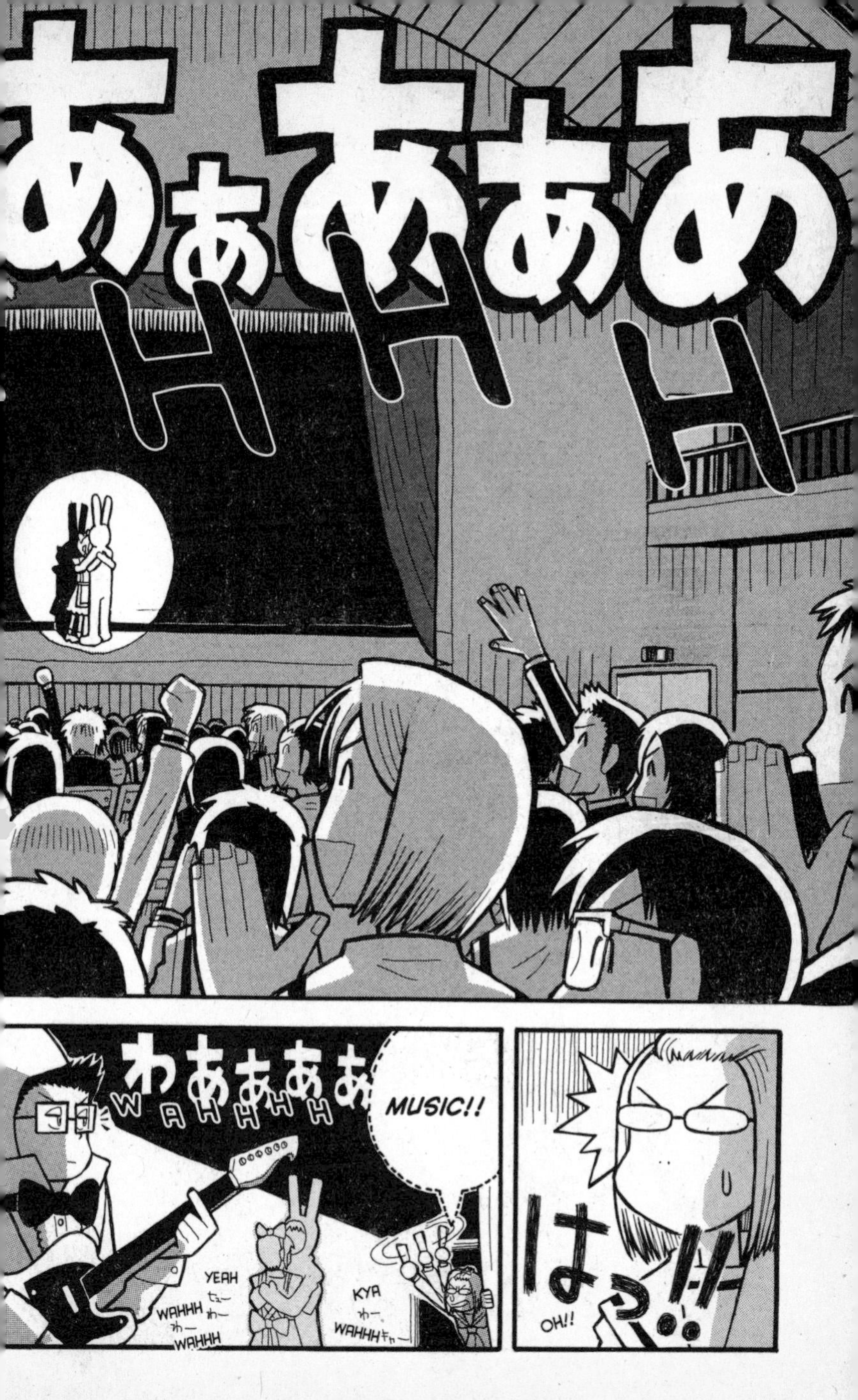

あぁあああ
AHHH
はっ!!
OH!!
MUSIC!!
わあぁあぁあ
WAHHHH
KYA
WAHHH
YEAH
WAHHH
WAHHH

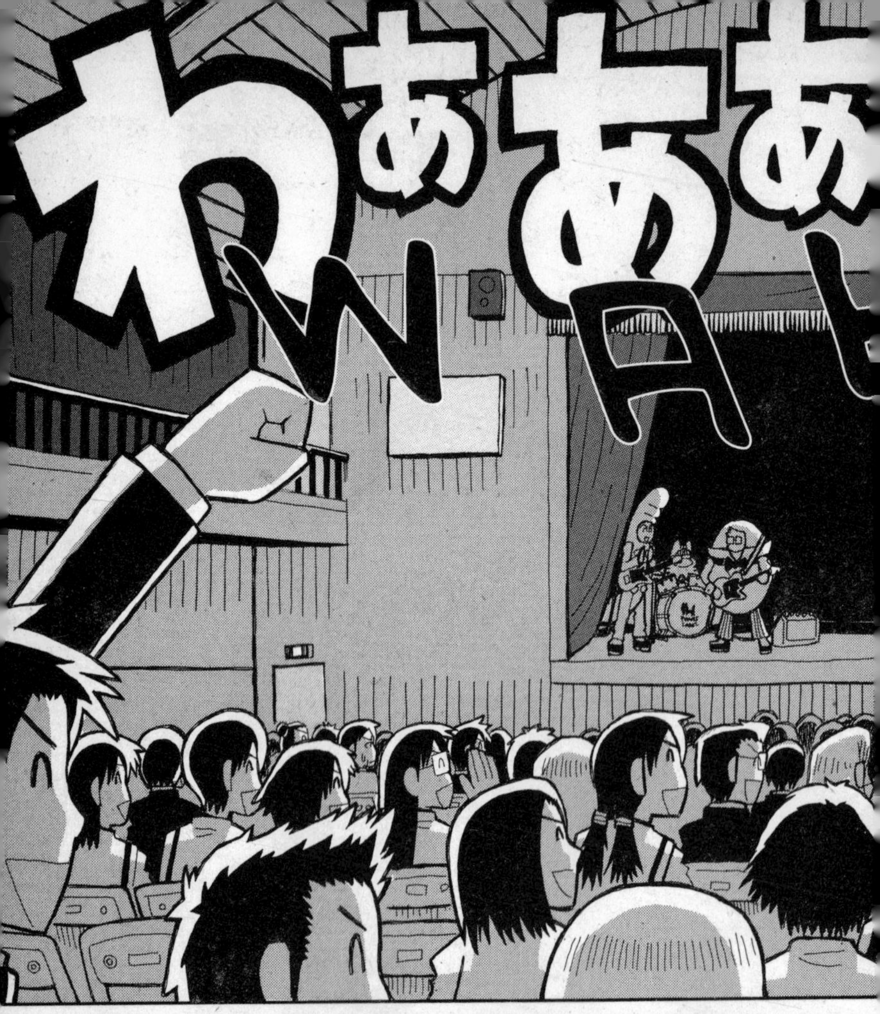
わあああ
WA
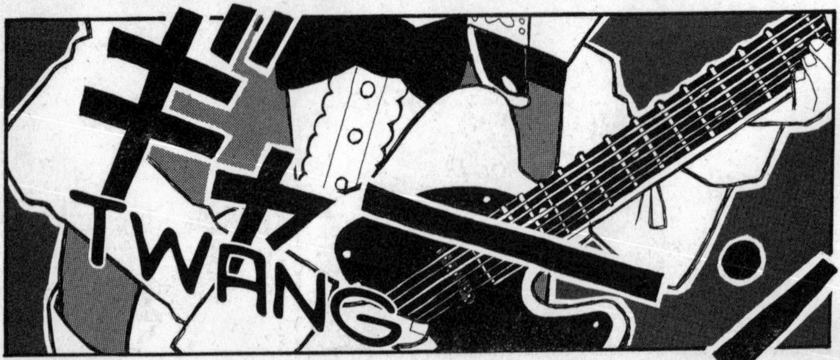
ギャーン
TWANG

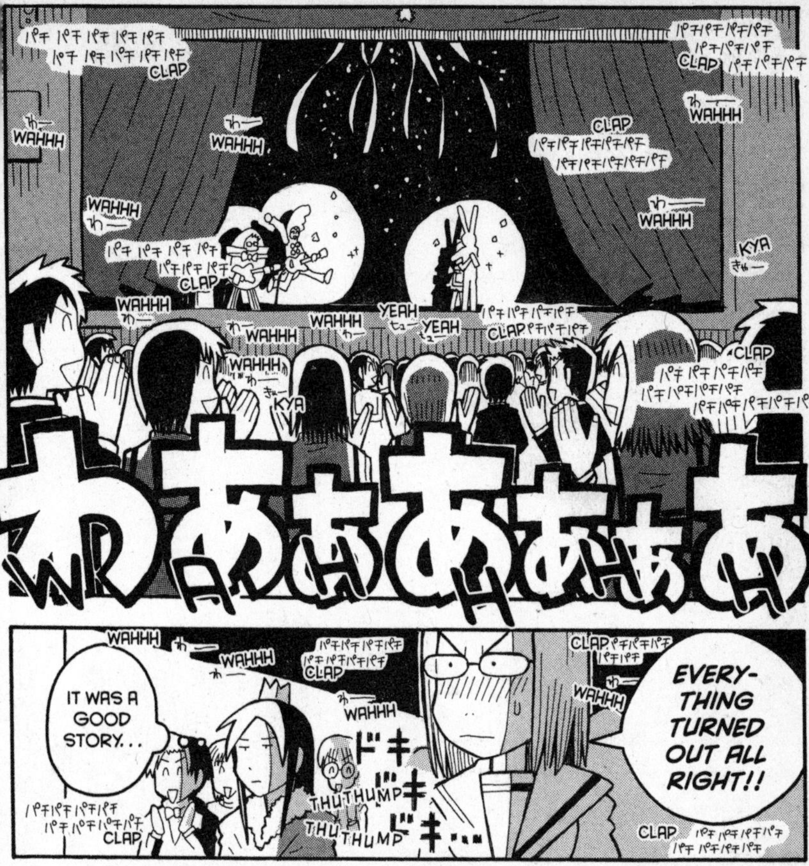
パチパチパチパチパチ パチパチパチパチパチ CLAP
WAHHH わー
CLAP パチパチパチパチパチ パチパチパチパチパチ
WAHHH わー
KYA きゃー
パチパチパチパチ パチパチパチパチ CLAP
YEAH ヒュー
WAHHH わー
CLAP パチパチパチパチ
WAHHH わー
KYA きゃー
わあああああああ
WAAHHHH
EVERY-THING TURNED OUT ALL RIGHT!!
CLAP パチパチパチパチ
WAHHH わー
ドキ ドキ...
THUTHUMP THUTHUMP
IT WAS A GOOD STORY...
パチパチパチパチ パチパチパチパチ CLAP
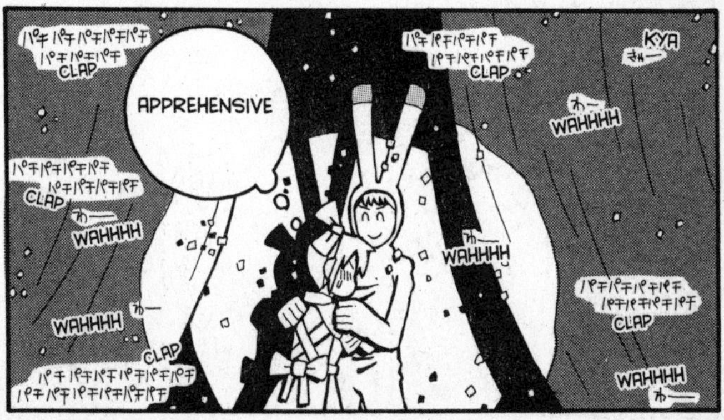
KYA きゃー
パチパチパチパチ パチパチパチパチ CLAP
APPREHENSIVE
パチパチパチパチ パチパチパチパチ CLAP
WAHHHH わー
WAHHHH わー
パチパチパチパチパチパチ パチパチパチパチパチパチ CLAP

TRACK 7 THE END.

CURTAIN CALL

おまけ

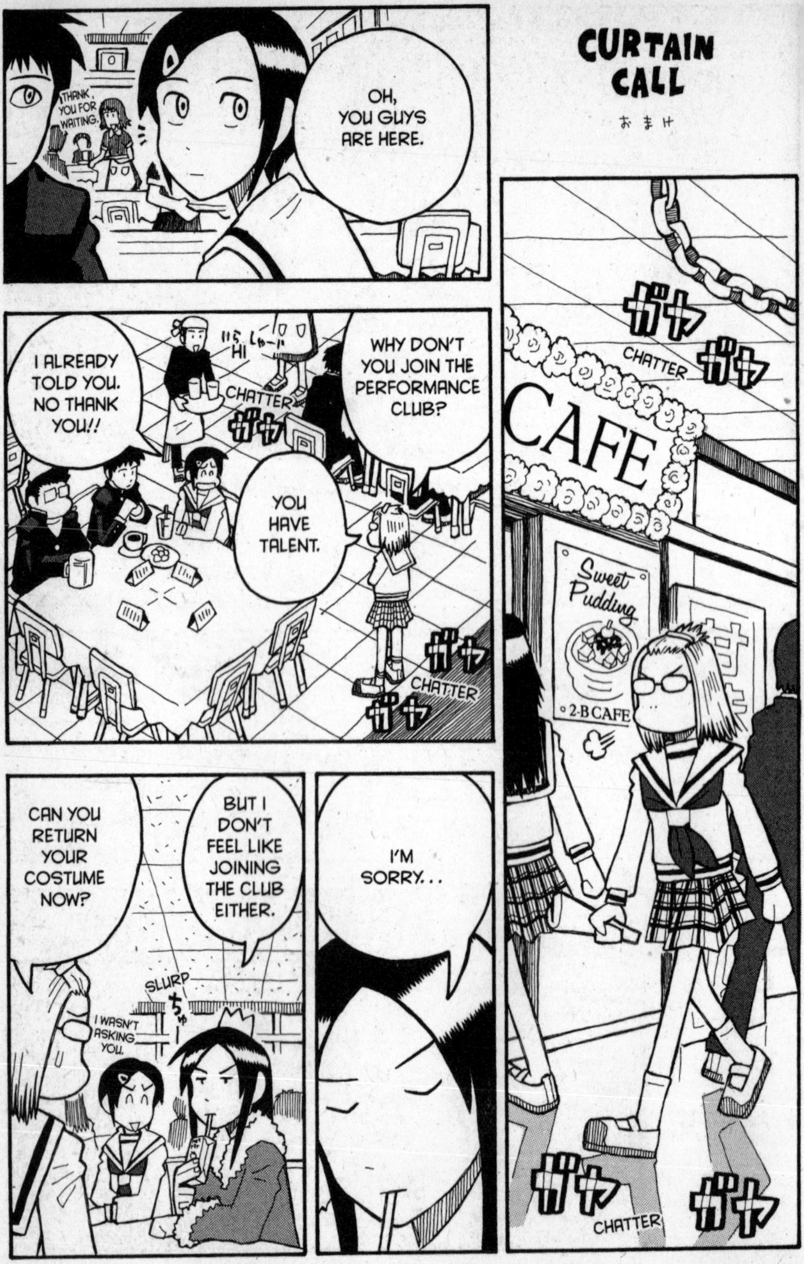
ガヤ
CHATTER
ガヤ
CAFE
Sweet Pudding
2-B CAFE
ガヤ
CHATTER
ガヤ
OH, YOU GUYS ARE HERE.
THANK YOU FOR WAITING.
WHY DON'T YOU JOIN THE PERFORMANCE CLUB?
いらっしゃーい
HI
YOU HAVE TALENT.
CHATTER
ガヤ
I ALREADY TOLD YOU. NO THANK YOU!!
ガヤ
CHATTER
ガヤ
I'M SORRY...
BUT I DON'T FEEL LIKE JOINING THE CLUB EITHER.
CAN YOU RETURN YOUR COSTUME NOW?
SLURP
ちゅ
I WASN'T ASKING YOU.

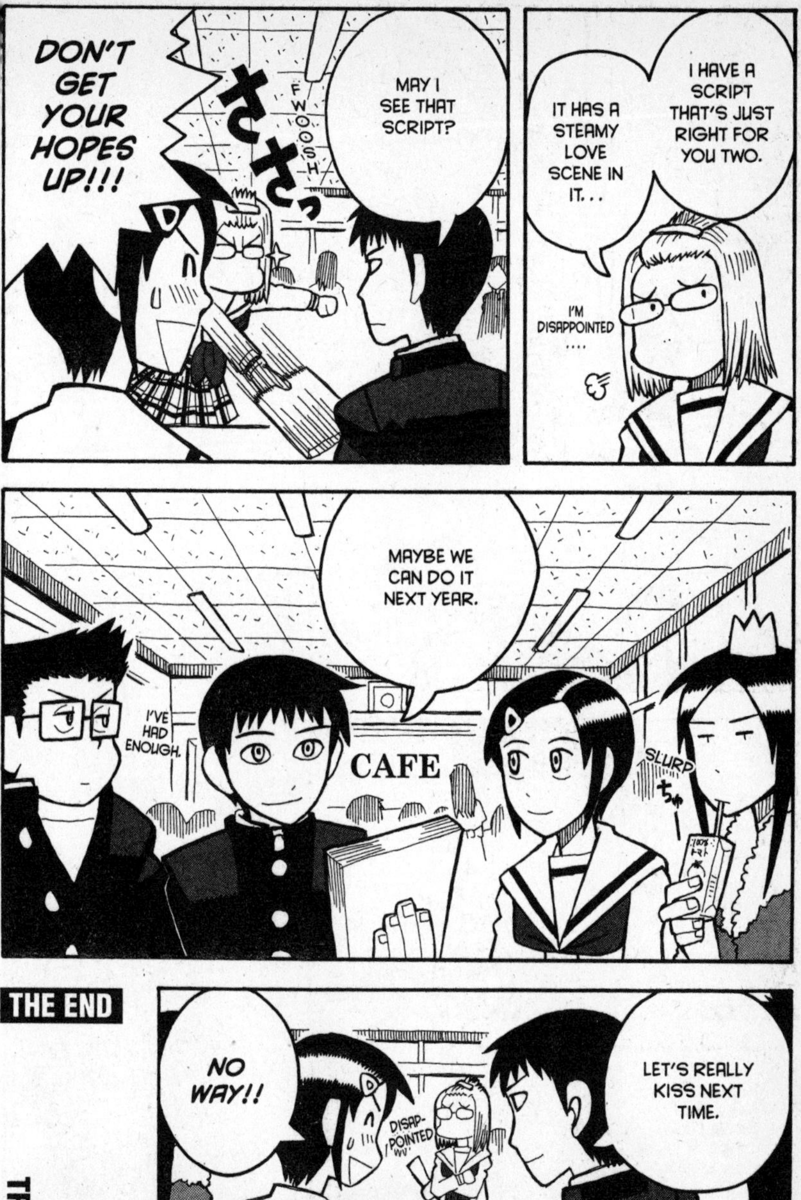
I HAVE A SCRIPT THAT'S JUST RIGHT FOR YOU TWO.
IT HAS A STEAMY LOVE SCENE IN IT. . .
I'M DISAPPOINTED . . . .
MAY I SEE THAT SCRIPT?
FWOOSH
ささっ
DON'T GET YOUR HOPES UP!!!
MAYBE WE CAN DO IT NEXT YEAR.
SLURP
ちゅ
CAFE
I'VE HAD ENOUGH.
LET'S REALLY KISS NEXT TIME.
DISAP-POINTED
NO WAY!!

THE END

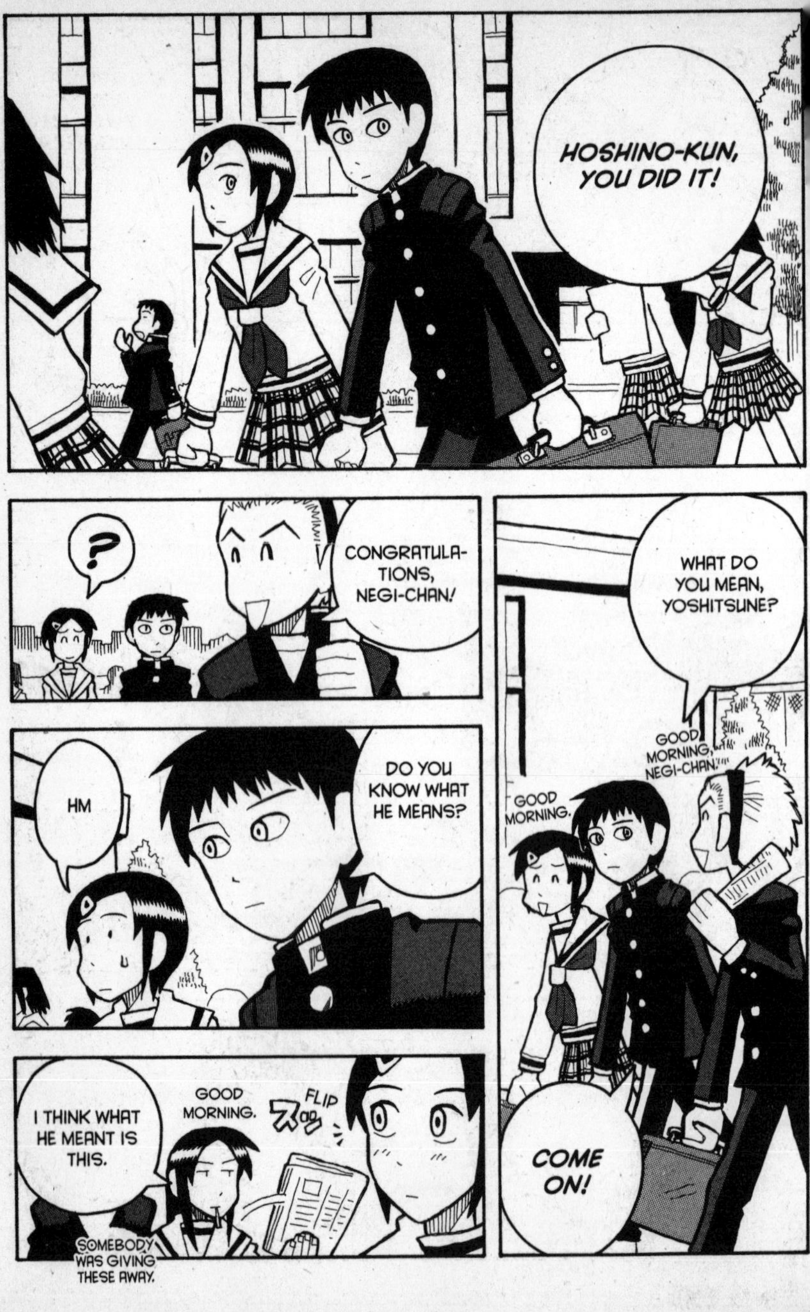
HOSHINO-KUN, YOU DID IT!
WHAT DO YOU MEAN, YOSHITSUNE?
GOOD MORNING, NEGI-CHAN!
GOOD MORNING.
COME ON!
CONGRATULATIONS, NEGI-CHAN!
?
DO YOU KNOW WHAT HE MEANS?
HM
FLIP
GOOD MORNING.
I THINK WHAT HE MEANT IS THIS.
SOMEBODY WAS GIVING THESE AWAY.

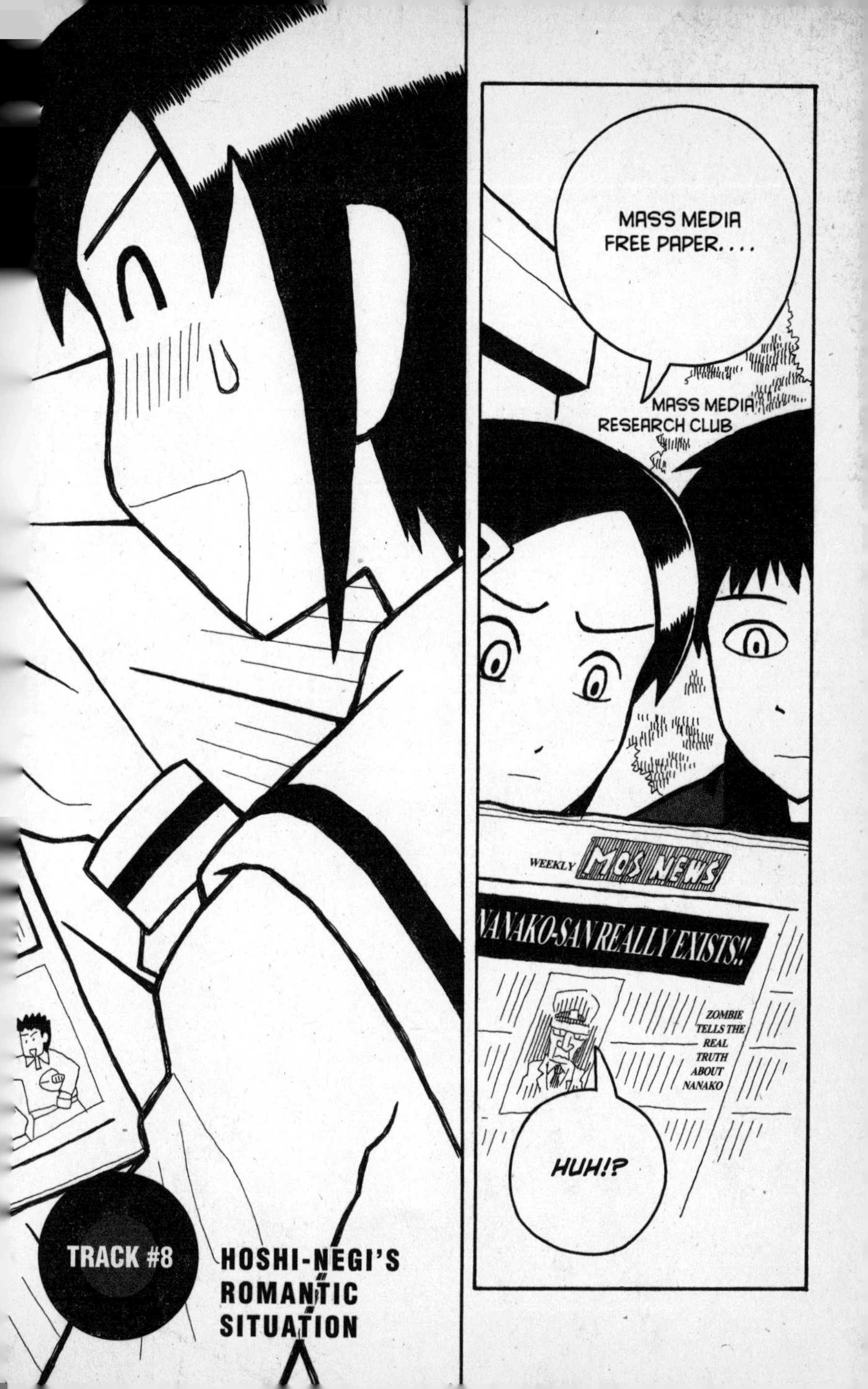
MASS MEDIA FREE PAPER....
MASS MEDIA RESEARCH CLUB
WEEKLY MOS NEWS
NANAKO-SAN REALLY EXISTS!!
ZOMBIE TELLS THE REAL TRUTH ABOUT NANAKO
HUH!?
TRACK #8
HOSHI-NEGI'S ROMANTIC SITUATION

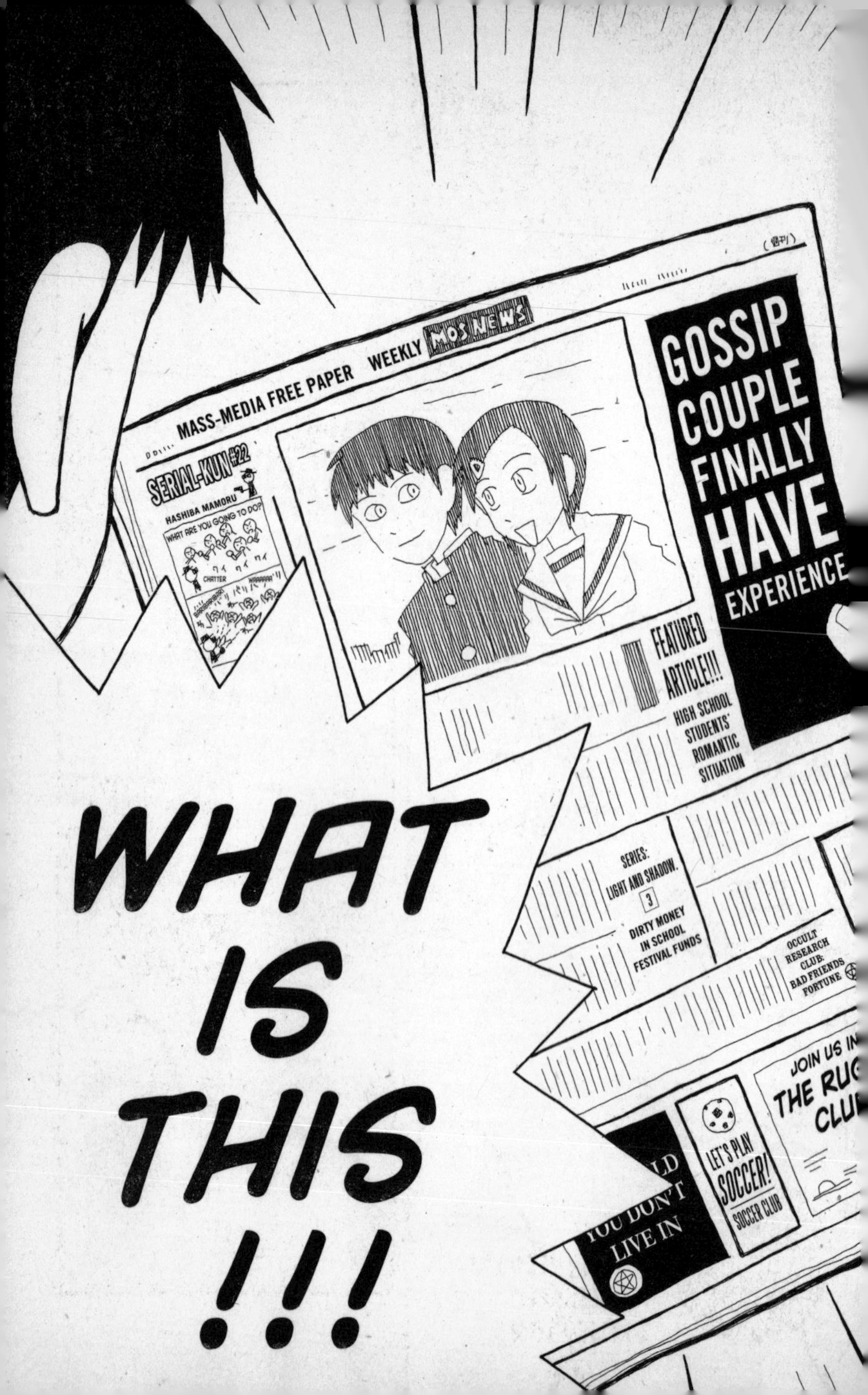

MASS-MEDIA FREE PAPER
WEEKLY MOS NEWS
SERIAL-KUN #22
HASHIBA MAMORU
WHAT ARE YOU GOING TO DO?
CHATTER
GOSSIP COUPLE FINALLY HAVE EXPERIENCE
FEATURED ARTICLE!!!
HIGH SCHOOL STUDENTS' ROMANTIC SITUATION
SERIES: LIGHT AND SHADOW. 3
DIRTY MONEY IN SCHOOL FESTIVAL FUNDS
OCCULT RESEARCH CLUB: BAD FRIENDS FORTUNE
JOIN US IN THE RUG CLUB
LET'S PLAY SOCCER! SOCCER CLUB
YOU DON'T LIVE IN
WHAT IS THIS !!!

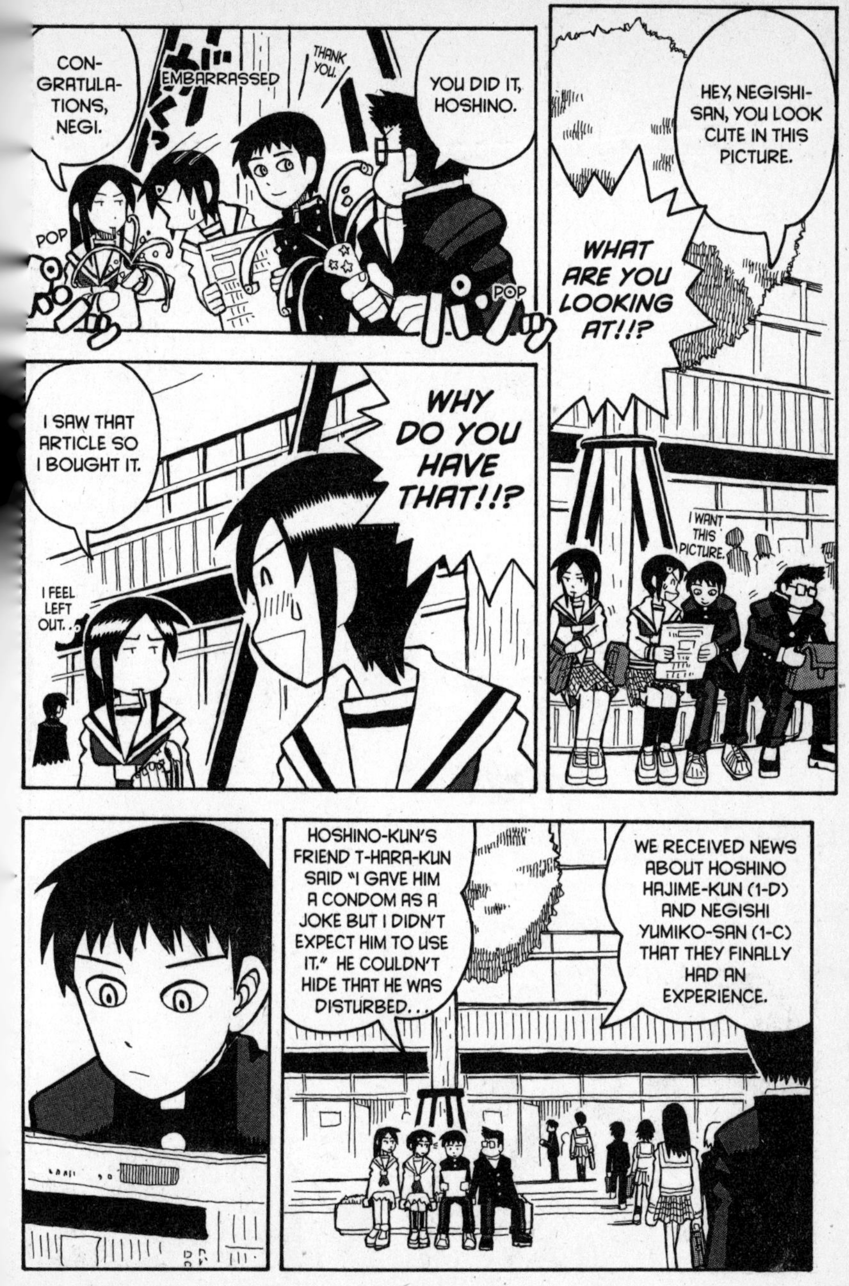
HEY, NEGISHI-SAN, YOU LOOK CUTE IN THIS PICTURE.
WHAT ARE YOU LOOKING AT!!?
I WANT THIS PICTURE.
YOU DID IT, HOSHINO.
THANK YOU.
EMBARRASSED
CONGRATULATIONS, NEGI.
POP
POP
WHY DO YOU HAVE THAT!!?
I SAW THAT ARTICLE SO I BOUGHT IT.
I FEEL LEFT OUT...
WE RECEIVED NEWS ABOUT HOSHINO HAJIME-KUN (1-D) AND NEGISHI YUMIKO-SAN (1-C) THAT THEY FINALLY HAD AN EXPERIENCE.
HOSHINO-KUN'S FRIEND T-HARA-KUN SAID "I GAVE HIM A CONDOM AS A JOKE BUT I DIDN'T EXPECT HIM TO USE IT." HE COULDN'T HIDE THAT HE WAS DISTURBED...

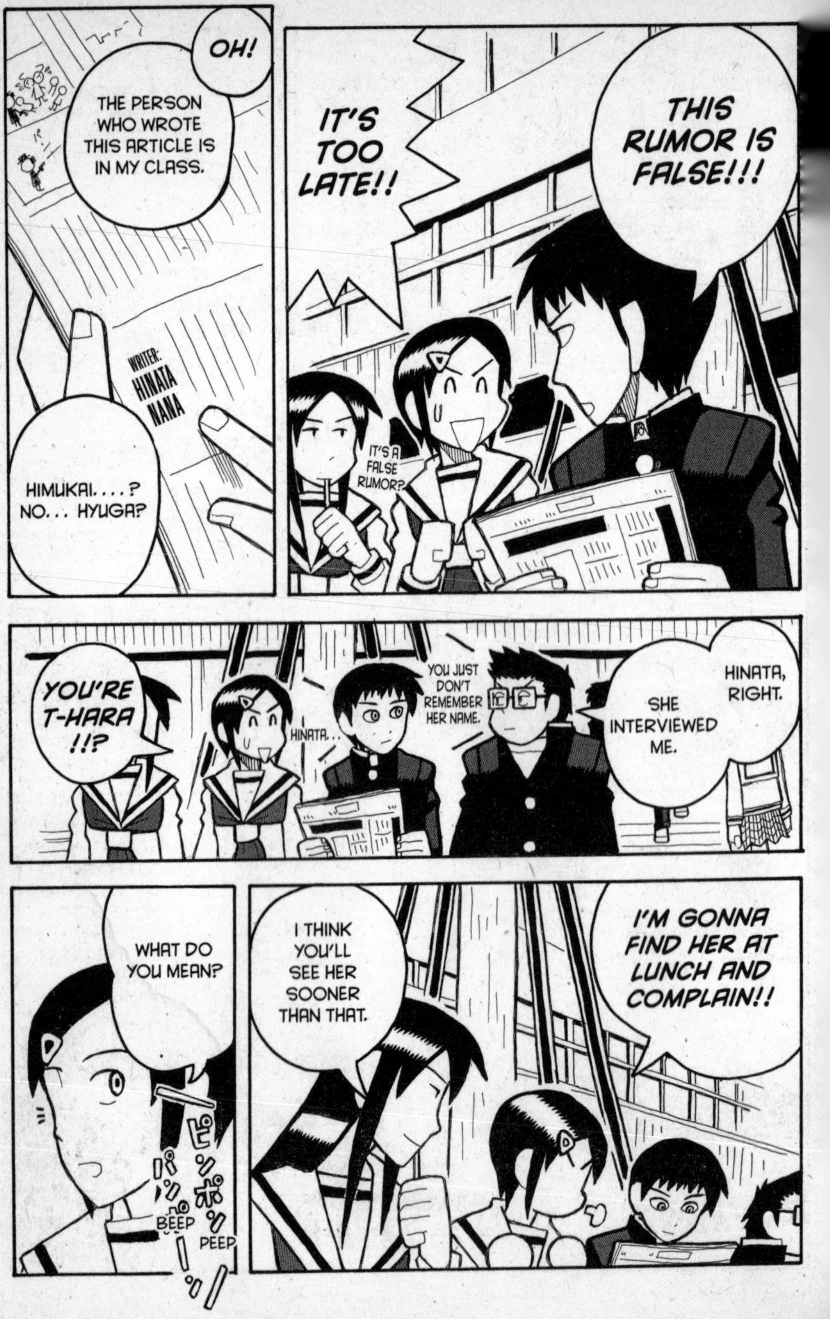
THIS RUMOR IS FALSE!!!
IT'S TOO LATE!!
IT'S A FALSE RUMOR?
OH!
THE PERSON WHO WROTE THIS ARTICLE IS IN MY CLASS.
WRITER: HINATA NANA
HIMUKAI....? NO... HYUGA?
HINATA, RIGHT.
SHE INTERVIEWED ME.
YOU JUST DON'T REMEMBER HER NAME.
HINATA...
YOU'RE T-HARA!!?
I'M GONNA FIND HER AT LUNCH AND COMPLAIN!!
I THINK YOU'LL SEE HER SOONER THAN THAT.
WHAT DO YOU MEAN?
BEEP
PEEP

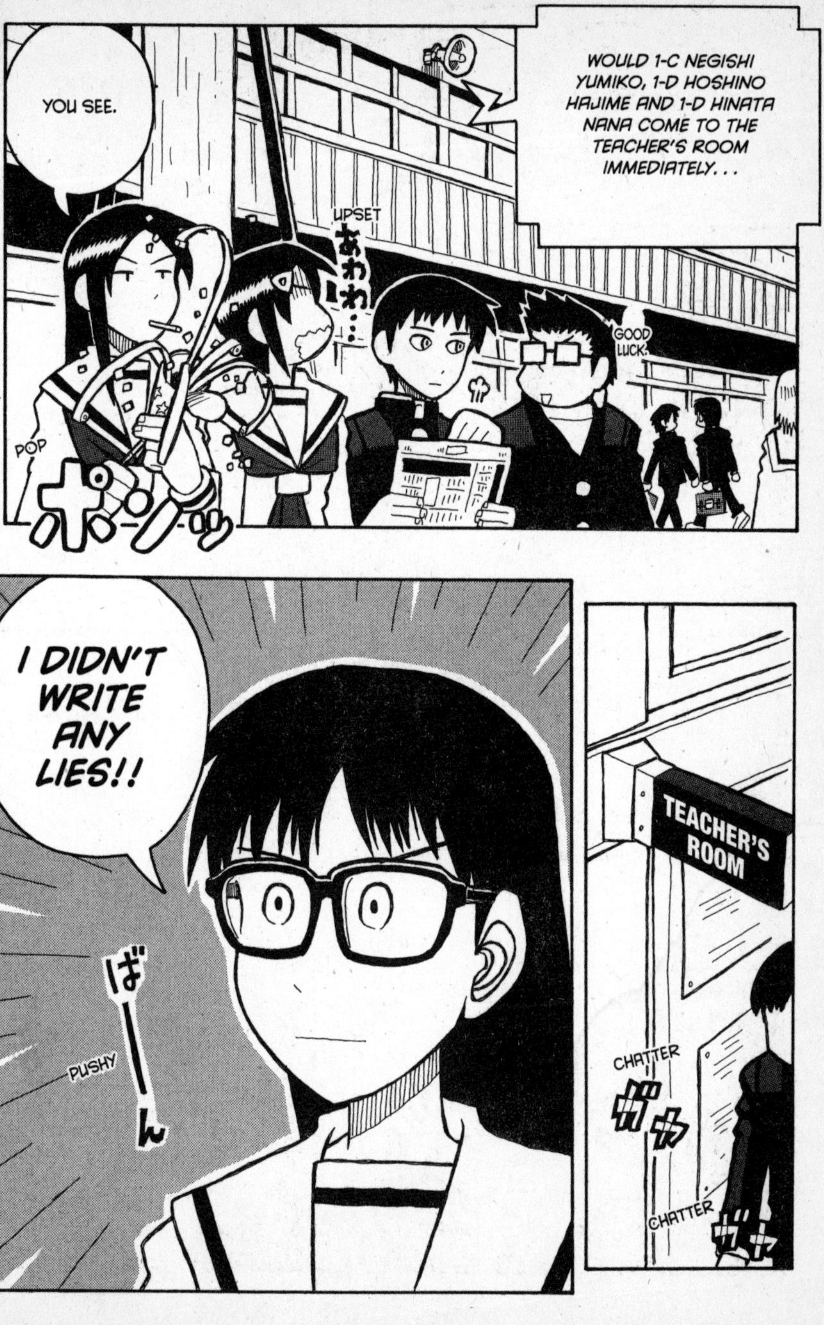

WOULD 1-C NEGISHI YUMIKO, 1-D HOSHINO HAJIME AND 1-D HINATA NANA COME TO THE TEACHER'S ROOM IMMEDIATELY...
GOOD LUCK.
UPSET
あわわ…
YOU SEE.
POP
TEACHER'S ROOM
CHATTER
CHATTER
I DIDN'T WRITE ANY LIES!!
PUSHY

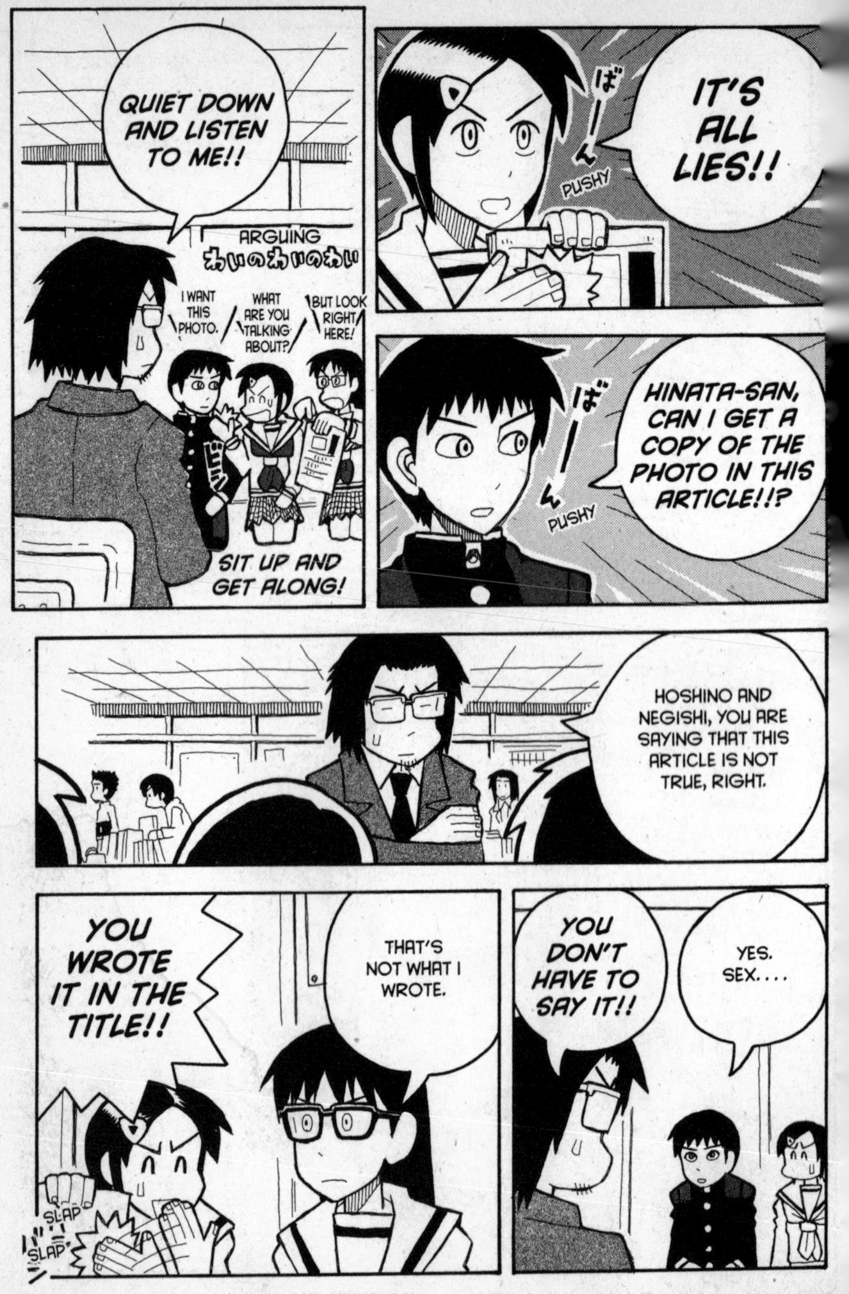
ばーん
PUSHY
IT'S ALL LIES!!
ばーん
PUSHY
HINATA-SAN, CAN I GET A COPY OF THE PHOTO IN THIS ARTICLE!!?
QUIET DOWN AND LISTEN TO ME!!
ARGUING
わいのわいのわい
BUT LOOK RIGHT HERE!
WHAT ARE YOU TALKING ABOUT?
I WANT THIS PHOTO.
SIT UP AND GET ALONG!
HOSHINO AND NEGISHI, YOU ARE SAYING THAT THIS ARTICLE IS NOT TRUE, RIGHT.
YES. SEX....
YOU DON'T HAVE TO SAY IT!!
THAT'S NOT WHAT I WROTE.
YOU WROTE IT IN THE TITLE!!
SLAP
SLAP

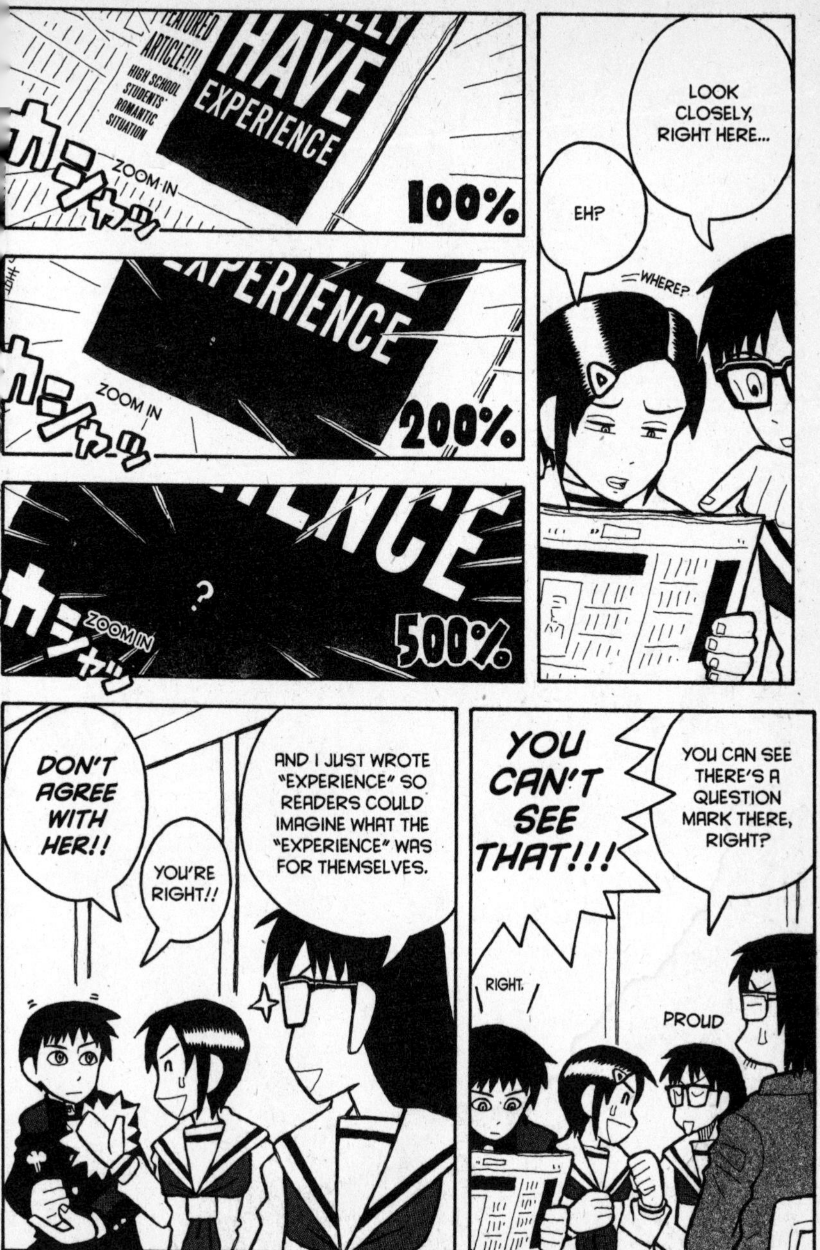
LOOK CLOSELY, RIGHT HERE...
EH?
WHERE?
FEATURED ARTICLE!!!
HIGH SCHOOL STUDENTS' ROMANTIC SITUATION
HAVE
EXPERIENCE
ZOOM IN
100%
ZOOM IN
200%
?
ZOOM IN
500%
YOU CAN SEE THERE'S A QUESTION MARK THERE, RIGHT?
YOU CAN'T SEE THAT!!!
PROUD
RIGHT.
AND I JUST WROTE "EXPERIENCE" SO READERS COULD IMAGINE WHAT THE "EXPERIENCE" WAS FOR THEMSELVES.
YOU'RE RIGHT!!
DON'T AGREE WITH HER!!

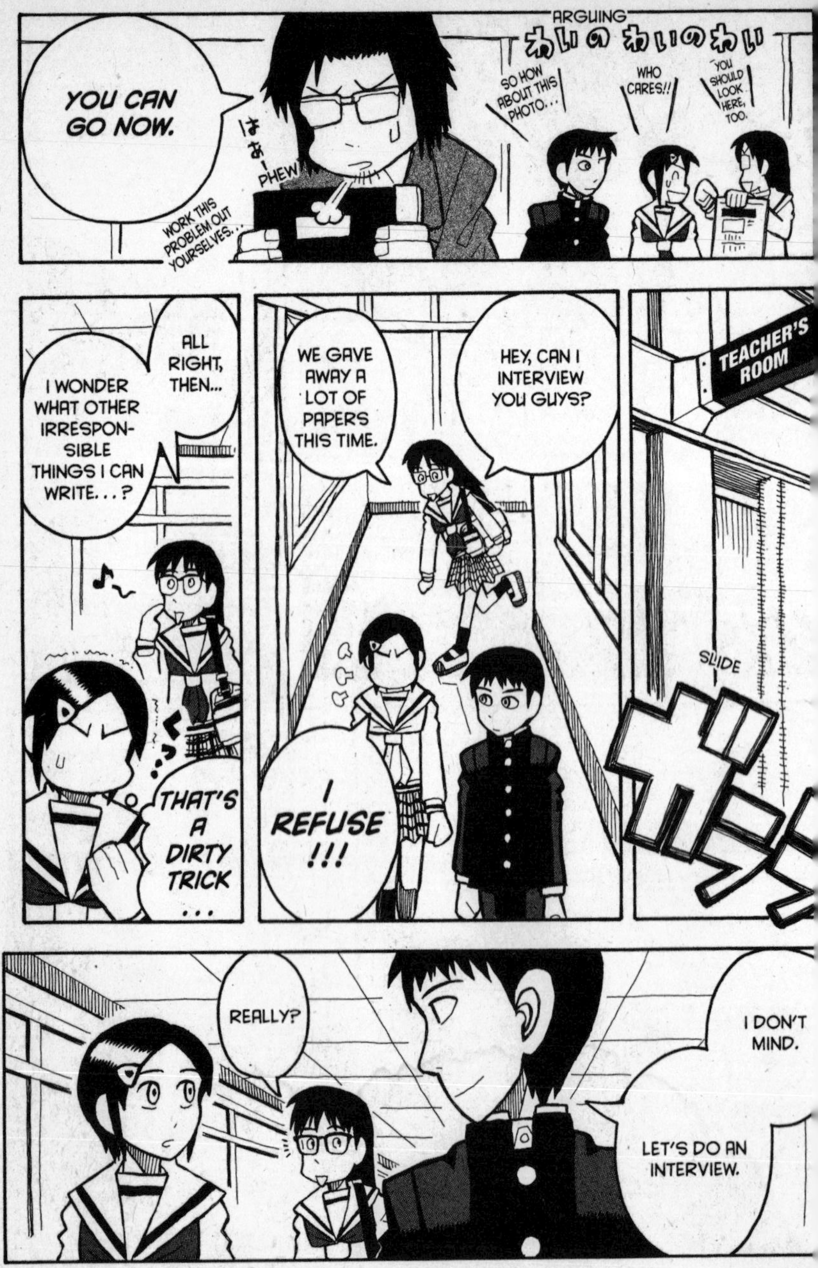
ARGUING
わいのわいのわい
YOU SHOULD LOOK HERE, TOO.
WHO CARES!!
SO HOW ABOUT THIS PHOTO...
はあ〜 PHEW
YOU CAN GO NOW.
WORK THIS PROBLEM OUT YOURSELVES...
TEACHER'S ROOM
SLIDE
HEY, CAN I INTERVIEW YOU GUYS?
WE GAVE AWAY A LOT OF PAPERS THIS TIME.
I REFUSE!!!
ALL RIGHT, THEN...
I WONDER WHAT OTHER IRRESPON-SIBLE THINGS I CAN WRITE...?
THAT'S A DIRTY TRICK...
I DON'T MIND.
LET'S DO AN INTERVIEW.
REALLY?

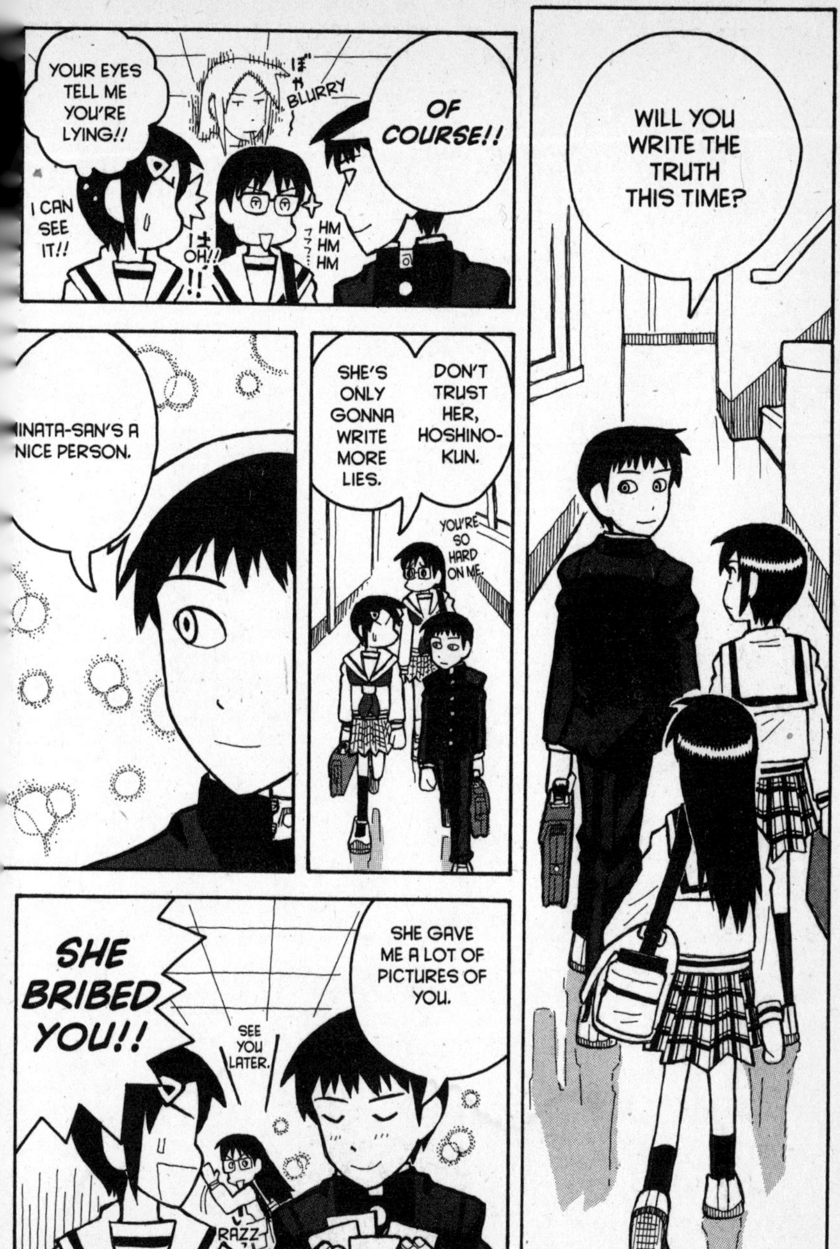
WILL YOU WRITE THE TRUTH THIS TIME?
OF COURSE!!
BLURRY
YOUR EYES TELL ME YOU'RE LYING!!
HM HM HM
OH!!
I CAN SEE IT!!
DON'T TRUST HER, HOSHINO-KUN.
SHE'S ONLY GONNA WRITE MORE LIES.
YOU'RE SO HARD ON ME.
INATA-SAN'S A NICE PERSON.
SHE GAVE ME A LOT OF PICTURES OF YOU.
SEE YOU LATER.
SHE BRIBED YOU!!
RAZZ

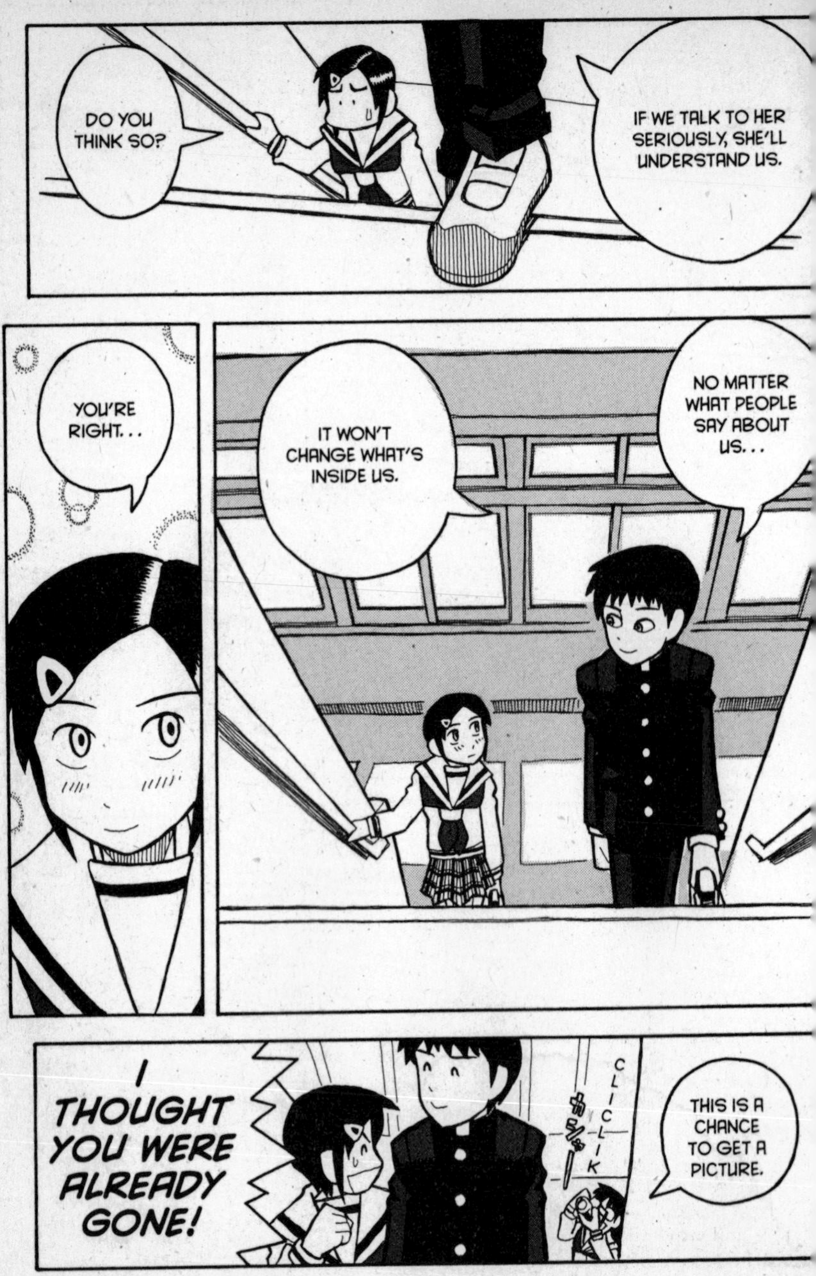
IF WE TALK TO HER SERIOUSLY, SHE'LL UNDERSTAND US.
DO YOU THINK SO?
NO MATTER WHAT PEOPLE SAY ABOUT US...
IT WON'T CHANGE WHAT'S INSIDE US.
YOU'RE RIGHT...
THIS IS A CHANCE TO GET A PICTURE.
CLICLIK
I THOUGHT YOU WERE ALREADY GONE!

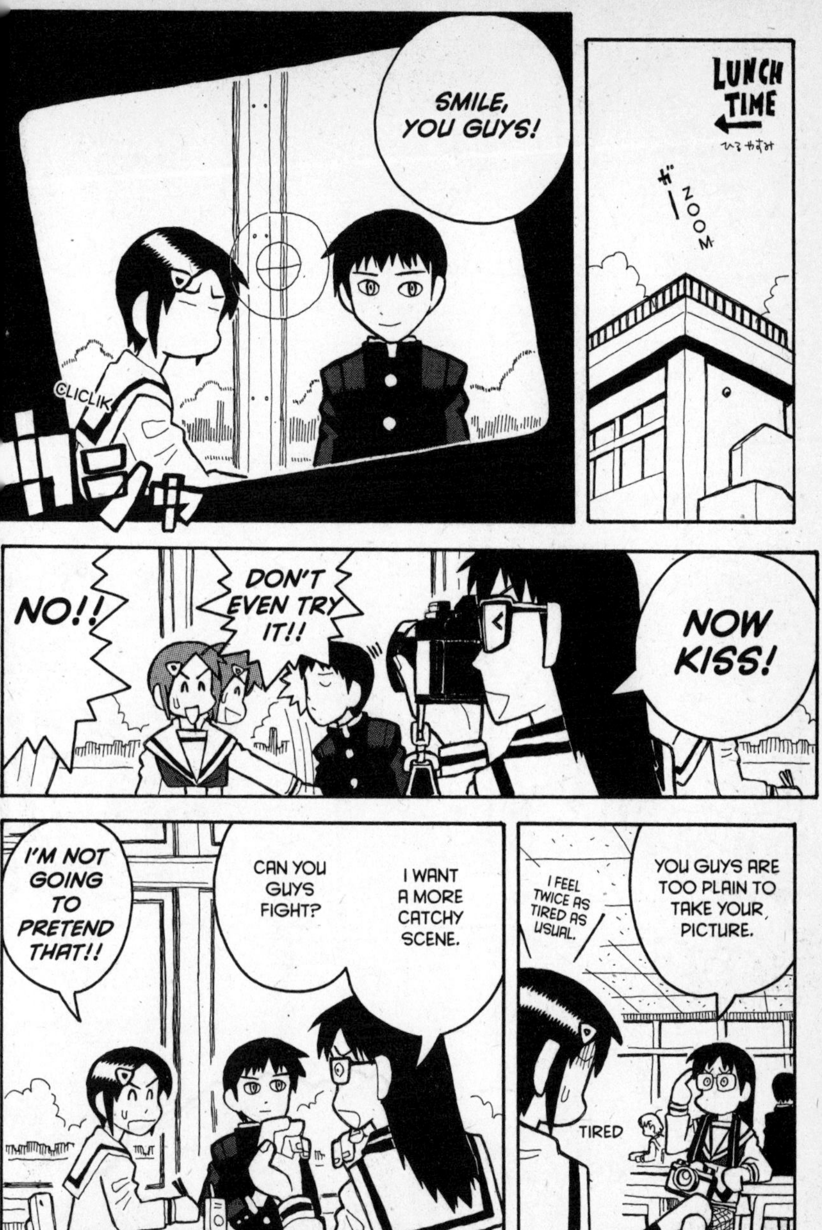
LUNCH TIME
ひるやすみ
ZOOM
SMILE, YOU GUYS!
CLICLIK
NOW KISS!
DON'T EVEN TRY IT!!
NO!!
YOU GUYS ARE TOO PLAIN TO TAKE YOUR PICTURE.
I FEEL TWICE AS TIRED AS USUAL.
TIRED
I WANT A MORE CATCHY SCENE.
CAN YOU GUYS FIGHT?
I'M NOT GOING TO PRETEND THAT!!

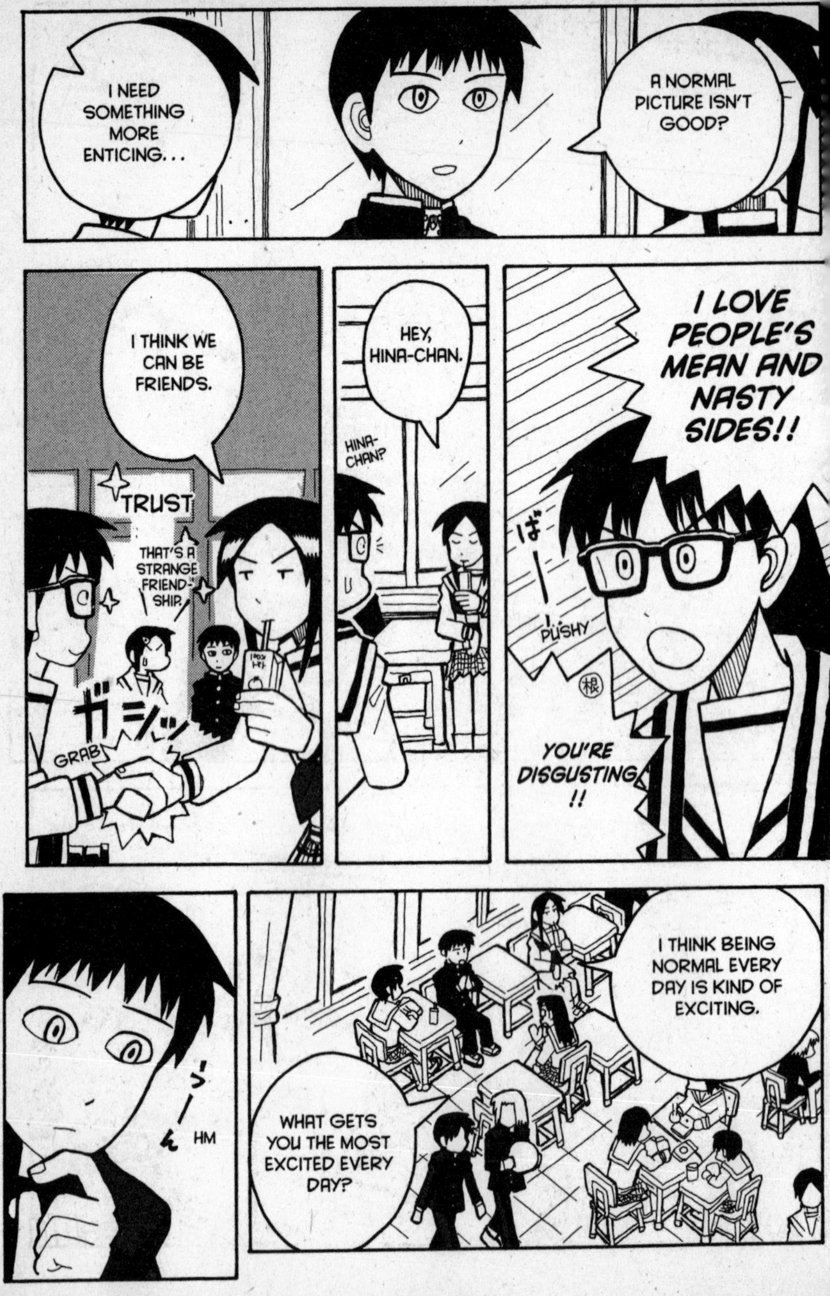
A NORMAL PICTURE ISN'T GOOD?
I NEED SOMETHING MORE ENTICING...
I LOVE PEOPLE'S MEAN AND NASTY SIDES!!
ばーー
PUSHY
YOU'RE DISGUSTING!!
HEY, HINA-CHAN.
HINA-CHAN?
I THINK WE CAN BE FRIENDS.
TRUST
THAT'S A STRANGE FRIENDSHIP.
ガシッ
GRAB
I THINK BEING NORMAL EVERY DAY IS KIND OF EXCITING.
WHAT GETS YOU THE MOST EXCITED EVERY DAY?
うーん
HM

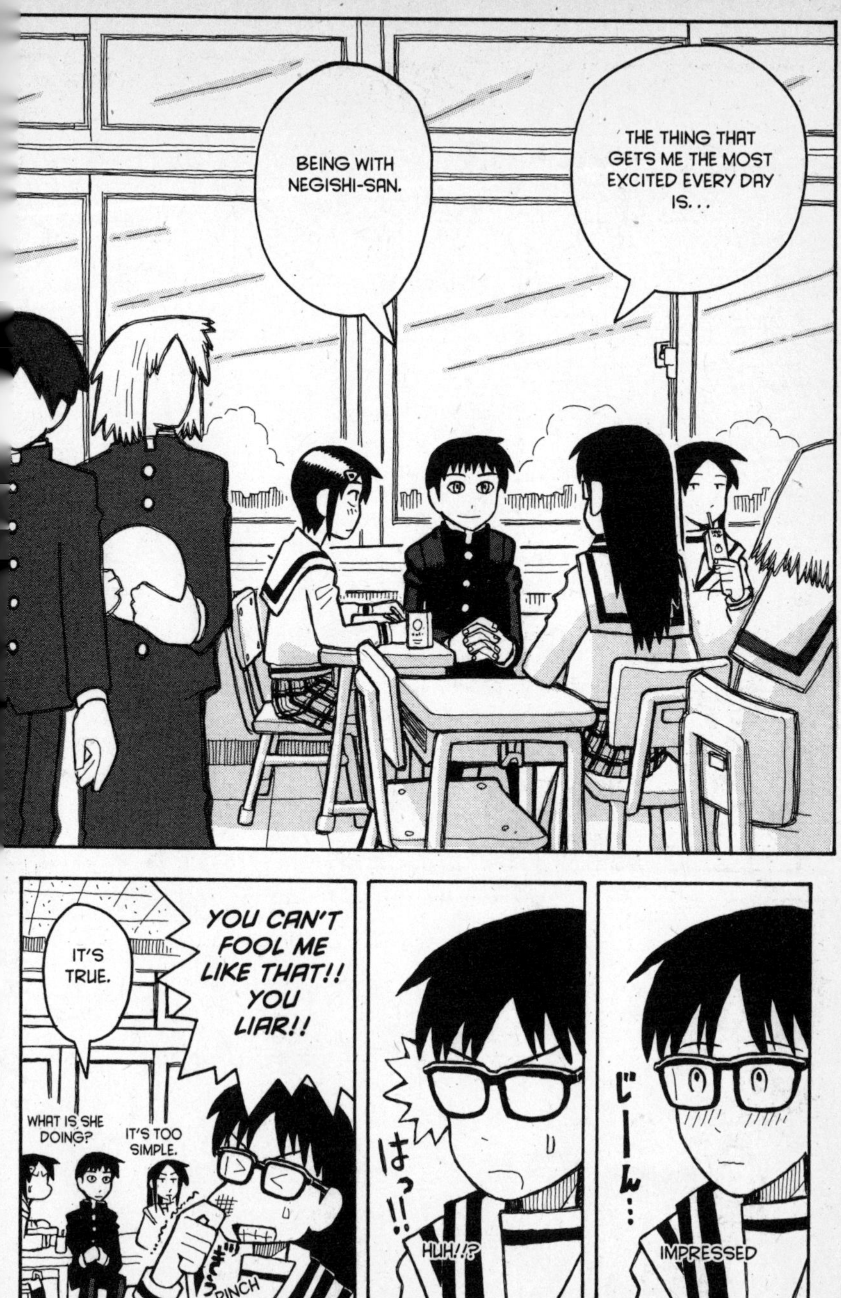
THE THING THAT GETS ME THE MOST EXCITED EVERY DAY IS...
BEING WITH NEGISHI-SAN.
じーん…
IMPRESSED
はっ!!
HUH!!?
YOU CAN'T FOOL ME LIKE THAT!! YOU LIAR!!
IT'S TRUE.
IT'S TOO SIMPLE.
WHAT IS SHE DOING?
PINCH

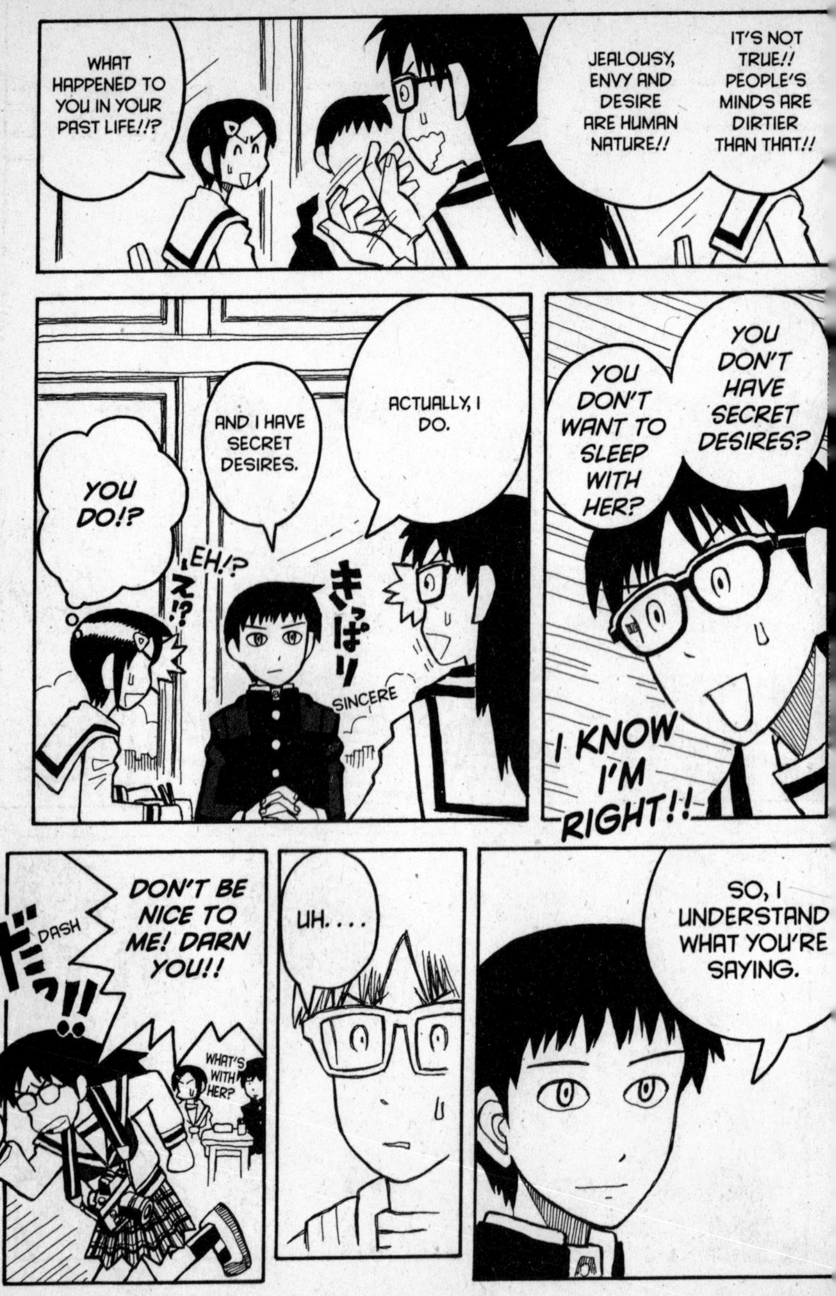
IT'S NOT TRUE!! PEOPLE'S MINDS ARE DIRTIER THAN THAT!!
JEALOUSY, ENVY AND DESIRE ARE HUMAN NATURE!!
WHAT HAPPENED TO YOU IN YOUR PAST LIFE!!?
YOU DON'T HAVE SECRET DESIRES?
YOU DON'T WANT TO SLEEP WITH HER?
I KNOW I'M RIGHT!!
ACTUALLY, I DO.
AND I HAVE SECRET DESIRES.
きっぱり
SINCERE
え!?
EH!?
YOU DO!?
SO, I UNDERSTAND WHAT YOU'RE SAYING.
UH. . . .
DON'T BE NICE TO ME! DARN YOU!!
だっ!!
DASH
WHAT'S WITH HER?

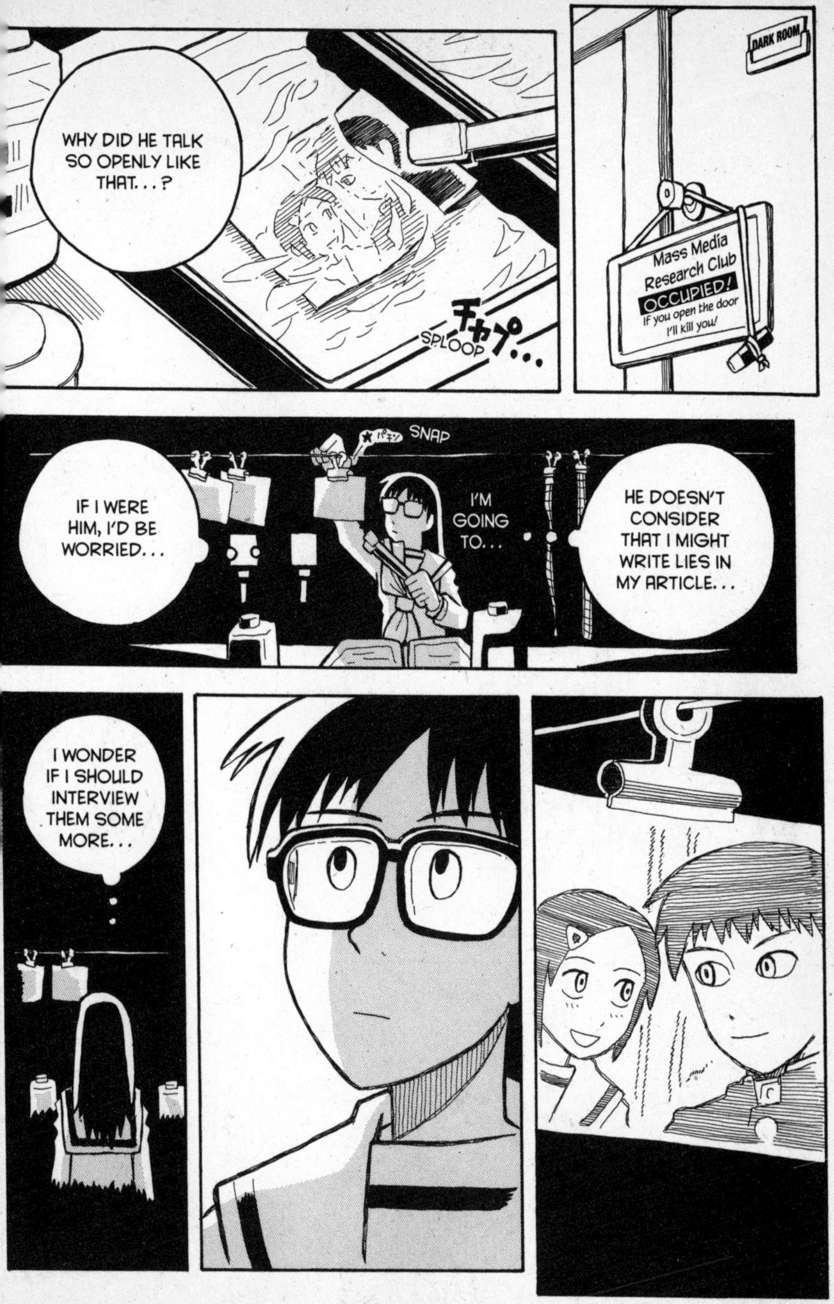
DARK ROOM
Mass Media Research Club
OCCUPIED!
If you open the door I'll kill you!
WHY DID HE TALK SO OPENLY LIKE THAT...?
チャプ...
SPLOOP
HE DOESN'T CONSIDER THAT I MIGHT WRITE LIES IN MY ARTICLE...
I'M GOING TO...
SNAP
IF I WERE HIM, I'D BE WORRIED...
I WONDER IF I SHOULD INTERVIEW THEM SOME MORE...

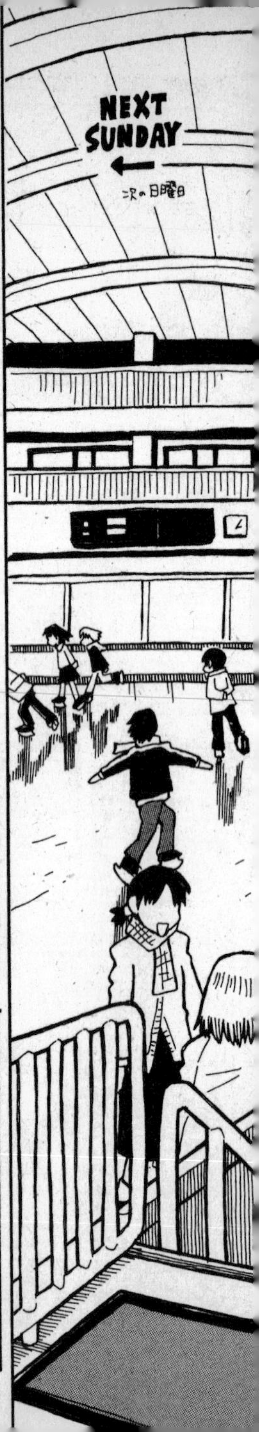
NEXT SUNDAY
次の日曜日

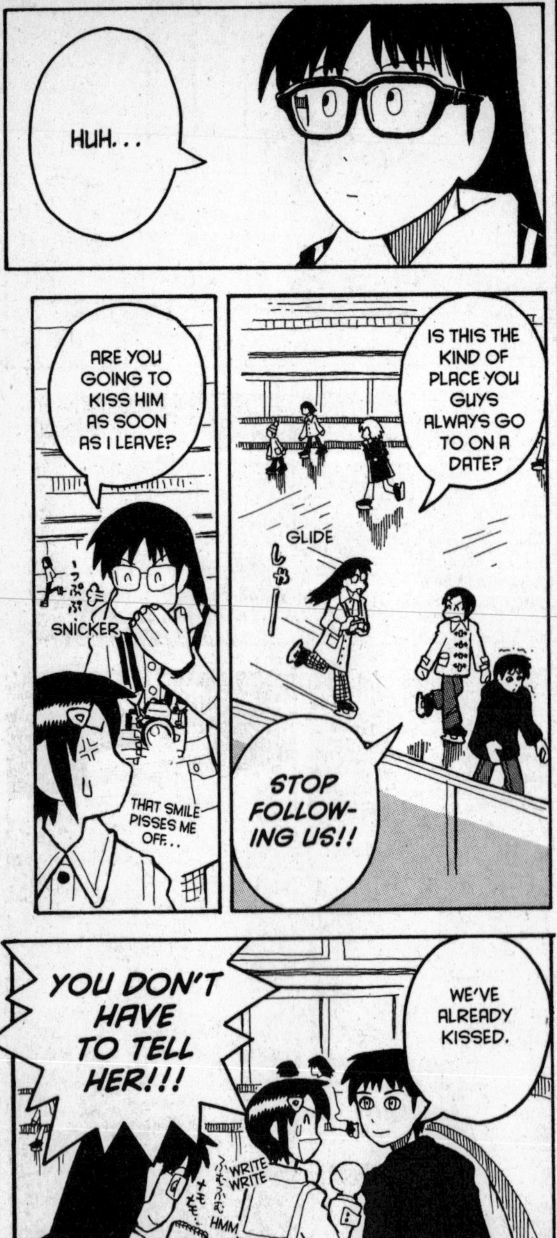
HUH...
IS THIS THE KIND OF PLACE YOU GUYS ALWAYS GO TO ON A DATE?
GLIDE
しゃー
STOP FOLLOWING US!!
ARE YOU GOING TO KISS HIM AS SOON AS I LEAVE?
うぷぷ
SNICKER
THAT SMILE PISSES ME OFF...
WE'VE ALREADY KISSED.
YOU DON'T HAVE TO TELL HER!!!
WRITE WRITE
ふむふむ
メモメモ...
HMM

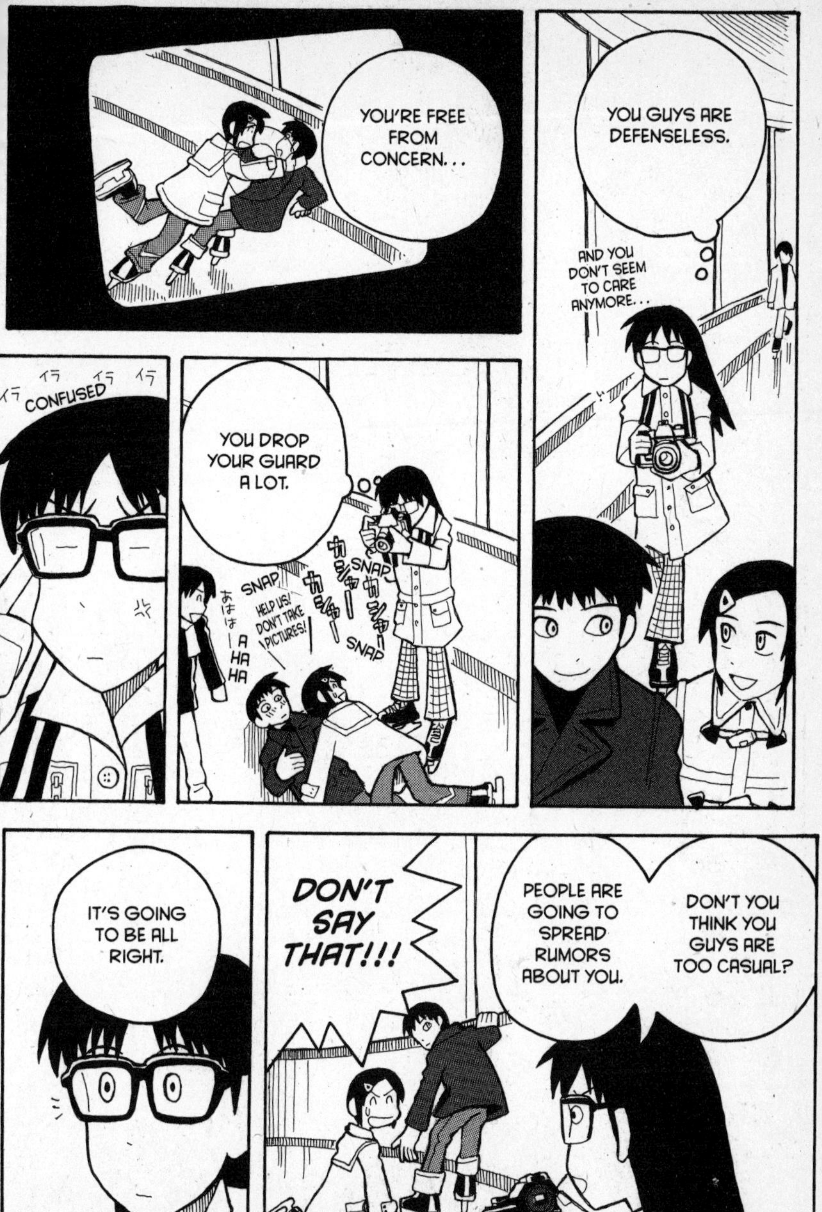
YOU GUYS ARE DEFENSELESS.
AND YOU DON'T SEEM TO CARE ANYMORE...
YOU'RE FREE FROM CONCERN...
YOU DROP YOUR GUARD A LOT.
カシャ カシャ
SNAP SNAP SNAP SNAP
HELP US! DON'T TAKE PICTURES!
おほほ
A HA HA
イラ イラ イラ イラ
CONFUSED
DON'T YOU THINK YOU GUYS ARE TOO CASUAL?
PEOPLE ARE GOING TO SPREAD RUMORS ABOUT YOU.
DON'T SAY THAT!!!
IT'S GOING TO BE ALL RIGHT.

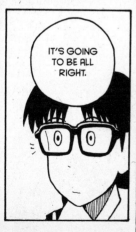

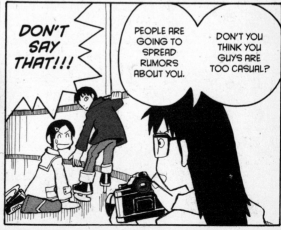

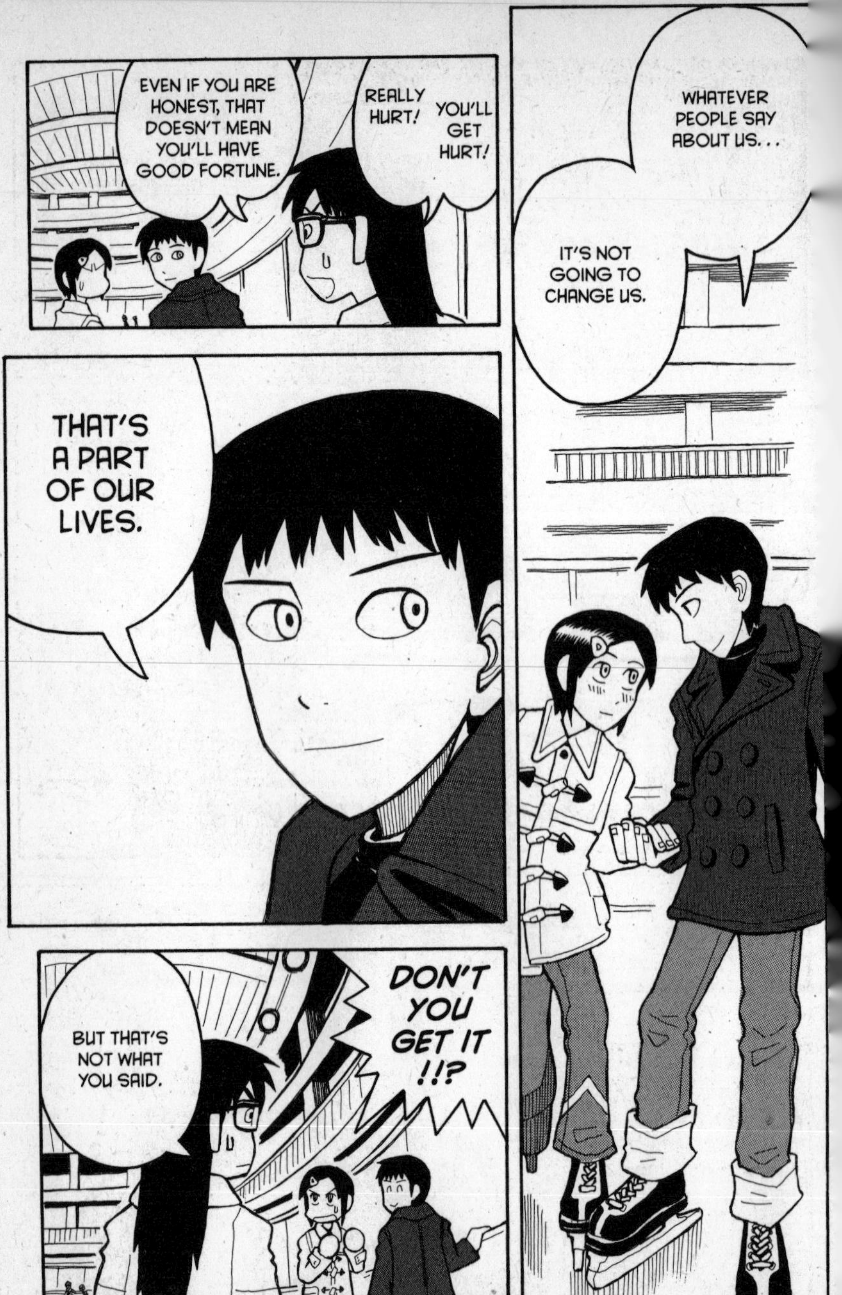
WHATEVER PEOPLE SAY ABOUT US...
IT'S NOT GOING TO CHANGE US.
YOU'LL GET HURT!
REALLY HURT!
EVEN IF YOU ARE HONEST, THAT DOESN'T MEAN YOU'LL HAVE GOOD FORTUNE.
THAT'S A PART OF OUR LIVES.
DON'T YOU GET IT !!?
BUT THAT'S NOT WHAT YOU SAID.

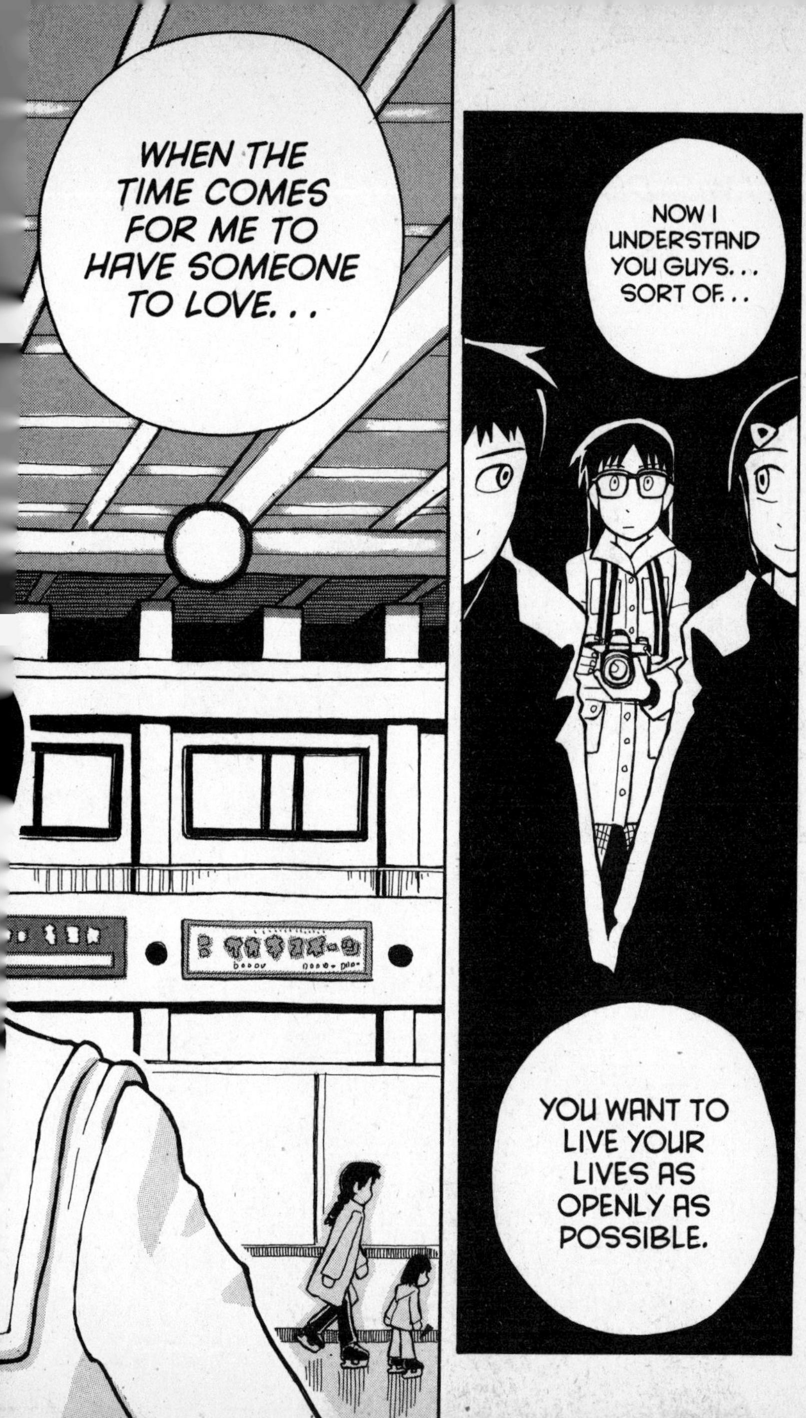
NOW I UNDERSTAND YOU GUYS... SORT OF...
YOU WANT TO LIVE YOUR LIVES AS OPENLY AS POSSIBLE.
WHEN THE TIME COMES FOR ME TO HAVE SOMEONE TO LOVE...

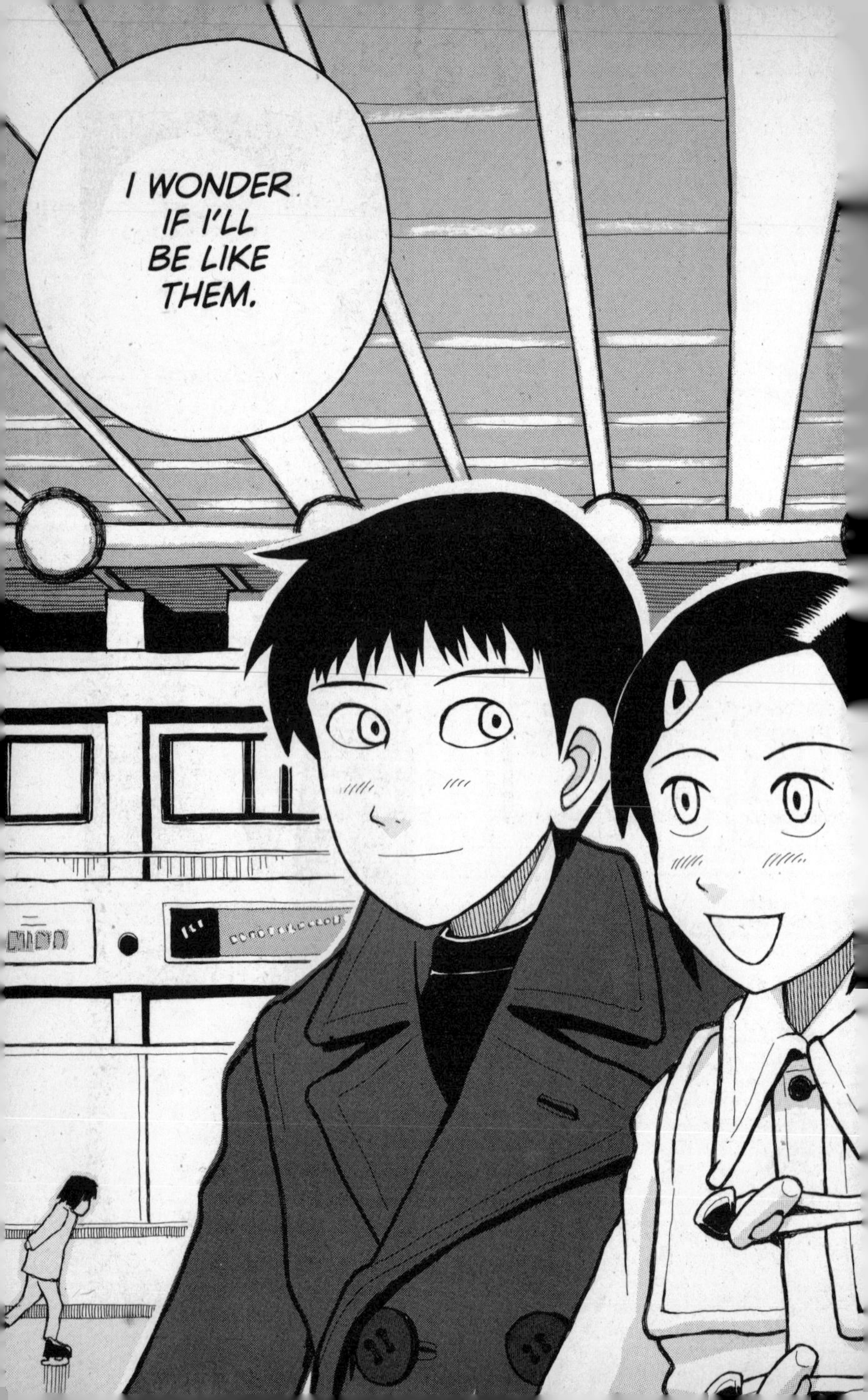
I WONDER IF I'LL BE LIKE THEM.

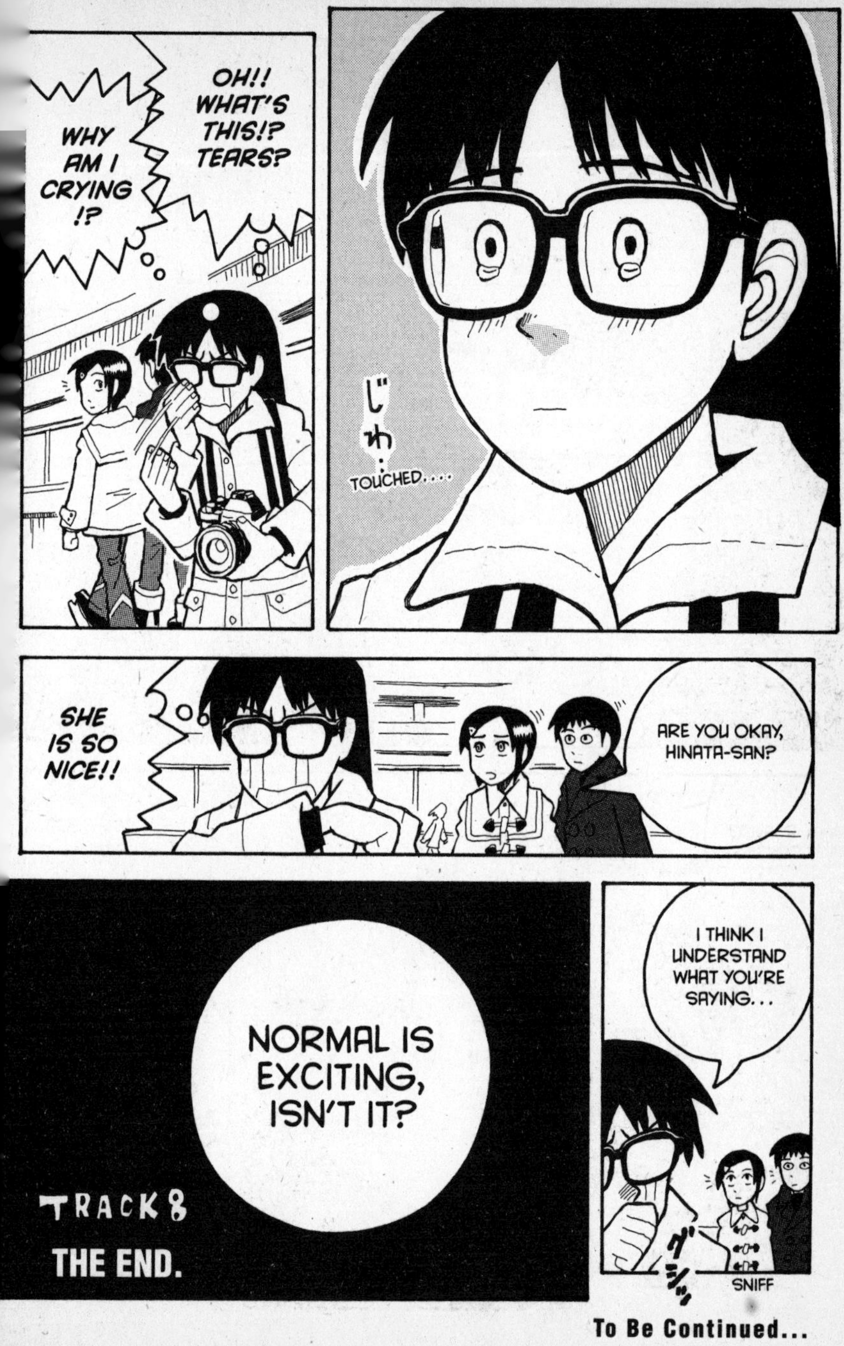
じわ
TOUCHED....
OH!! WHAT'S THIS!? TEARS?
WHY AM I CRYING !?
ARE YOU OKAY, HINATA-SAN?
SHE IS SO NICE!!
I THINK I UNDERSTAND WHAT YOU'RE SAYING...
SNIFF
NORMAL IS EXCITING, ISN'T IT?
TRACK 8
THE END.

To Be Continued...

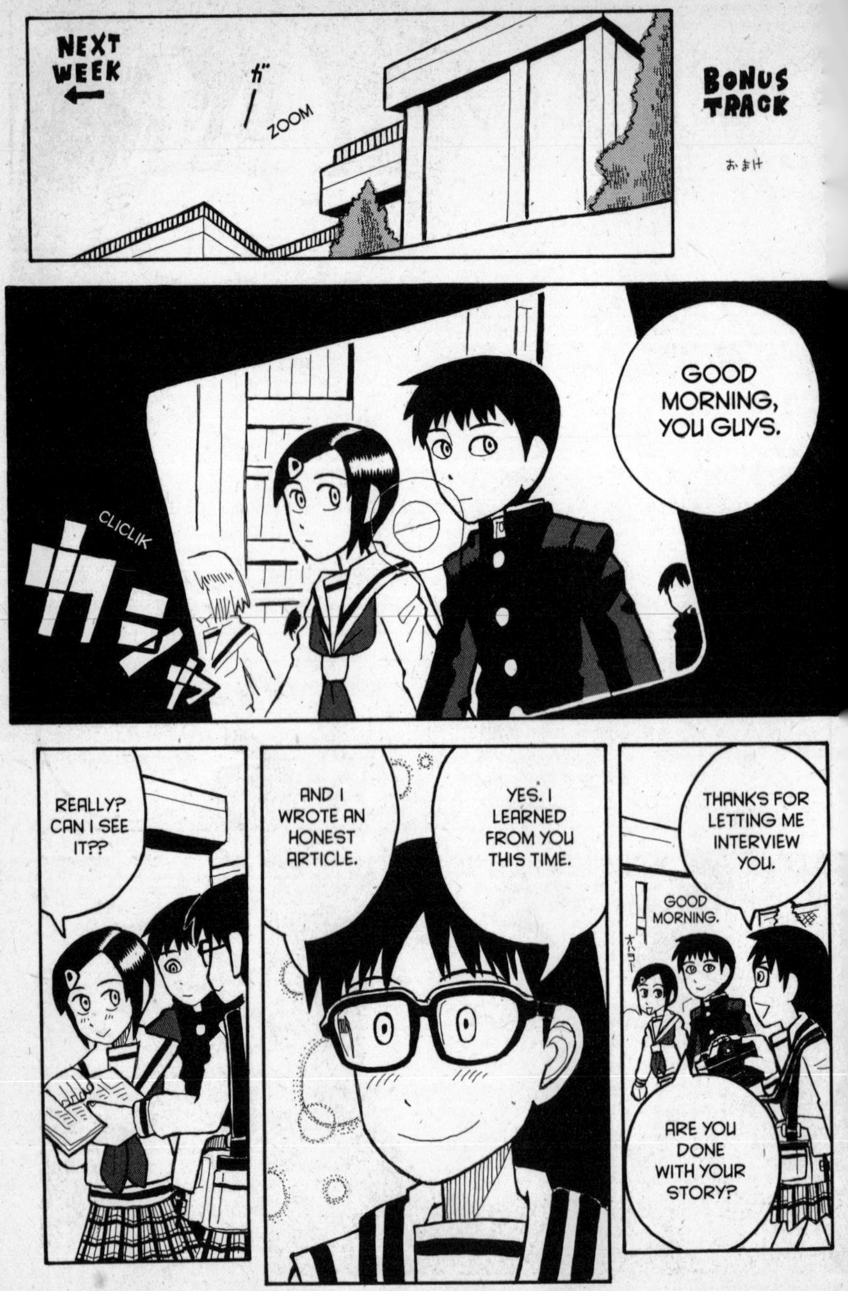
BONUS TRACK
おまけ
ガー
ZOOM
NEXT WEEK ←
GOOD MORNING, YOU GUYS.
CLICLIK
THANKS FOR LETTING ME INTERVIEW YOU.
GOOD MORNING.
オハヨー
ARE YOU DONE WITH YOUR STORY?
YES. I LEARNED FROM YOU THIS TIME.
AND I WROTE AN HONEST ARTICLE.
REALLY? CAN I SEE IT??

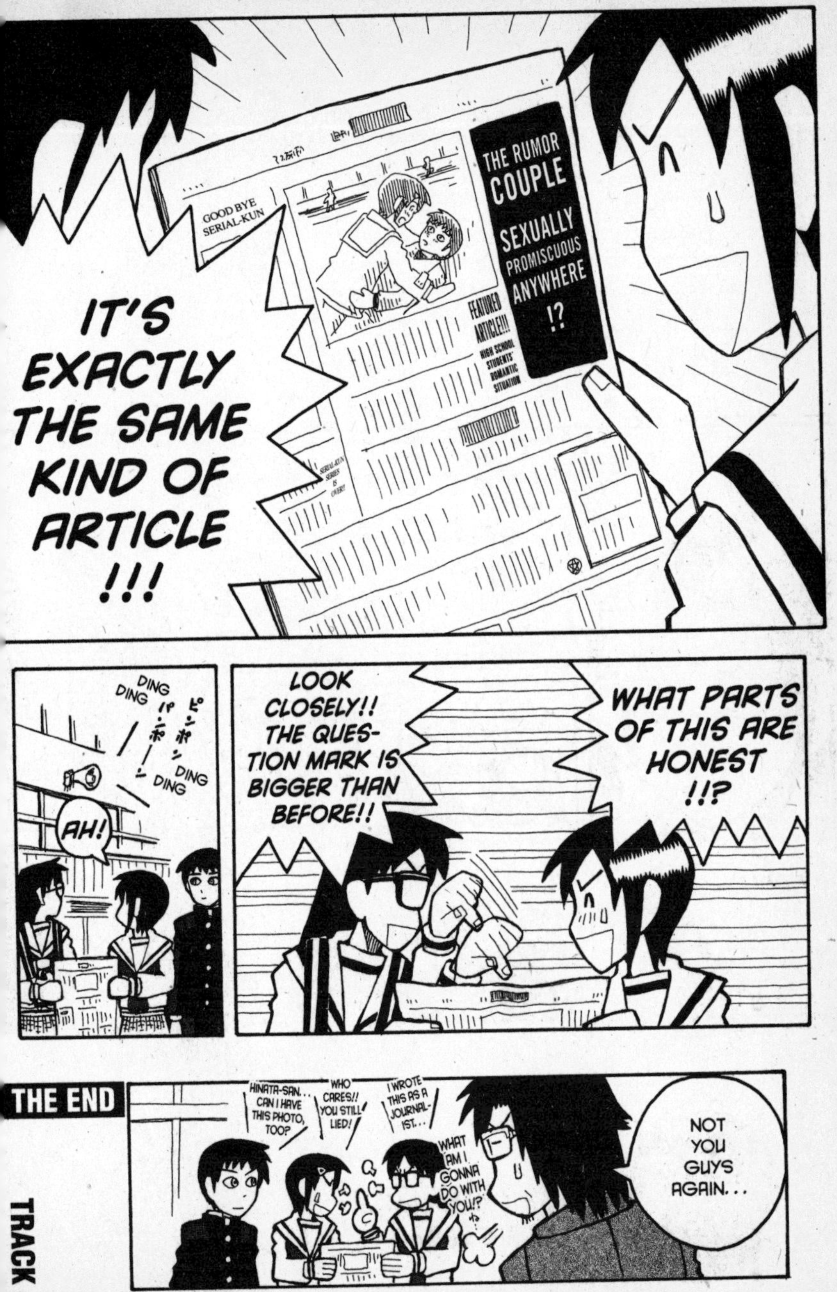
THE RUMOR COUPLE
SEXUALLY PROMISCUOUS ANYWHERE !?
FEATURED ARTICLE!!!
HIGH SCHOOL STUDENTS' ROMANTIC SITUATION
GOOD BYE SERIAL-KUN
SERIAL-KUN SERIES IS OVER!!
IT'S EXACTLY THE SAME KIND OF ARTICLE !!!
WHAT PARTS OF THIS ARE HONEST !!?
LOOK CLOSELY!! THE QUES-TION MARK IS BIGGER THAN BEFORE!!
DING DING
DING DING
AH!
NOT YOU GUYS AGAIN...
WHAT AM I GONNA DO WITH YOU!?
I WROTE THIS AS A JOURNAL-IST...
WHO CARES!! YOU STILL LIED!
HINATA-SAN... CAN I HAVE THIS PHOTO, TOO?

THE END

TRACK #8 ▶▶ END

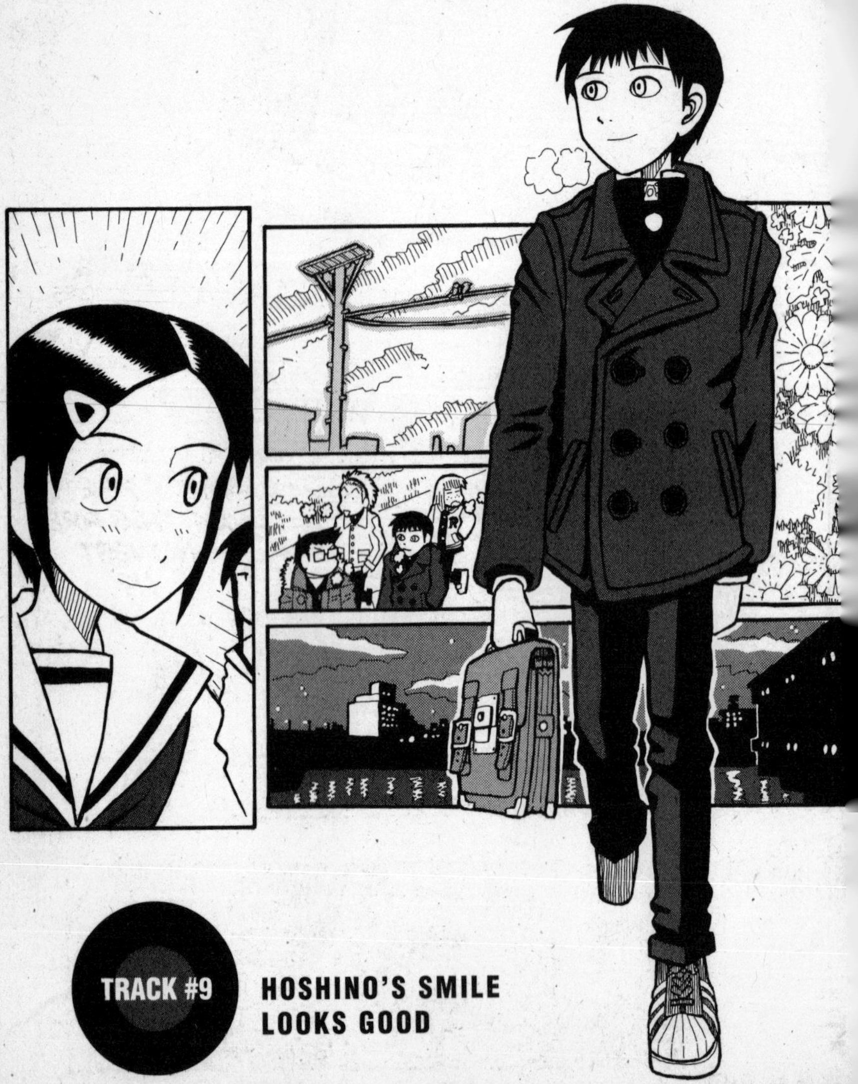

TRACK #9

HOSHINO'S SMILE LOOKS GOOD

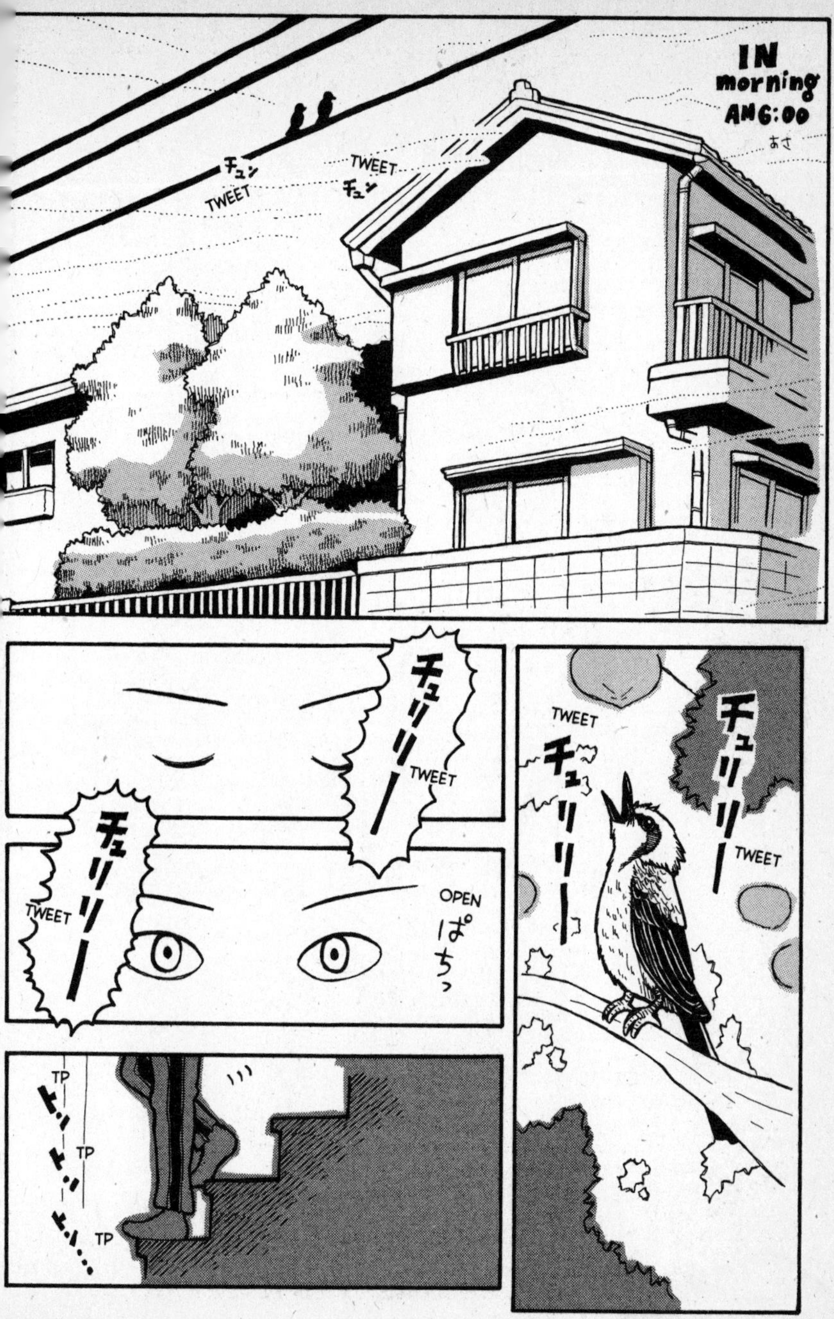
IN morning AM6:00
あさ
TWEET
チュン
チュン
TWEET
チュリリー
TWEET
TWEET
チュリリー
チュリリー
TWEET
OPEN
ぱちっ
チュリリー
TWEET
TP
トッ
TP
トッ
TP
トッ…

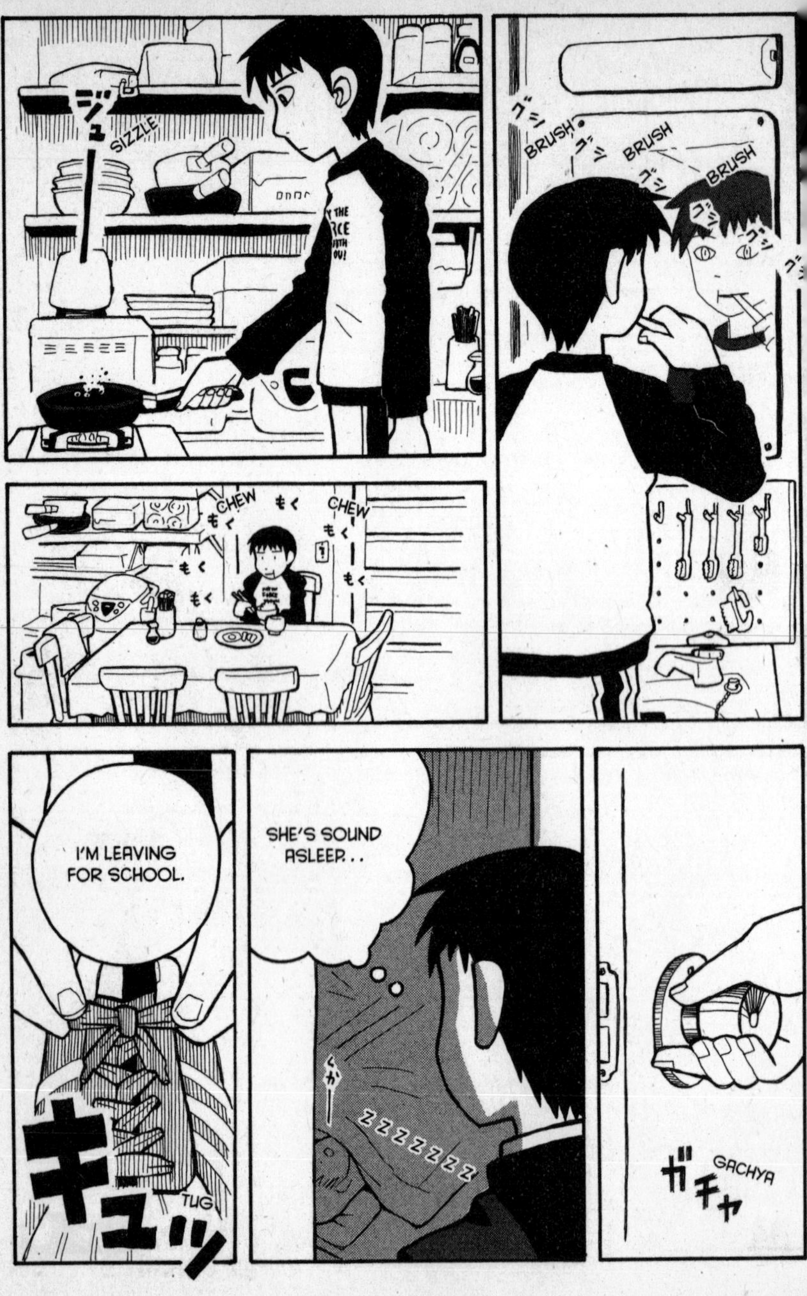

BRUSH
BRUSH
BRUSH
ジュ
SIZZLE
CHEW
CHEW
ガチャ
GACHYA
SHE'S SOUND ASLEEP...
ZZZZZZZ
I'M LEAVING FOR SCHOOL.
キュッ
TUG

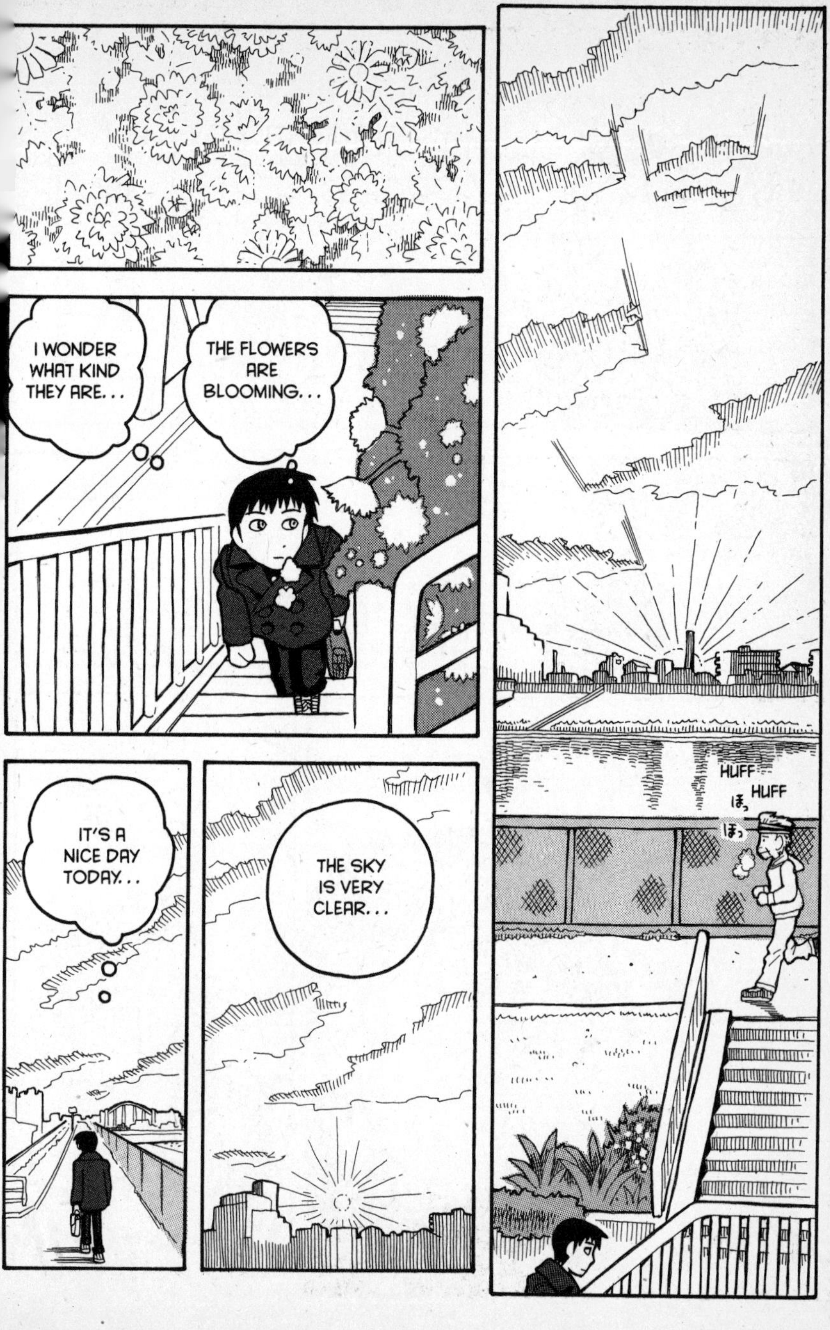
HUFF
HUFF
ほっ
ほっ
THE FLOWERS ARE BLOOMING...
I WONDER WHAT KIND THEY ARE...
THE SKY IS VERY CLEAR...
IT'S A NICE DAY TODAY...

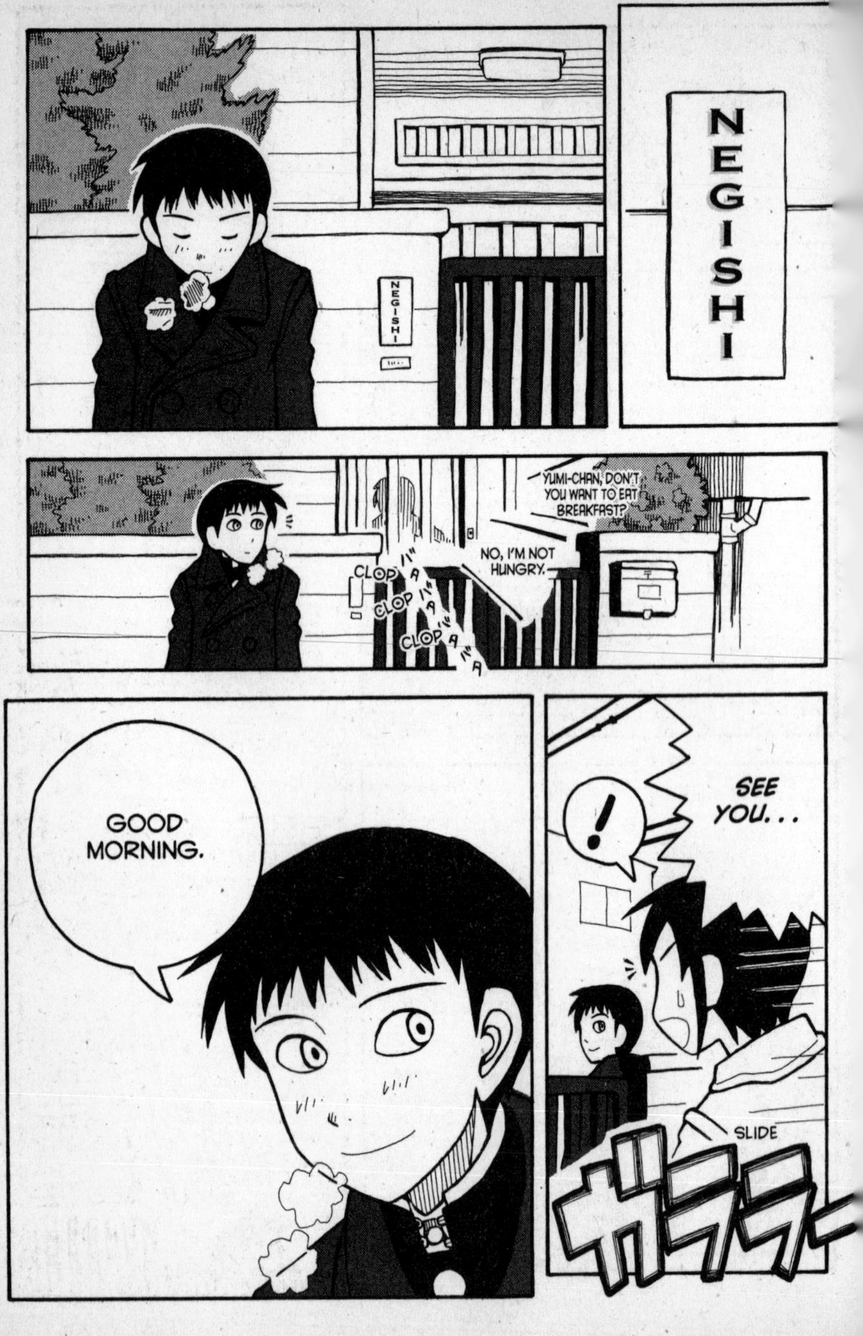
NEGISHI
NEGISHI
YUMI-CHAN, DON'T YOU WANT TO EAT BREAKFAST?
NO, I'M NOT HUNGRY.
CLOP CLOP CLOP
SEE YOU. . .
!
SLIDE
GOOD MORNING.

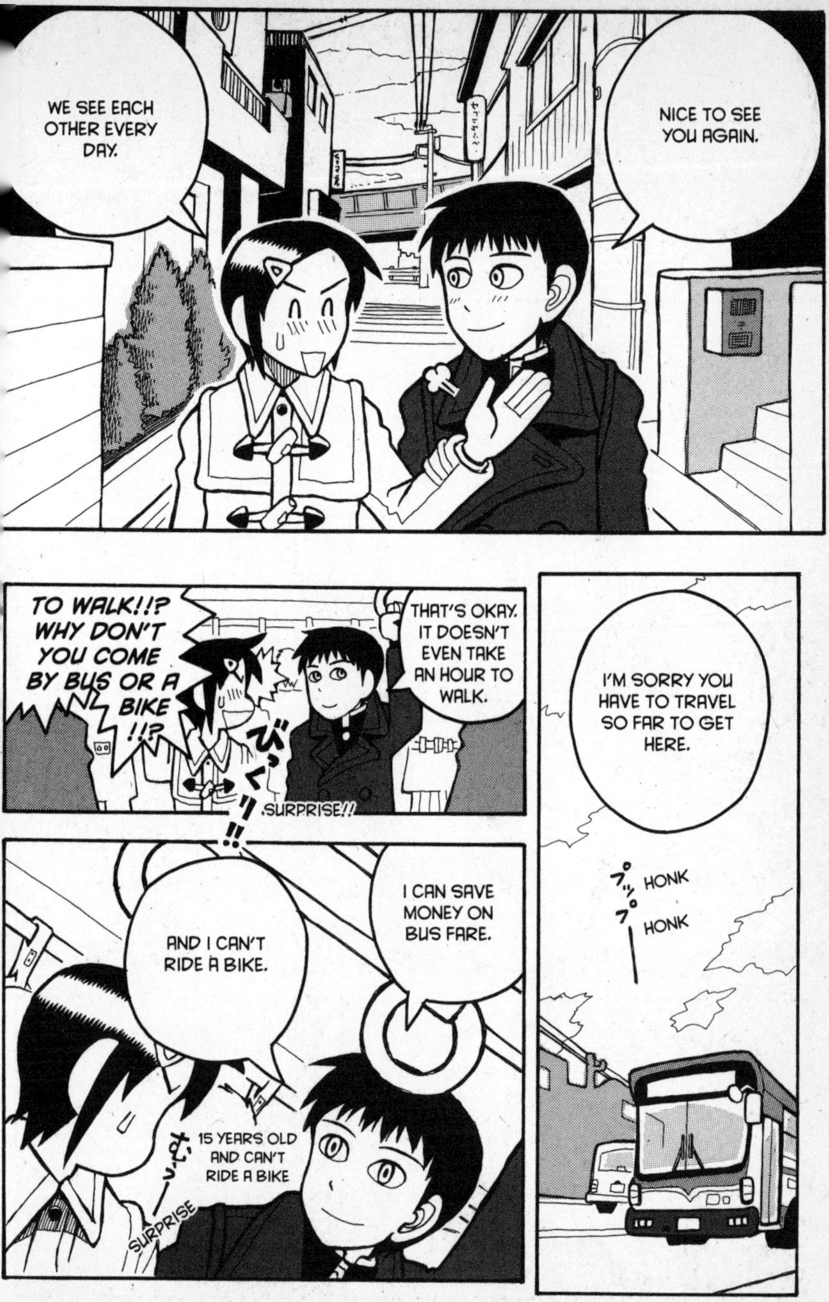
NICE TO SEE YOU AGAIN.
WE SEE EACH OTHER EVERY DAY.
I'M SORRY YOU HAVE TO TRAVEL SO FAR TO GET HERE.
HONK
HONK
THAT'S OKAY. IT DOESN'T EVEN TAKE AN HOUR TO WALK.
TO WALK!!? WHY DON'T YOU COME BY BUS OR A BIKE!!?
SURPRISE!!
I CAN SAVE MONEY ON BUS FARE.
AND I CAN'T RIDE A BIKE.
15 YEARS OLD AND CAN'T RIDE A BIKE
SURPRISE

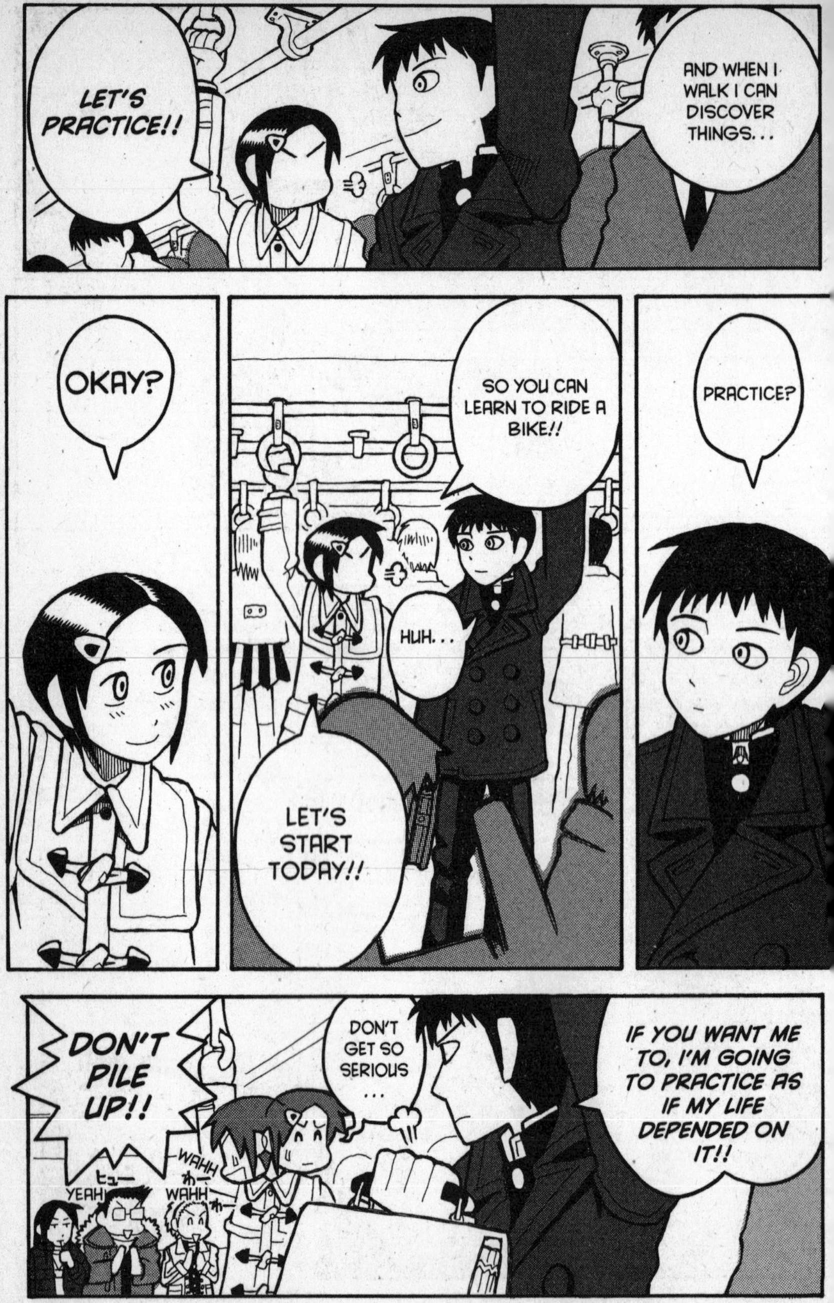
AND WHEN I WALK I CAN DISCOVER THINGS...
LET'S PRACTICE!!
PRACTICE?
SO YOU CAN LEARN TO RIDE A BIKE!!
HUH...
LET'S START TODAY!!
OKAY?
IF YOU WANT ME TO, I'M GOING TO PRACTICE AS IF MY LIFE DEPENDED ON IT!!
DON'T GET SO SERIOUS...
DON'T PILE UP!!
WAHH わー
WAHH わー
ヒュー YEAH

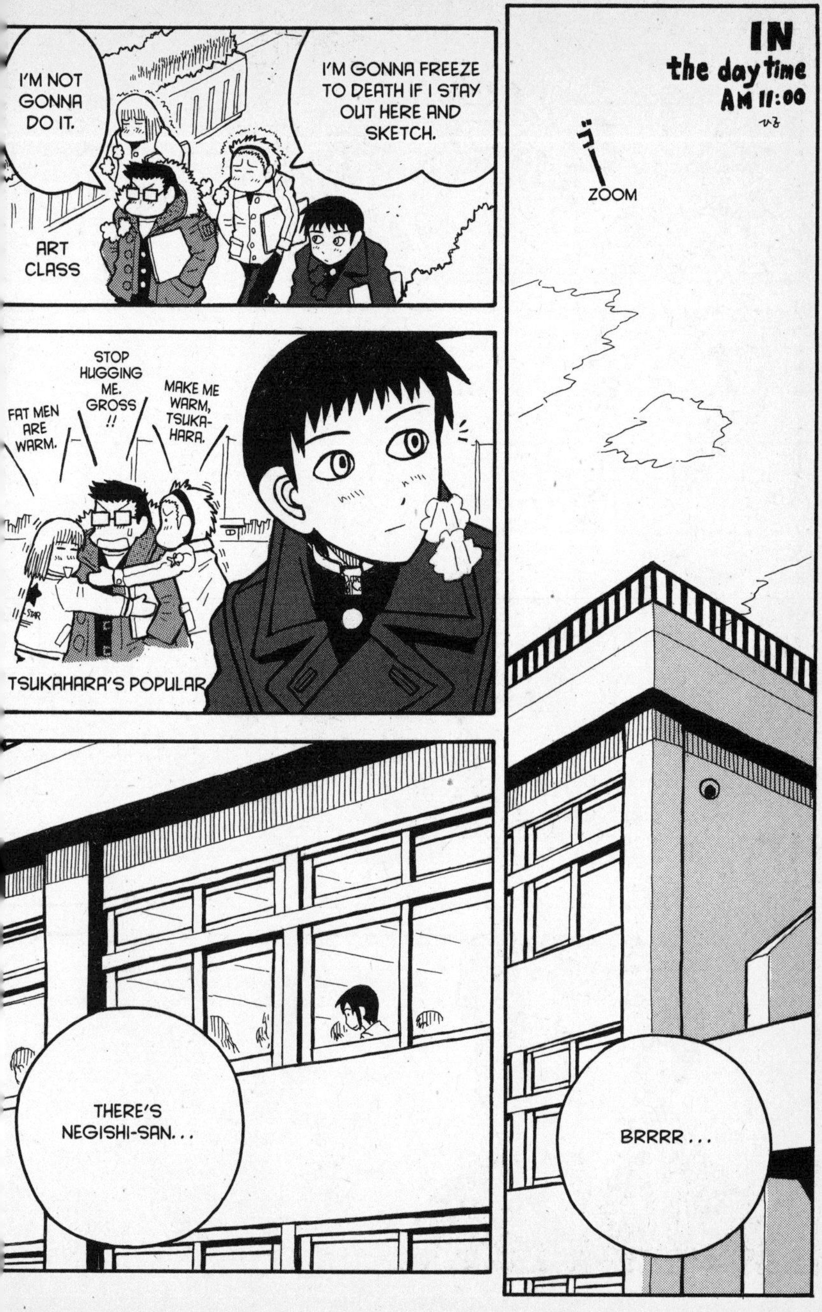
IN
the day time
AM 11:00
ZOOM
BRRRR...
I'M GONNA FREEZE TO DEATH IF I STAY OUT HERE AND SKETCH.
I'M NOT GONNA DO IT.
ART CLASS
MAKE ME WARM, TSUKAHARA.
STOP HUGGING ME. GROSS!!
FAT MEN ARE WARM.
STAR
TSUKAHARA'S POPULAR
THERE'S NEGISHI-SAN...

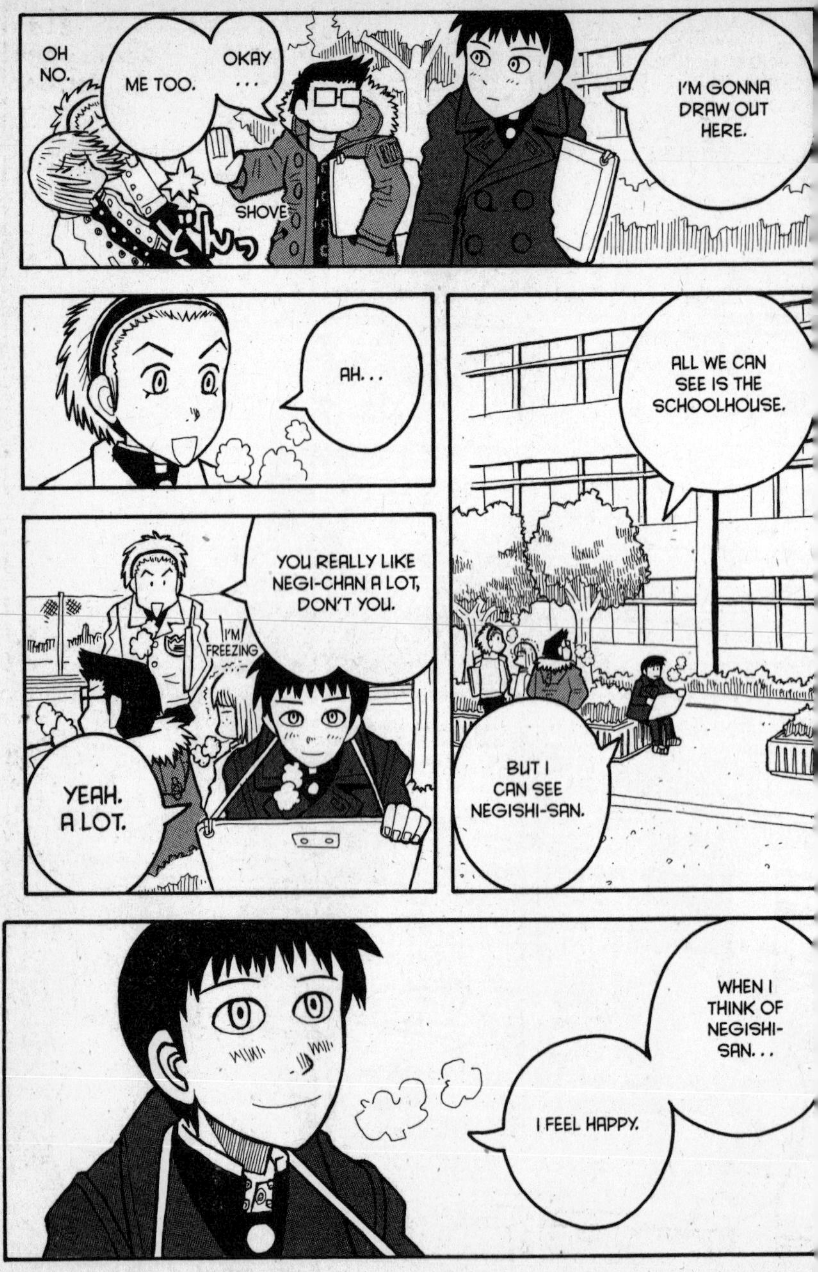
I'M GONNA DRAW OUT HERE.
OKAY...
ME TOO.
OH NO.
SHOVE
どんっ
ALL WE CAN SEE IS THE SCHOOLHOUSE.
BUT I CAN SEE NEGISHI-SAN.
AH...
YOU REALLY LIKE NEGI-CHAN A LOT, DON'T YOU.
I'M FREEZING
YEAH. A LOT.
WHEN I THINK OF NEGISHI-SAN...
I FEEL HAPPY.

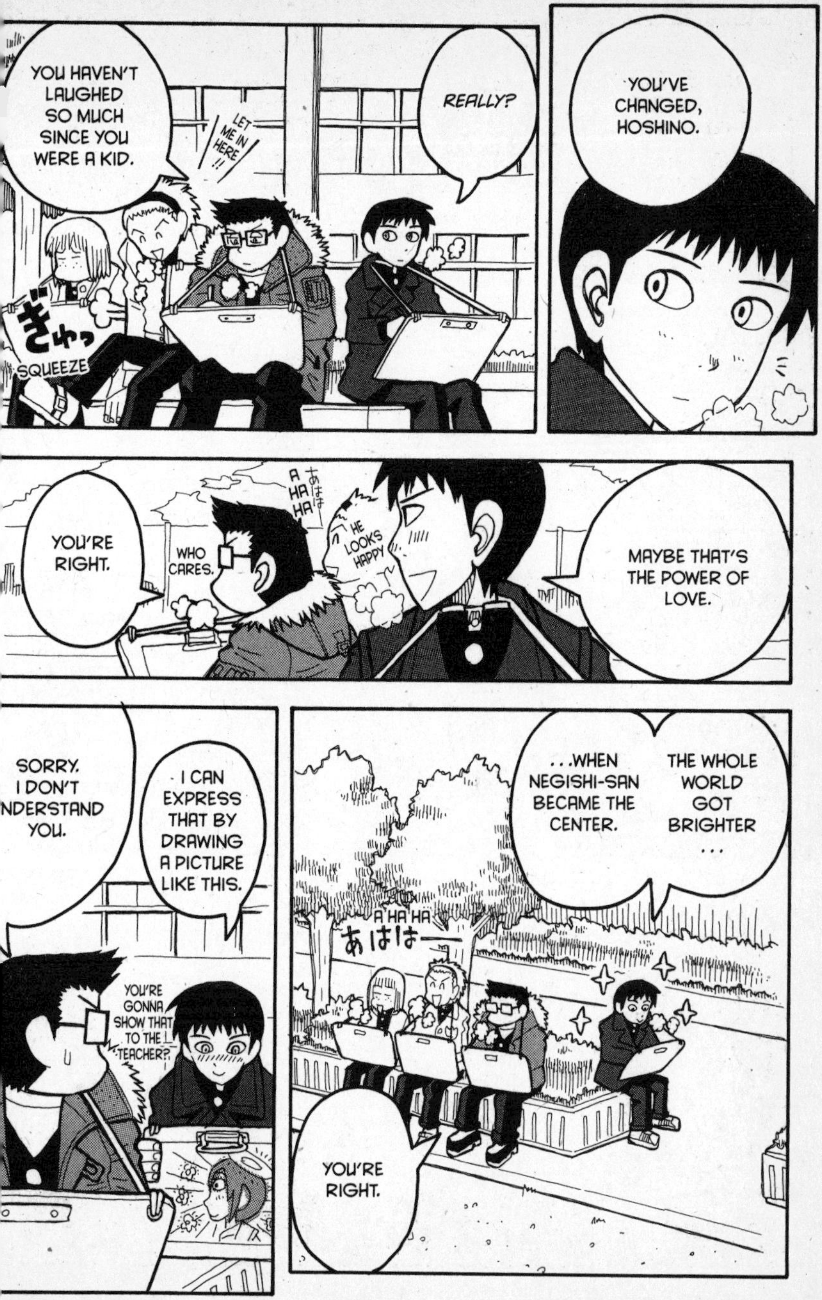
YOU'VE CHANGED, HOSHINO.
REALLY?
LET ME IN HERE!!
YOU HAVEN'T LAUGHED SO MUCH SINCE YOU WERE A KID.
ぎゅっ
SQUEEZE
MAYBE THAT'S THE POWER OF LOVE.
HE LOOKS HAPPY
あはは
A HA HA
WHO CARES.
YOU'RE RIGHT.
THE WHOLE WORLD GOT BRIGHTER ...
...WHEN NEGISHI-SAN BECAME THE CENTER.
あはは―
A HA HA
YOU'RE RIGHT.
I CAN EXPRESS THAT BY DRAWING A PICTURE LIKE THIS.
SORRY. I DON'T NDERSTAND YOU.
YOU'RE GONNA SHOW THAT TO THE TEACHER?

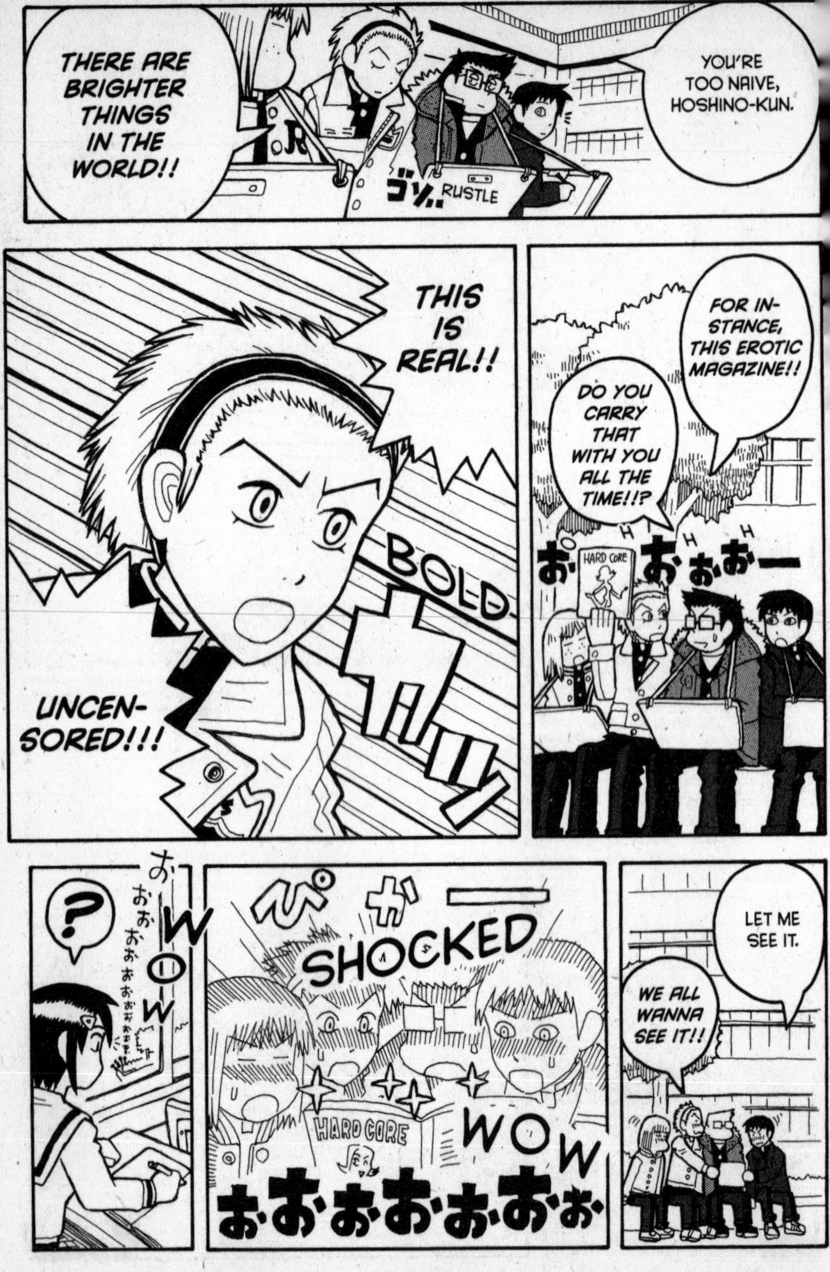
YOU'RE TOO NAIVE, HOSHINO-KUN.
THERE ARE BRIGHTER THINGS IN THE WORLD!!
ゴソ..
RUSTLE
FOR IN-STANCE, THIS EROTIC MAGAZINE!!
DO YOU CARRY THAT WITH YOU ALL THE TIME!!?
HARD CORE
お おぉおー
H H H
THIS IS REAL!!
BOLD
UNCEN-SORED!!!
LET ME SEE IT.
WE ALL WANNA SEE IT!!
ぴかー
SHOCKED
HARD CORE
WOW
おおおおおおぉ
?
WOW
お

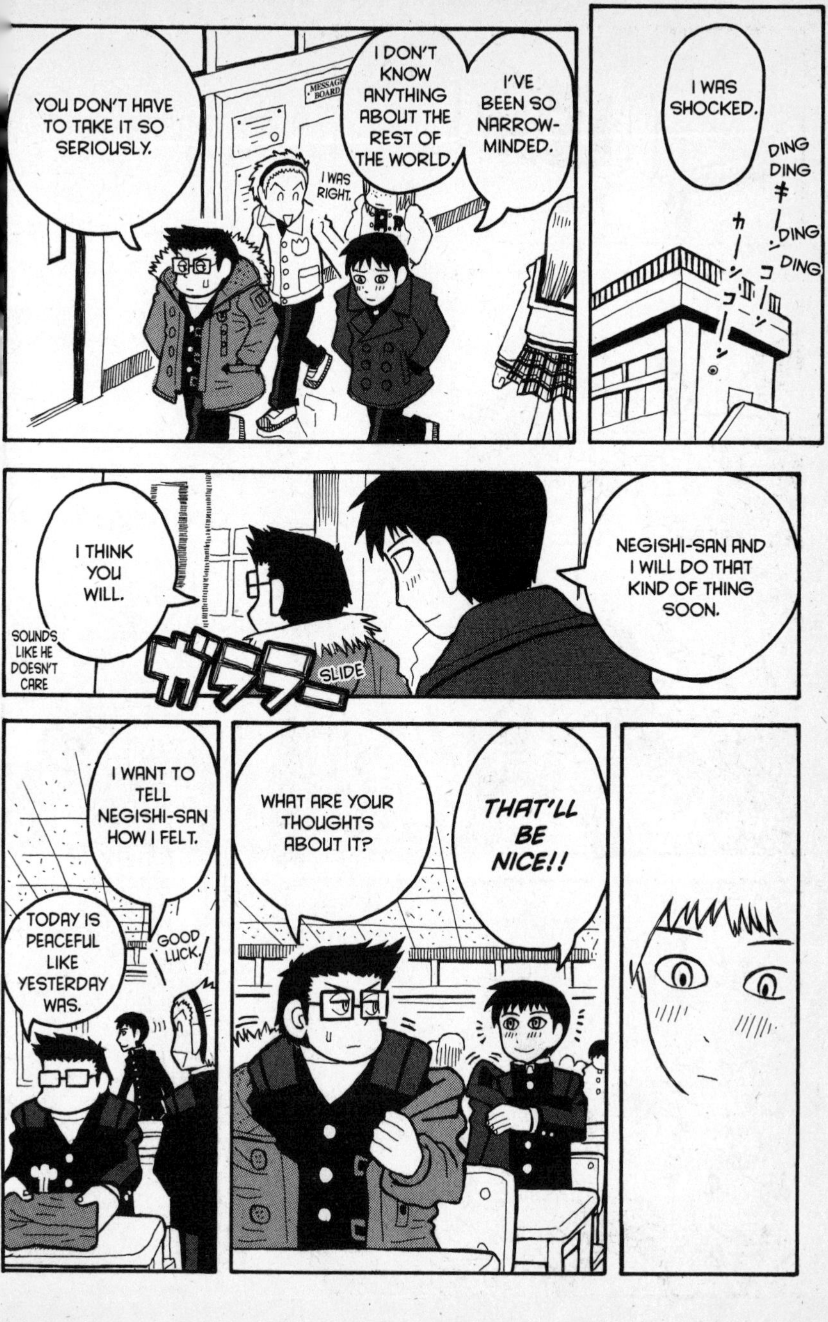
I WAS SHOCKED.
DING DING
DING DING
I'VE BEEN SO NARROW-MINDED.
I DON'T KNOW ANYTHING ABOUT THE REST OF THE WORLD.
MESSAGE BOARD
I WAS RIGHT.
YOU DON'T HAVE TO TAKE IT SO SERIOUSLY.
NEGISHI-SAN AND I WILL DO THAT KIND OF THING SOON.
I THINK YOU WILL.
SOUNDS LIKE HE DOESN'T CARE
SLIDE
THAT'LL BE NICE!!
WHAT ARE YOUR THOUGHTS ABOUT IT?
I WANT TO TELL NEGISHI-SAN HOW I FELT.
GOOD LUCK.
TODAY IS PEACEFUL LIKE YESTERDAY WAS.

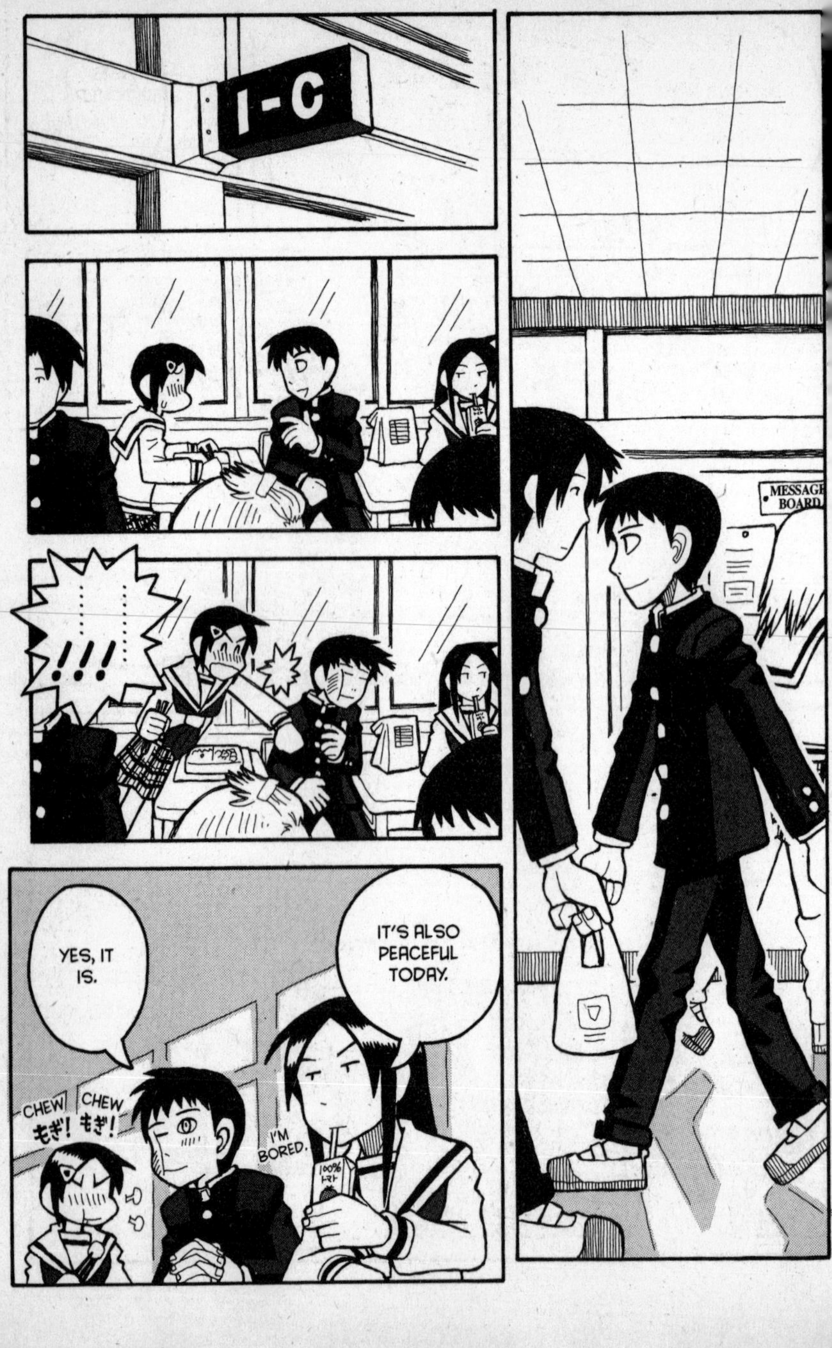
MESSAG
BOARD
I-C
......
!!!
IT'S ALSO PEACEFUL TODAY.
YES, IT IS.
I'M BORED.
100% トマト
CHEW もぎ!
CHEW もぎ!

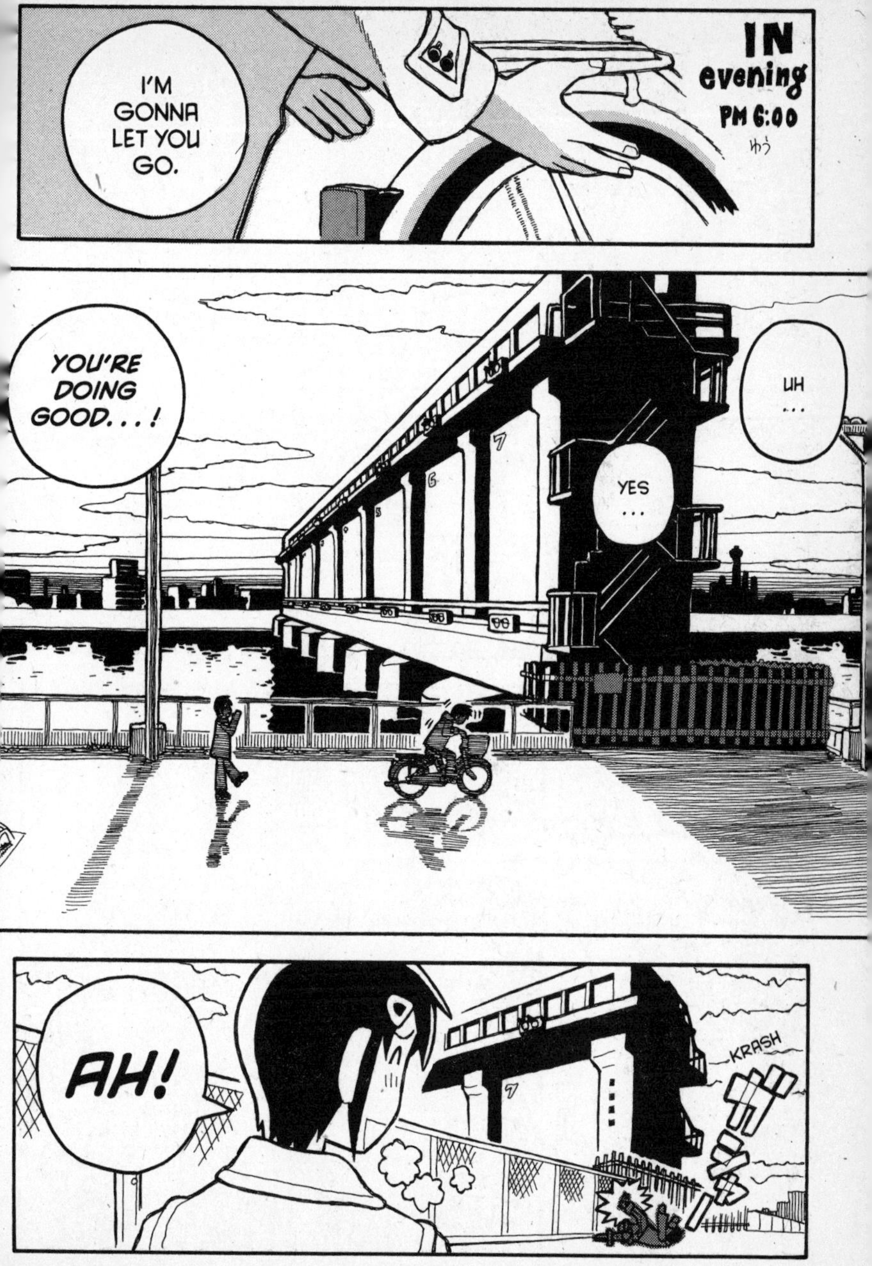
IN evening PM 6:00
ゆう
I'M GONNA LET YOU GO.
UH ...
YES ...
YOU'RE DOING GOOD...!
KRASH
AH!

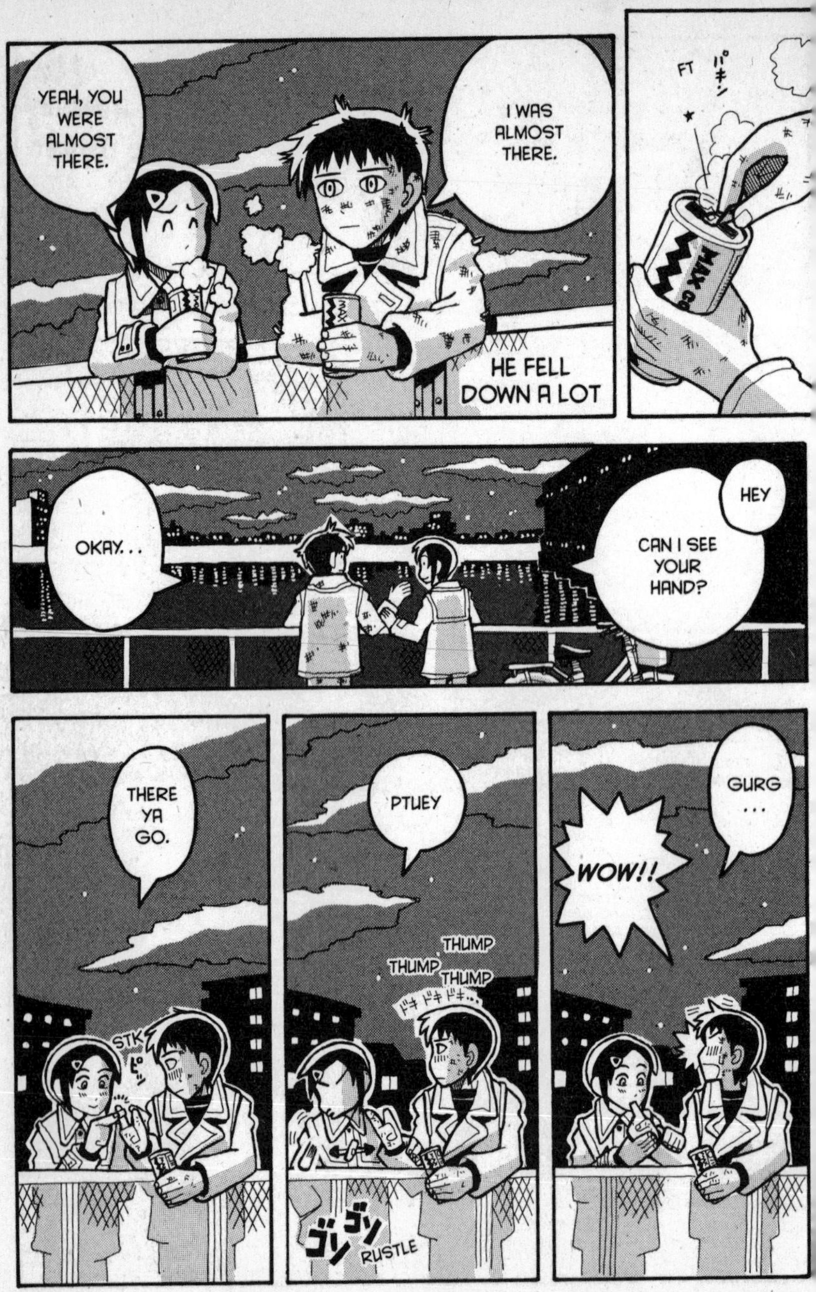
FT
パキン
I WAS ALMOST THERE.
YEAH, YOU WERE ALMOST THERE.
HE FELL DOWN A LOT
HEY
CAN I SEE YOUR HAND?
OKAY...
GURG ...
WOW!!
PTUEY
THUMP
THUMP
THUMP
ドキドキドキ...
ゴソゴソ
RUSTLE
THERE YA GO.
STK
ピッ

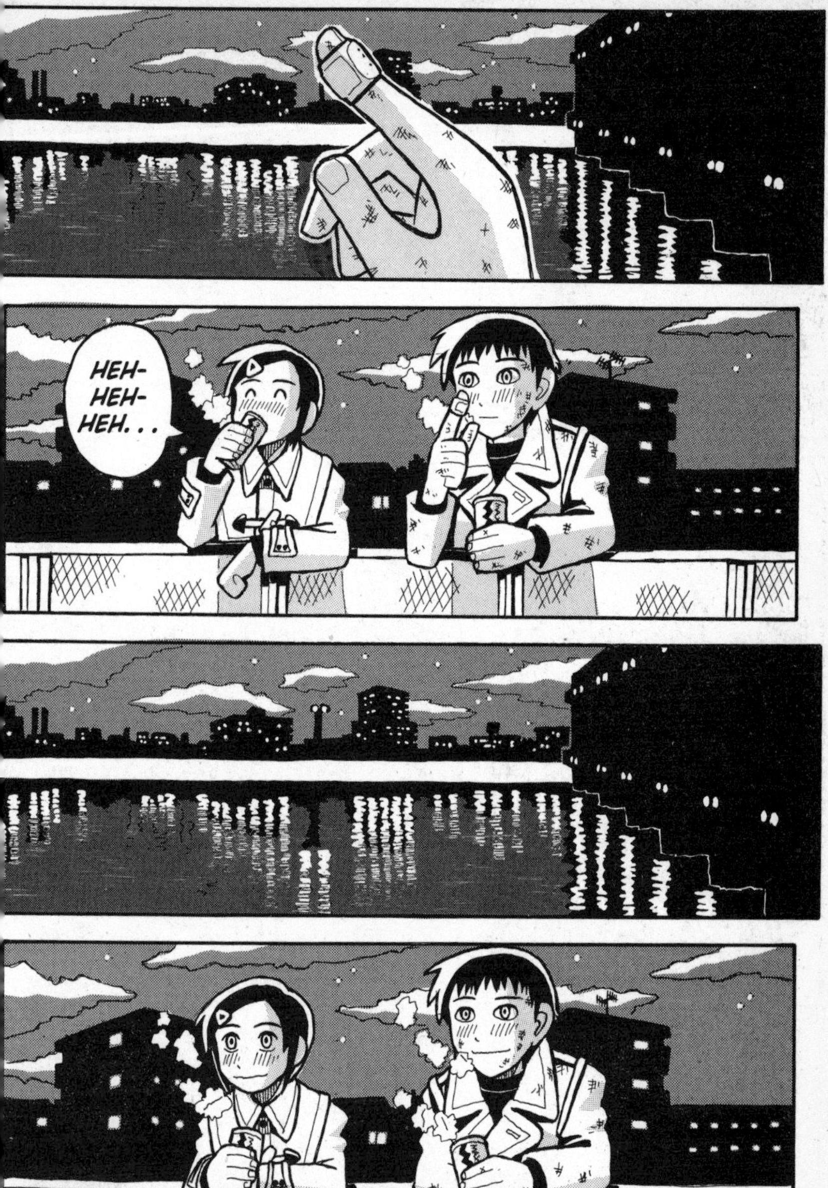
HEH-
HEH-
HEH. . .

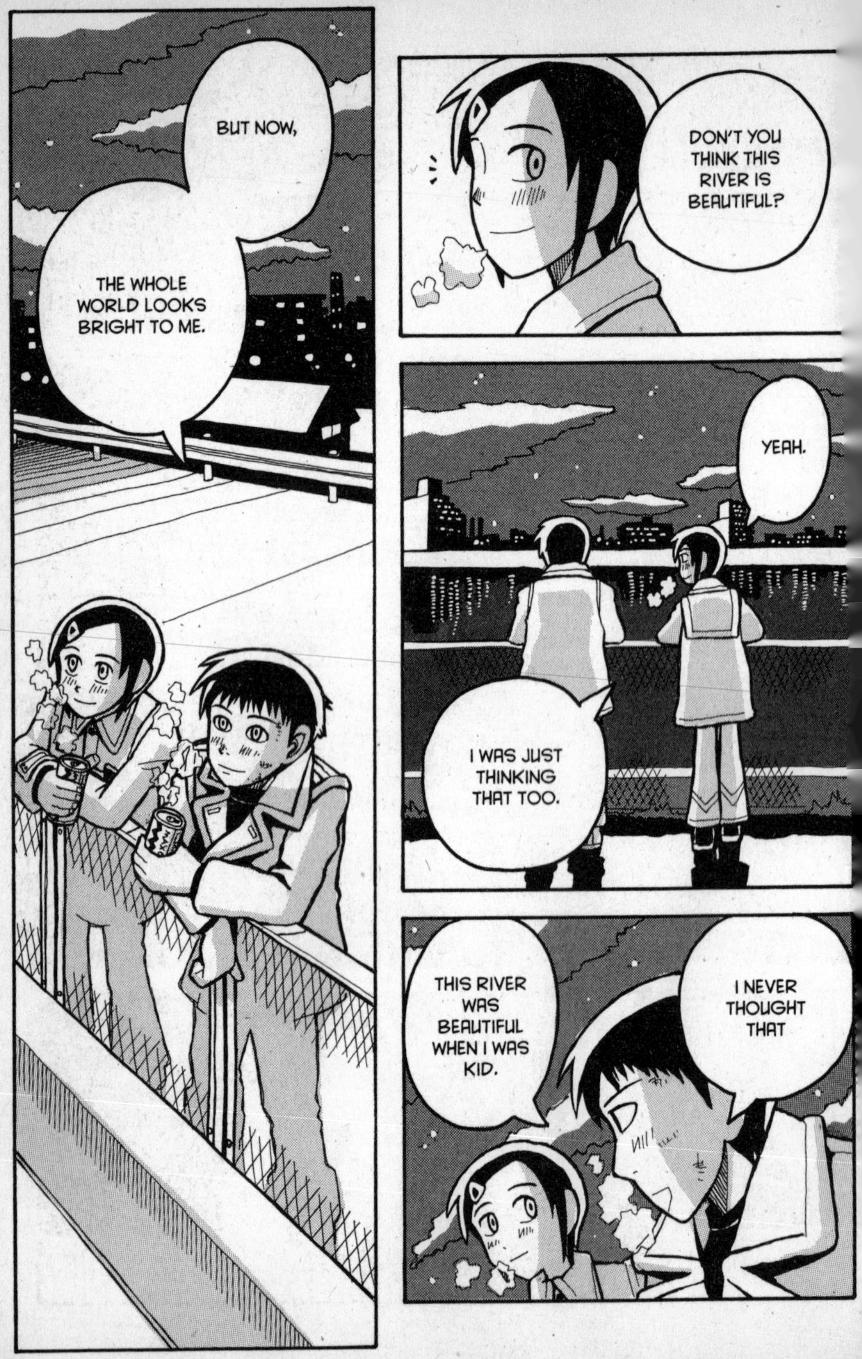
DON'T YOU THINK THIS RIVER IS BEAUTIFUL?
YEAH.
I WAS JUST THINKING THAT TOO.
I NEVER THOUGHT THAT
THIS RIVER WAS BEAUTIFUL WHEN I WAS KID.
BUT NOW,
THE WHOLE WORLD LOOKS BRIGHT TO ME.

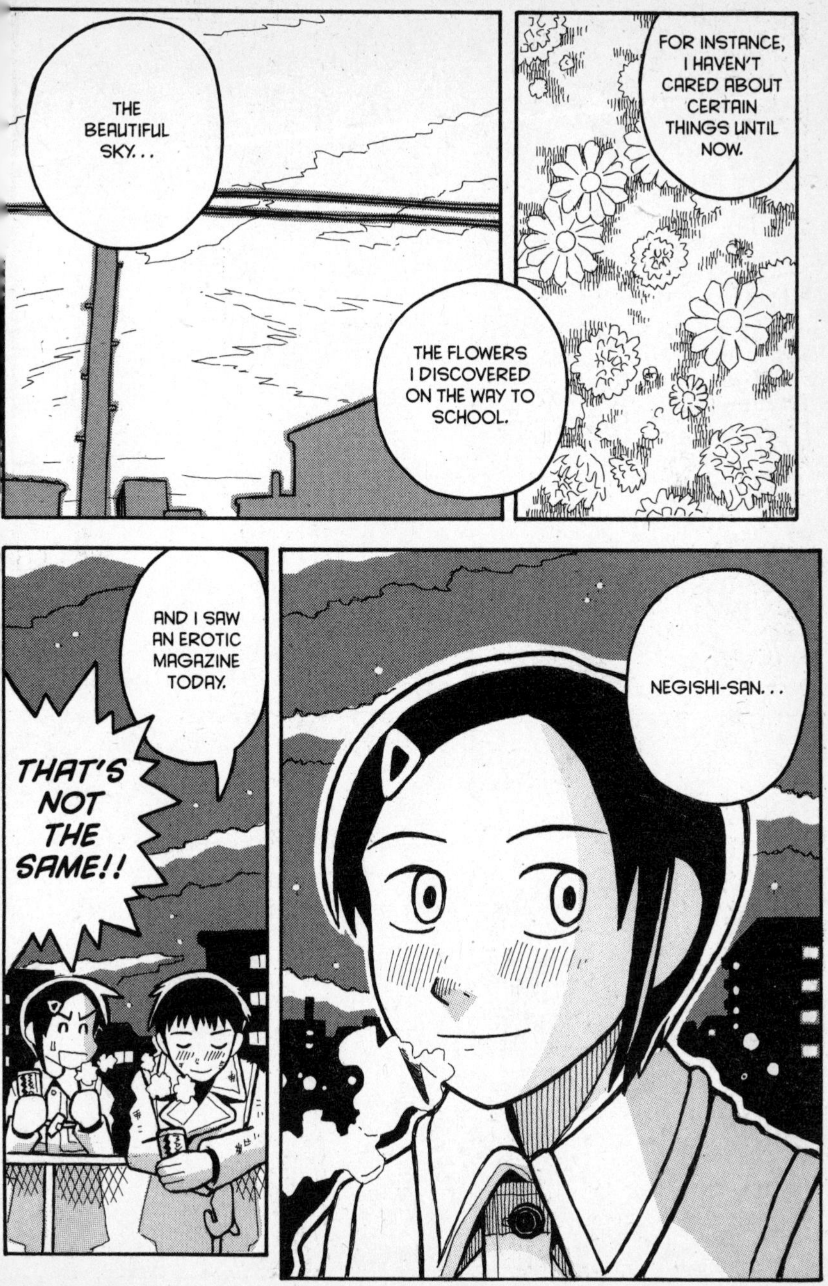
FOR INSTANCE, I HAVEN'T CARED ABOUT CERTAIN THINGS UNTIL NOW.
THE FLOWERS I DISCOVERED ON THE WAY TO SCHOOL.
THE BEAUTIFUL SKY...
NEGISHI-SAN...
AND I SAW AN EROTIC MAGAZINE TODAY.
THAT'S NOT THE SAME!!

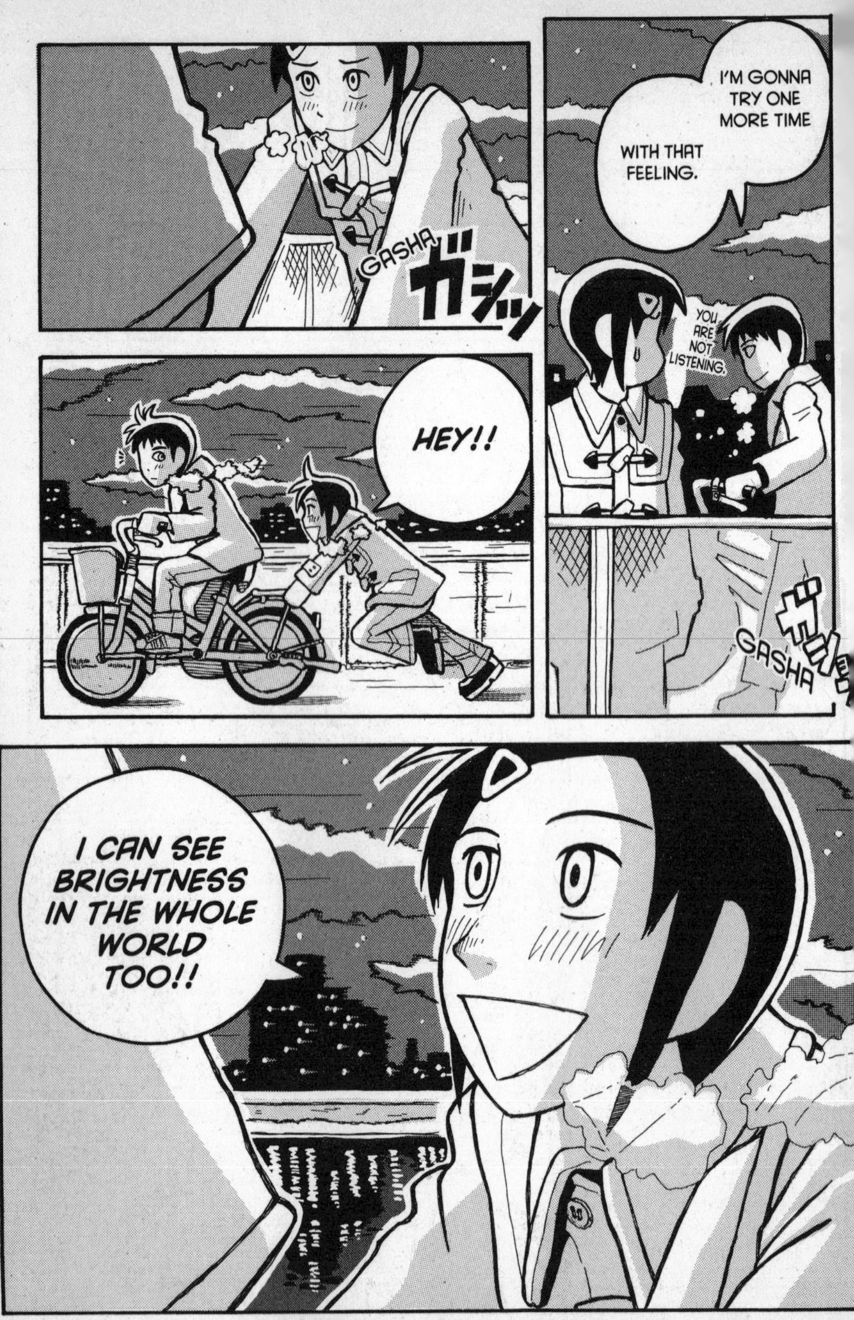
I'M GONNA TRY ONE MORE TIME
WITH THAT FEELING.
YOU ARE NOT LISTENING.
GASHA
GASHA
ガシッ
HEY!!
I CAN SEE BRIGHTNESS IN THE WHOLE WORLD TOO!!

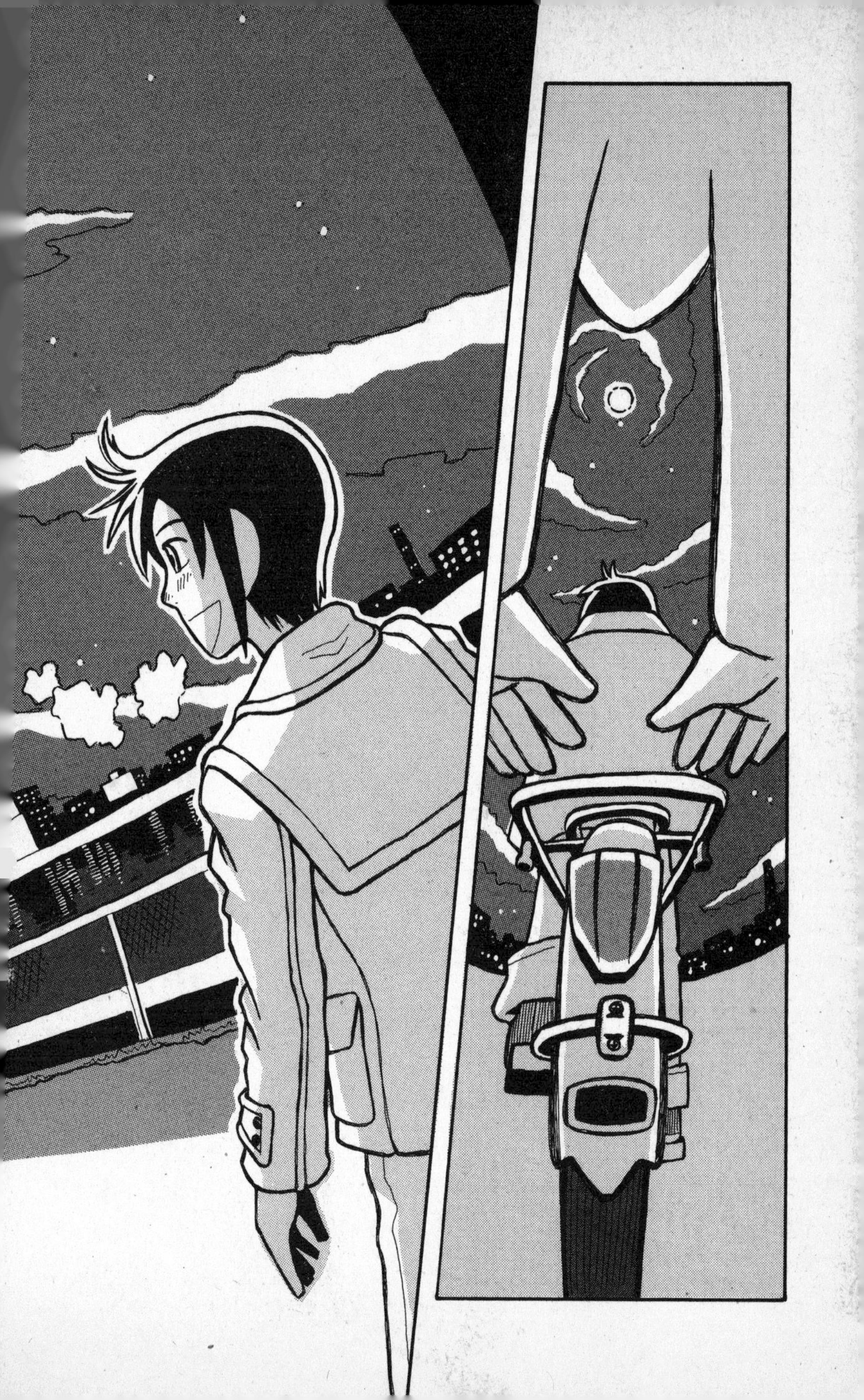

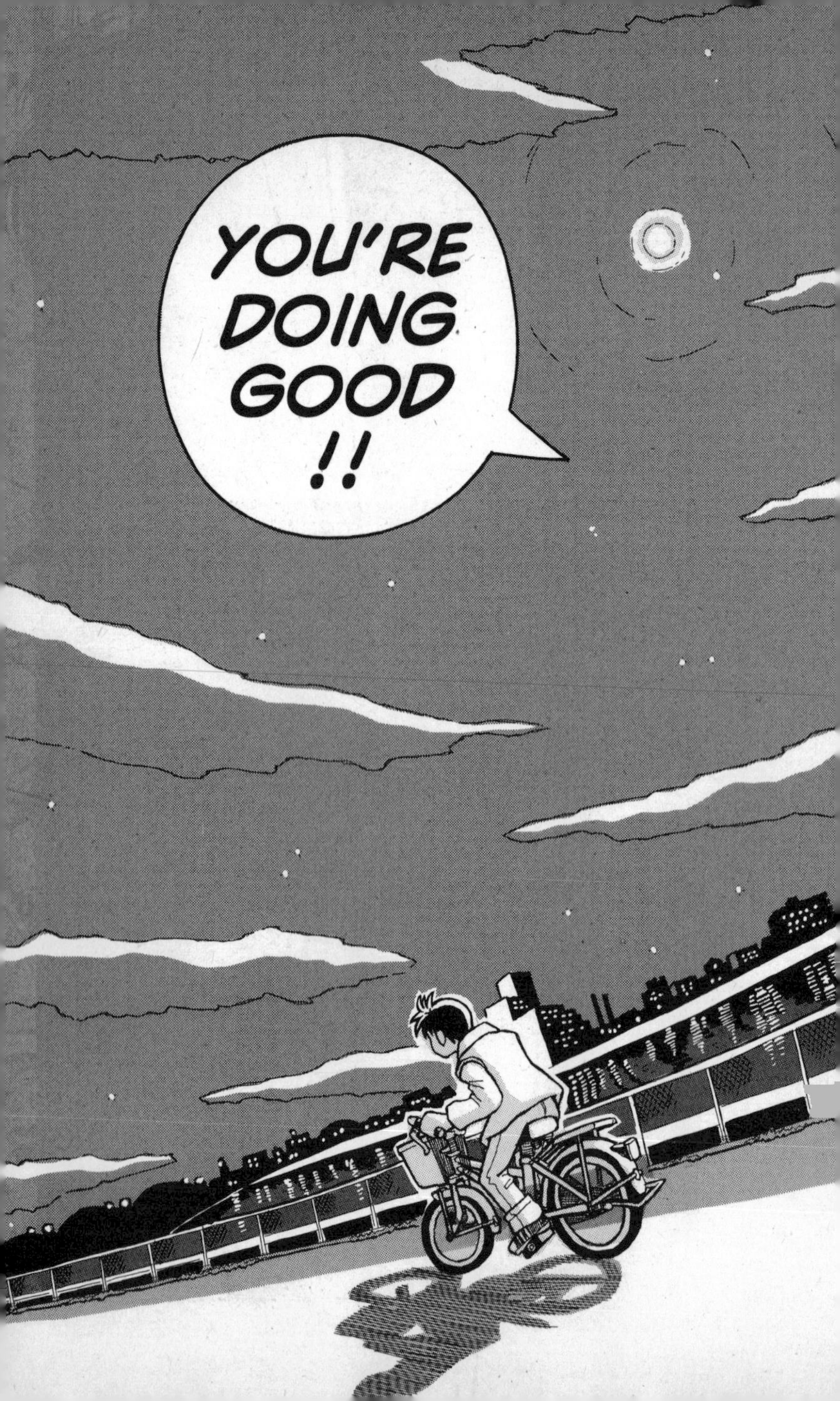
YOU'RE DOING GOOD !!

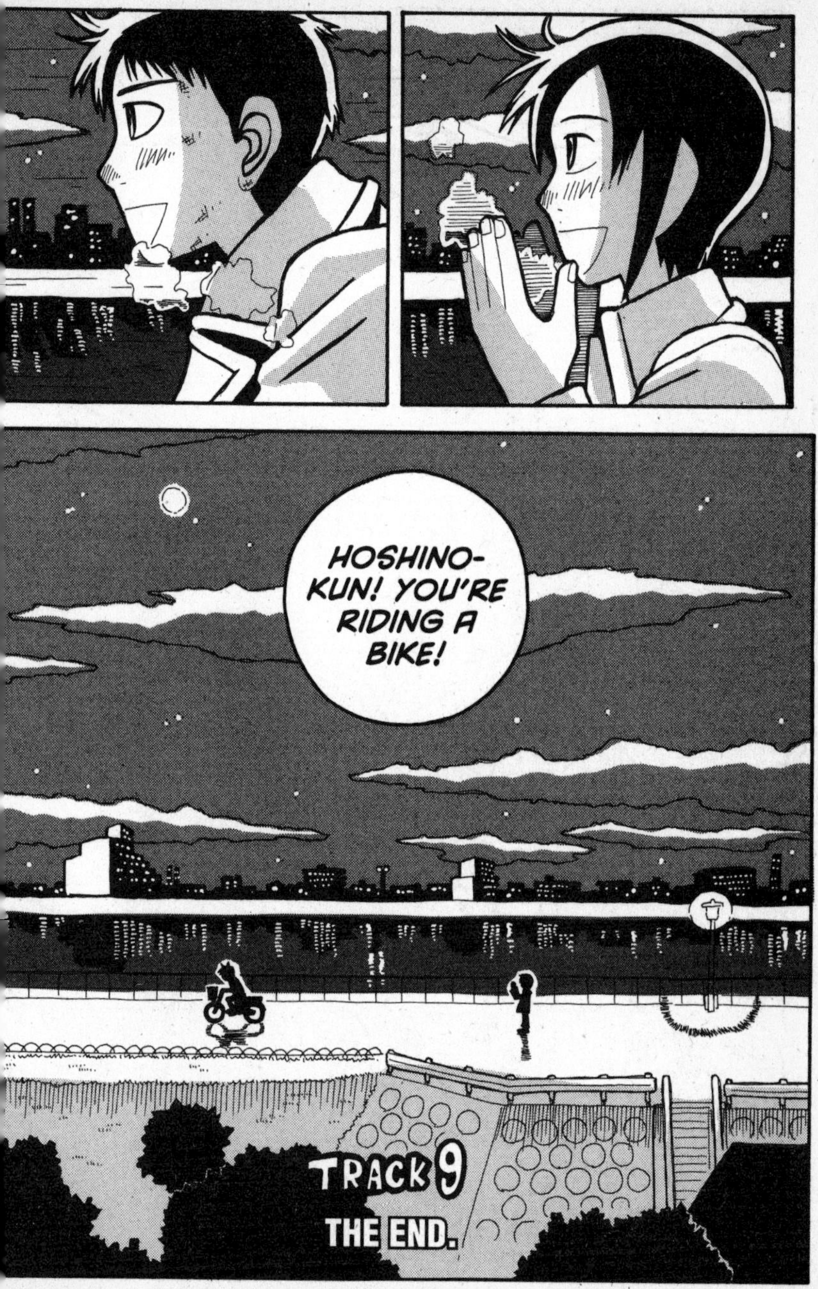
HOSHINO-KUN! YOU'RE RIDING A BIKE!
TRACK 9
THE END.

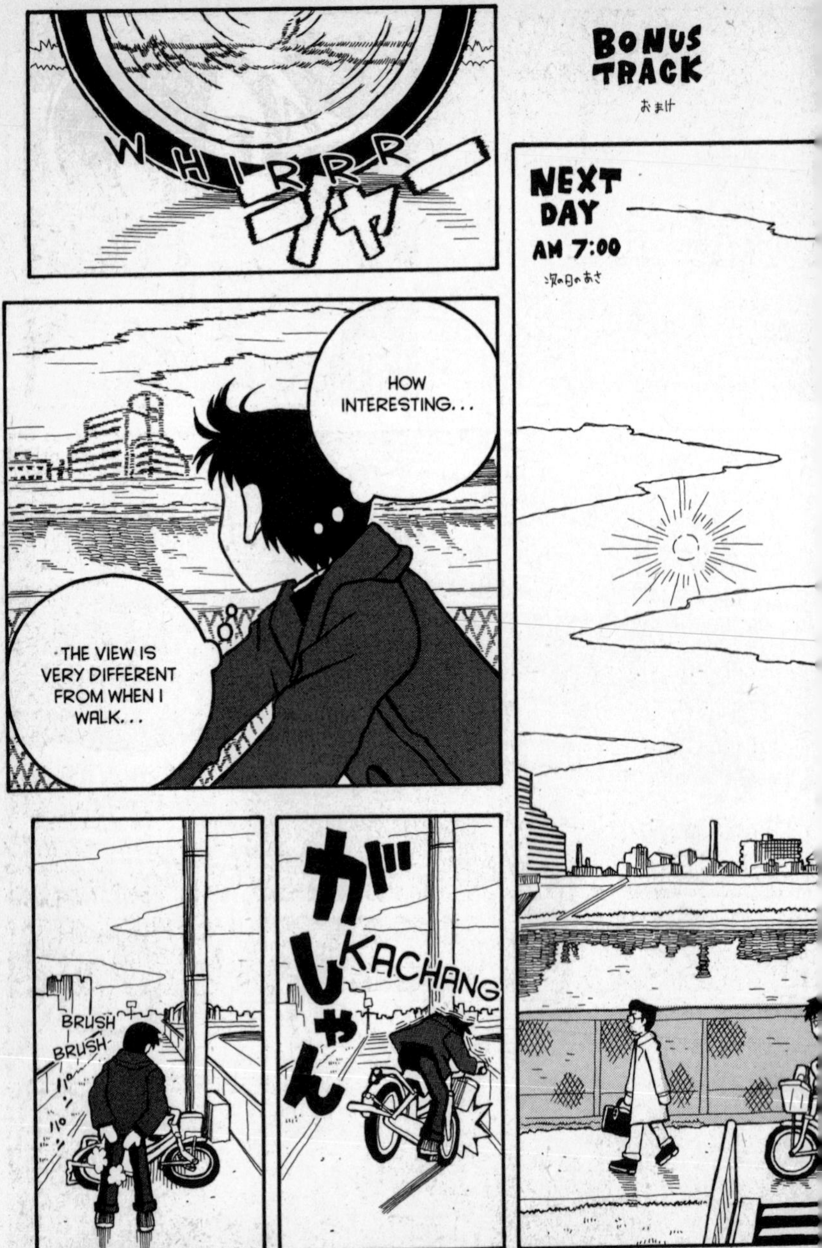
BONUS TRACK
おまけ
NEXT DAY
AM 7:00
次の日のあさ
WHIRRR
HOW INTERESTING...
THE VIEW IS VERY DIFFERENT FROM WHEN I WALK...
がしゃん
KACHANG
BRUSH
BRUSH

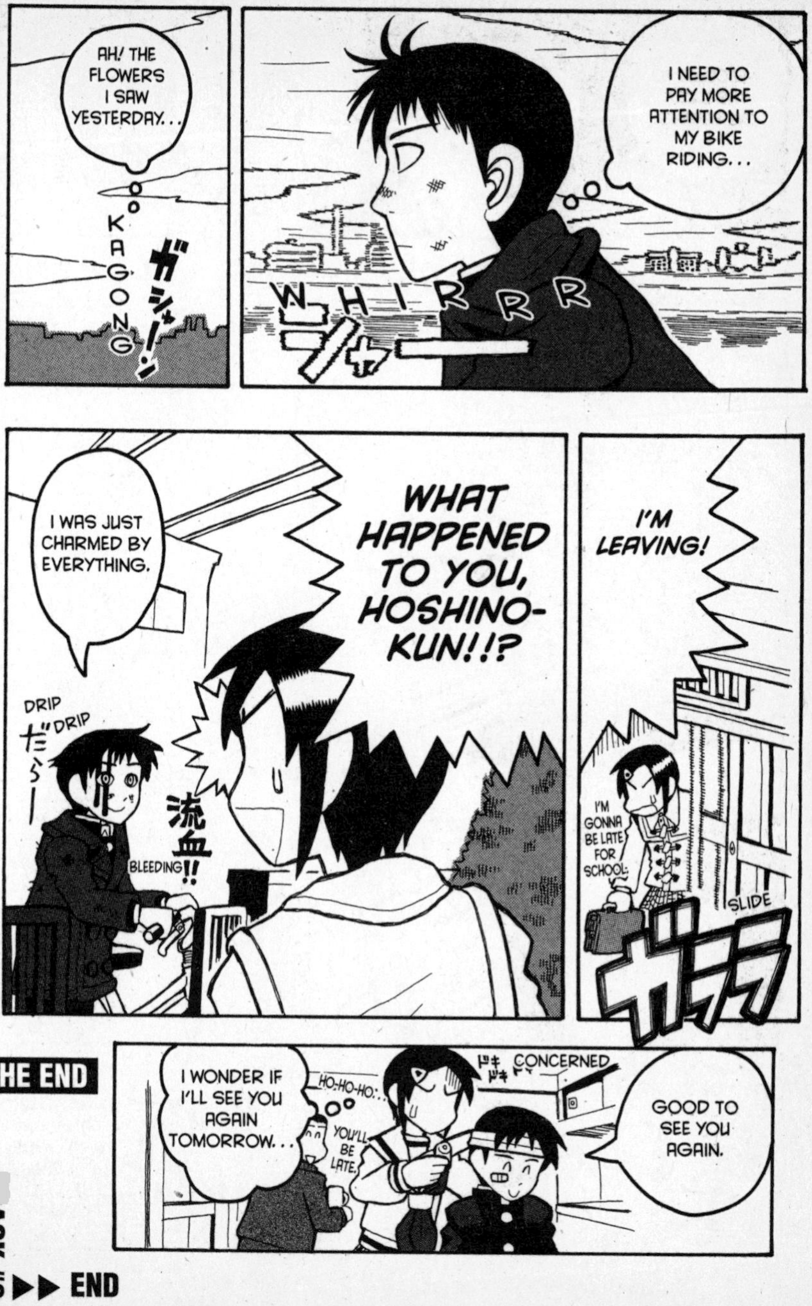
I NEED TO PAY MORE ATTENTION TO MY BIKE RIDING...
WHIRRR
AH! THE FLOWERS I SAW YESTERDAY...
KAGONG
I'M LEAVING!
I'M GONNA BE LATE FOR SCHOOL.
SLIDE
WHAT HAPPENED TO YOU, HOSHINO-KUN!!?
I WAS JUST CHARMED BY EVERYTHING.
DRIP DRIP
流血
BLEEDING!!
GOOD TO SEE YOU AGAIN.
CONCERNED
HO-HO-HO...
YOU'LL BE LATE.
I WONDER IF I'LL SEE YOU AGAIN TOMORROW...

HE END

▶▶ END

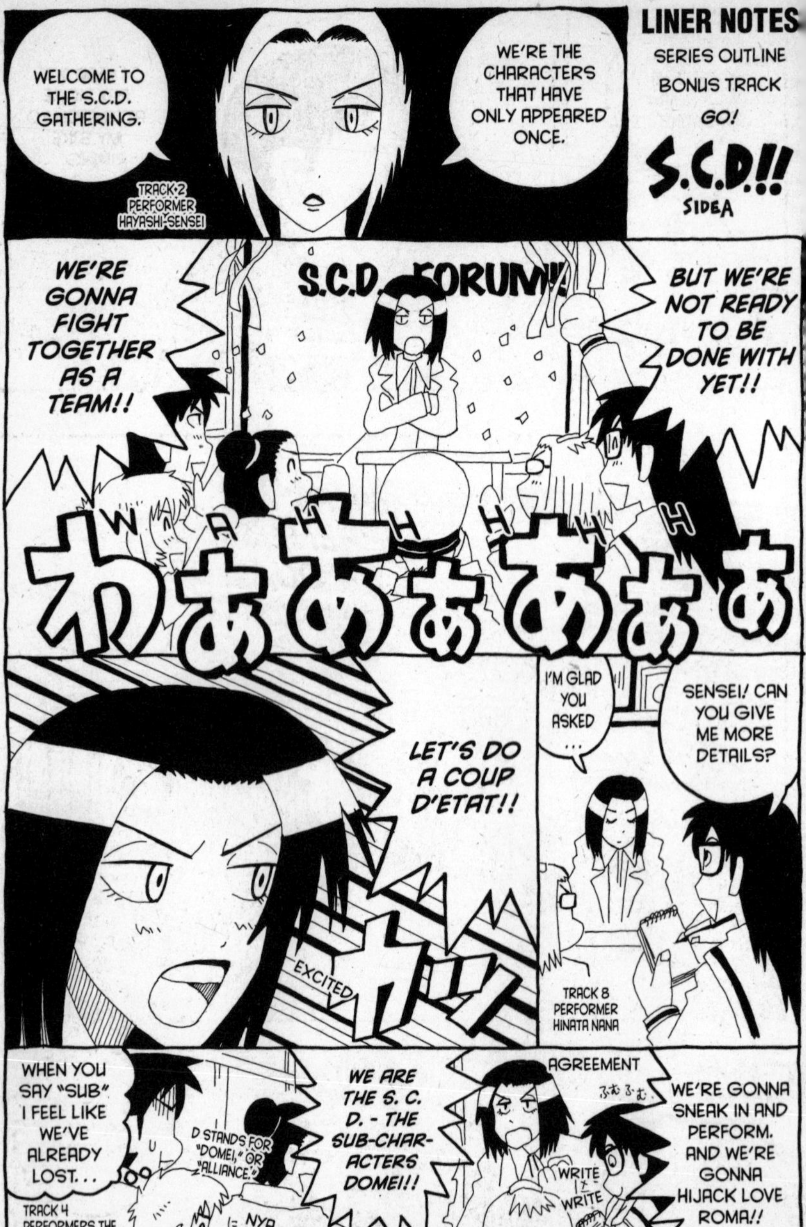
LINER NOTES
SERIES OUTLINE
BONUS TRACK
GO!
S.C.D!!
SIDE A
WE'RE THE CHARACTERS THAT HAVE ONLY APPEARED ONCE.
WELCOME TO THE S.C.D. GATHERING.
TRACK 2 PERFORMER HAYASHI-SENSEI
BUT WE'RE NOT READY TO BE DONE WITH YET!!
S.C.D. FORUM!!
WE'RE GONNA FIGHT TOGETHER AS A TEAM!!
WAHHHHH
わああぁあぁあ
SENSEI! CAN YOU GIVE ME MORE DETAILS?
I'M GLAD YOU ASKED ...
TRACK 8 PERFORMER HINATA NANA
LET'S DO A COUP D'ETAT!!
EXCITED
ガッ
WE'RE GONNA SNEAK IN AND PERFORM. AND WE'RE GONNA HIJACK LOVE ROMA!!
AGREEMENT
ふむふむ
WRITE WRITE
WE ARE THE S. C. D. - THE SUB-CHARACTERS DOMEI!!
D STANDS FOR "DOMEI," OR "ALLIANCE."
NYA
WHEN YOU SAY "SUB" I FEEL LIKE WE'VE ALREADY LOST...
TRACK 4 PERFORMERS THE NEGISHI FAMILY

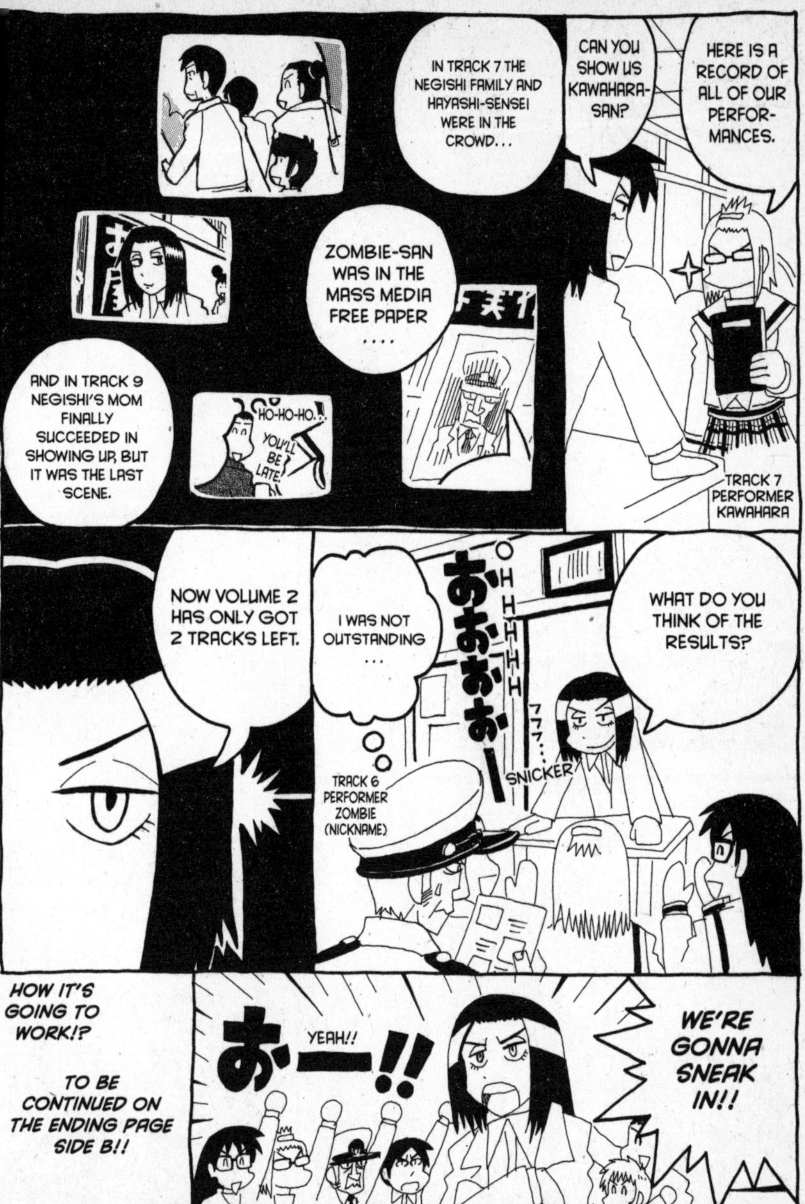
HERE IS A RECORD OF ALL OF OUR PERFORMANCES.
CAN YOU SHOW US KAWAHARA-SAN?
TRACK 7 PERFORMER KAWAHARA
IN TRACK 7 THE NEGISHI FAMILY AND HAYASHI-SENSEI WERE IN THE CROWD...
ZOMBIE-SAN WAS IN THE MASS MEDIA FREE PAPER ....
HO-HO-HO.!
YOU'LL BE LATE!
AND IN TRACK 9 NEGISHI'S MOM FINALLY SUCCEEDED IN SHOWING UP, BUT IT WAS THE LAST SCENE.
WHAT DO YOU THINK OF THE RESULTS?
おおおおー
OHHHHHHH
フフフ...
SNICKER
I WAS NOT OUTSTANDING ...
TRACK 6 PERFORMER ZOMBIE (NICKNAME)
NOW VOLUME 2 HAS ONLY GOT 2 TRACKS LEFT.
WE'RE GONNA SNEAK IN!!
おー!!
YEAH!!
HOW IT'S GOING TO WORK!?
TO BE CONTINUED ON THE ENDING PAGE SIDE B!!

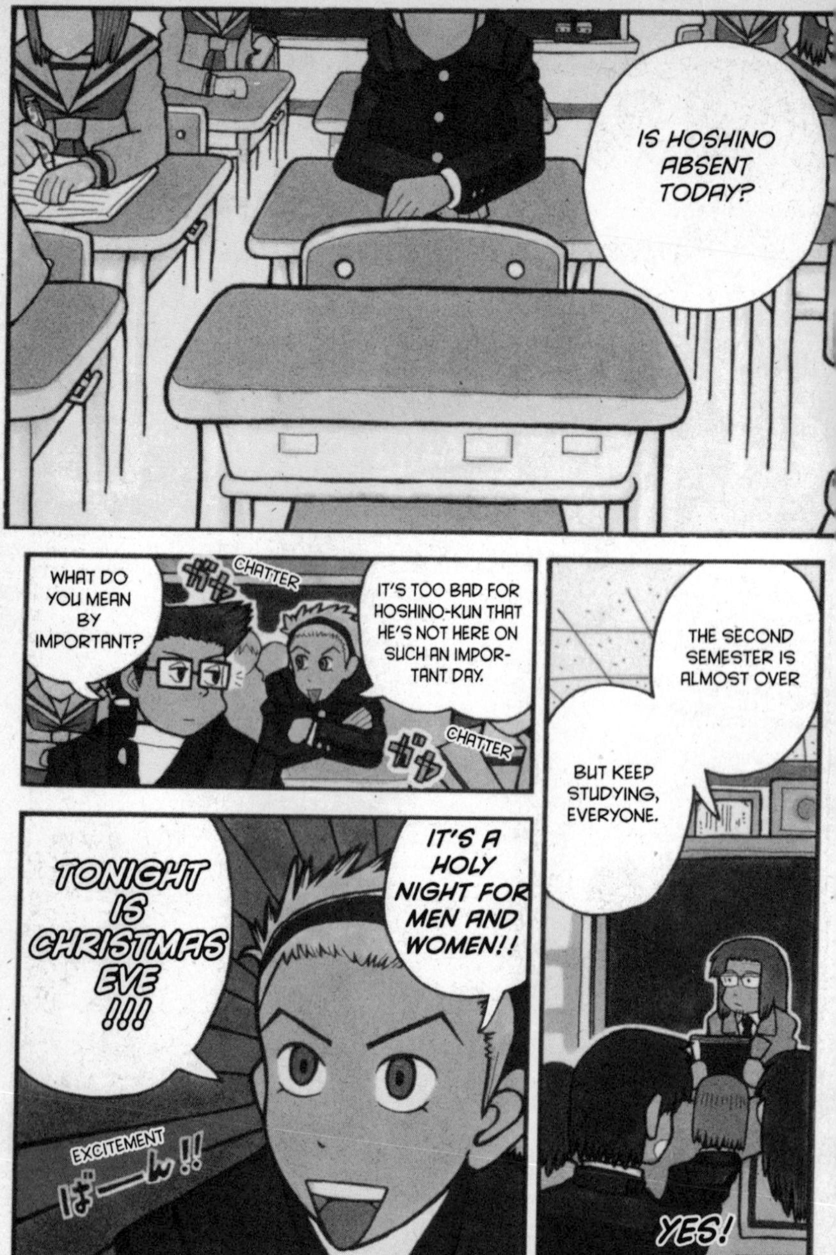
IS HOSHINO ABSENT TODAY?
THE SECOND SEMESTER IS ALMOST OVER
BUT KEEP STUDYING, EVERYONE.
YES!
IT'S TOO BAD FOR HOSHINO-KUN THAT HE'S NOT HERE ON SUCH AN IMPORTANT DAY.
CHATTER
WHAT DO YOU MEAN BY IMPORTANT?
CHATTER
IT'S A HOLY NIGHT FOR MEN AND WOMEN!!
TONIGHT IS CHRISTMAS EVE!!!
EXCITEMENT
ばーん!!

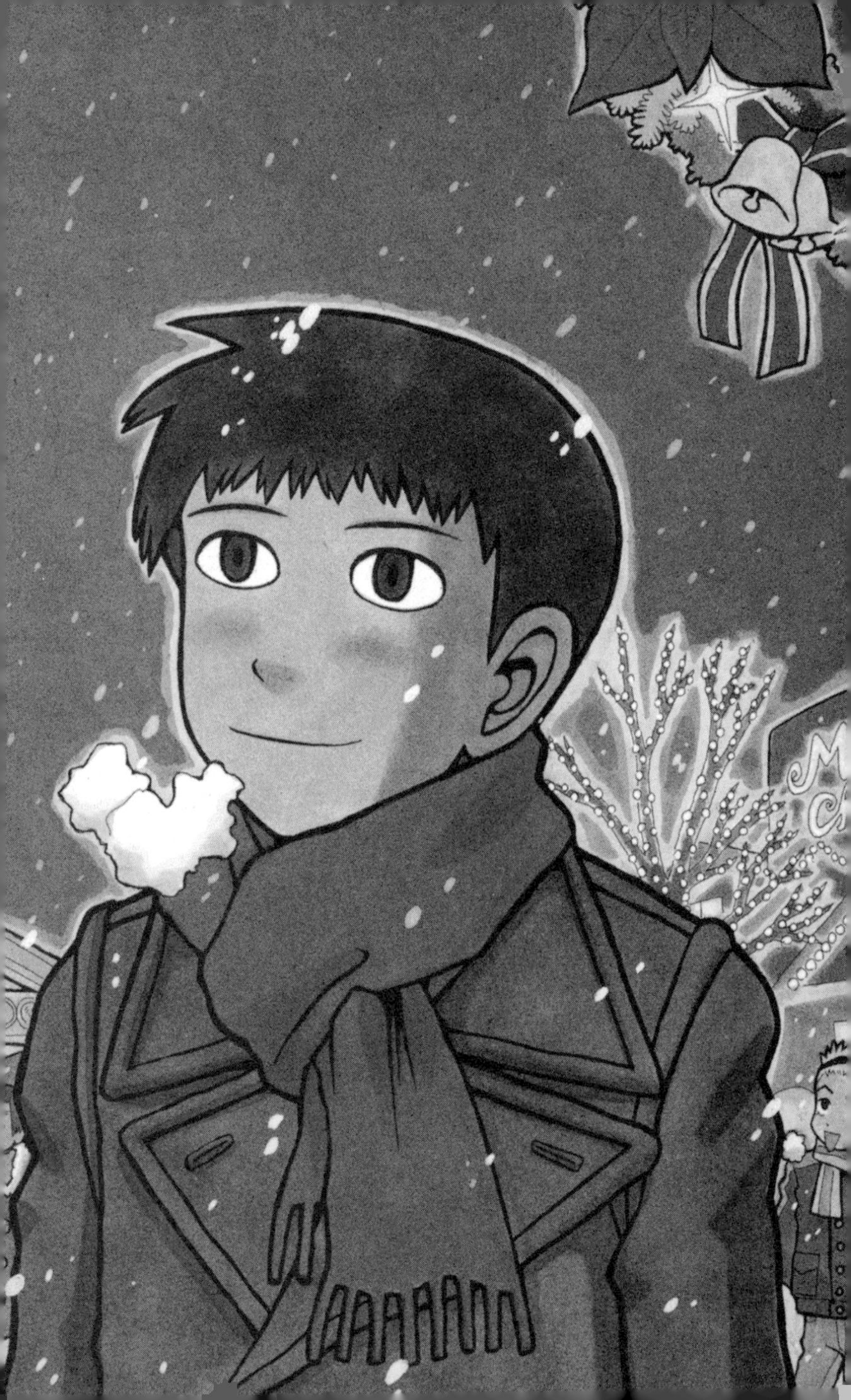

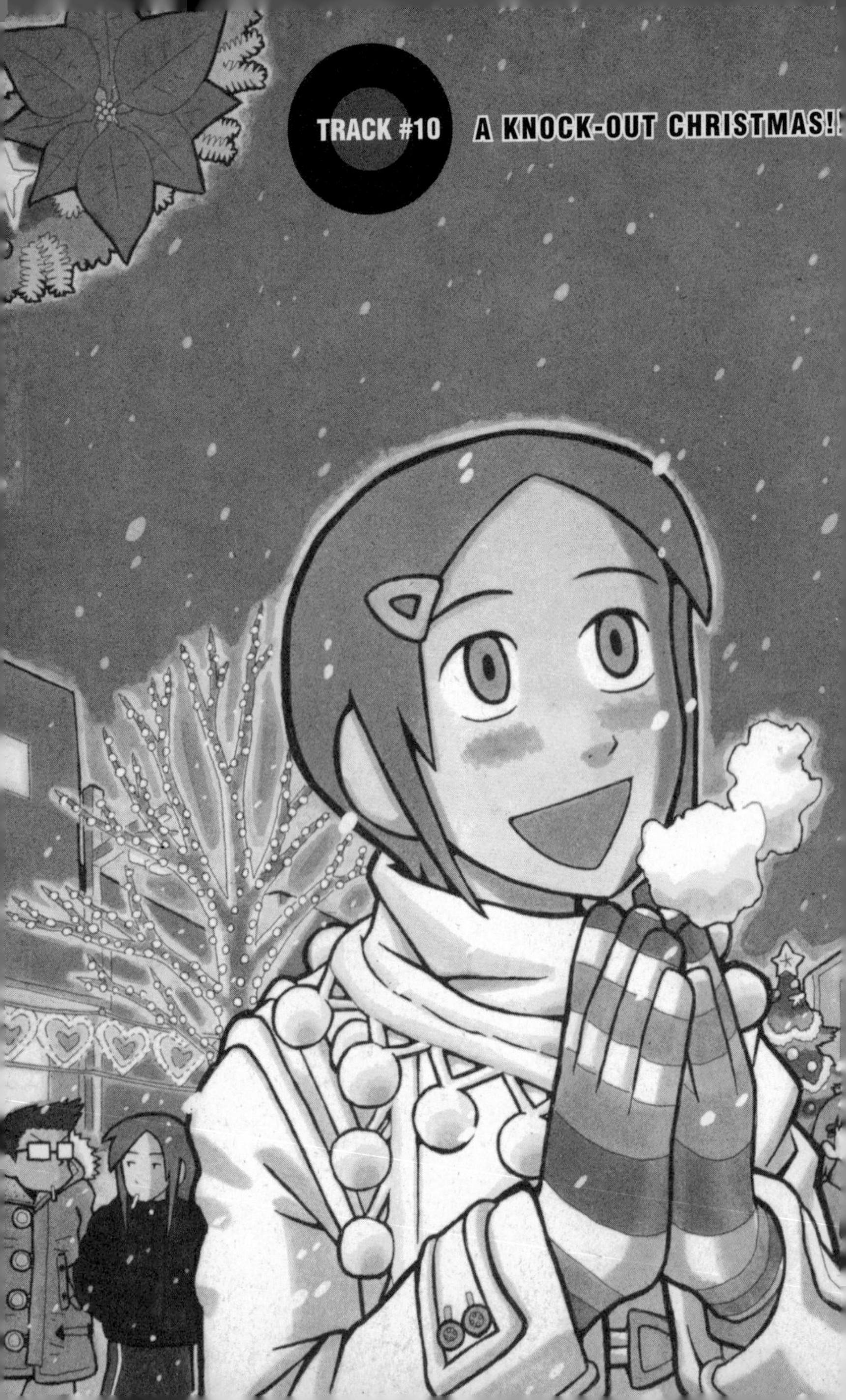
TRACK #10
A KNOCK-OUT CHRISTMAS!!

LINER NOTES

2004 PROMOTIONAL POSTER
AFTERNOON FEBRUARY ISSUE

THE FEBRUARY ISSUE OF *AFTERNOON* HAD A LOT OF COLOR PAGES, INCLUDING THE COVER (FIRST PAGE WHEN YOU OPEN THE COMIC), THIS POSTER AND 3 COLOR PAGES IN THIS EPISODE (THE CHRISTMAS ONE). AND I ALSO HAVE A BAD MEMORY OF SCREWING UP THE DRAWINGS ON THE PREVIOUS 2 PAGES. I HAD TO START ALL OVER AND DRAW THEM ONE MORE TIME. I WAS SO BUSY I THOUGHT I WOULD DIE, BUT I MADE IT THROUGH SOMEHOW. I IMPRESSED MYSELF.

TOYODA MINORU

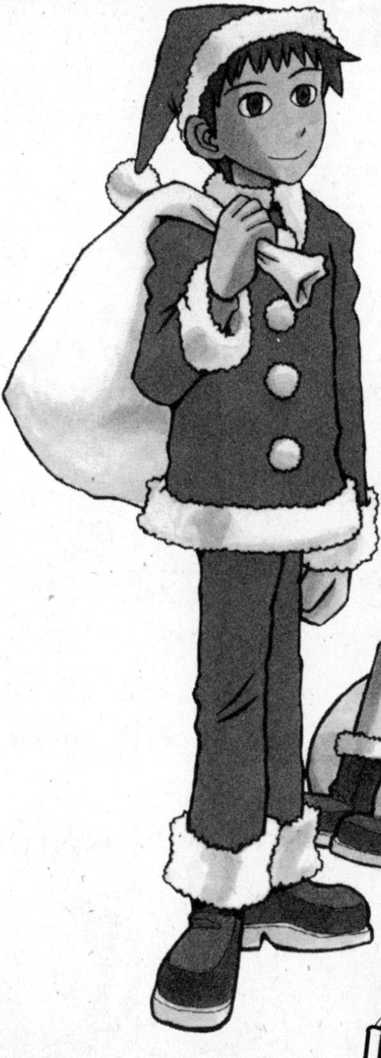

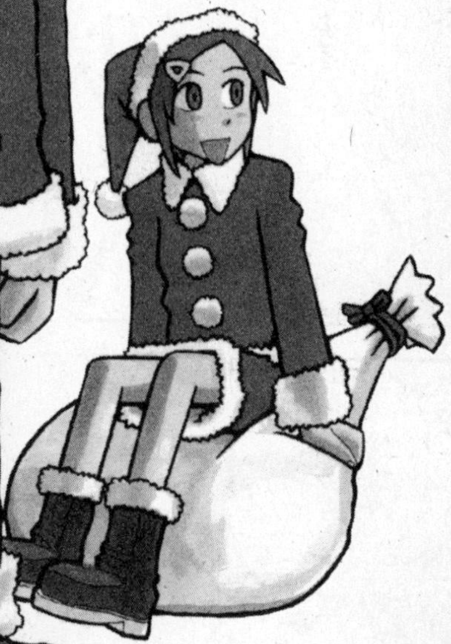

LOVE ROMA

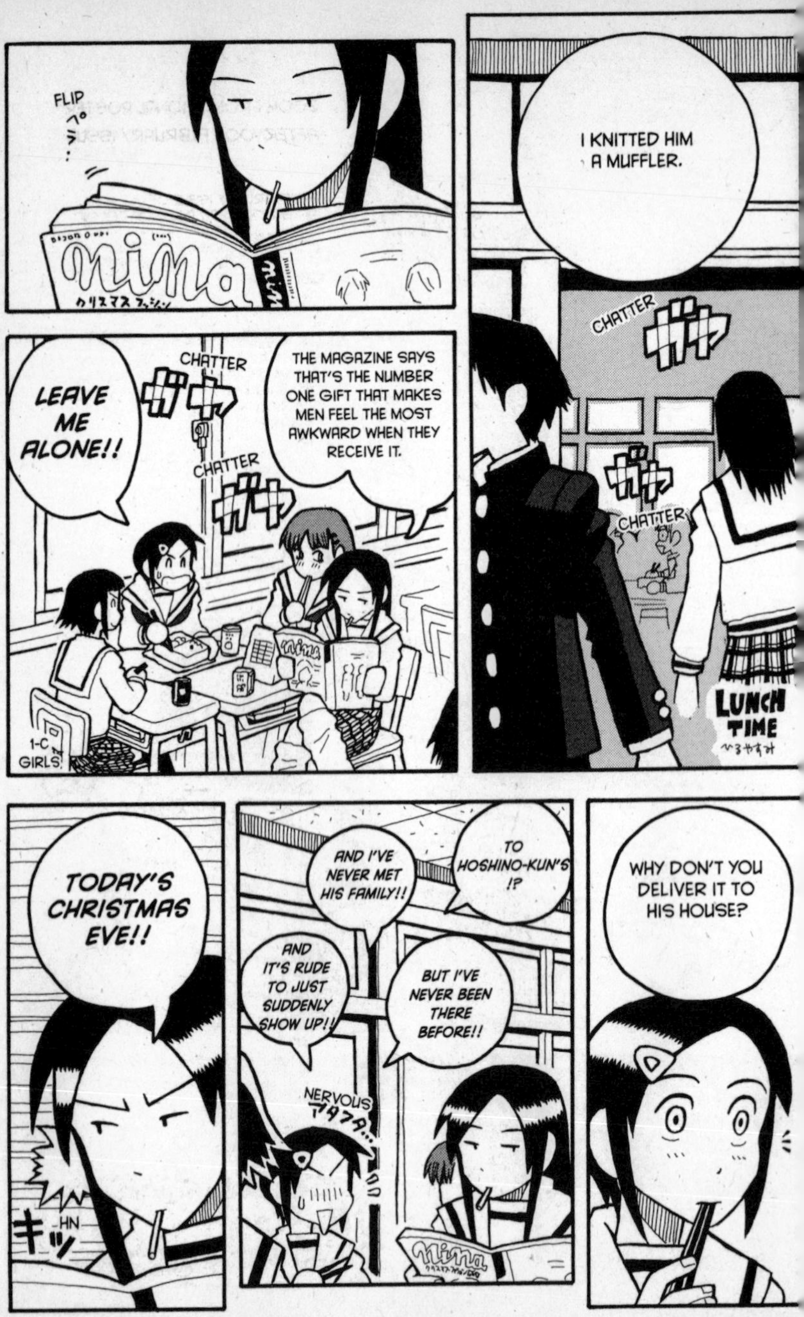
I KNITTED HIM A MUFFLER.
CHATTER
CHATTER
LUNCH TIME
ひるやすみ
FLIP
ぺら…
nima
クリスマスファッション
THE MAGAZINE SAYS THAT'S THE NUMBER ONE GIFT THAT MAKES MEN FEEL THE MOST AWKWARD WHEN THEY RECEIVE IT.
CHATTER
LEAVE ME ALONE!!
CHATTER
1-C GIRLS
WHY DON'T YOU DELIVER IT TO HIS HOUSE?
TO HOSHINO-KUN'S !?
AND I'VE NEVER MET HIS FAMILY!!
BUT I'VE NEVER BEEN THERE BEFORE!!
AND IT'S RUDE TO JUST SUDDENLY SHOW UP!!
NERVOUS
アタフタ…
nima
TODAY'S CHRISTMAS EVE!!
HN
キッ

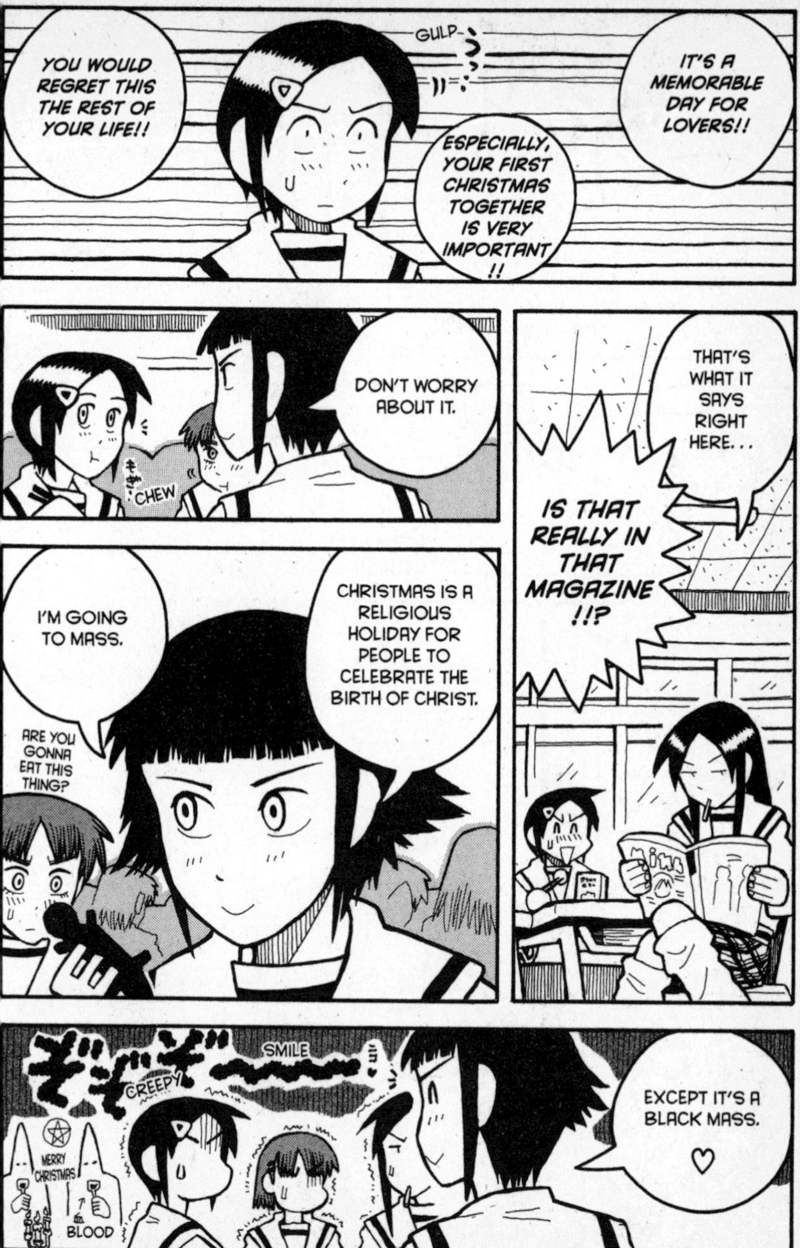
IT'S A MEMORABLE DAY FOR LOVERS!!
GULP
ESPECIALLY, YOUR FIRST CHRISTMAS TOGETHER IS VERY IMPORTANT!!
YOU WOULD REGRET THIS THE REST OF YOUR LIFE!!
THAT'S WHAT IT SAYS RIGHT HERE...
IS THAT REALLY IN THAT MAGAZINE!!?
DON'T WORRY ABOUT IT.
CHEW
CHRISTMAS IS A RELIGIOUS HOLIDAY FOR PEOPLE TO CELEBRATE THE BIRTH OF CHRIST.
I'M GOING TO MASS.
ARE YOU GONNA EAT THIS THING?
EXCEPT IT'S A BLACK MASS. ♥
SMILE
CREEPY
MERRY CHRISTMAS
BLOOD

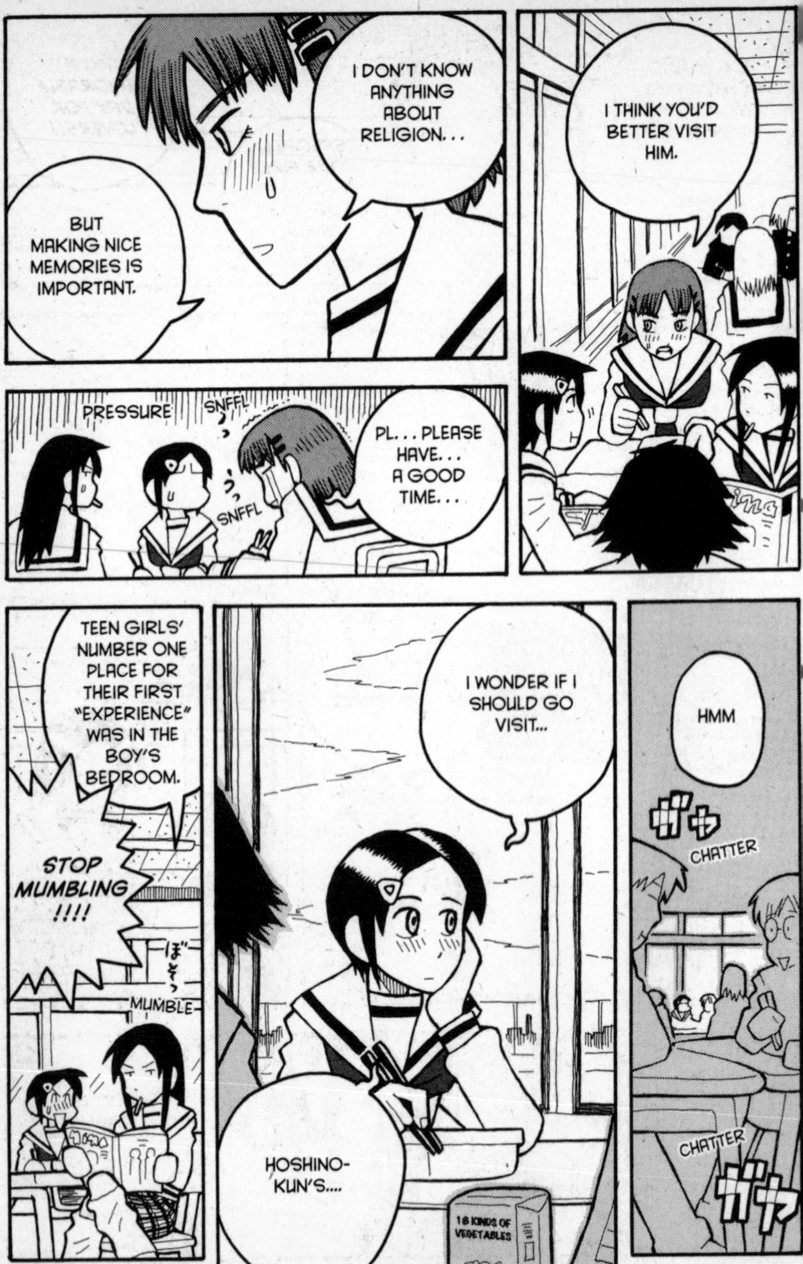
I THINK YOU'D BETTER VISIT HIM.
I DON'T KNOW ANYTHING ABOUT RELIGION...
BUT MAKING NICE MEMORIES IS IMPORTANT.
SNFFL
PL... PLEASE HAVE... A GOOD TIME...
PRESSURE
SNFFL
HMM
ガヤ
CHATTER
CHATTER
ガヤ
I WONDER IF I SHOULD GO VISIT...
HOSHINO-KUN'S....
18 KINDS OF VEGETABLES
TEEN GIRLS' NUMBER ONE PLACE FOR THEIR FIRST "EXPERIENCE" WAS IN THE BOY'S BEDROOM.
STOP MUMBLING !!!!
ぼそっ
MUMBLE

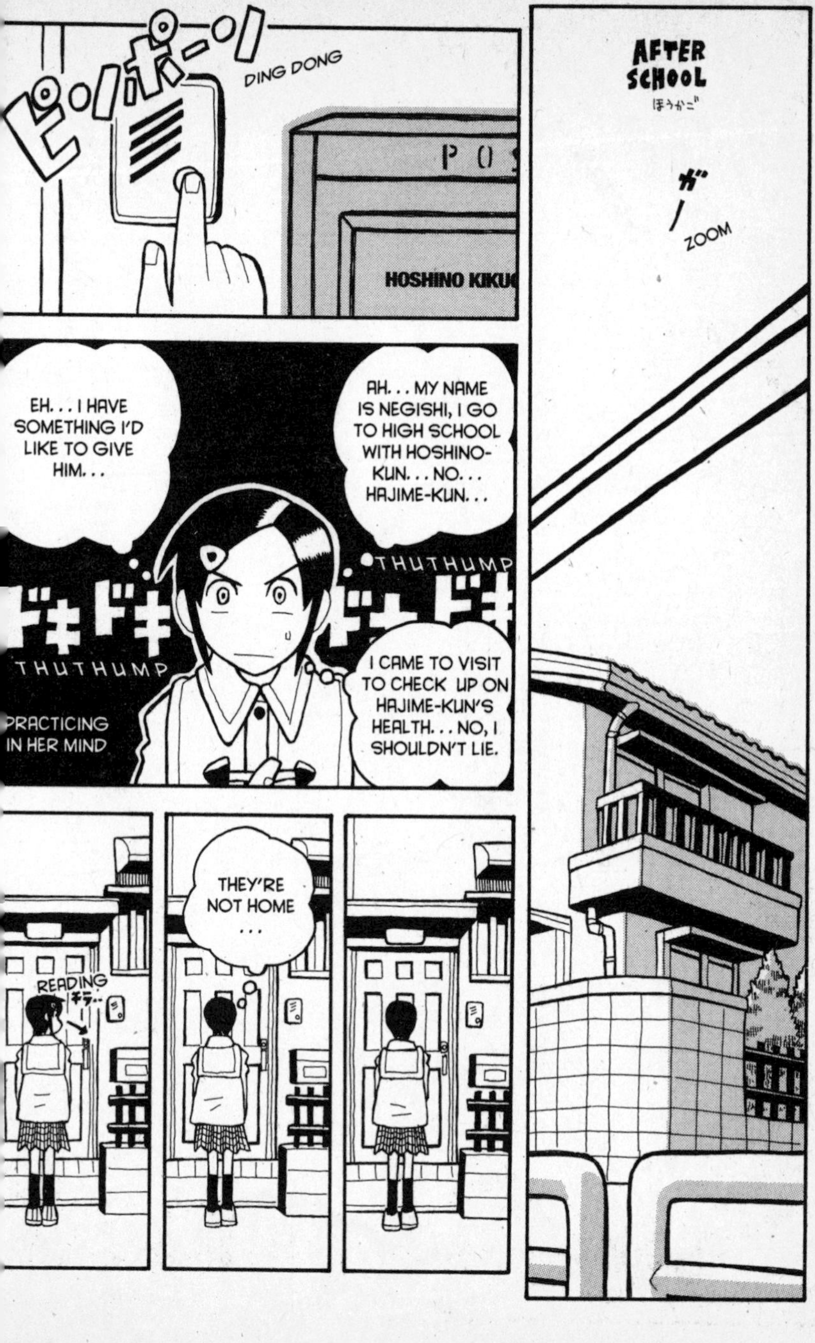
AFTER SCHOOL
ほうかご
ZOOM
DING DONG
POS
HOSHINO KIKU
AH... MY NAME IS NEGISHI, I GO TO HIGH SCHOOL WITH HOSHINO-KUN... NO... HAJIME-KUN...
EH... I HAVE SOMETHING I'D LIKE TO GIVE HIM...
THUTHUMP
ドキドキ
I CAME TO VISIT TO CHECK UP ON HAJIME-KUN'S HEALTH... NO, I SHOULDN'T LIE.
ドキドキ
THUTHUMP
PRACTICING IN HER MIND
THEY'RE NOT HOME ...
READING

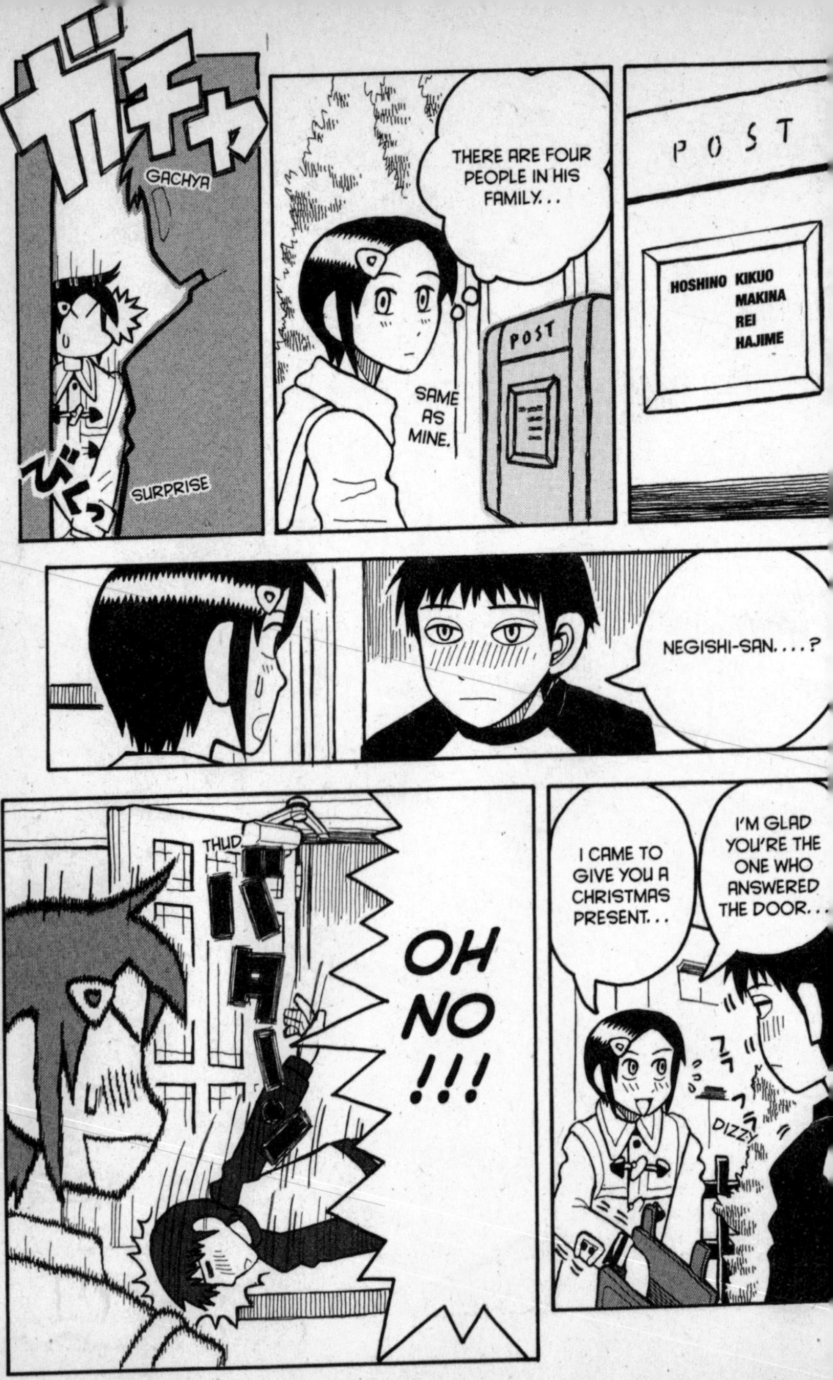
POST
HOSHINO KIKUO
MAKINA
REI
HAJIME
THERE ARE FOUR PEOPLE IN HIS FAMILY...
POST
SAME AS MINE.
ガチャ
GACHYA
びくっ
SURPRISE
NEGISHI-SAN....?
I'M GLAD YOU'RE THE ONE WHO ANSWERED THE DOOR...
I CAME TO GIVE YOU A CHRISTMAS PRESENT...
DIZZY
OH NO!!!
THUD

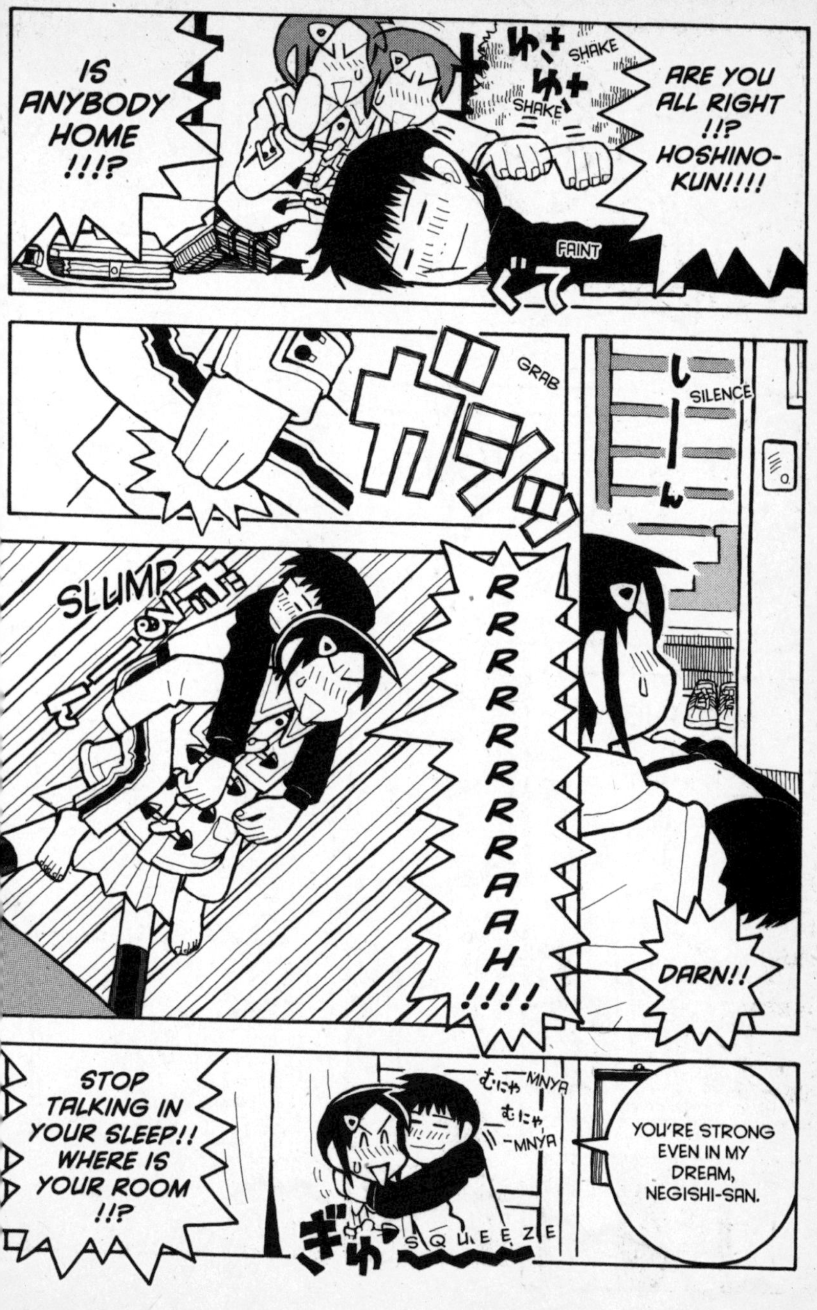
ARE YOU ALL RIGHT !!? HOSHINO-KUN!!!!
ゆさゆさ
SHAKE
SHAKE
IS ANYBODY HOME !!!?
FAINT
しーん
SILENCE
GRAB
DARN!!
RRRRRRRRAAH!!!!
SLUMP
YOU'RE STRONG EVEN IN MY DREAM, NEGISHI-SAN.
むにゃ
MNYA
むにゃ
MNYA
STOP TALKING IN YOUR SLEEP!! WHERE IS YOUR ROOM !!?
ぎゅ
SQUEEZE

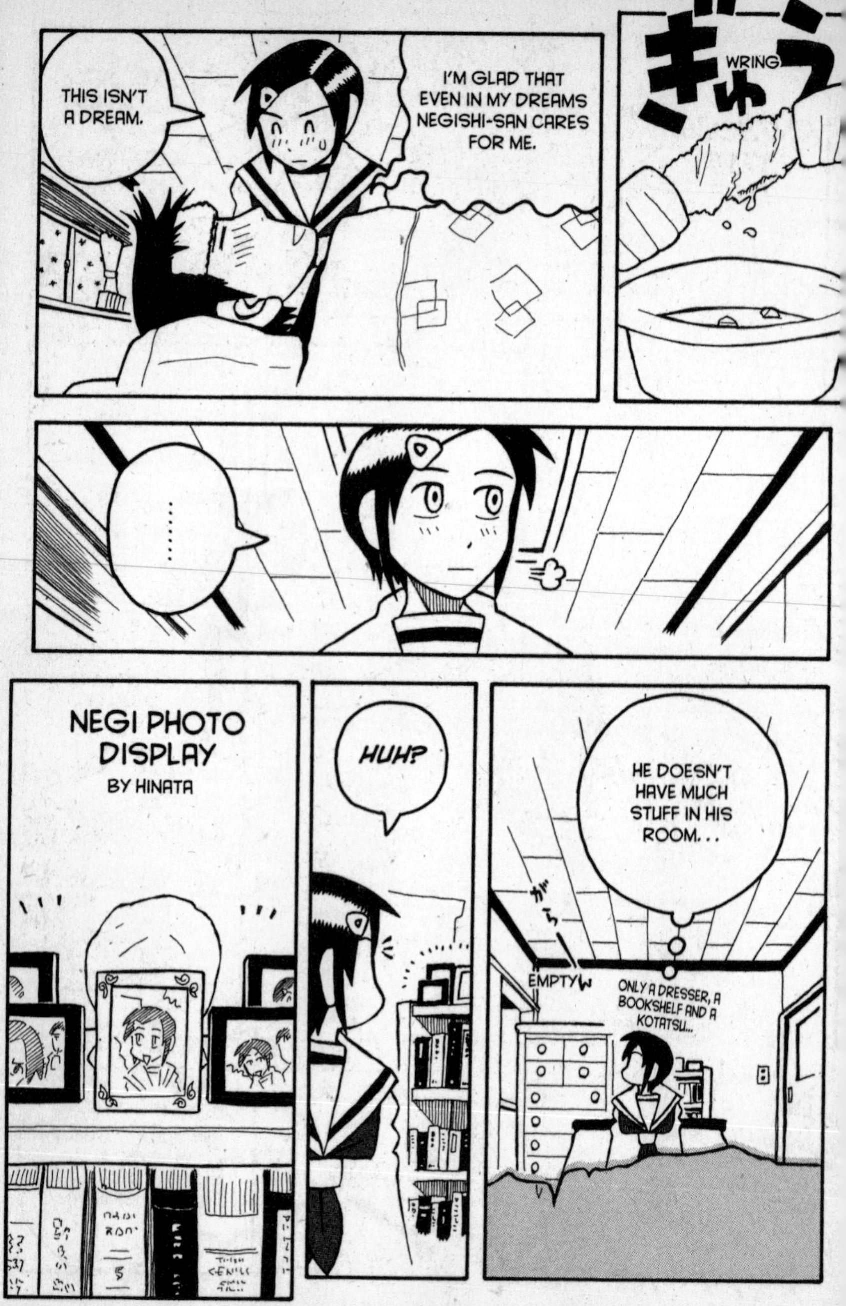
ぎゅう
WRING
I'M GLAD THAT EVEN IN MY DREAMS NEGISHI-SAN CARES FOR ME.
THIS ISN'T A DREAM.
......
HE DOESN'T HAVE MUCH STUFF IN HIS ROOM...
がらー
EMPTY
ONLY A DRESSER, A BOOKSHELF AND A KOTATSU...
HUH?
NEGI PHOTO DISPLAY
BY HINATA

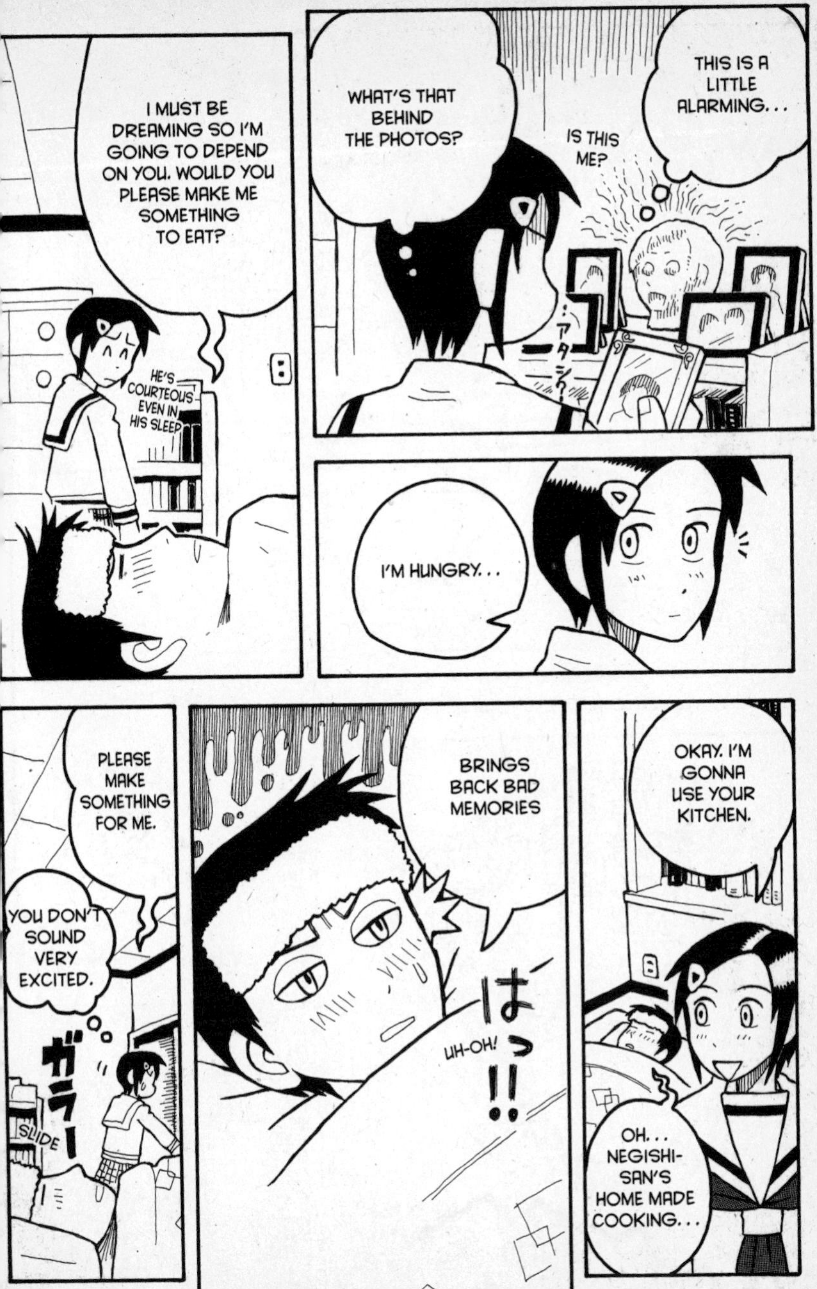
THIS IS A LITTLE ALARMING...
IS THIS ME?
WHAT'S THAT BEHIND THE PHOTOS?
I'M HUNGRY...
I MUST BE DREAMING SO I'M GOING TO DEPEND ON YOU. WOULD YOU PLEASE MAKE ME SOMETHING TO EAT?
HE'S COURTEOUS EVEN IN HIS SLEEP
OKAY. I'M GONNA USE YOUR KITCHEN.
OH... NEGISHI-SAN'S HOME MADE COOKING...
BRINGS BACK BAD MEMORIES
はっ!!
UH-OH!
PLEASE MAKE SOMETHING FOR ME.
YOU DON'T SOUND VERY EXCITED.
ガラー
SLIDE

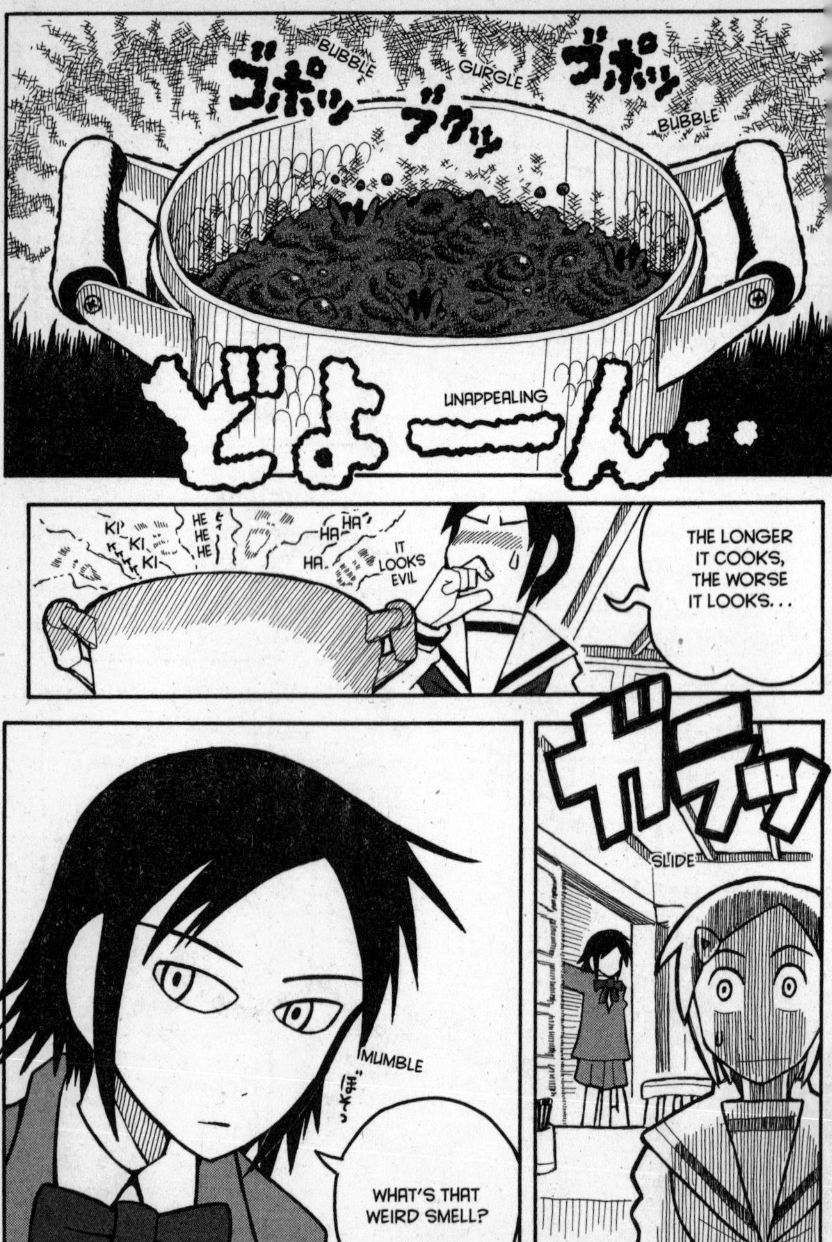

BUBBLE
GURGLE
BUBBLE
UNAPPEALING
THE LONGER IT COOKS, THE WORSE IT LOOKS...
IT LOOKS EVIL
HA HA HA
HE HE HE
KI KI KI
SLIDE
MUMBLE
WHAT'S THAT WEIRD SMELL?

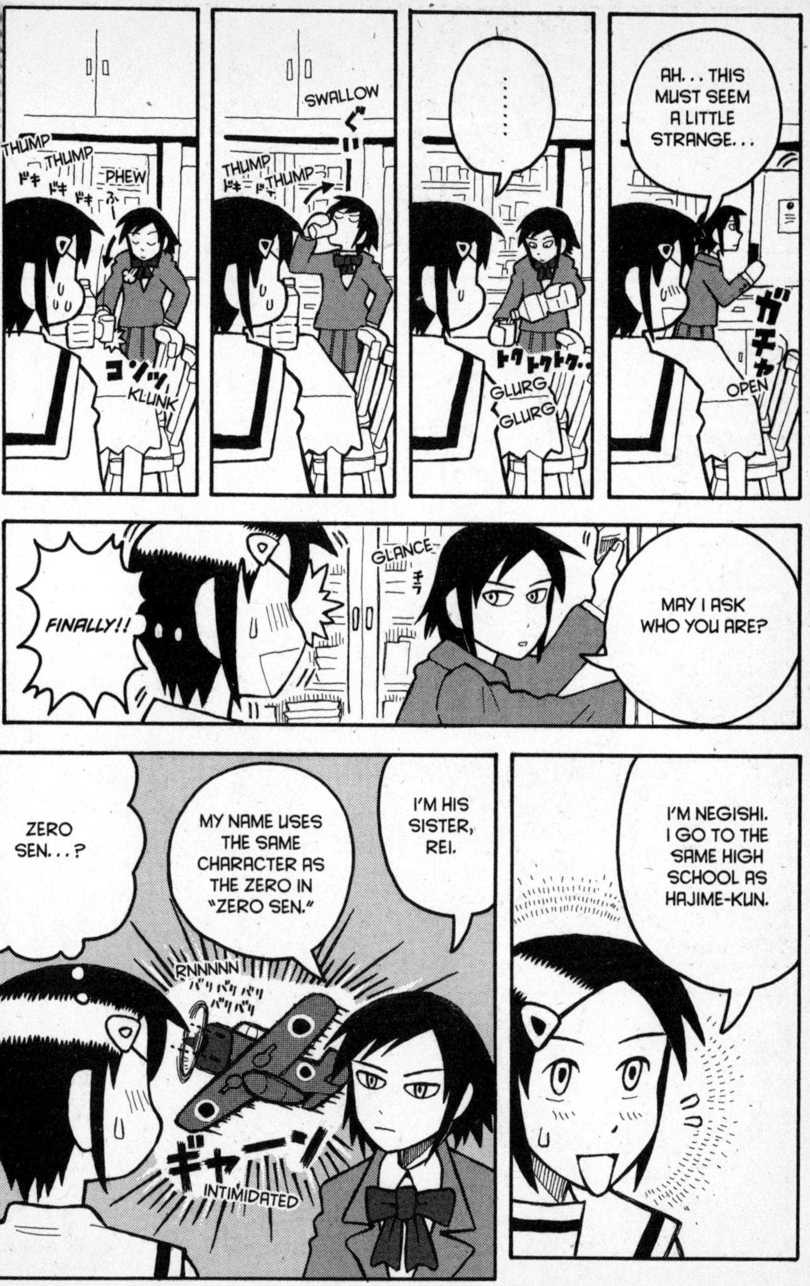
AH. . . THIS MUST SEEM A LITTLE STRANGE. . .
ガチャ
OPEN
. . . . . .
トクトクトク. .
GLURG GLURG
SWALLOW
THUMP THUMP
THUMP THUMP
PHEW
コンッ
KLUNK
MAY I ASK WHO YOU ARE?
GLANCE
FINALLY!!
I'M NEGISHI. I GO TO THE SAME HIGH SCHOOL AS HAJIME-KUN.
I'M HIS SISTER, REI.
MY NAME USES THE SAME CHARACTER AS THE ZERO IN "ZERO SEN."
RNNNNN
INTIMIDATED
ZERO SEN. . .?

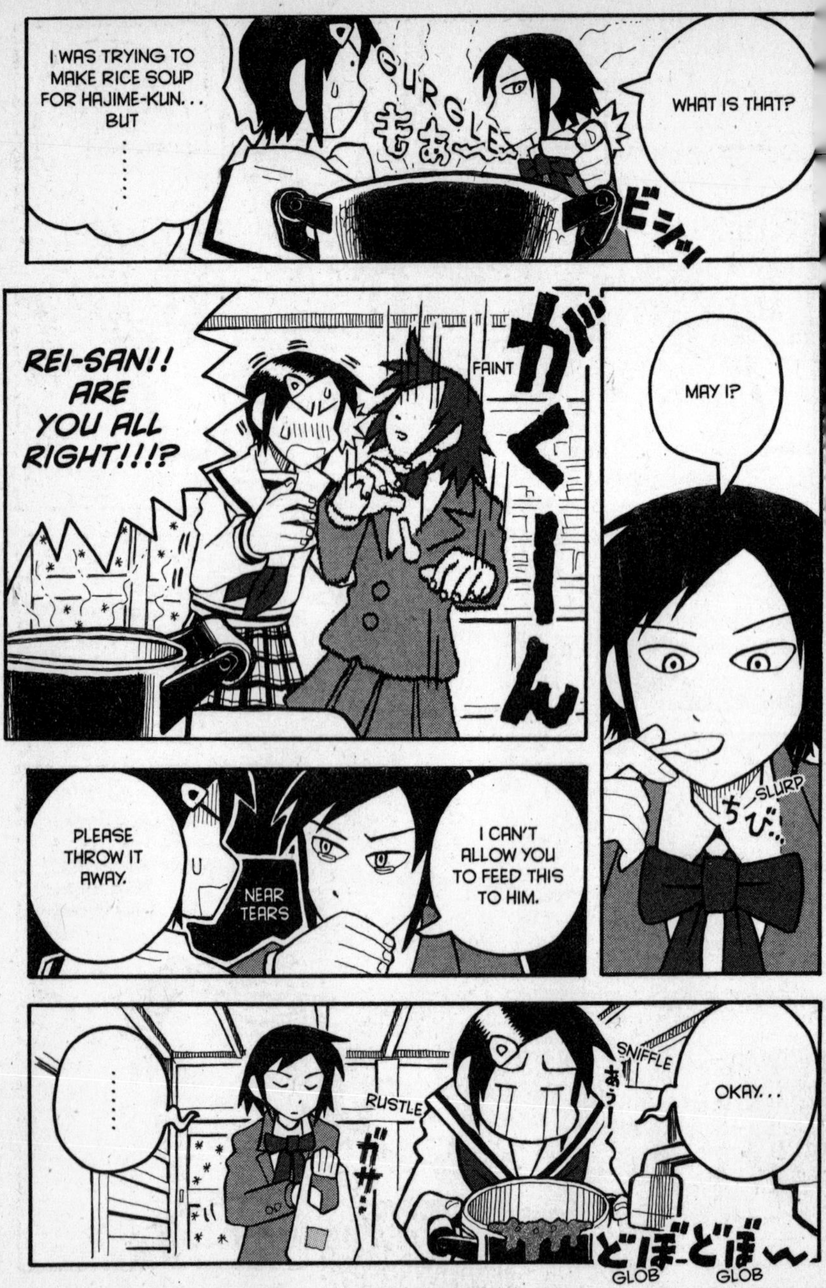
WHAT IS THAT?
ビシッ
GURGLE
もあ〜
I WAS TRYING TO MAKE RICE SOUP FOR HAJIME-KUN... BUT
......
MAY I?
ちび…
SLURP
がくーん
FAINT
REI-SAN!! ARE YOU ALL RIGHT!!!?
I CAN'T ALLOW YOU TO FEED THIS TO HIM.
NEAR TEARS
PLEASE THROW IT AWAY.
OKAY...
SNIFFLE
あぅ〜
どぼどぼ〜
GLOB GLOB
ガサ
RUSTLE
......

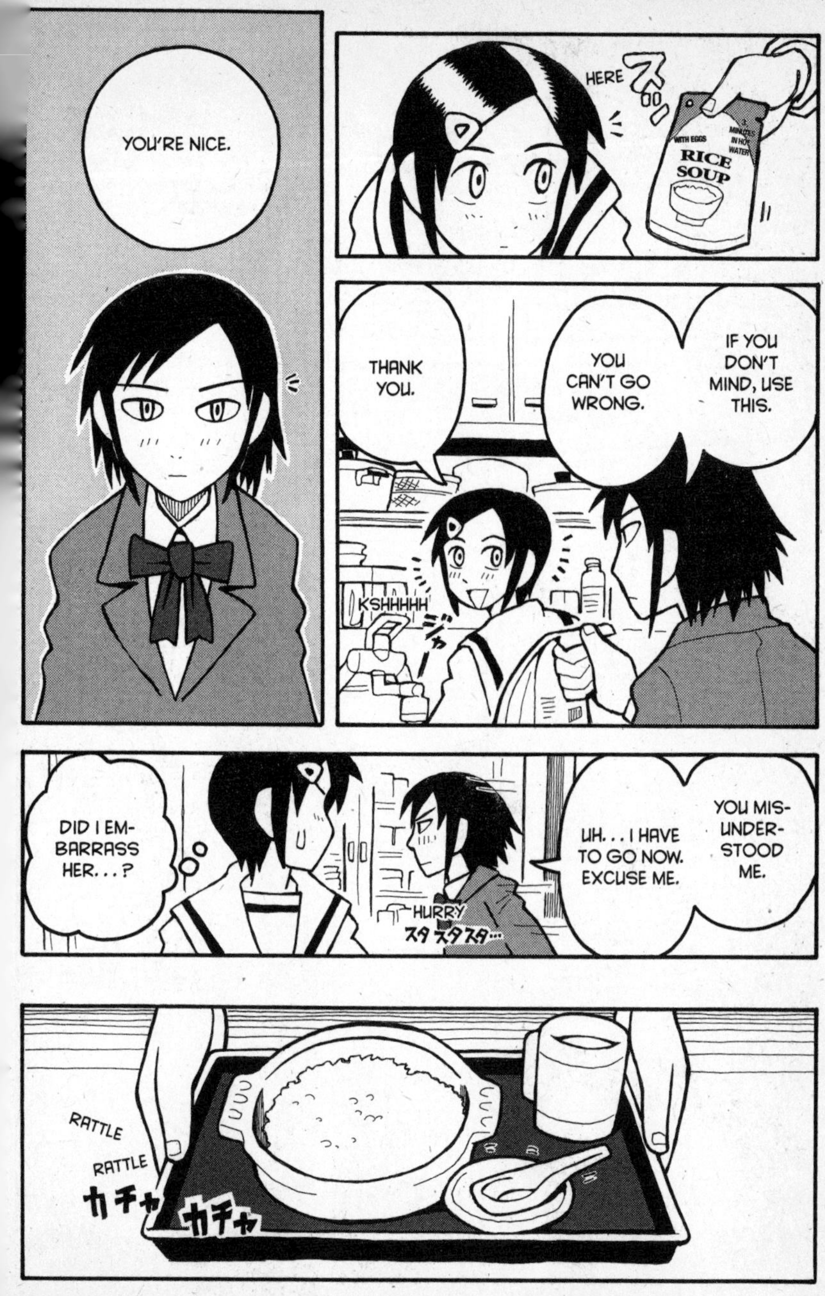
HERE
WITH EGGS
RICE SOUP
3 MINUTES IN HOT WATER
IF YOU DON'T MIND, USE THIS.
YOU CAN'T GO WRONG.
THANK YOU.
KSHHHHH
ジャ
YOU'RE NICE.
YOU MIS-UNDER-STOOD ME.
UH. . . I HAVE TO GO NOW. EXCUSE ME.
HURRY
スタスタスタ…
DID I EM-BARRASS HER. . . ?
RATTLE
RATTLE
カチャ
カチャ

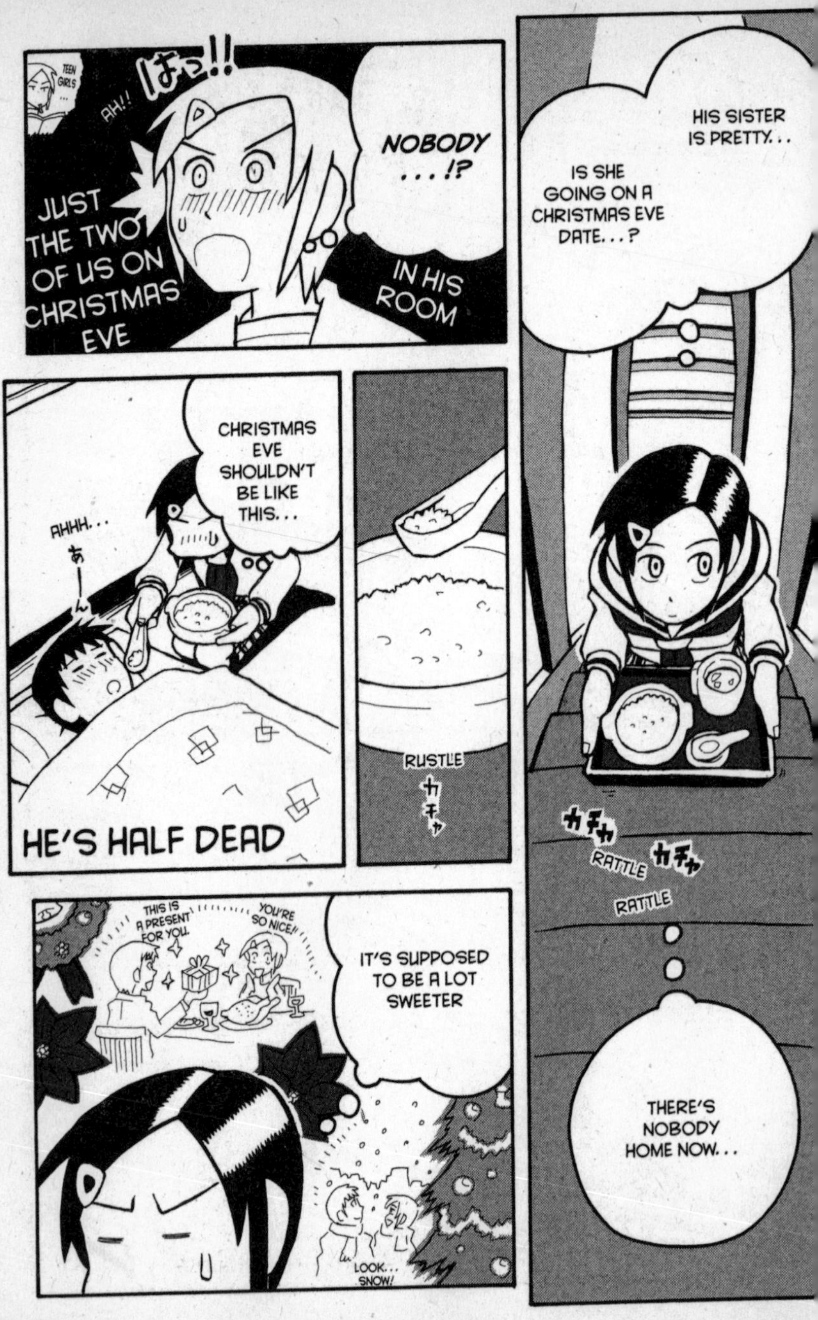
HIS SISTER IS PRETTY...
IS SHE GOING ON A CHRISTMAS EVE DATE...?
カチャ
RATTLE
カチャ
RATTLE
THERE'S NOBODY HOME NOW...
NOBODY ...!?
IN HIS ROOM
はっ!!
AH!!
TEEN GIRLS ...
JUST THE TWO OF US ON CHRISTMAS EVE
RUSTLE
カチャ
CHRISTMAS EVE SHOULDN'T BE LIKE THIS...
AHHH...
あーん
HE'S HALF DEAD
IT'S SUPPOSED TO BE A LOT SWEETER
YOU'RE SO NICE!!
THIS IS A PRESENT FOR YOU.
LOOK... SNOW!

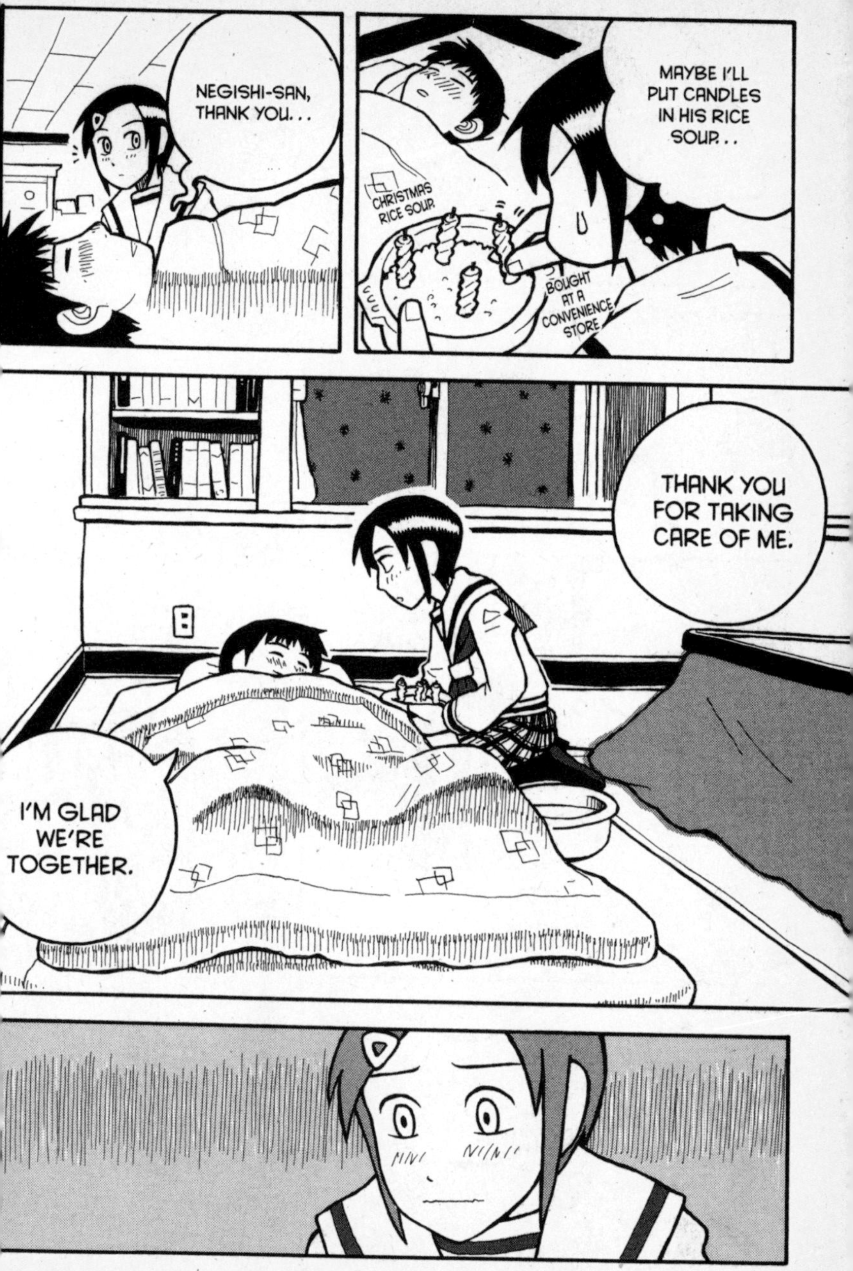
MAYBE I'LL PUT CANDLES IN HIS RICE SOUP. . .
CHRISTMAS RICE SOUP.
BOUGHT AT A CONVENIENCE STORE
NEGISHI-SAN, THANK YOU. . .
THANK YOU FOR TAKING CARE OF ME.
I'M GLAD WE'RE TOGETHER.

GENTLY

WATERY
じわ..

I'M SORRY, HOSHINO-KUN.

SNIFFLE
ぐすっ

MORE TEARS....?

HUH!? TEARS...?

SNIFF
ぐすっ

SNIFF
ぐすっ

SNIFF

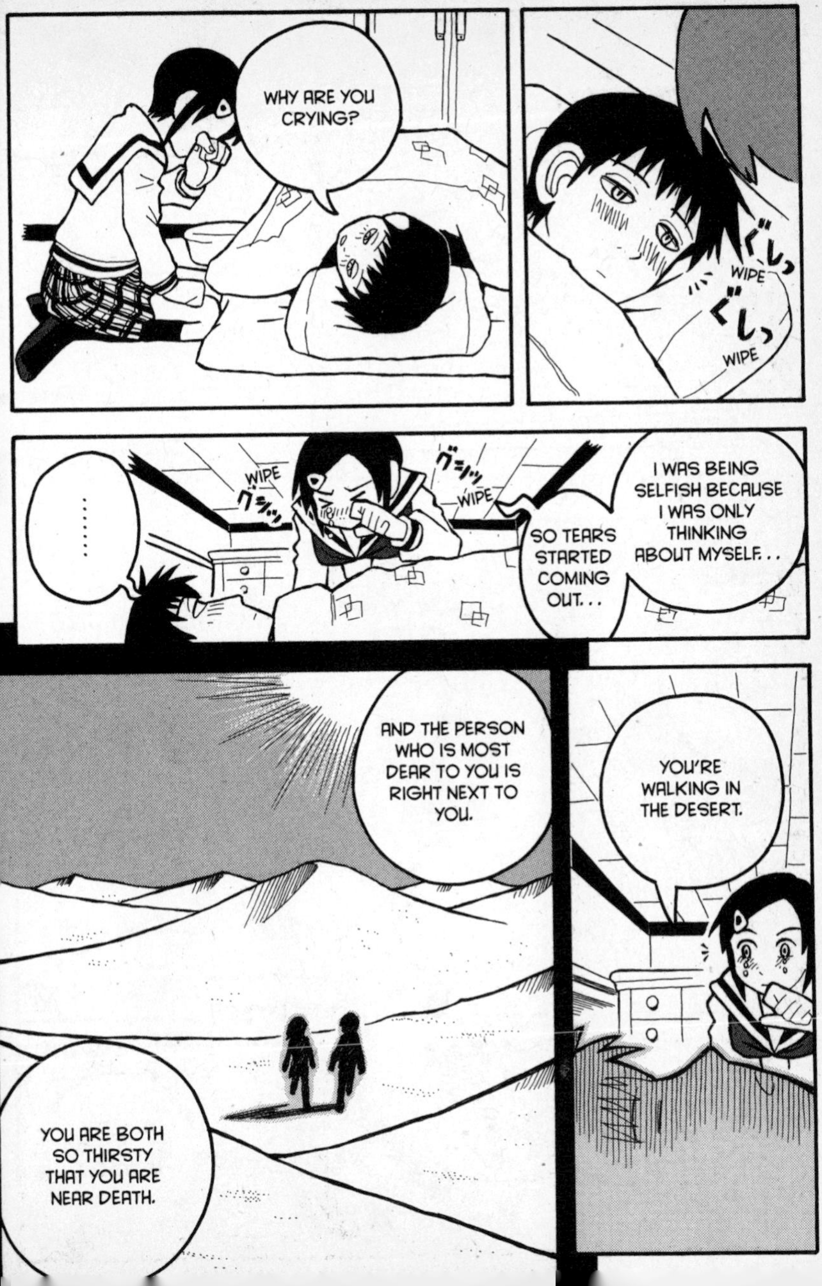

ぐしっ
WIPE
ぐしっ
WIPE
WHY ARE YOU CRYING?
I WAS BEING SELFISH BECAUSE I WAS ONLY THINKING ABOUT MYSELF...
SO TEARS STARTED COMING OUT...
WIPE
WIPE
......
YOU'RE WALKING IN THE DESERT.
AND THE PERSON WHO IS MOST DEAR TO YOU IS RIGHT NEXT TO YOU.
YOU ARE BOTH SO THIRSTY THAT YOU ARE NEAR DEATH.

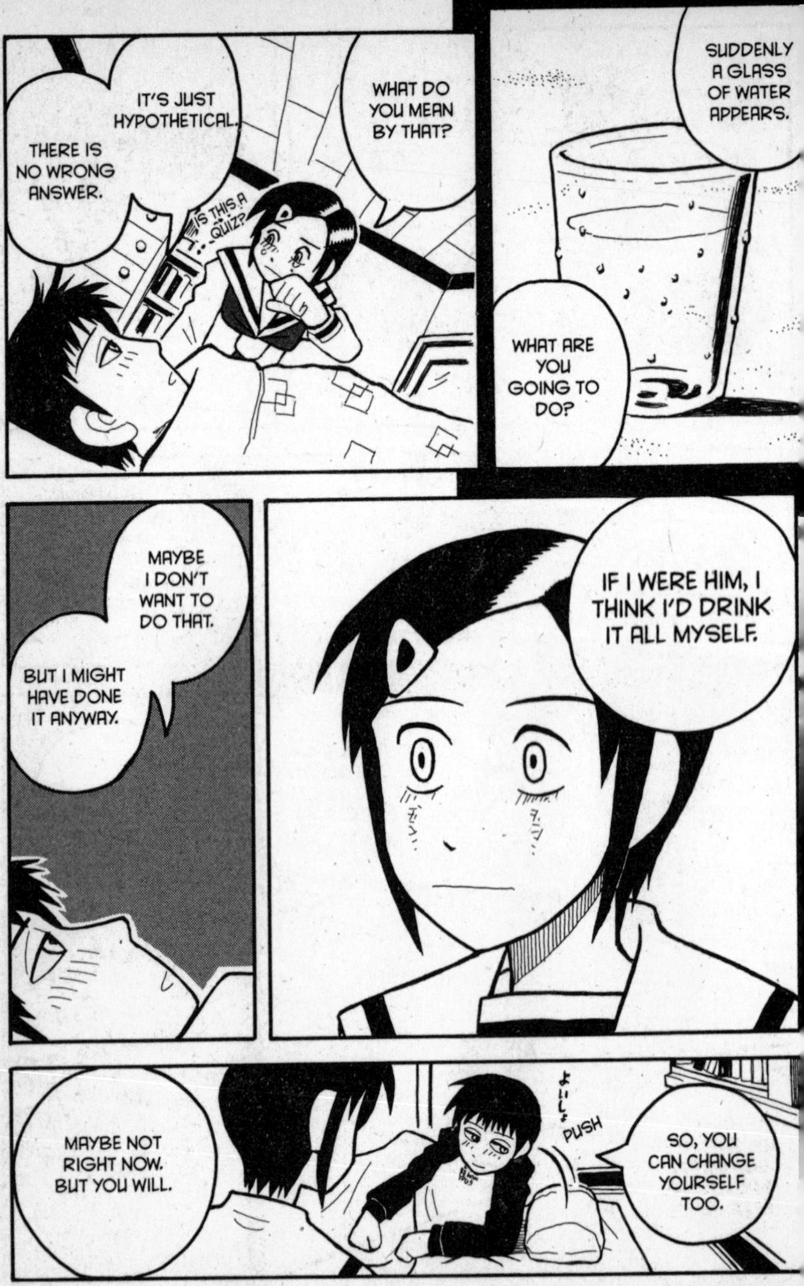
SUDDENLY A GLASS OF WATER APPEARS.
WHAT ARE YOU GOING TO DO?
WHAT DO YOU MEAN BY THAT?
IT'S JUST HYPOTHETICAL.
THERE IS NO WRONG ANSWER.
IS THIS A QUIZ?
IF I WERE HIM, I THINK I'D DRINK IT ALL MYSELF.
MAYBE I DON'T WANT TO DO THAT.
BUT I MIGHT HAVE DONE IT ANYWAY.
SO, YOU CAN CHANGE YOURSELF TOO.
よいしょ
PUSH
MAYBE NOT RIGHT NOW. BUT YOU WILL.

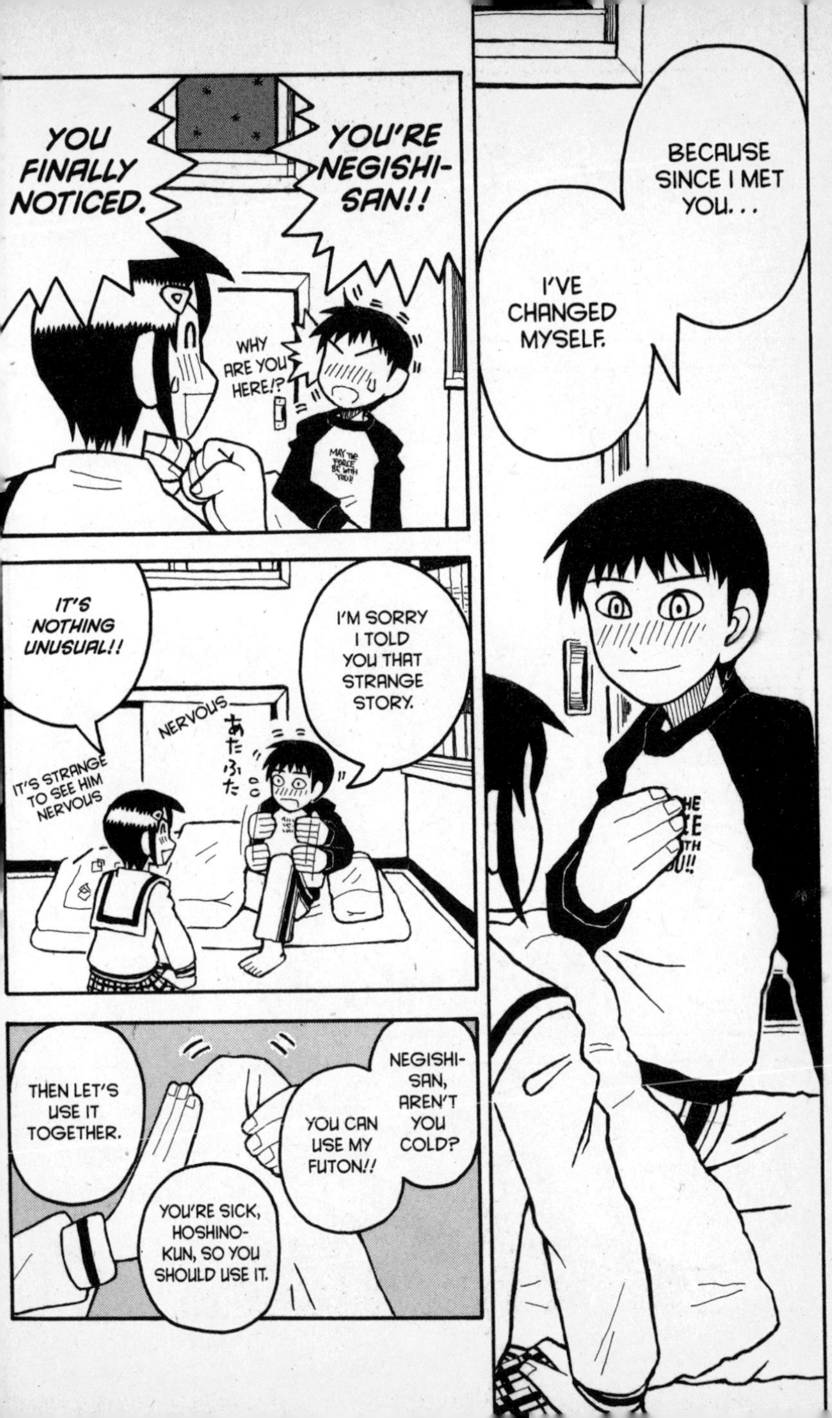
YOU'RE NEGISHI-SAN!!
YOU FINALLY NOTICED.
WHY ARE YOU HERE!?
MAY THE FORCE BE WITH YOU!!
I'M SORRY I TOLD YOU THAT STRANGE STORY.
IT'S NOTHING UNUSUAL!!
NERVOUS
あたふた
IT'S STRANGE TO SEE HIM NERVOUS
NEGISHI-SAN, AREN'T YOU COLD?
YOU CAN USE MY FUTON!!
YOU'RE SICK, HOSHINO-KUN, SO YOU SHOULD USE IT.
THEN LET'S USE IT TOGETHER.
BECAUSE SINCE I MET YOU...
I'VE CHANGED MYSELF.

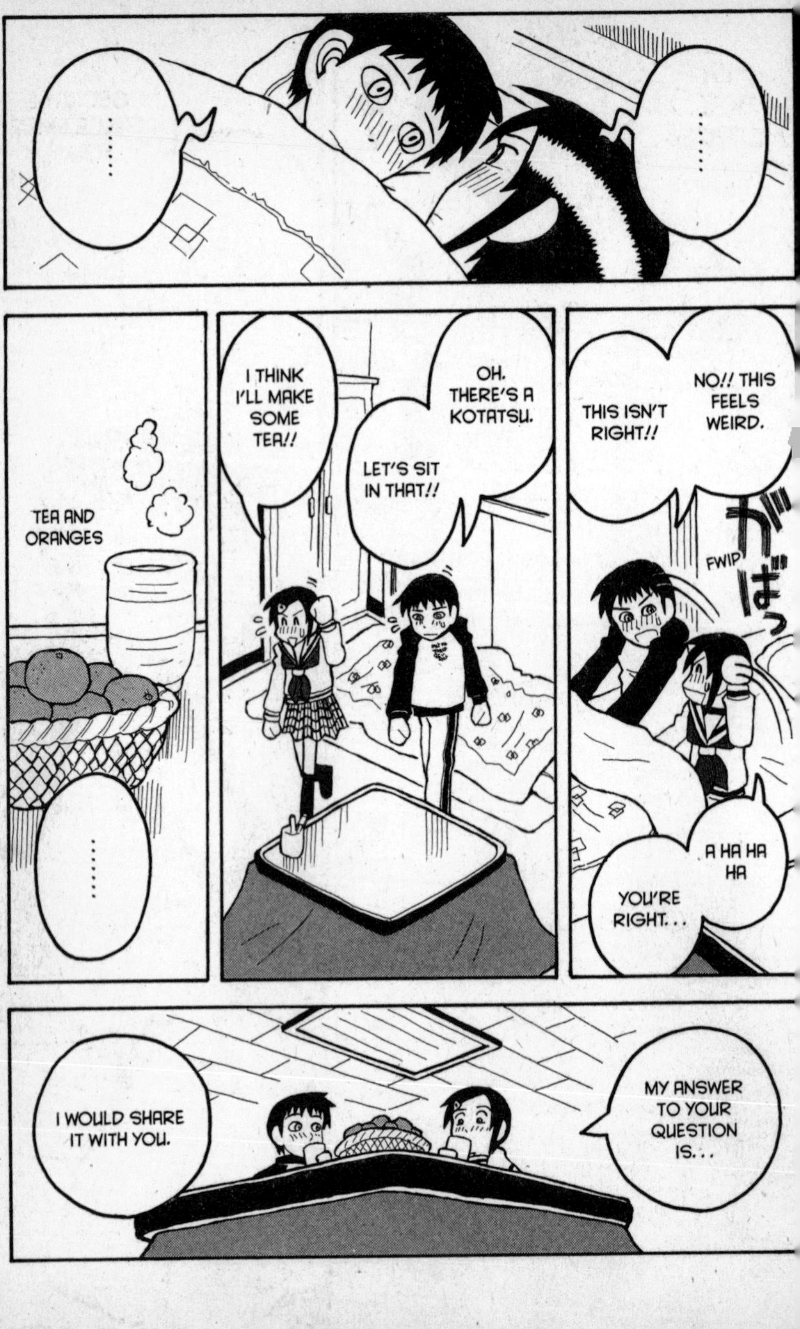
......
......
NO!! THIS FEELS WEIRD.
THIS ISN'T RIGHT!!
がばっ
FWIP
A HA HA HA
YOU'RE RIGHT...
OH. THERE'S A KOTATSU.
LET'S SIT IN THAT!!
I THINK I'LL MAKE SOME TEA!!
TEA AND ORANGES
......
MY ANSWER TO YOUR QUESTION IS...
I WOULD SHARE IT WITH YOU.

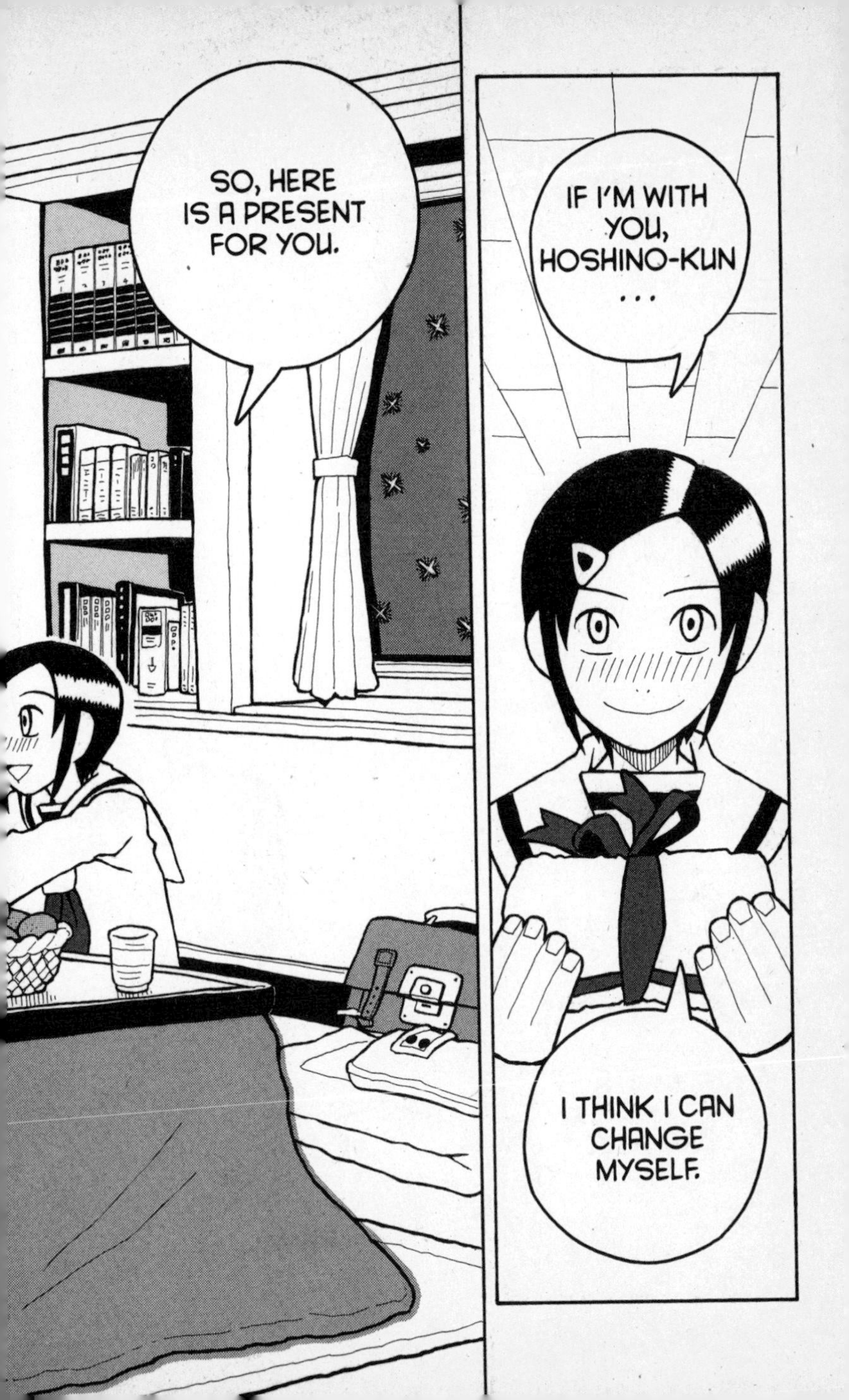
IF I'M WITH YOU, HOSHINO-KUN . . .
I THINK I CAN CHANGE MYSELF.
SO, HERE IS A PRESENT FOR YOU.

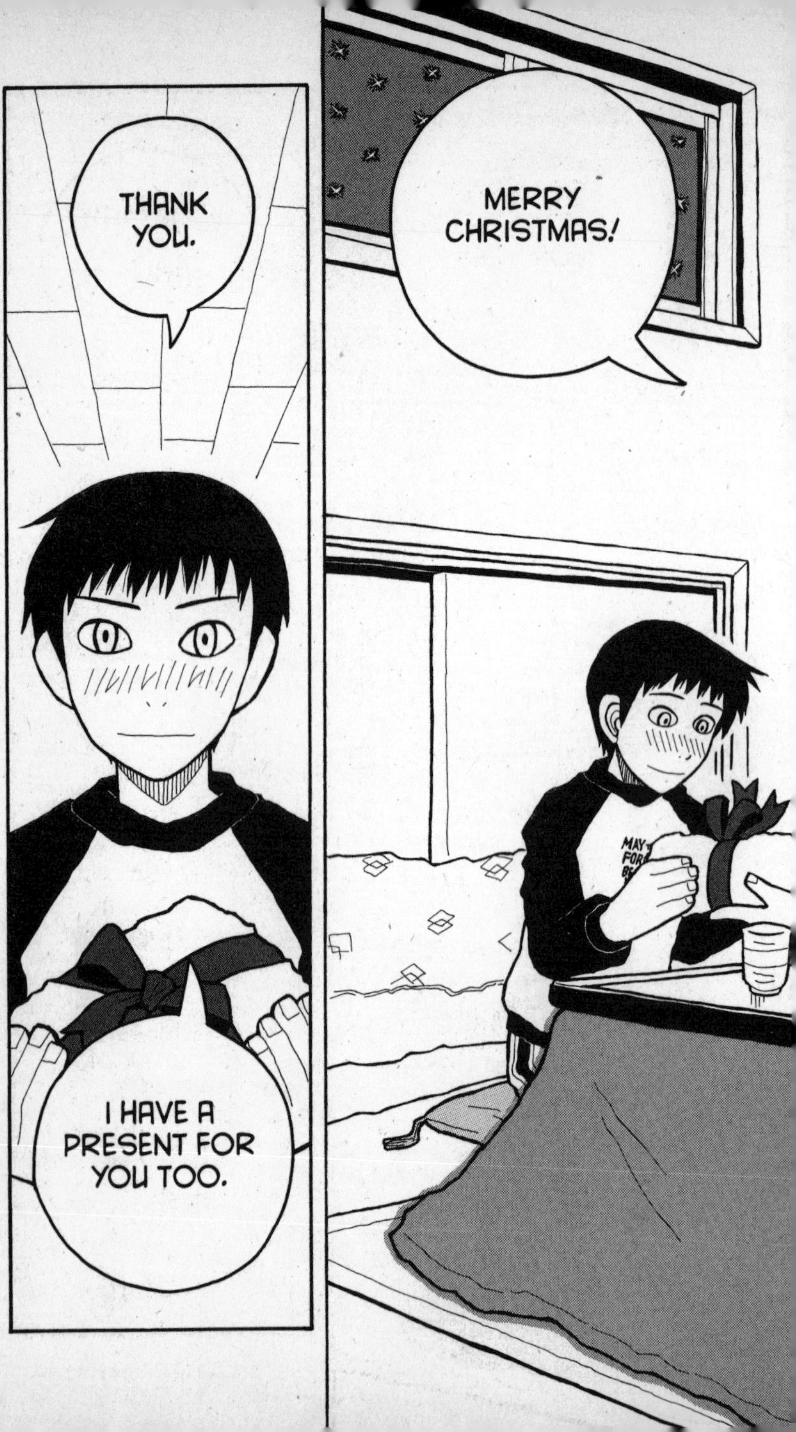
MERRY CHRISTMAS!
THANK YOU.
I HAVE A PRESENT FOR YOU TOO.

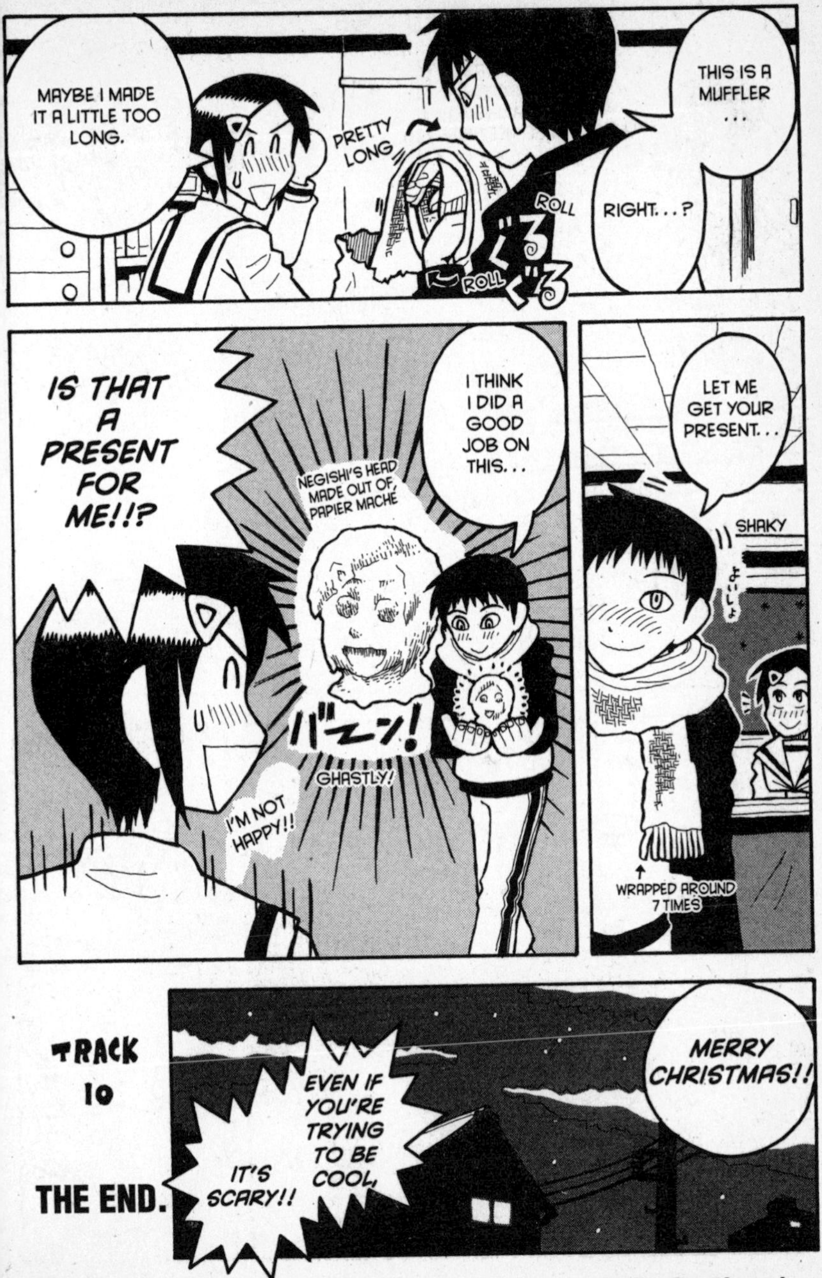
THIS IS A MUFFLER . . .
RIGHT. . . ?
ROLL
ROLL
PRETTY LONG
MAYBE I MADE IT A LITTLE TOO LONG.
LET ME GET YOUR PRESENT. . .
SHAKY
よいしょ
WRAPPED AROUND 7 TIMES
I THINK I DID A GOOD JOB ON THIS. . .
NEGISHI'S HEAD MADE OUT OF PAPIER MACHE
IS THAT A PRESENT FOR ME!!?
GHASTLY!
I'M NOT HAPPY!!
MERRY CHRISTMAS!!
EVEN IF YOU'RE TRYING TO BE COOL,
IT'S SCARY!!

TRACK 10

THE END.

To Be Continued...

BONUS TRACK

おまけ

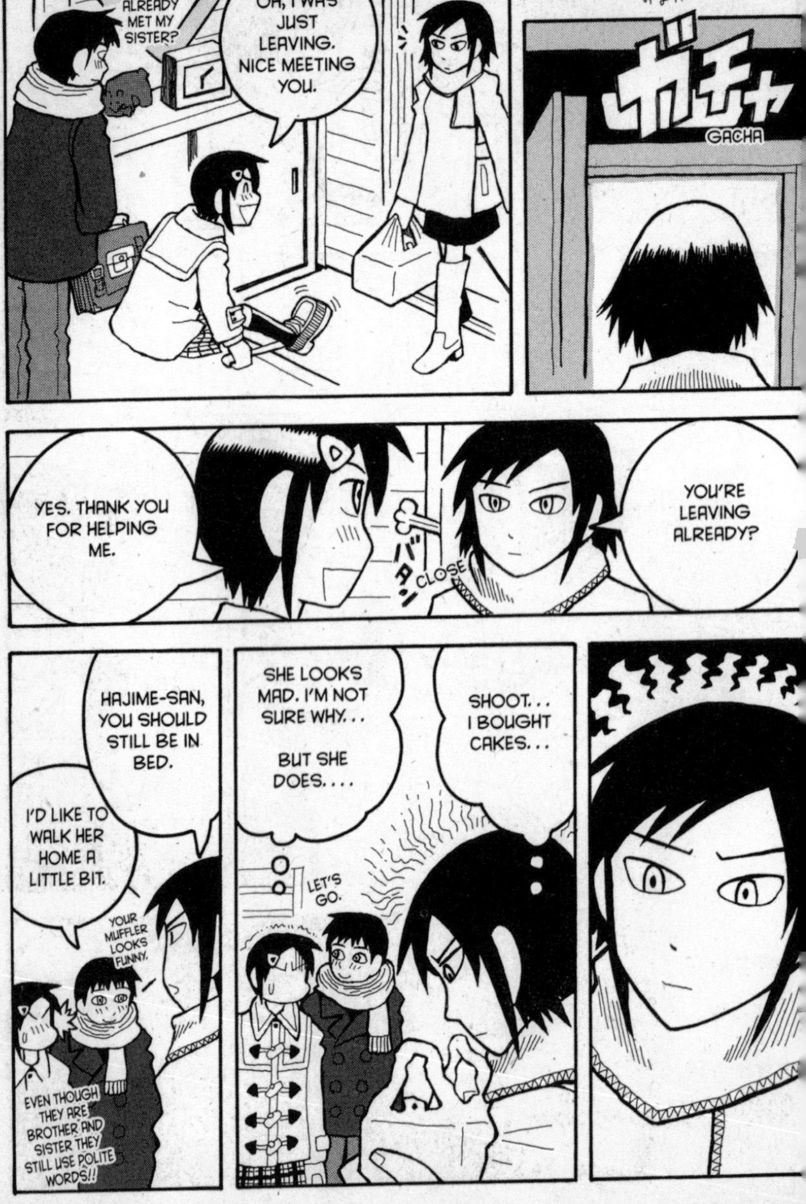
ガチャ
GACHA
OH, I WAS JUST LEAVING. NICE MEETING YOU.
YOU'VE ALREADY MET MY SISTER?
YOU'RE LEAVING ALREADY?
バタン
CLOSE
YES. THANK YOU FOR HELPING ME.
SHOOT... I BOUGHT CAKES...
SHE LOOKS MAD. I'M NOT SURE WHY...
BUT SHE DOES....
LET'S GO.
HAJIME-SAN, YOU SHOULD STILL BE IN BED.
I'D LIKE TO WALK HER HOME A LITTLE BIT.
YOUR MUFFLER LOOKS FUNNY.
EVEN THOUGH THEY ARE BROTHER AND SISTER THEY STILL USE POLITE WORDS!!

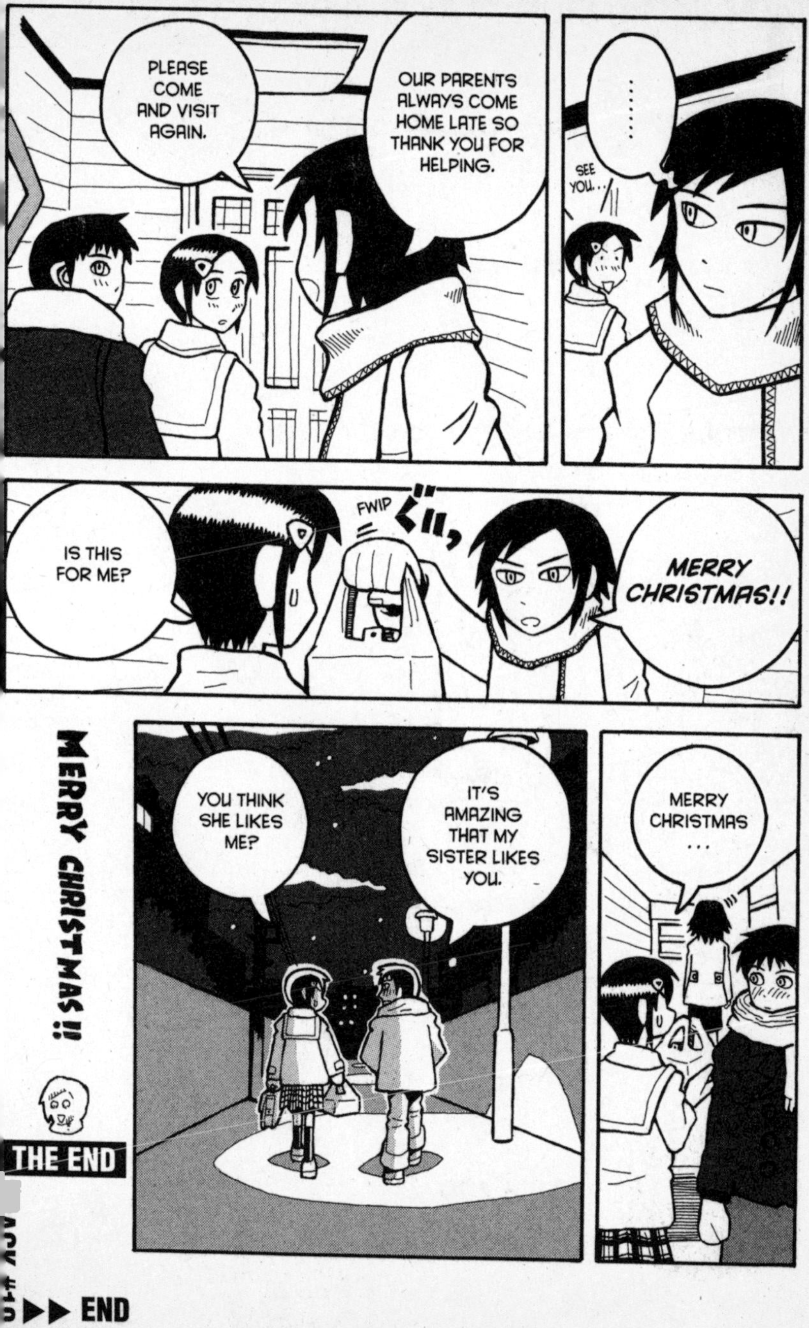
......
SEE YOU...
OUR PARENTS ALWAYS COME HOME LATE SO THANK YOU FOR HELPING.
PLEASE COME AND VISIT AGAIN.
MERRY CHRISTMAS!!
FWIP
IS THIS FOR ME?
MERRY CHRISTMAS ...
IT'S AMAZING THAT MY SISTER LIKES YOU.
YOU THINK SHE LIKES ME?
MERRY CHRISTMAS!!
THE END
ACK #16 ▶▶ END

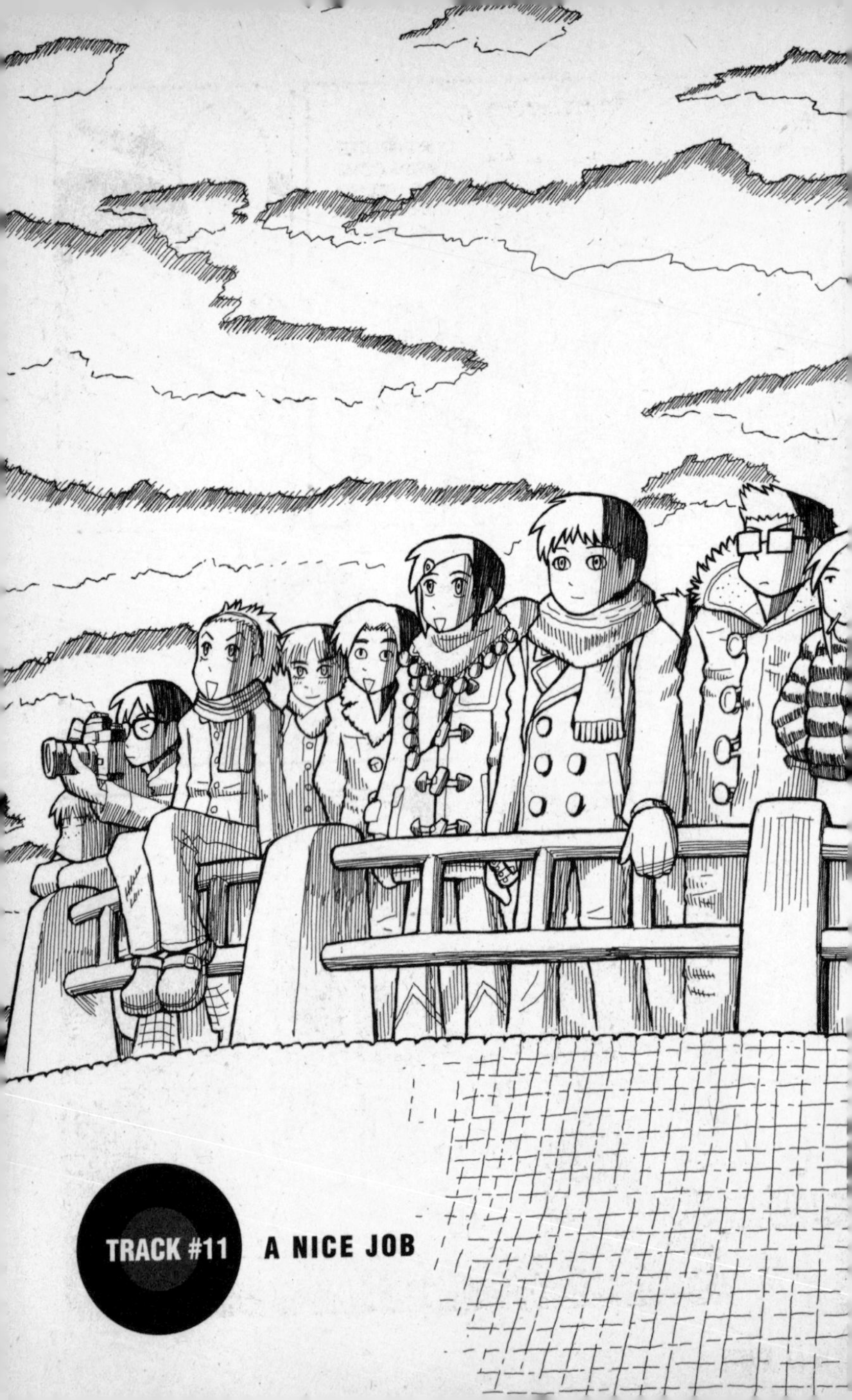

TRACK #11 A NICE JOB

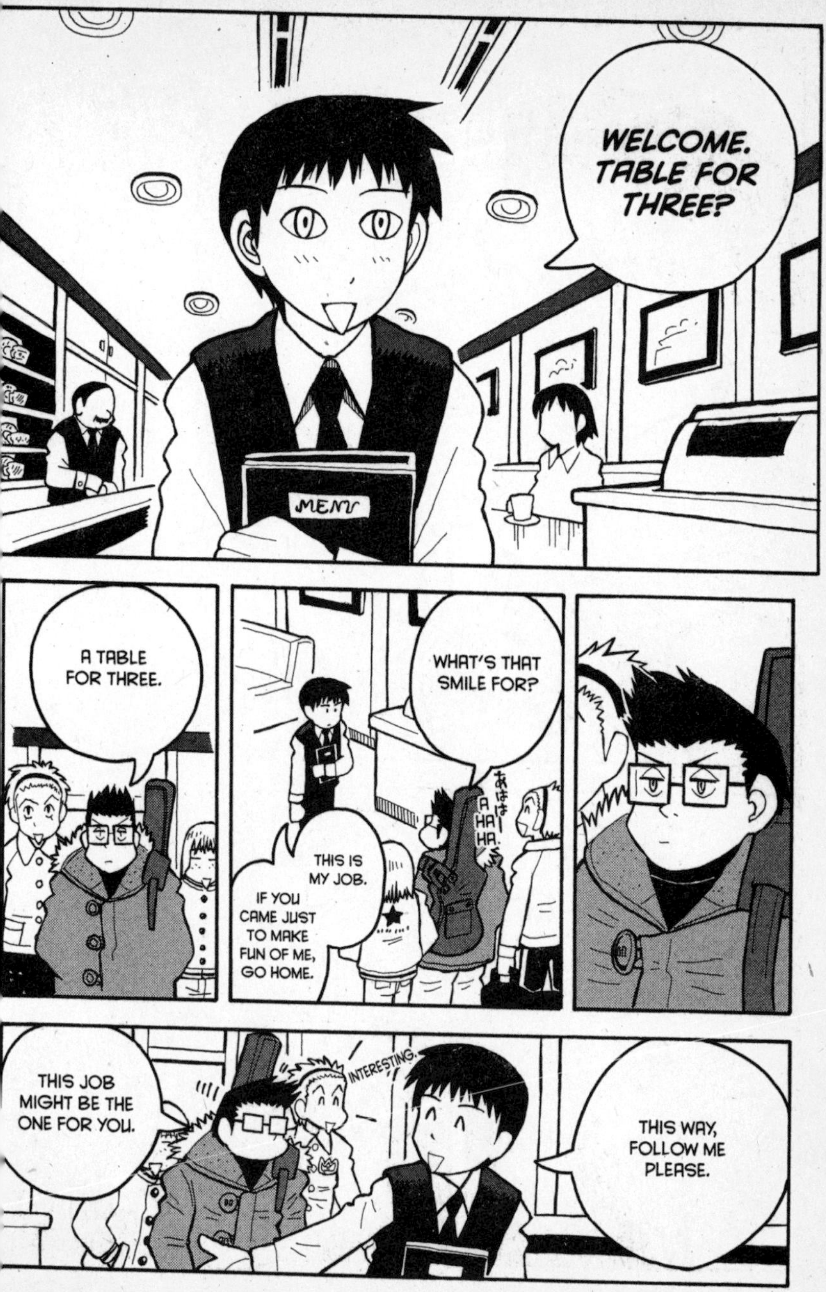
WELCOME. TABLE FOR THREE?
WHAT'S THAT SMILE FOR?
あはは
A HA HA.
THIS IS MY JOB.
IF YOU CAME JUST TO MAKE FUN OF ME, GO HOME.
A TABLE FOR THREE.
THIS WAY, FOLLOW ME PLEASE.
INTERESTING.
THIS JOB MIGHT BE THE ONE FOR YOU.

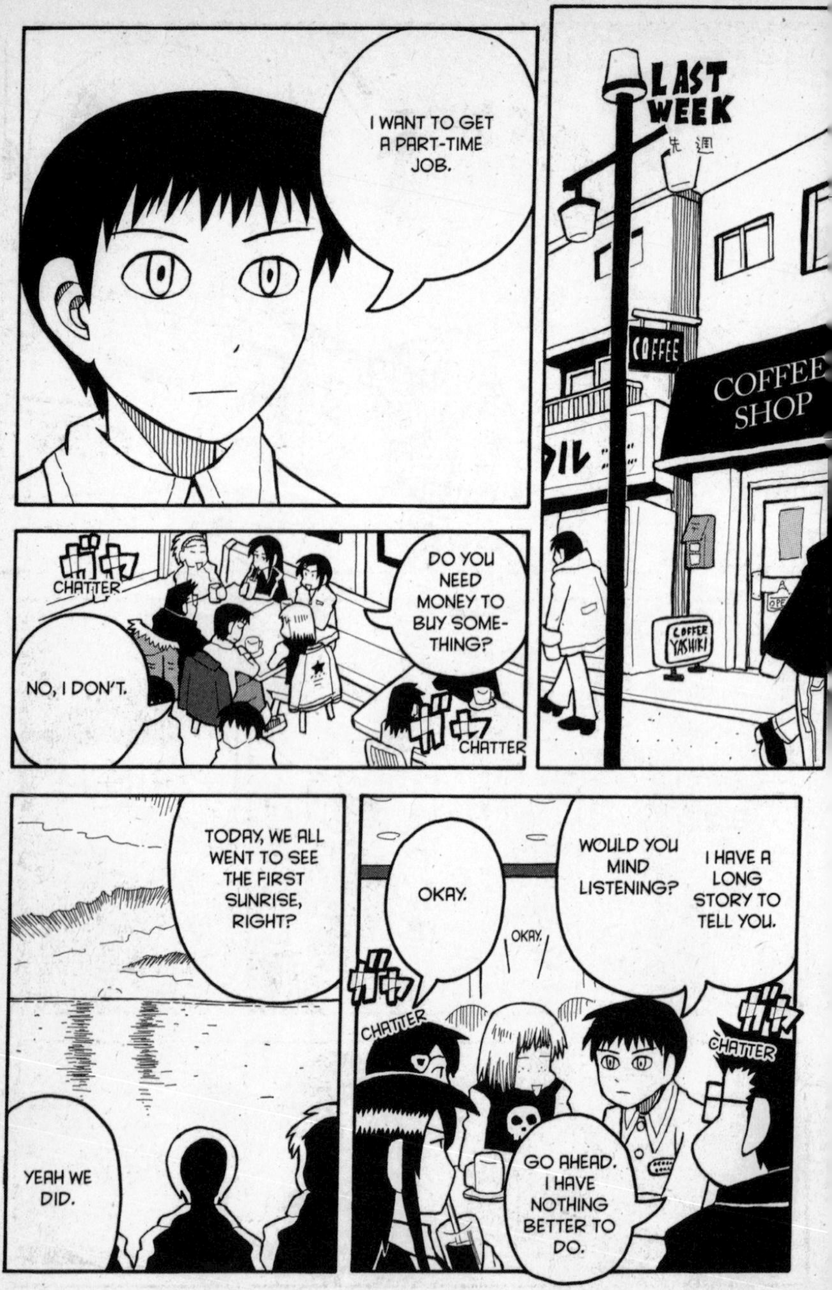
LAST WEEK
先週
COFFEE
COFFEE SHOP
COFFEE YASHIKI
I WANT TO GET A PART-TIME JOB.
CHATTER
DO YOU NEED MONEY TO BUY SOME-THING?
NO, I DON'T.
CHATTER
I HAVE A LONG STORY TO TELL YOU.
WOULD YOU MIND LISTENING?
CHATTER
OKAY.
OKAY.
CHATTER
GO AHEAD. I HAVE NOTHING BETTER TO DO.
TODAY, WE ALL WENT TO SEE THE FIRST SUNRISE, RIGHT?
YEAH WE DID.

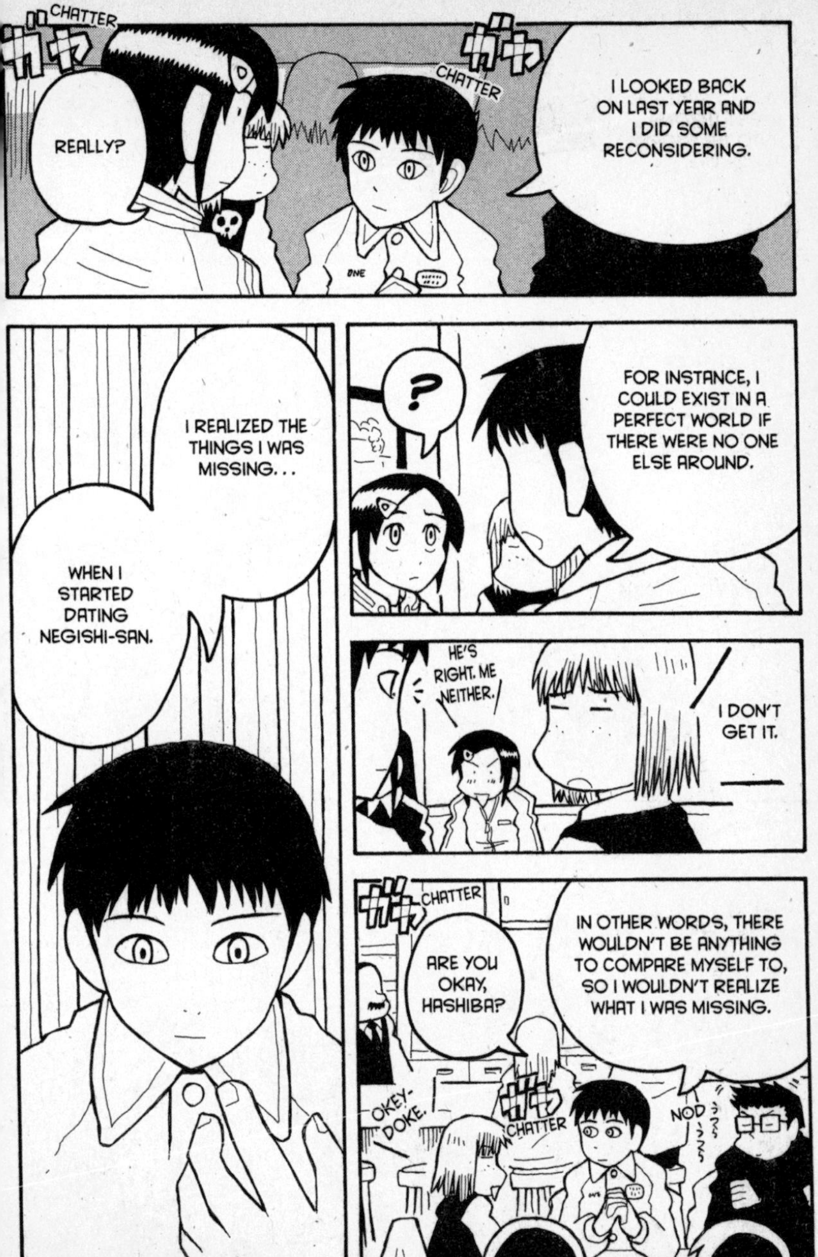
CHATTER
I LOOKED BACK ON LAST YEAR AND I DID SOME RECONSIDERING.
CHATTER
REALLY?
FOR INSTANCE, I COULD EXIST IN A PERFECT WORLD IF THERE WERE NO ONE ELSE AROUND.
?
I DON'T GET IT.
HE'S RIGHT. ME NEITHER.
IN OTHER WORDS, THERE WOULDN'T BE ANYTHING TO COMPARE MYSELF TO, SO I WOULDN'T REALIZE WHAT I WAS MISSING.
NOD
CHATTER
ARE YOU OKAY, HASHIBA?
CHATTER
OKEY-DOKE.
I REALIZED THE THINGS I WAS MISSING. . .
WHEN I STARTED DATING NEGISHI-SAN.

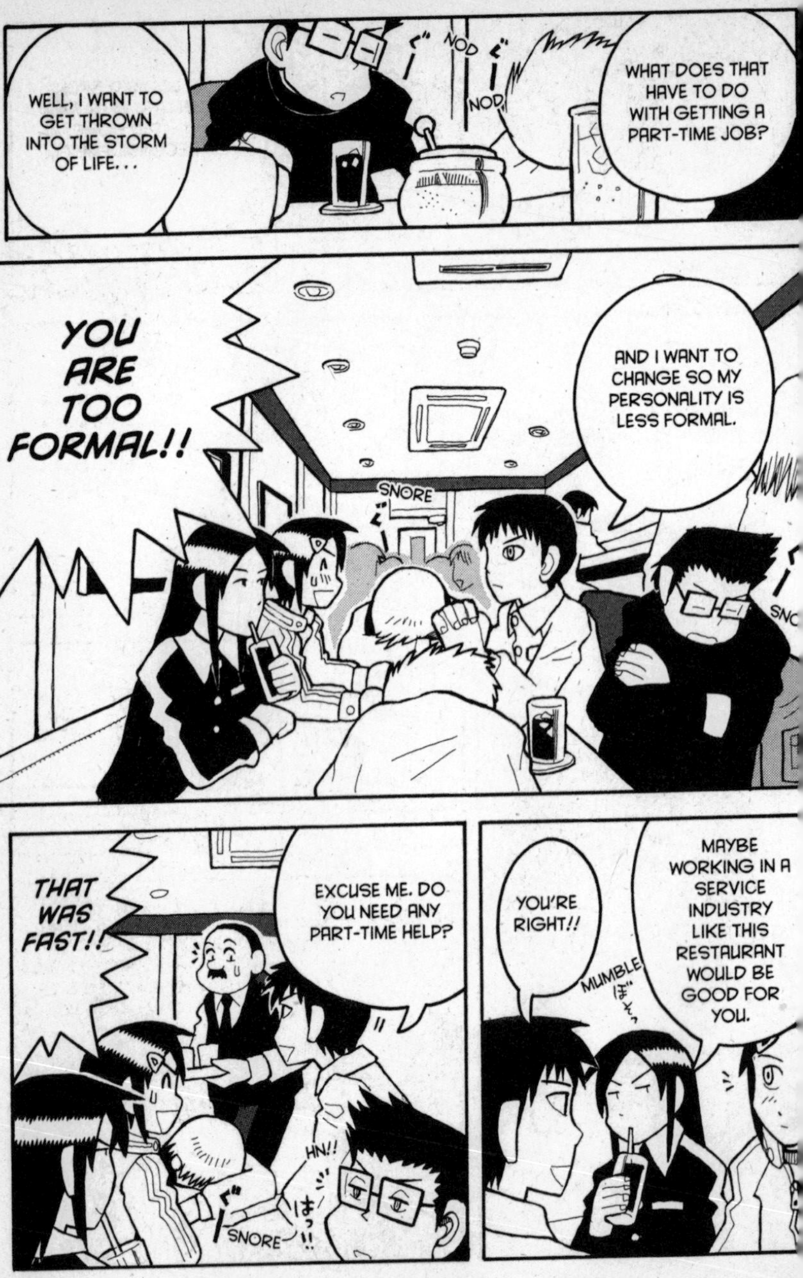

WHAT DOES THAT HAVE TO DO WITH GETTING A PART-TIME JOB?
NOD
NOD
WELL, I WANT TO GET THROWN INTO THE STORM OF LIFE...
AND I WANT TO CHANGE SO MY PERSONALITY IS LESS FORMAL.
SNORE
YOU ARE TOO FORMAL!!
MAYBE WORKING IN A SERVICE INDUSTRY LIKE THIS RESTAURANT WOULD BE GOOD FOR YOU.
MUMBLE
ぼそっ
YOU'RE RIGHT!!
EXCUSE ME. DO YOU NEED ANY PART-TIME HELP?
THAT WAS FAST!!
HN!!
はっ!!
SNORE

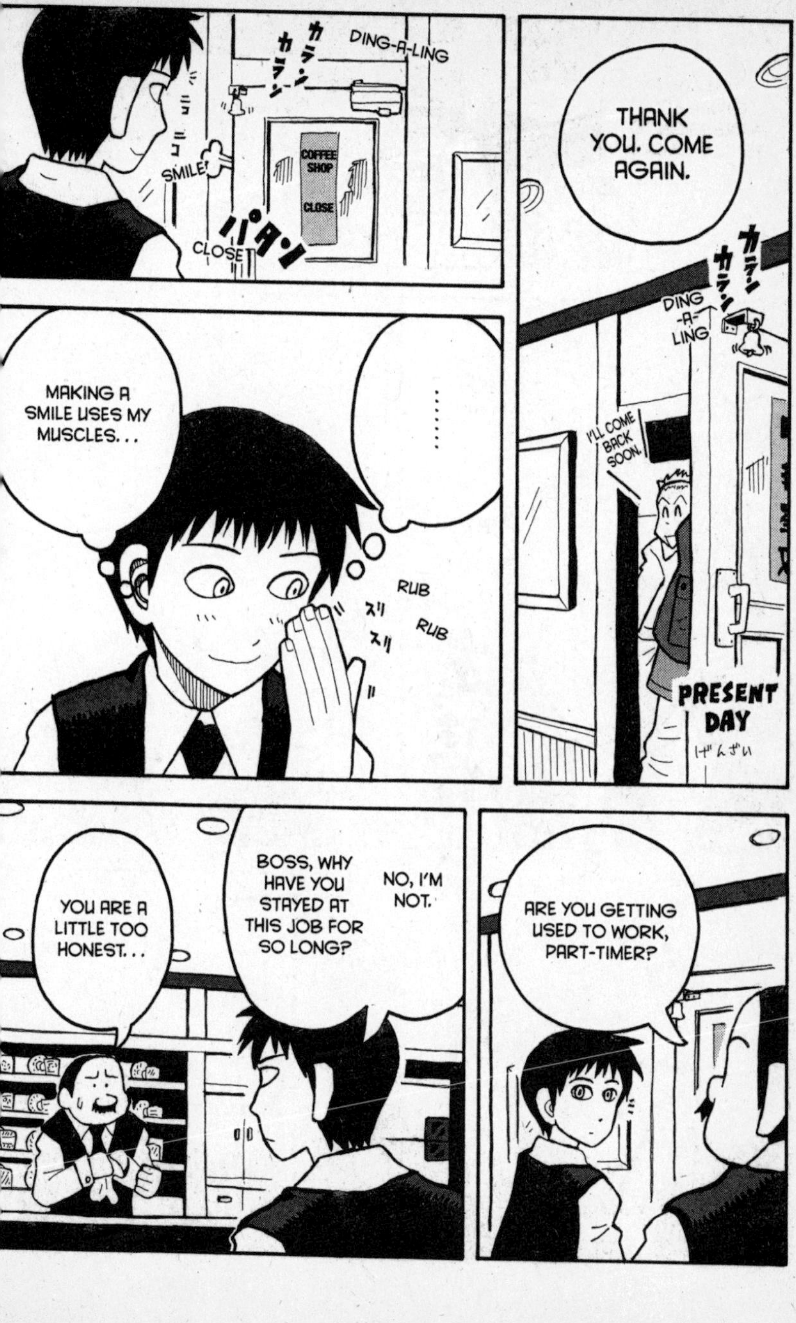
THANK YOU. COME AGAIN.
カラン カラン
DING-A-LING
I'LL COME BACK SOON.
PRESENT DAY
げんざい
カラン カラン
DING-A-LING
ニコ ニコ
SMILE
COFFEE SHOP
CLOSE
パタン
CLOSE
......
MAKING A SMILE USES MY MUSCLES...
スリ スリ
RUB RUB
ARE YOU GETTING USED TO WORK, PART-TIMER?
NO, I'M NOT.
BOSS, WHY HAVE YOU STAYED AT THIS JOB FOR SO LONG?
YOU ARE A LITTLE TOO HONEST...

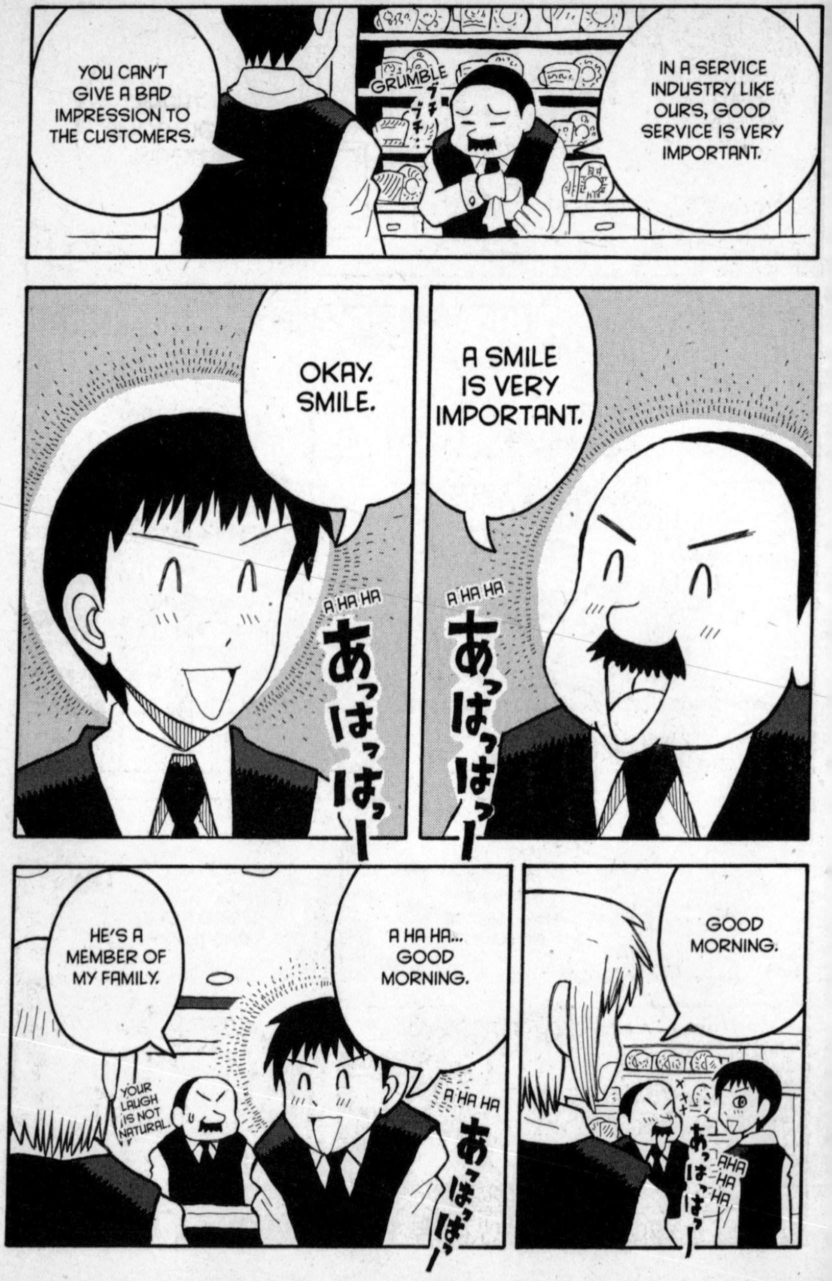
IN A SERVICE INDUSTRY LIKE OURS, GOOD SERVICE IS VERY IMPORTANT.
GRUMBLE
ブチブチ…
YOU CAN'T GIVE A BAD IMPRESSION TO THE CUSTOMERS.
A SMILE IS VERY IMPORTANT.
A HA HA
あっはっはっー
OKAY. SMILE.
A HA HA
あっはっはっー
GOOD MORNING.
AHA HA HA
あっはっはっー
A HA HA... GOOD MORNING.
A HA HA
あっはっぱっー
HE'S A MEMBER OF MY FAMILY.
YOUR LAUGH IS NOT NATURAL.

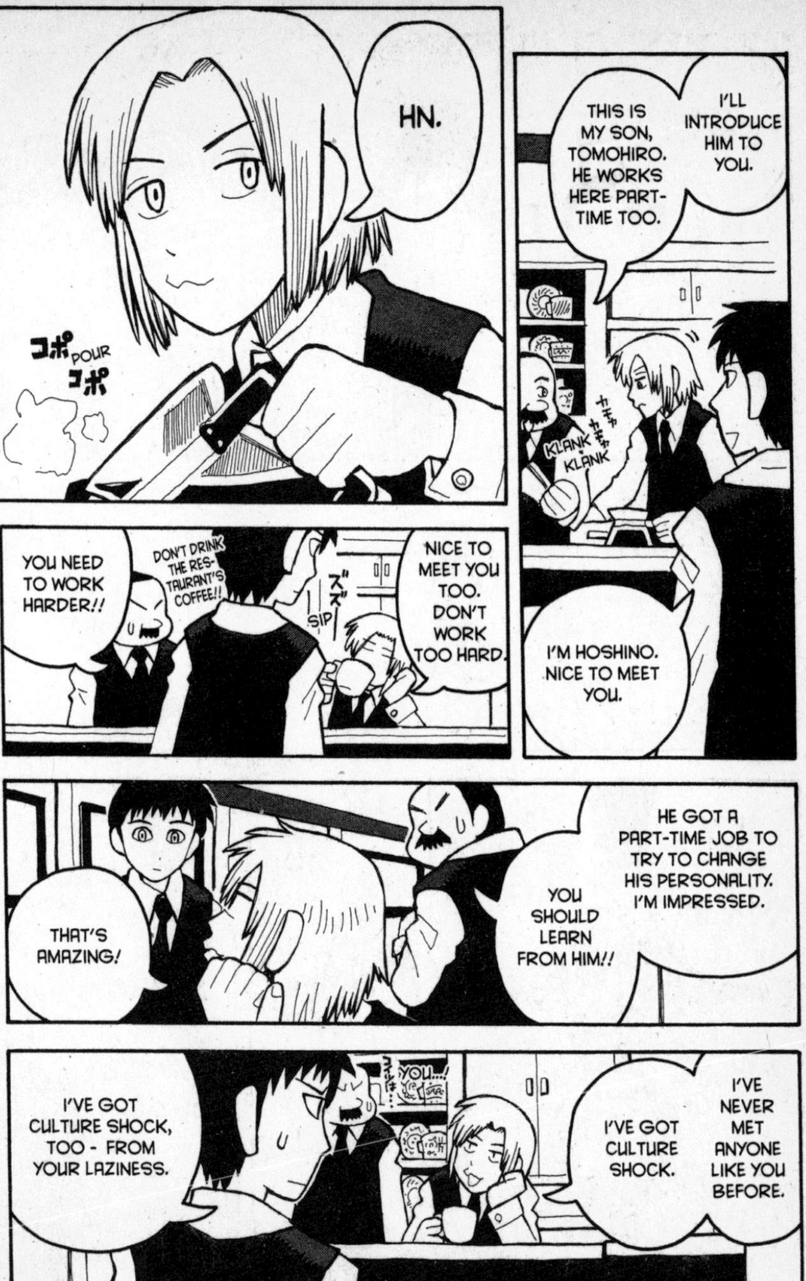
I'LL INTRODUCE HIM TO YOU.
THIS IS MY SON, TOMOHIRO. HE WORKS HERE PART-TIME TOO.
カチャ KLANK
カチャ KLANK
I'M HOSHINO. NICE TO MEET YOU.
HN.
コポ POUR コポ
NICE TO MEET YOU TOO. DON'T WORK TOO HARD.
ズズ SIP
DON'T DRINK THE RES-TAURANT'S COFFEE!!
YOU NEED TO WORK HARDER!!
HE GOT A PART-TIME JOB TO TRY TO CHANGE HIS PERSONALITY. I'M IMPRESSED.
YOU SHOULD LEARN FROM HIM!!
THAT'S AMAZING!
I'VE NEVER MET ANYONE LIKE YOU BEFORE.
I'VE GOT CULTURE SHOCK.
YOU...!
I'VE GOT CULTURE SHOCK, TOO - FROM YOUR LAZINESS.

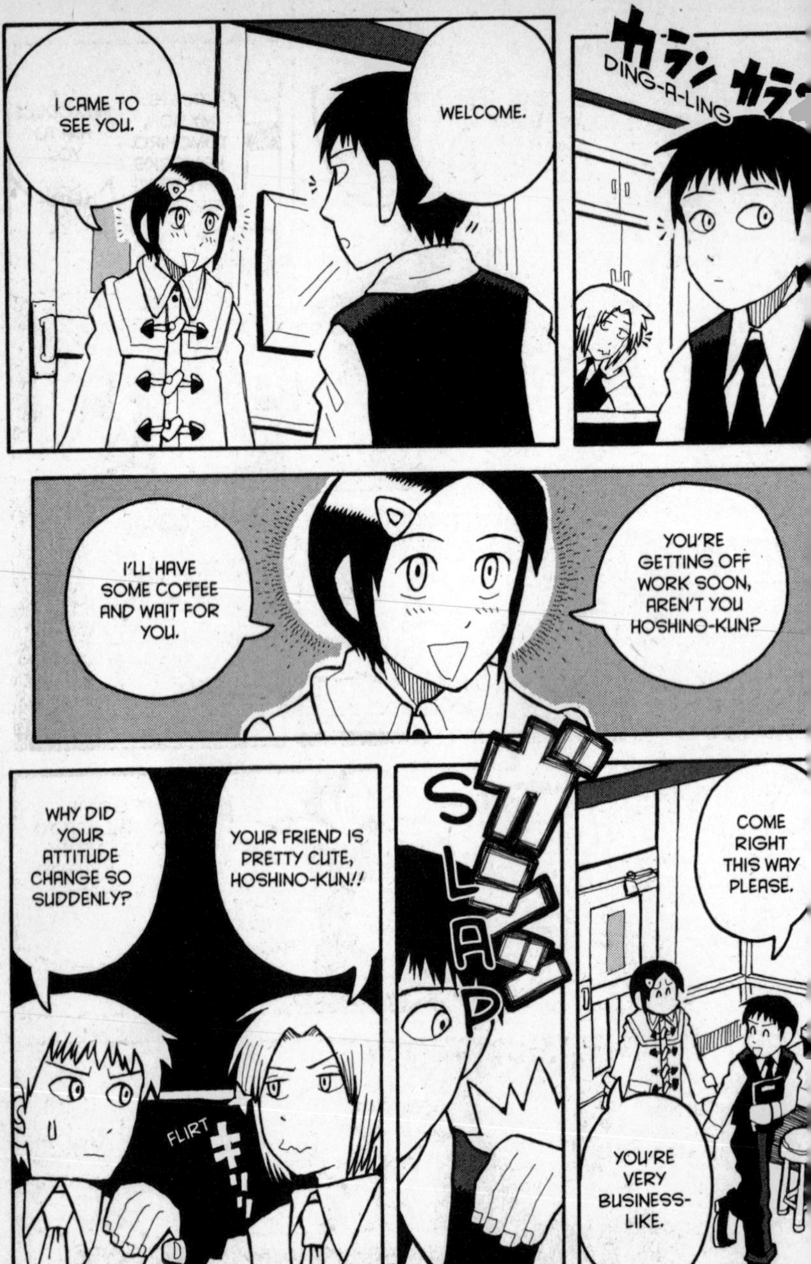
カラン
DING-A-LING
WELCOME.
I CAME TO SEE YOU.
YOU'RE GETTING OFF WORK SOON, AREN'T YOU HOSHINO-KUN?
I'LL HAVE SOME COFFEE AND WAIT FOR YOU.
COME RIGHT THIS WAY PLEASE.
YOU'RE VERY BUSINESS-LIKE.
SLAP
YOUR FRIEND IS PRETTY CUTE, HOSHINO-KUN!!
WHY DID YOUR ATTITUDE CHANGE SO SUDDENLY?
FLIRT

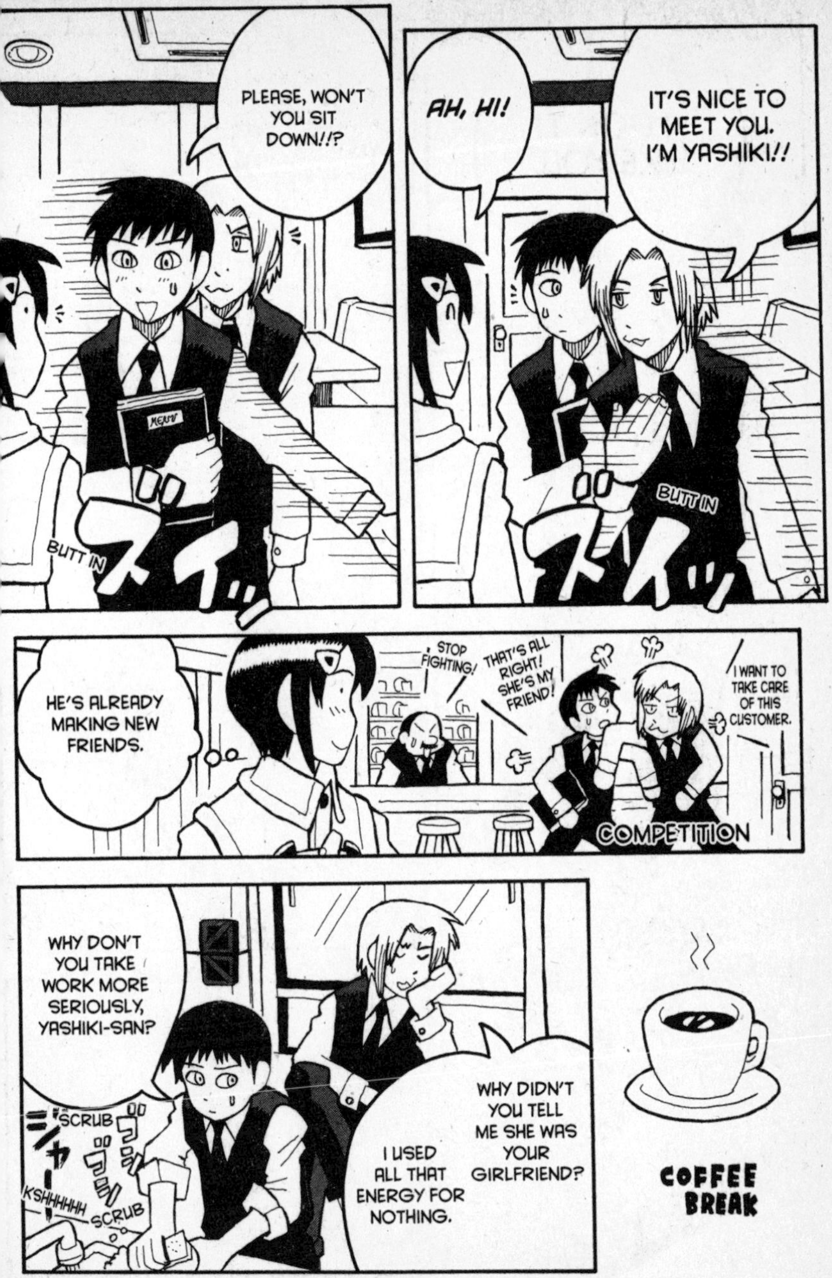
IT'S NICE TO MEET YOU. I'M YASHIKI!!
AH, HI!
BUTT IN
PLEASE, WON'T YOU SIT DOWN!!?
BUTT IN
I WANT TO TAKE CARE OF THIS CUSTOMER.
THAT'S ALL RIGHT! SHE'S MY FRIEND!
STOP FIGHTING!
COMPETITION
HE'S ALREADY MAKING NEW FRIENDS.
COFFEE BREAK
WHY DIDN'T YOU TELL ME SHE WAS YOUR GIRLFRIEND?
I USED ALL THAT ENERGY FOR NOTHING.
WHY DON'T YOU TAKE WORK MORE SERIOUSLY, YASHIKI-SAN?
SCRUB
KSHHHHHH
SCRUB

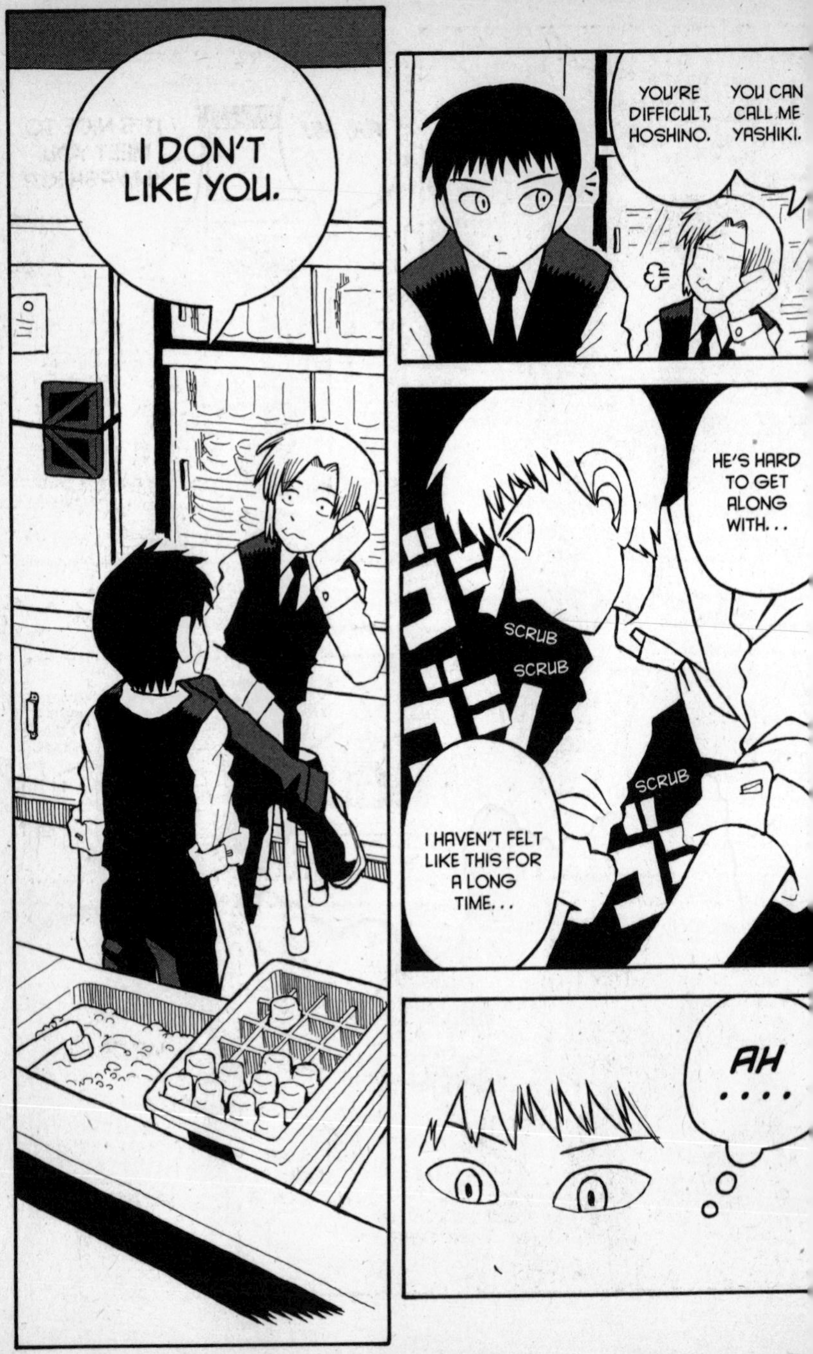
YOU CAN CALL ME YASHIKI.
YOU'RE DIFFICULT, HOSHINO.
HE'S HARD TO GET ALONG WITH...
SCRUB
SCRUB
SCRUB
I HAVEN'T FELT LIKE THIS FOR A LONG TIME...
AH ....
I DON'T LIKE YOU.

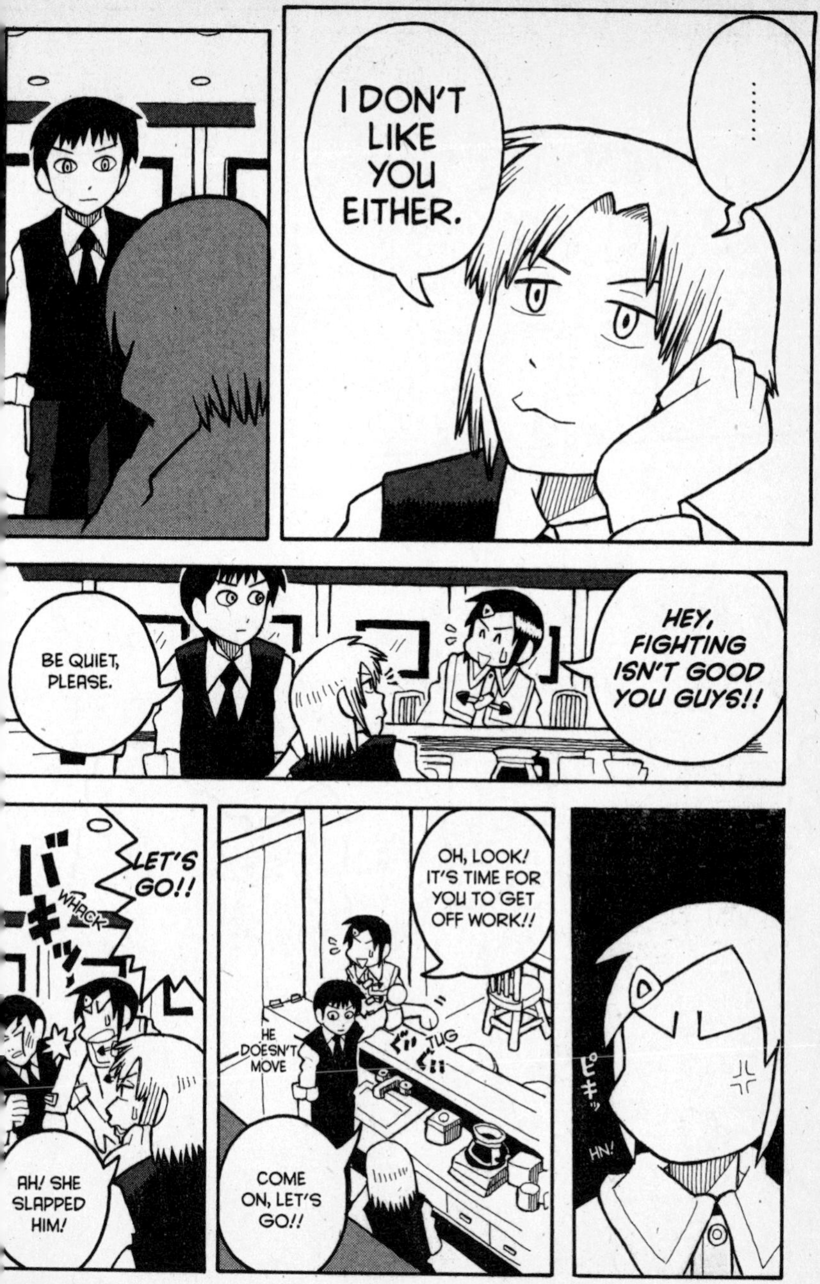
......
I DON'T LIKE YOU EITHER.
HEY, FIGHTING ISN'T GOOD YOU GUYS!!
BE QUIET, PLEASE.
ピキッ
HN!
OH, LOOK! IT'S TIME FOR YOU TO GET OFF WORK!!
ぐぃ
TUG
ぐぃ
HE DOESN'T MOVE
COME ON, LET'S GO!!
LET'S GO!!
バキッ
WHACK
AH! SHE SLAPPED HIM!

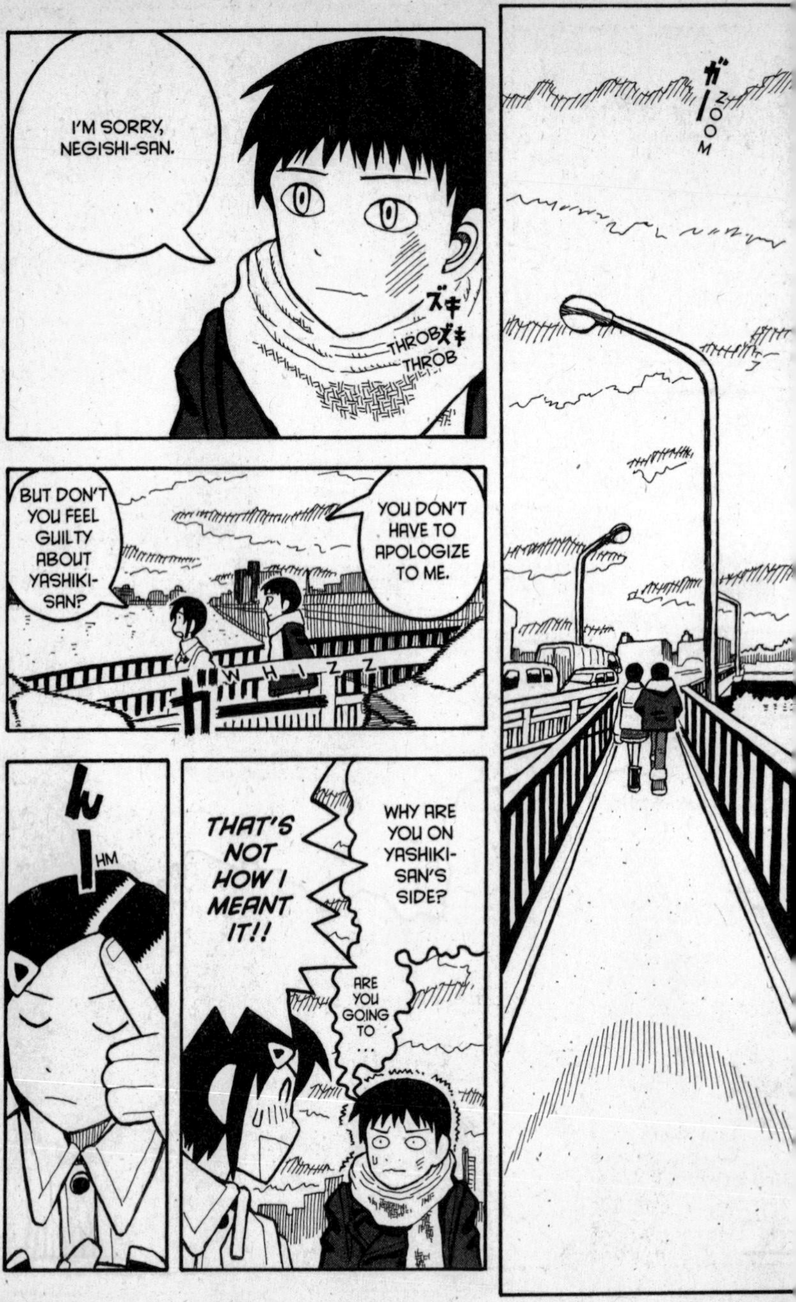
ZOOM
I'M SORRY, NEGISHI-SAN.
THROB THROB
YOU DON'T HAVE TO APOLOGIZE TO ME.
BUT DON'T YOU FEEL GUILTY ABOUT YASHIKI-SAN?
WHIZZ
WHY ARE YOU ON YASHIKI-SAN'S SIDE?
ARE YOU GOING TO . . .
THAT'S NOT HOW I MEANT IT!!
HM

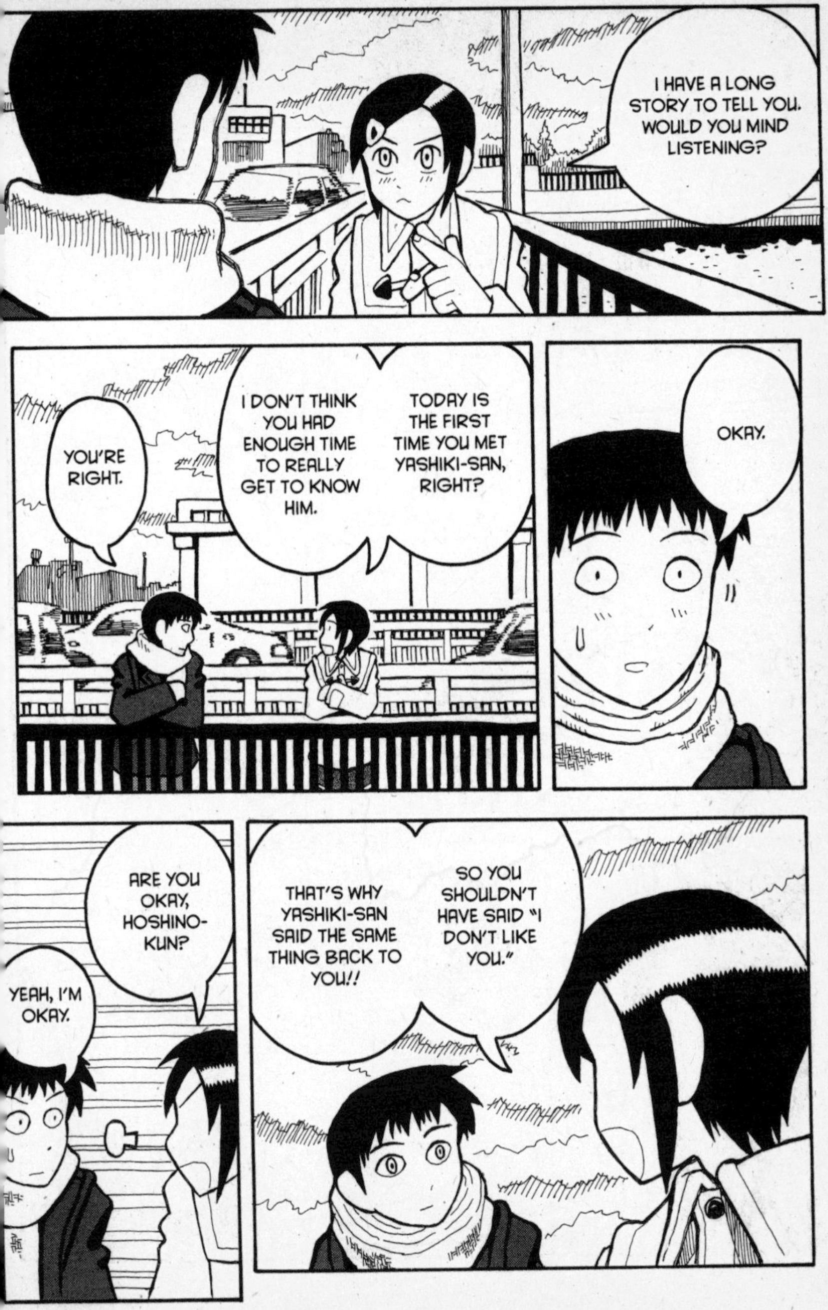
I HAVE A LONG STORY TO TELL YOU. WOULD YOU MIND LISTENING?
OKAY.
TODAY IS THE FIRST TIME YOU MET YASHIKI-SAN, RIGHT?
I DON'T THINK YOU HAD ENOUGH TIME TO REALLY GET TO KNOW HIM.
YOU'RE RIGHT.
SO YOU SHOULDN'T HAVE SAID "I DON'T LIKE YOU."
THAT'S WHY YASHIKI-SAN SAID THE SAME THING BACK TO YOU!!
ARE YOU OKAY, HOSHINO-KUN?
YEAH, I'M OKAY.

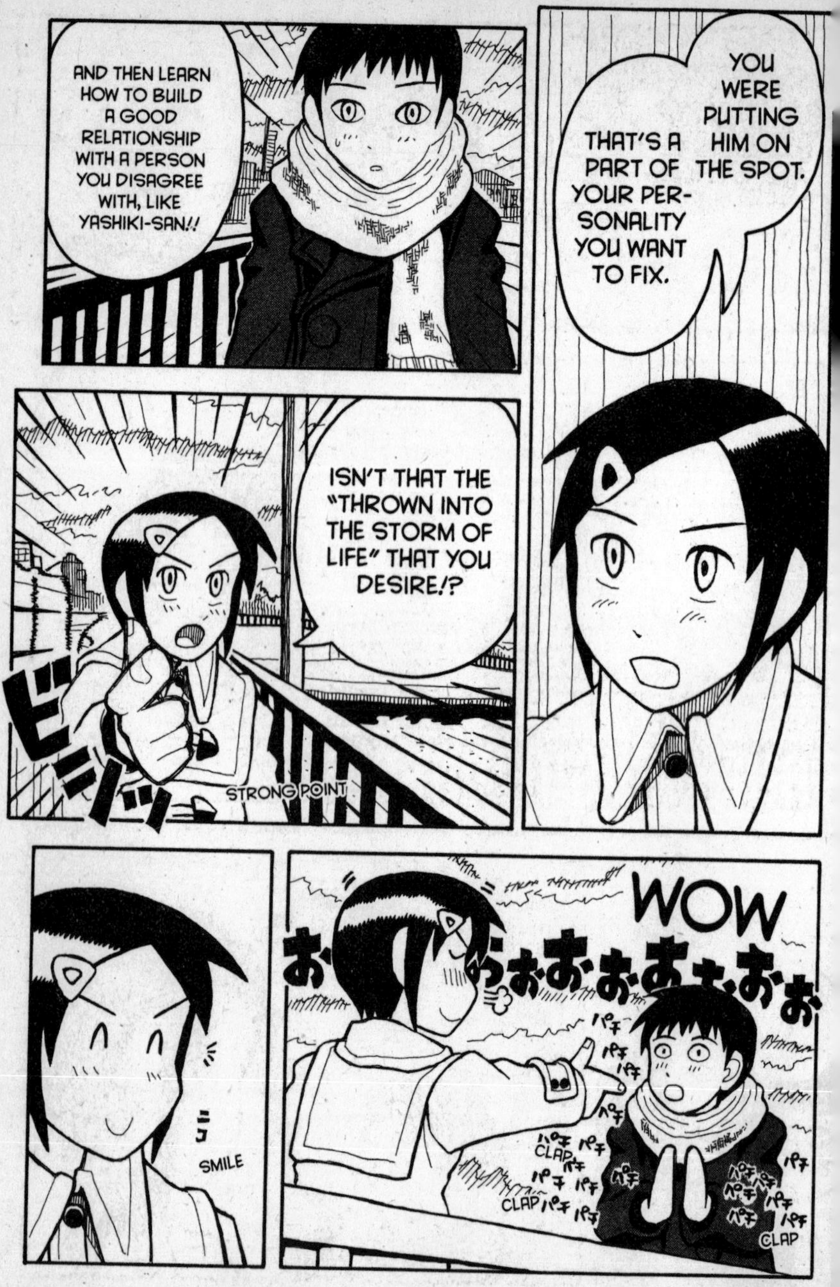

YOU WERE PUTTING HIM ON THE SPOT.
THAT'S A PART OF YOUR PERSONALITY YOU WANT TO FIX.
AND THEN LEARN HOW TO BUILD A GOOD RELATIONSHIP WITH A PERSON YOU DISAGREE WITH, LIKE YASHIKI-SAN!!
ISN'T THAT THE "THROWN INTO THE STORM OF LIFE" THAT YOU DESIRE!?
STRONG POINT
WOW
CLAP
CLAP
CLAP
SMILE

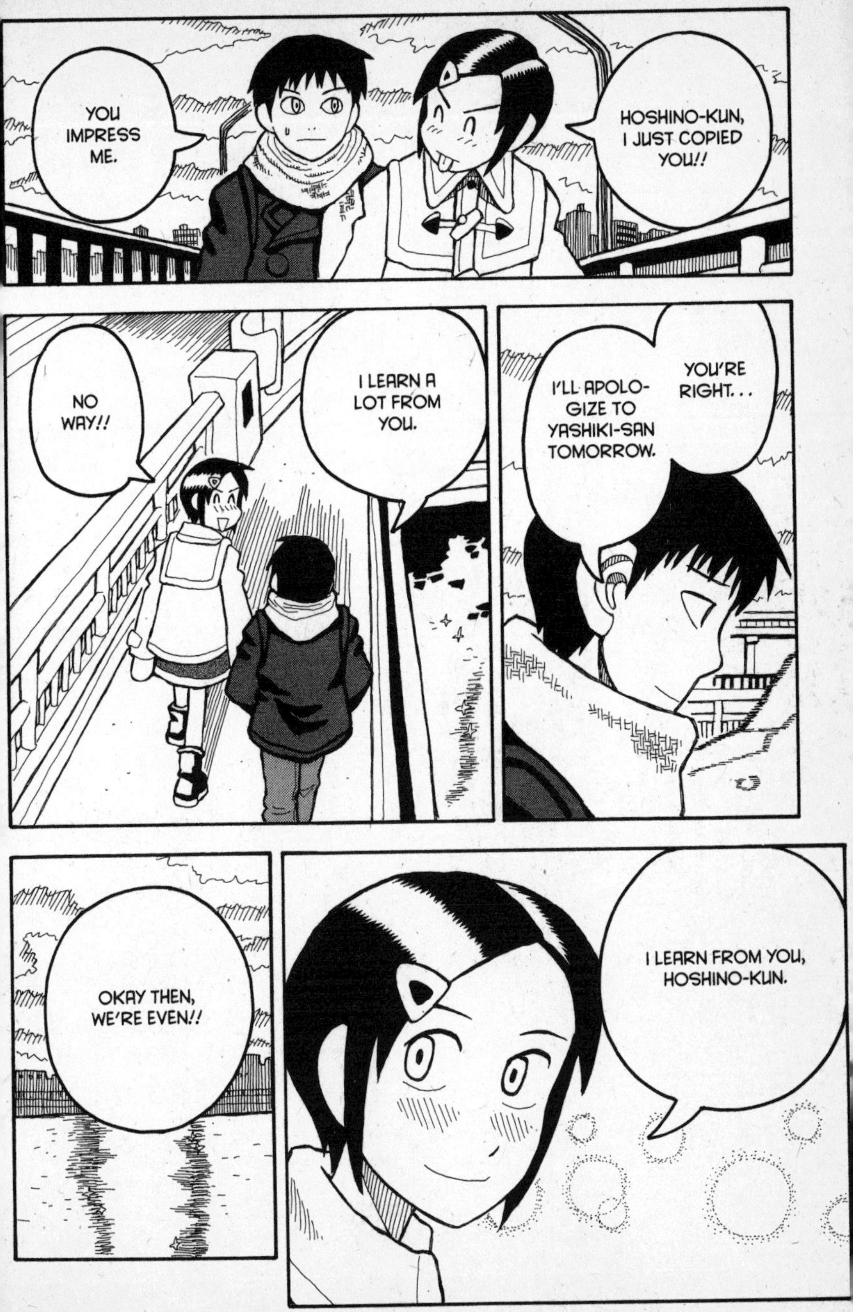
HOSHINO-KUN, I JUST COPIED YOU!!
YOU IMPRESS ME.
YOU'RE RIGHT...
I'LL APOLO-GIZE TO YASHIKI-SAN TOMORROW.
I LEARN A LOT FROM YOU.
NO WAY!!
I LEARN FROM YOU, HOSHINO-KUN.
OKAY THEN, WE'RE EVEN!!

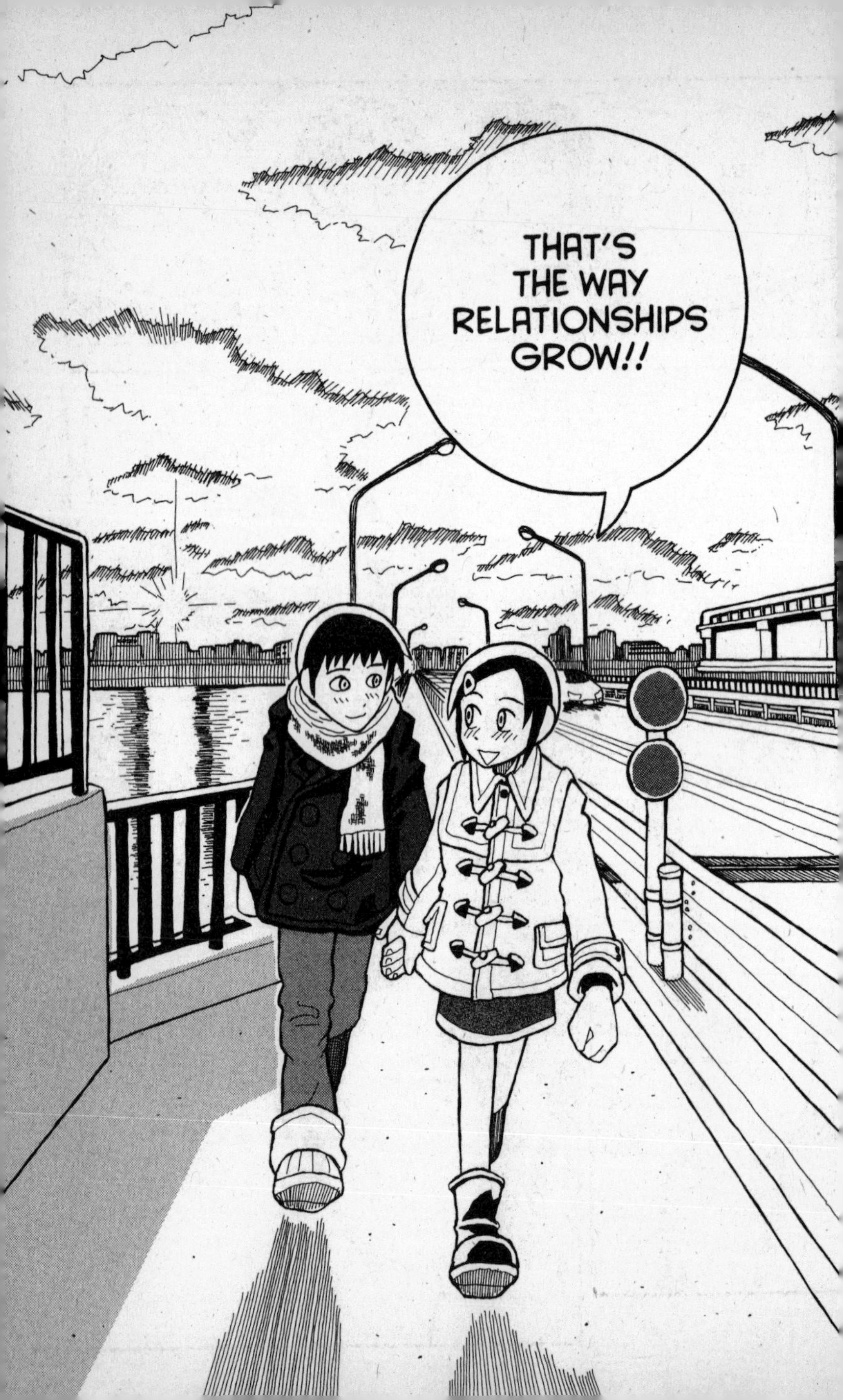
THAT'S THE WAY RELATIONSHIPS GROW!!

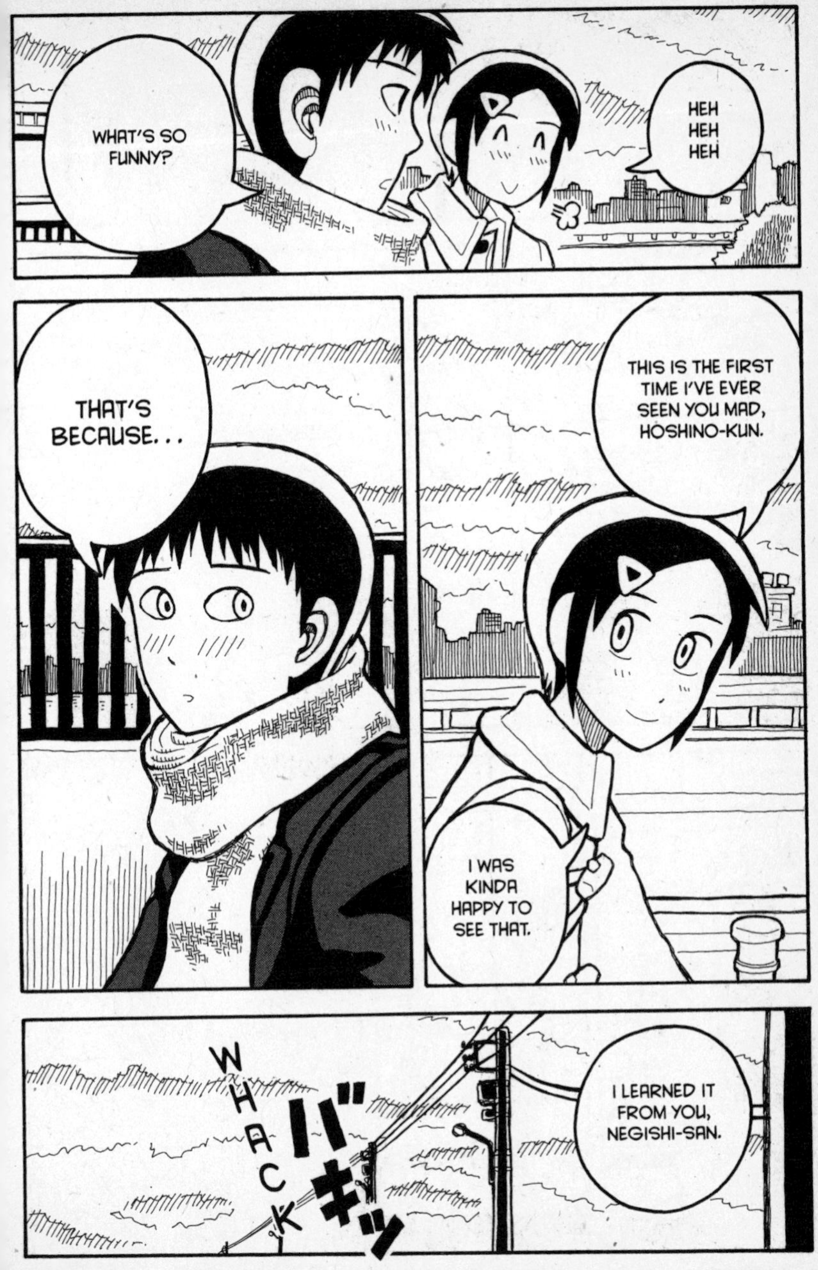
HEH HEH HEH
WHAT'S SO FUNNY?
THIS IS THE FIRST TIME I'VE EVER SEEN YOU MAD, HOSHINO-KUN.
I WAS KINDA HAPPY TO SEE THAT.
THAT'S BECAUSE...
I LEARNED IT FROM YOU, NEGISHI-SAN.
WHACK
バキッ

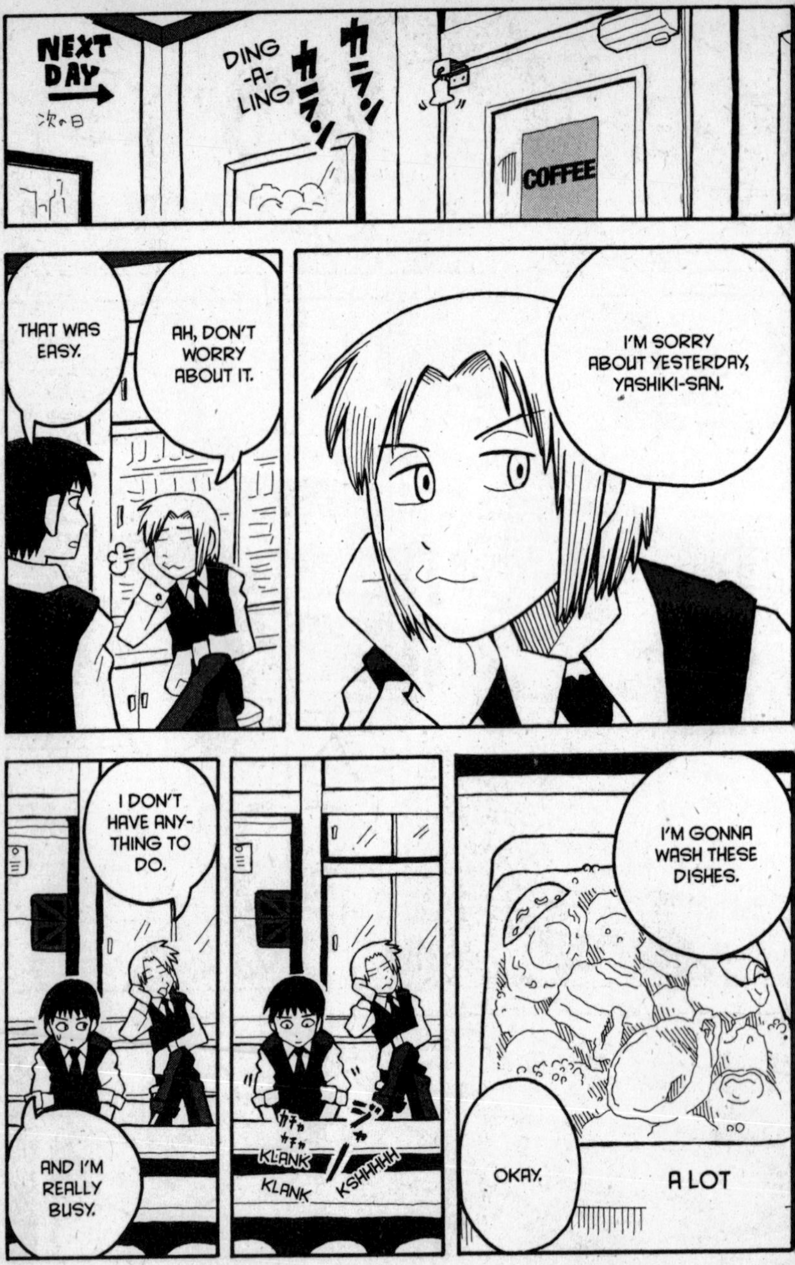
NEXT DAY
次の日
カラン
カラン
DING -A- LING
COFFEE
I'M SORRY ABOUT YESTERDAY, YASHIKI-SAN.
AH, DON'T WORRY ABOUT IT.
THAT WAS EASY.
I'M GONNA WASH THESE DISHES.
OKAY.
A LOT
ジャ
KSHHHH
カチャ カチャ
KLANK KLANK
I DON'T HAVE ANY-THING TO DO.
AND I'M REALLY BUSY.

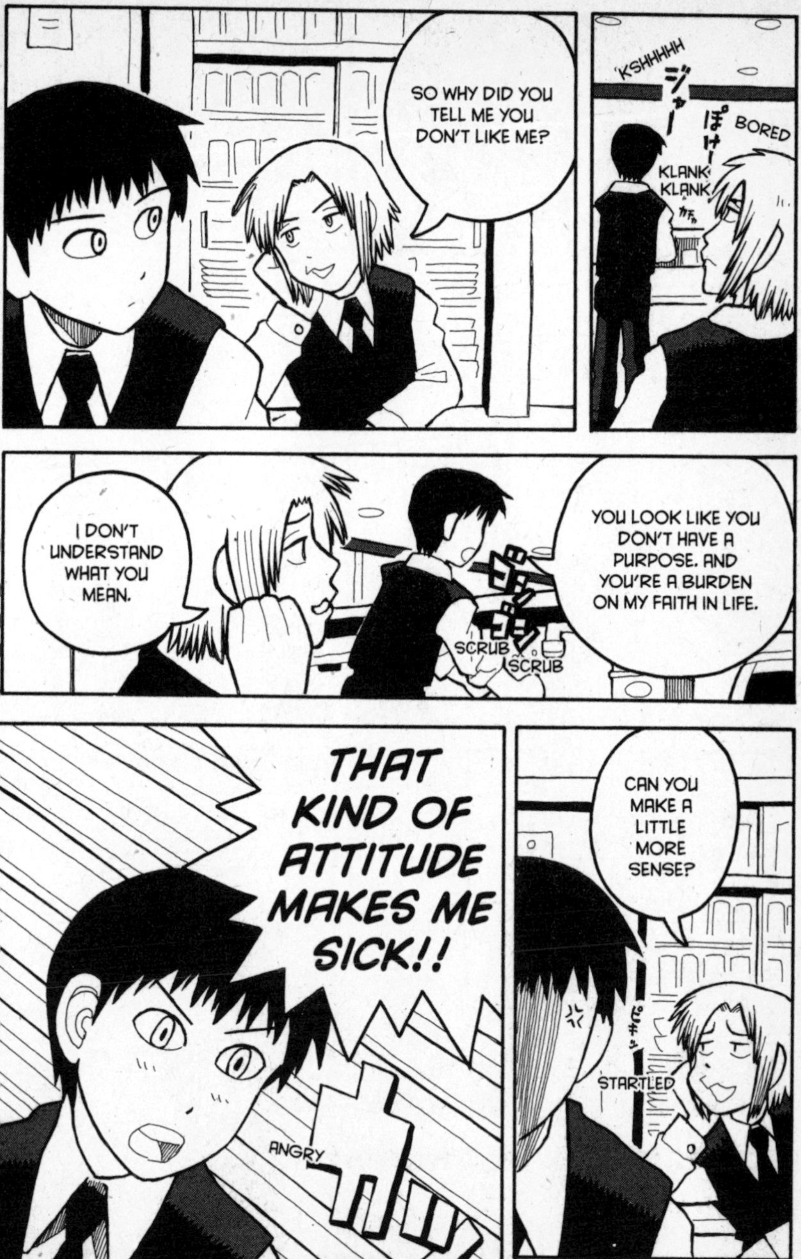
KSHHHHH
ジャー
ぽけー
BORED
KLANK KLANK
SO WHY DID YOU TELL ME YOU DON'T LIKE ME?
YOU LOOK LIKE YOU DON'T HAVE A PURPOSE. AND YOU'RE A BURDEN ON MY FAITH IN LIFE.
SCRUB SCRUB
I DON'T UNDERSTAND WHAT YOU MEAN.
CAN YOU MAKE A LITTLE MORE SENSE?
STARTLED
THAT KIND OF ATTITUDE MAKES ME SICK!!
ANGRY

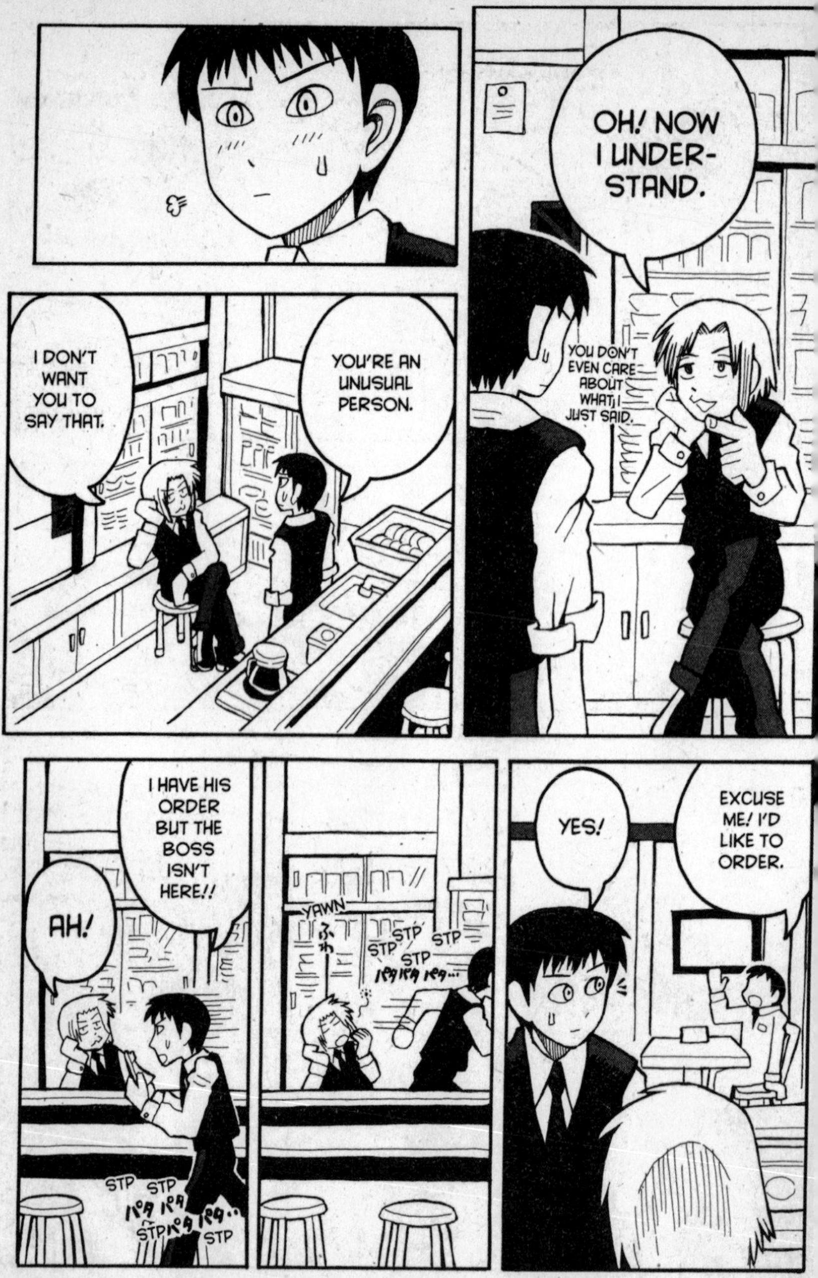
OH! NOW I UNDER-STAND.
YOU DON'T EVEN CARE ABOUT WHAT I JUST SAID.
YOU'RE AN UNUSUAL PERSON.
I DON'T WANT YOU TO SAY THAT.
EXCUSE ME! I'D LIKE TO ORDER.
YES!
YAWN
ふわ
STP STP STP STP
パタパタ パタ…
I HAVE HIS ORDER BUT THE BOSS ISN'T HERE!!
AH!
STP STP
パタ パタ
STP パタ パタ…
STP

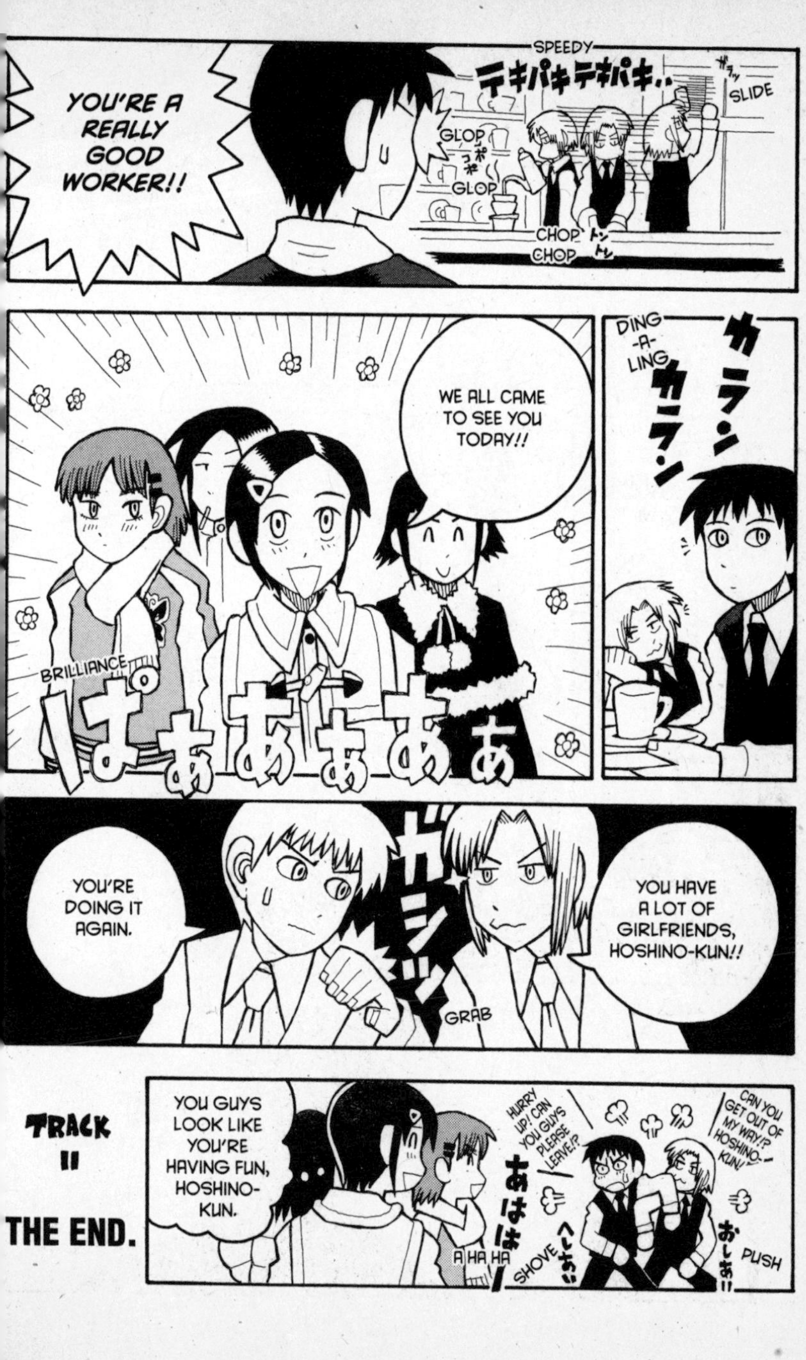
SPEEDY
テキパキテキパキ
ガラッ SLIDE
GLOP コポ GLOP
CHOP トントン CHOP
YOU'RE A REALLY GOOD WORKER!!
DING-A-LING
カランカラン
WE ALL CAME TO SEE YOU TODAY!!
BRILLIANCE
ぱあああああ
YOU HAVE A LOT OF GIRLFRIENDS, HOSHINO-KUN!!
ガシッ
GRAB
YOU'RE DOING IT AGAIN.
CAN YOU GET OUT OF MY WAY!? HOSHINO-KUN!
おしあ!! PUSH
HURRY UP! CAN YOU GUYS PLEASE LEAVE!?
へしあい SHOVE
あはは! A HA HA
YOU GUYS LOOK LIKE YOU'RE HAVING FUN, HOSHINO-KUN.

TRACK 11

THE END.

BONUS TRACK

おまけ

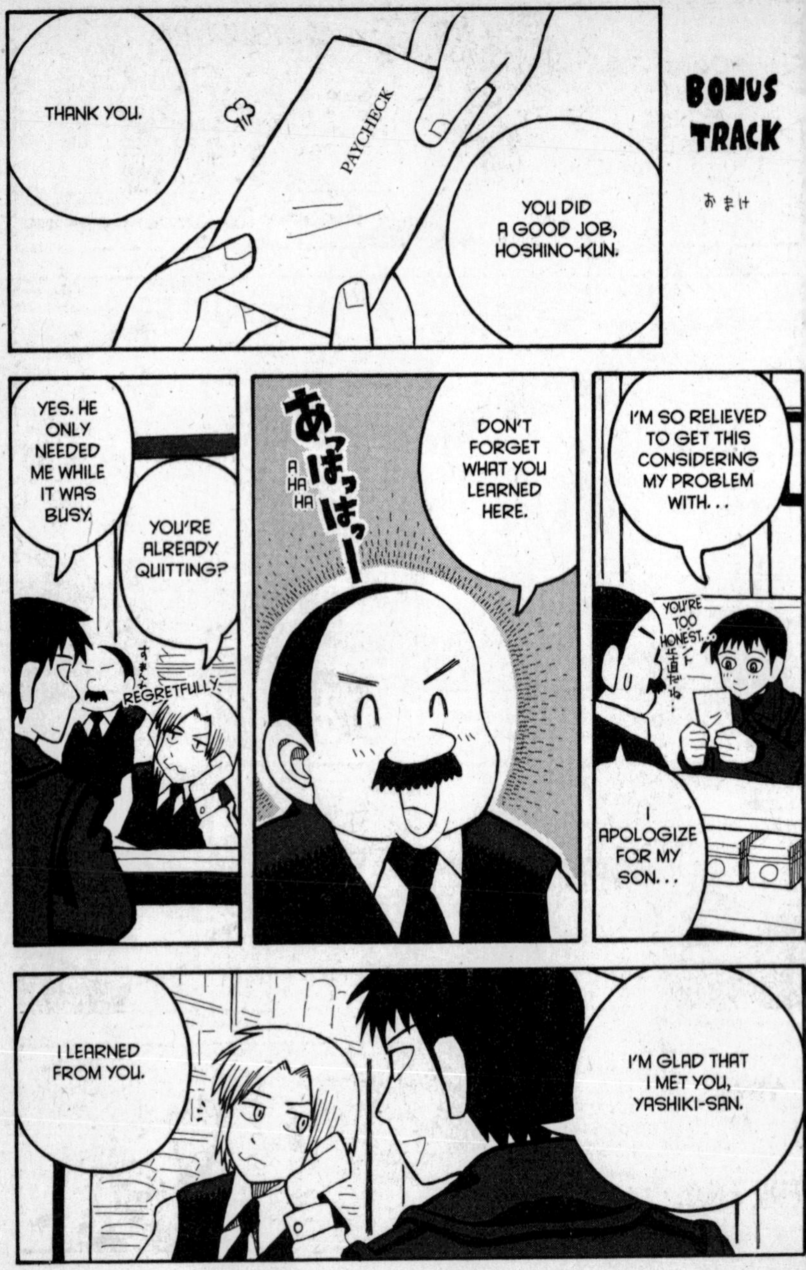
YOU DID A GOOD JOB, HOSHINO-KUN.
PAYCHECK
THANK YOU.
I'M SO RELIEVED TO GET THIS CONSIDERING MY PROBLEM WITH. . .
YOU'RE TOO HONEST. . .
I APOLOGIZE FOR MY SON. . .
DON'T FORGET WHAT YOU LEARNED HERE.
あっはっはー
A HA HA
YOU'RE ALREADY QUITTING?
YES. HE ONLY NEEDED ME WHILE IT WAS BUSY.
REGRETFULLY
I'M GLAD THAT I MET YOU, YASHIKI-SAN.
I LEARNED FROM YOU.

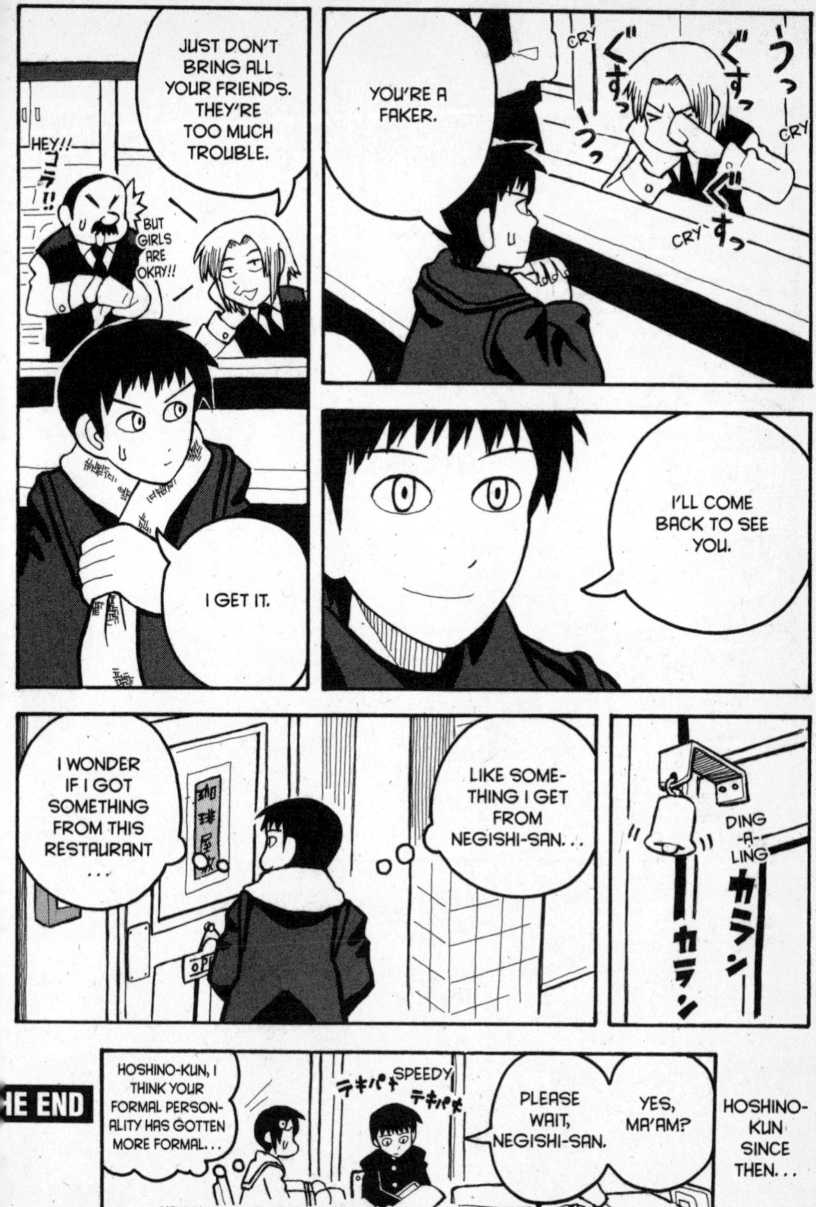
YOU'RE A FAKER.
うっ ぐすっ CRY
CRY
ぐすっ CRY
ぐすっ CRY
うっ
JUST DON'T BRING ALL YOUR FRIENDS. THEY'RE TOO MUCH TROUBLE.
HEY!! コラ!!
BUT GIRLS ARE OKAY!!
I'LL COME BACK TO SEE YOU.
I GET IT.
DING-A-LING カラン
カラン
LIKE SOMETHING I GET FROM NEGISHI-SAN...
I WONDER IF I GOT SOMETHING FROM THIS RESTAURANT...
HOSHINO-KUN SINCE THEN...
YES, MA'AM?
PLEASE WAIT, NEGISHI-SAN.
テキパキ SPEEDY テキパキ
HOSHINO-KUN, I THINK YOUR FORMAL PERSONALITY HAS GOTTEN MORE FORMAL...
HE TALKS LIKE HE'S SERVING AT THE RESTAURANT
HE END

▶▶ END ▶▶ LOVE ROMA 2 ▶▶ END

SERIES OUTLINE
BONUS TRACK

GO! S.C.D.!! SIDE B

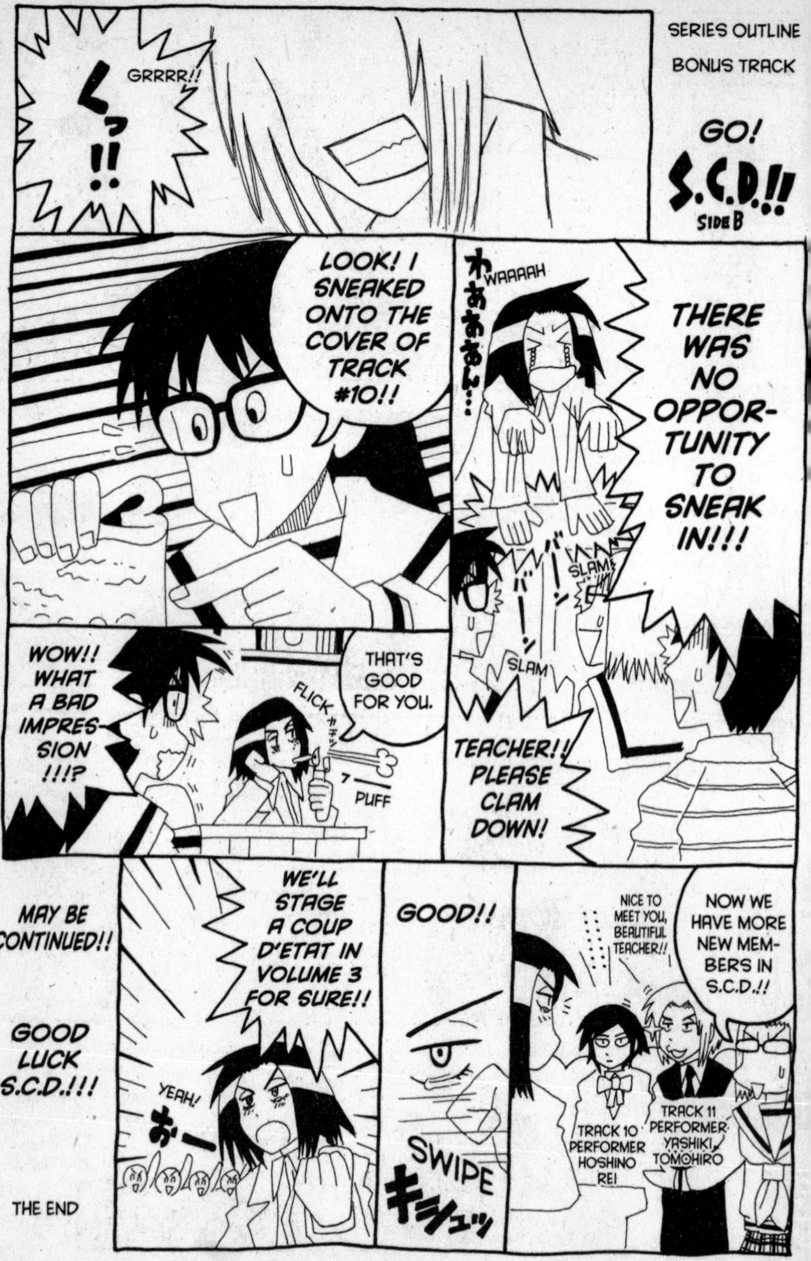

くっ!!
GRRRR!!
わああああん…
WAAAAAH
THERE WAS NO OPPORTUNITY TO SNEAK IN!!!
バーン
SLAM
バーン
SLAM
TEACHER!! PLEASE CLAM DOWN!
LOOK! I SNEAKED ONTO THE COVER OF TRACK #10!!
THAT'S GOOD FOR YOU.
カチッ
FLICK
PUFF
WOW!! WHAT A BAD IMPRESSION!!!?
NOW WE HAVE MORE NEW MEMBERS IN S.C.D.!!
NICE TO MEET YOU, BEAUTIFUL TEACHER!!
TRACK 11 PERFORMER YASHIKI TOMOHIRO
TRACK 10 PERFORMER HOSHINO REI
GOOD!!
キシュッ
SWIPE
WE'LL STAGE A COUP D'ETAT IN VOLUME 3 FOR SURE!!
おー
YEAH!

MAY BE CONTINUED!!

GOOD LUCK S.C.D.!!!

THE END

LINER NOTES

2

SERIES OUTLINE

BONUS TRACK AND EXPLANATION

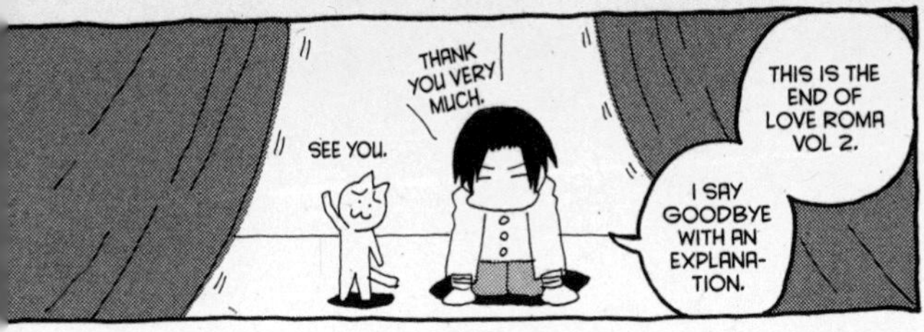

THIS IS THE END OF LOVE ROMA VOL 2.
I SAY GOODBYE WITH AN EXPLANATION.
THANK YOU VERY MUCH.
SEE YOU.

EXPLANATION

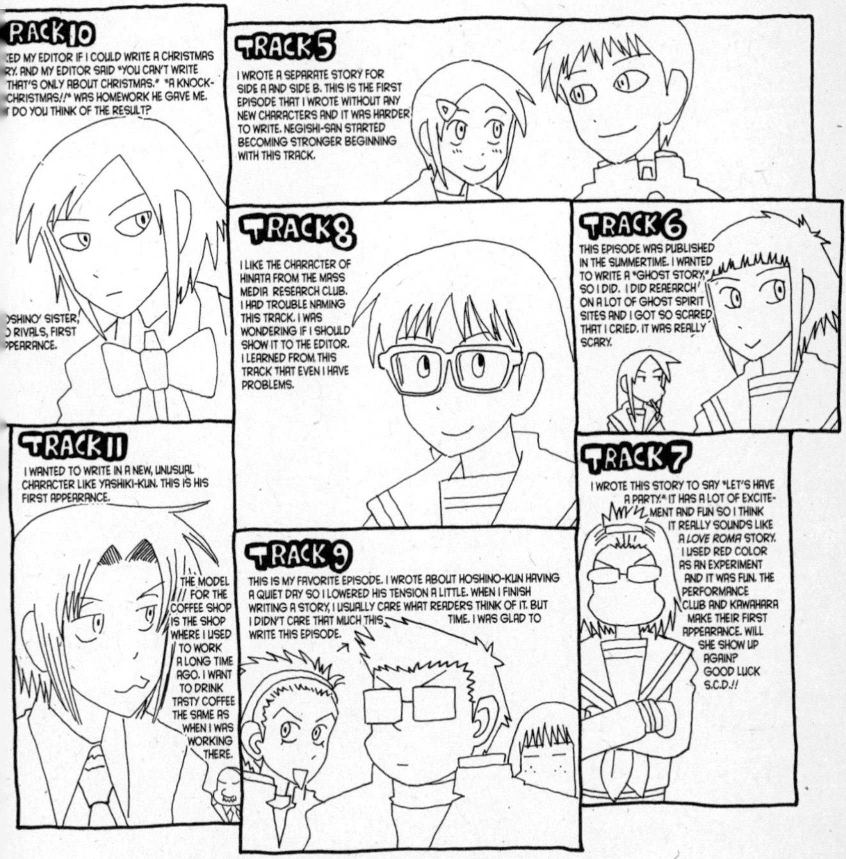

TRACK 5
I WROTE A SEPARATE STORY FOR SIDE A AND SIDE B. THIS IS THE FIRST EPISODE THAT I WROTE WITHOUT ANY NEW CHARACTERS AND IT WAS HARDER TO WRITE. NEGISHI-SAN STARTED BECOMING STRONGER BEGINNING WITH THIS TRACK.
TRACK 6
THIS EPISODE WAS PUBLISHED IN THE SUMMERTIME. I WANTED TO WRITE A "GHOST STORY," SO I DID. I DID REAEARCH ON A LOT OF GHOST SPIRIT SITES AND I GOT SO SCARED THAT I CRIED. IT WAS REALLY SCARY.
TRACK 8
I LIKE THE CHARACTER OF HINATA FROM THE MASS MEDIA RESEARCH CLUB. I HAD TROUBLE NAMING THIS TRACK. I WAS WONDERING IF I SHOULD SHOW IT TO THE EDITOR. I LEARNED FROM THIS TRACK THAT EVEN I HAVE PROBLEMS.
TRACK 7
I WROTE THIS STORY TO SAY "LET'S HAVE A PARTY." IT HAS A LOT OF EXCITEMENT AND FUN SO I THINK IT REALLY SOUNDS LIKE A *LOVE ROMA* STORY. I USED RED COLOR AS AN EXPERIMENT AND IT WAS FUN. THE PERFORMANCE CLUB AND KAWAHARA MAKE THEIR FIRST APPEARANCE. WILL SHE SHOW UP AGAIN? GOOD LUCK S.C.D.!!
TRACK 9
THIS IS MY FAVORITE EPISODE. I WROTE ABOUT HOSHINO-KUN HAVING A QUIET DAY SO I LOWERED HIS TENSION A LITTLE. WHEN I FINISH WRITING A STORY, I USUALLY CARE WHAT READERS THINK OF IT. BUT I DIDN'T CARE THAT MUCH THIS TIME. I WAS GLAD TO WRITE THIS EPISODE.
RACK 10
KED MY EDITOR IF I COULD WRITE A CHRISTMAS RY. AND MY EDITOR SAID "YOU CAN'T WRITE THAT'S ONLY ABOUT CHRISTMAS." "A KNOCK-CHRISTMAS!!" WAS HOMEWORK HE GAVE ME. T DO YOU THINK OF THE RESULT?
OSHINO' SISTER, O RIVALS, FIRST PPEARANCE.
TRACK 11
I WANTED TO WRITE IN A NEW, UNUSUAL CHARACTER LIKE YASHIKI-KUN. THIS IS HIS FIRST APPEARANCE.
THE MODEL FOR THE COFFEE SHOP IS THE SHOP WHERE I USED TO WORK A LONG TIME AGO. I WANT TO DRINK TASTY COFFEE THE SAME AS WHEN I WAS WORKING THERE.

I'M REALLY APPRECIATIVE TO EVERYBODY THAT BOUGHT AND READ THIS BOOK.
LOVE. HP "NET TOKAYIWASOU TEMPORARY"

HTTP://MEMBERS.EDOGAWA.HOME.NE.JP/POO1007/
FUNUKE LABEL

FUNUKE LABEL

AUTHOR PROFILE

MINORU TOYODA

MANGA DEBUT

The first episode of *Love Roma* in Kodansha's *Afternoon* magazine.

AWARDS

Toyoda won a prize for *Reonizumu* in 2000, but he won first place for *Love Roma* in 2002. The award was the "Afternoon Shiki Prize," which is awarded to new cartoonists.

DATE OF BIRTH

Oct. 7, 1971

STATUS

Living with his parents.

FAVORITE THING

Nothing but comics.

LEAST FAVORITE THING

The Occult.

ASPIRATIONS

Toyoda hopes that his comics will overcome differences in language or culture and will be enjoyed by a large number of people.

HIDDEN TRACK

In Japan, virtually all manga are printed with a dust jacket. In the original *tankoban* (the Japanese term for a trade paperback) for *Love Roma*, the "hidden tracks" are hidden under the dust jacket, printed on the physical cover of the book itself. While this does happen in Japan from time to time, it remains uncommon; most covers are either black-and-white versions of the color cover on the dust jacket, or just the logo of the magazine in which the story was serialized.

This track features a Japanese cultural reference that needs a little explanation. (Like most jokes, it takes a little of the humor away if you have to explain it, but it was either this or changing it to an American pop culture reference). Besides, we kept the reference in volume 1, so it would have been pretty silly to change it here.

This sequence once again uses the "*tsukkomi* and *boke*" humor that is so popular in Japan. *Tsukomu*, meaning to dig at, is the inspiration for half of a comedic style in Japan known as "*tsukkomi* and *boke*." One person plays the role of the *tsukkomi* and the other is the *boke*. The *boke* will say something stupid or make a silly mistake then the *tsukkomi* will correct them, usually accompanied by a smack on the head. In this strip, Negishi is going crazy hitting everyone because someone did a stupid *boke* to her and she's retaliating by doing *tsukkomi* to everyone (hitting them on the head). The only way to stop her is to do a *boke* that she'll like.

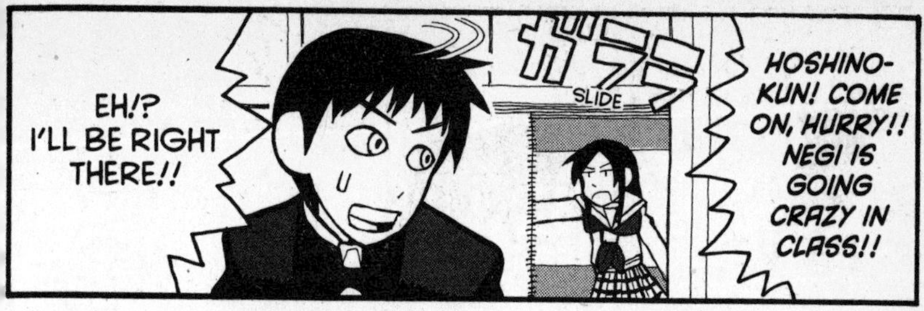
HOSHINO-KUN! COME ON, HURRY!! NEGI IS GOING CRAZY IN CLASS!!
ガララ
SLIDE
EH!? I'LL BE RIGHT THERE!!

LOVE ROMA **HIDDEN TRACK** **LET'S BE BOKÉ FOR NEGISHI-SAN"**

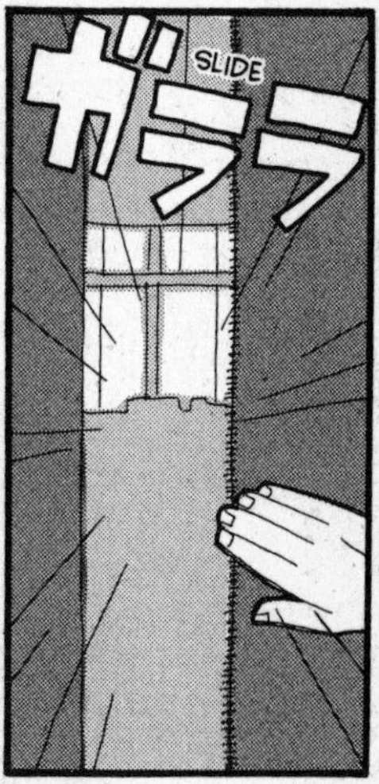
ガララ
SLIDE

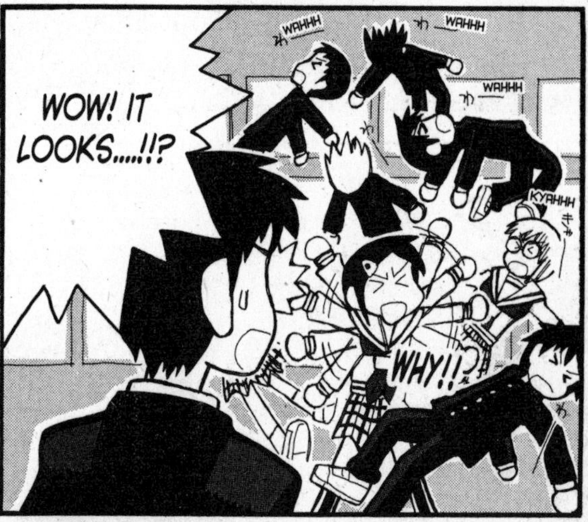
WAHHH
WAHHH
WAHHH
KYAHHH
WOW! IT LOOKS....!!?
WHY!!

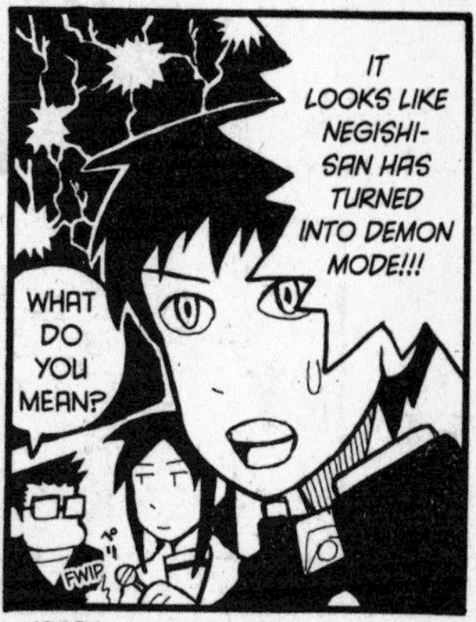
IT LOOKS LIKE NEGISHI-SAN HAS TURNED INTO DEMON MODE!!!
WHAT DO YOU MEAN?
FWIP

NOSEY

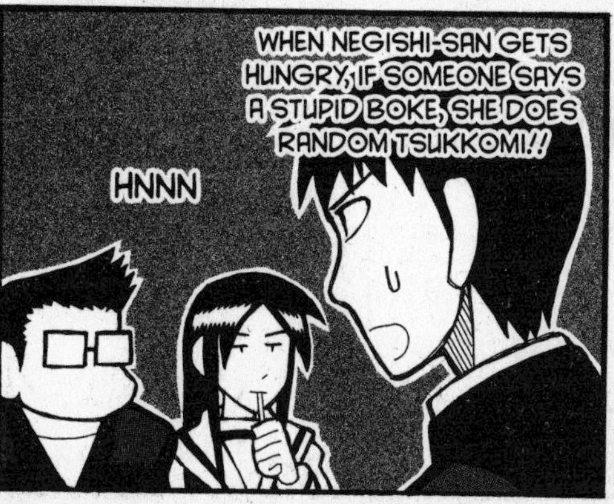
WHEN NEGISHI-SAN GETS HUNGRY, IF SOMEONE SAYS A STUPID BOKE, SHE DOES RANDOM TSUKKOMI!!
HNNN

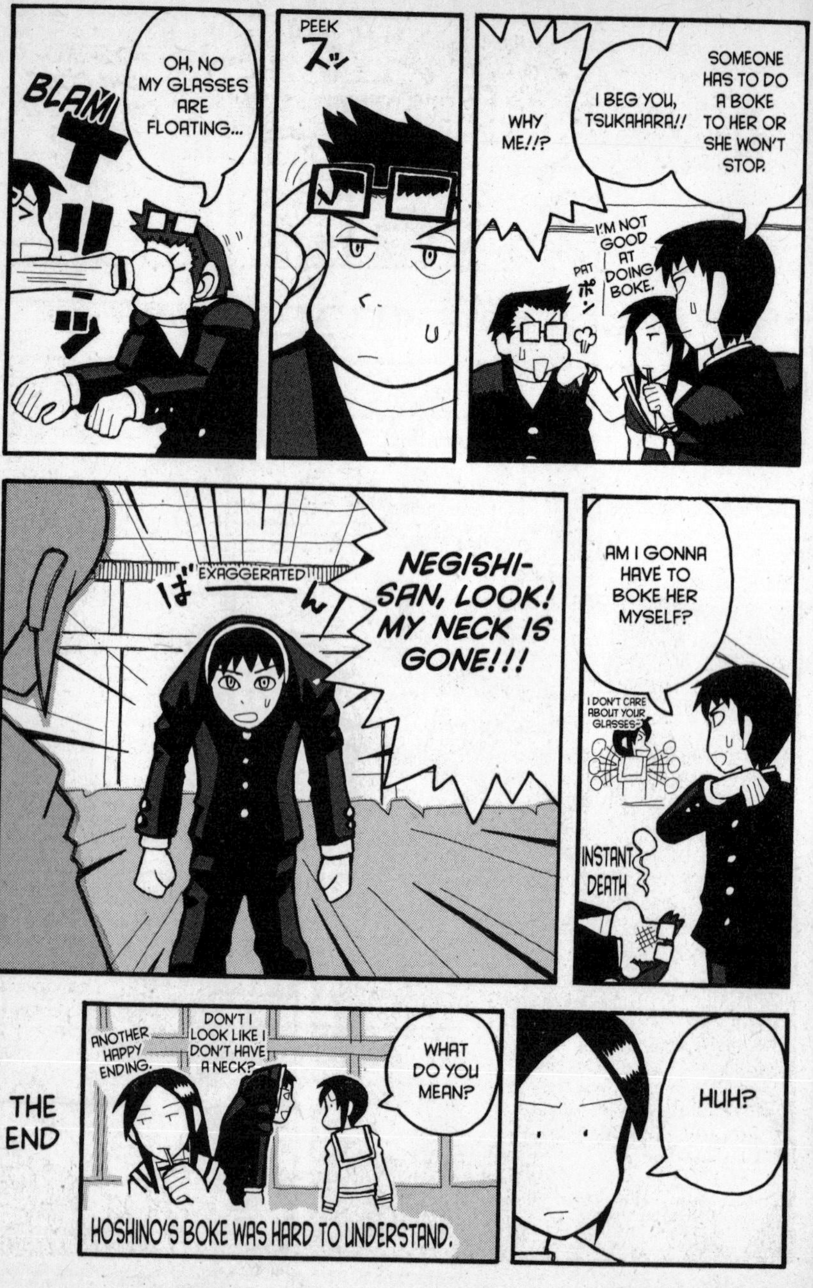
SOMEONE HAS TO DO A BOKE TO HER OR SHE WON'T STOP.
I BEG YOU, TSUKAHARA!!
WHY ME!!?
I'M NOT GOOD AT DOING BOKE.
PAT
ポン
PEEK
スッ
OH, NO MY GLASSES ARE FLOATING...
BLAM
AM I GONNA HAVE TO BOKE HER MYSELF?
I DON'T CARE ABOUT YOUR GLASSES-
INSTANT DEATH
NEGISHI-SAN, LOOK! MY NECK IS GONE!!!
EXAGGERATED
ば――ん
HUH?
WHAT DO YOU MEAN?
DON'T I LOOK LIKE I DON'T HAVE A NECK?
ANOTHER HAPPY ENDING.
HOSHINO'S BOKE WAS HARD TO UNDERSTAND.
THE END

HOSHINO-KUN'S DINNER

TRACK 10
LATER ON

NEGISHI-SAN SAID MY SISTER IS A NICE PERSON.
SHE MISUNDER-STOOD ME.
もく もく もく
CHEW CHEW
SHE LOOKS UNFRIENDLY BUT MAYBE IT WAS JUST AWKWARD.
REI-SAN! REI-SAN!
SHE'S SEEMS LIKE A VERY WARM PERSON. THAT'S WHAT NEGISHI SAID.
A HA HA
あはは—
.....I'M HAPPY TO HEAR THAT.....
ぼそっ
MUMBLE
DID YOU SAY SOME-THING?
NO, NOTHING
STOP TALKING, JUST EAT.
もく
CHEW
CHEW CHEW
もく もく

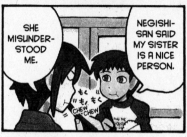

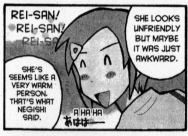

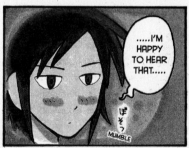

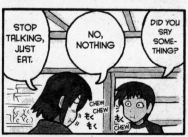

THE END

Translation Notes

Japanese is a tricky language for most Westerners, and translation is often more art than science. For your edification and reading pleasure, here are notes on some of the places where we could have gon in a different direction in our translation of the work, or where a Japanese cultural reference is used.

Like a Fish in Water, page 5

This expression is used by Yoshitsune because he is so excited to talk about sex, he has been given a new lease on life—like when a fish is thrown back into the water. The Japanese idiom is *mizu o eta sakana no yoda.*

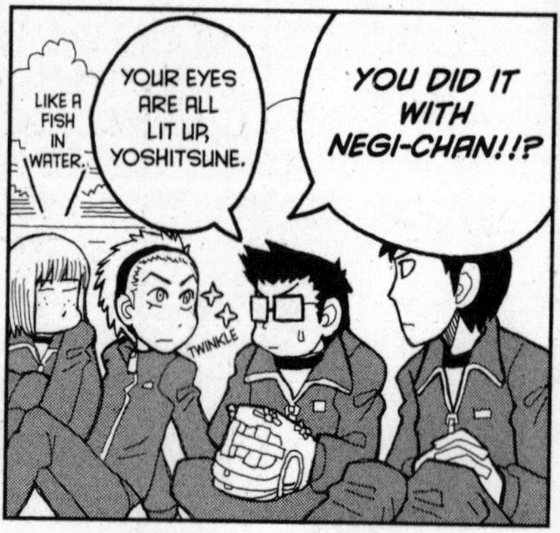
YOU DID IT WITH NEGI-CHAN!!?
YOUR EYES ARE ALL LIT UP, YOSHITSUNE.
LIKE A FISH IN WATER.
TWINKLE

Me, Myself and I, page 20

In English, "I" means "I" no matter if it is said by a male or female speaker. In kanji, one of the Japanese alphabets, there can be two different words depending on the gender of the speaker, and in the original Japanese, the text in the balloon reflects this. Unfortunately, there's not any way for us to show this in English; fortunately, it's not really a big deal here.

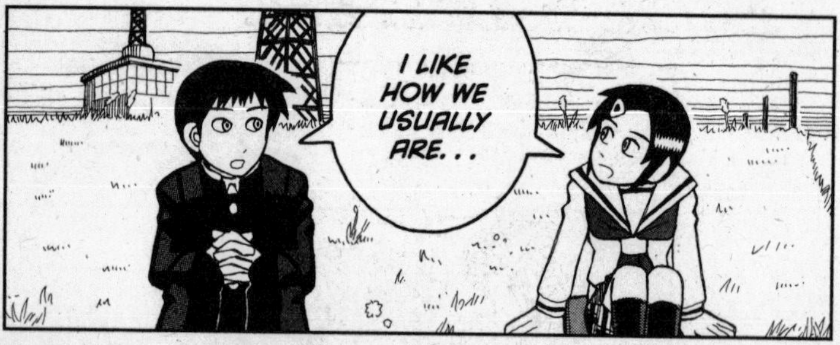
I LIKE HOW WE USUALLY ARE. . .

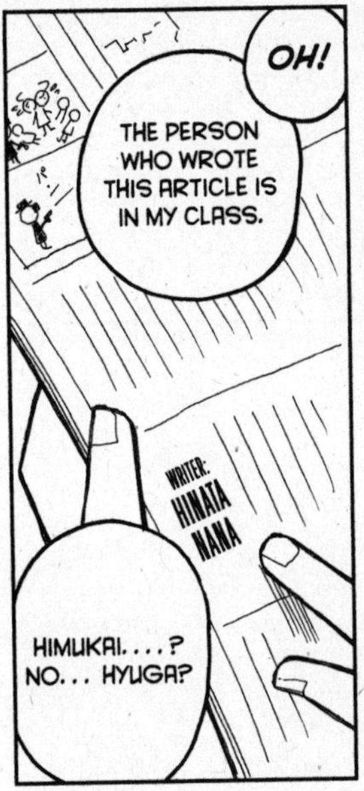
OH!
THE PERSON WHO WROTE THIS ARTICLE IS IN MY CLASS.
WRITER: HINATA NANA
HIMUKAI....? NO... HYUGA?

Himukai...?, page 85

Pronunciation of Japanese kanji can be very confusing as illustrated in this panel. Kanji, which number in the thousands, were derived from the Chinese and were adapted to fit the same words or ideas in Japanese. The result is that each kanji will have a Chinese pronunciation as well as one or more Japanese pronunciations. Familiarity is their guide but as illustrated here, personal names can be tricky. Hoshino is trying to read the name of a classmate but does not know how the kanji (Chinese characters) should be read.

Domei, page 129

Domei means "alliance" in English. In the acronym S.C.D., Toyoda chose to use the English words "Sub-Characters," for the S and C, then used Japanese for the D.

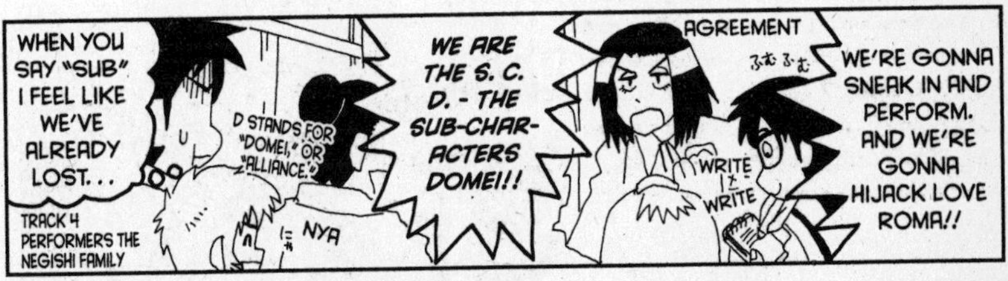
WE'RE GONNA SNEAK IN AND PERFORM. AND WE'RE GONNA HIJACK LOVE ROMA!!
AGREEMENT
ふむふむ
WRITE WRITE
WE ARE THE S. C. D. - THE SUB-CHARACTERS DOMEI!!
D STANDS FOR "DOMEI," OR "ALLIANCE."
NYA
WHEN YOU SAY "SUB" I FEEL LIKE WE'VE ALREADY LOST...
TRACK 4 PERFORMERS THE NEGISHI FAMILY

Christmas, page 131

In Japan Christmas is not celebrated as in America. It is more of a celebration for lovers than for a religious celebration. This is what Yoshitsune is referring to when he says it's a "holy" night for men and women. It's usually an important "date" night.

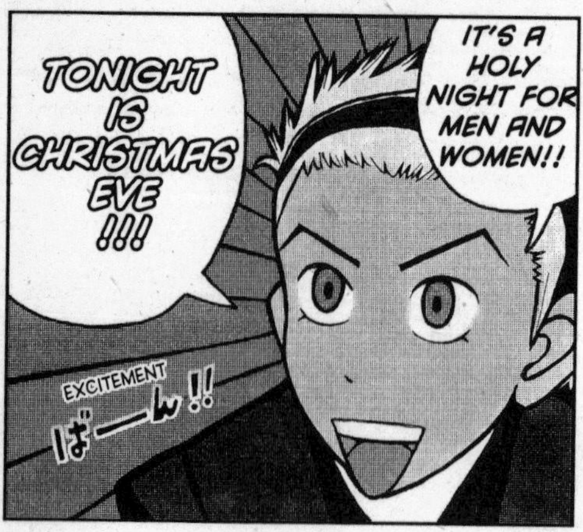

IT'S A HOLY NIGHT FOR MEN AND WOMEN!!
TONIGHT IS CHRISTMAS EVE!!!
EXCITEMENT
ばーん!!

Zero Sen, page 144

Here is another example of the variations found for pronunciations of kanji in Japanese. Rei is explaining that her name, although pronounced "Rei," uses the same kanji as the "Zero" part in "Zero sen," which is where the nickname for the Japanese "Zero" fighter planes in World War 2 came from. All kanji have more than one pronunciation which can make reading Japanese a challenge even for the Japanese.

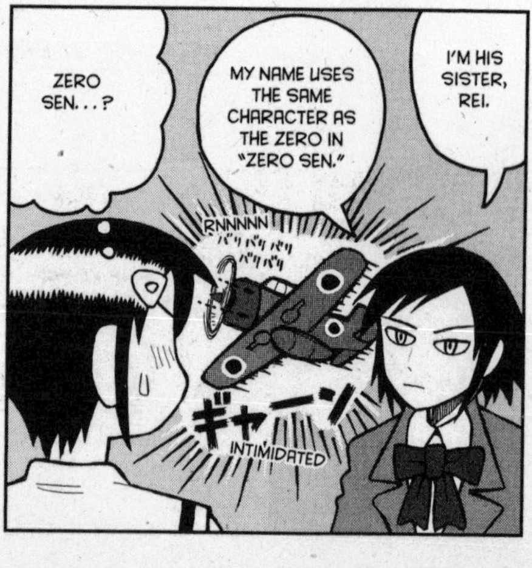

I'M HIS SISTER, REI.
MY NAME USES THE SAME CHARACTER AS THE ZERO IN "ZERO SEN."
ZERO SEN...?
RNNNNN
ギャーン
INTIMIDATED

Preview of Love Roma Volume 3

We're pleased to present you a preview from *Love Roma* Volume 3. This volume will be available in English in summer 2006, but for now you'll have to make do with Japanese!

珍しいですね こんな時季に

もうすぐ春なのにね——

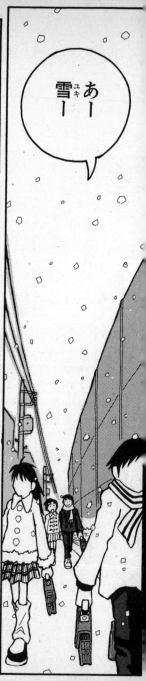

あー雪ー

恐ろしいもの?

そういえば もう一年も終わりですね

その前に恐ろしいものがあるよー

オハヨー

テスト‼

test /tést/ 图
検査・試験

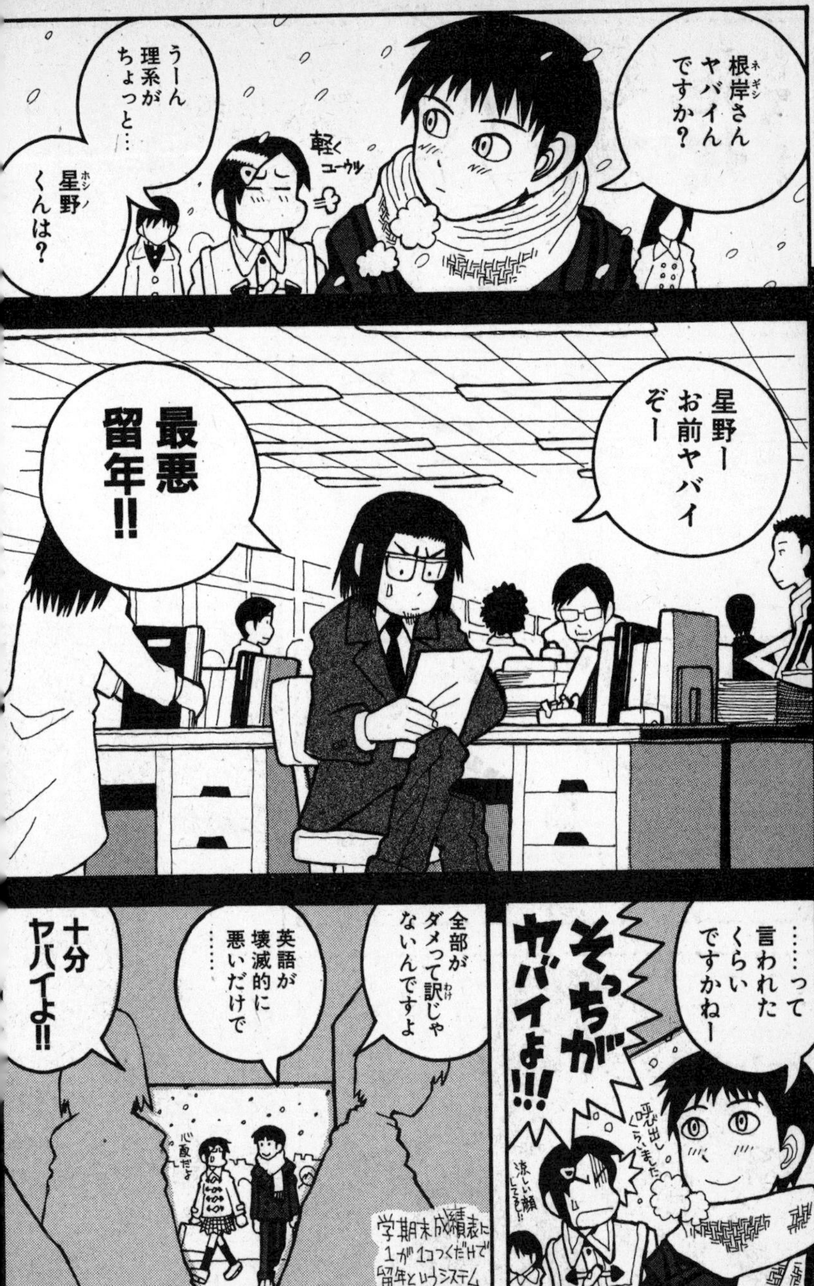
根岸さん ヤバイん ですか？
軽くユーウツ
うーん 理系が ちょっと…
星野くんは？
星野ー お前ヤバイ ぞー
最悪 留年!!
……って 言われた くらい ですかねー
そっちがヤバイよ!!!
呼び出しくらいました
涼しい顔してる!!
全部が ダメって訳じゃ ないんですよ
英語が 壊滅的に 悪いだけで ……
十分 ヤバイよ!!
心配だよ
学期末成績表に 1が1コつくだけで 留年というシステム

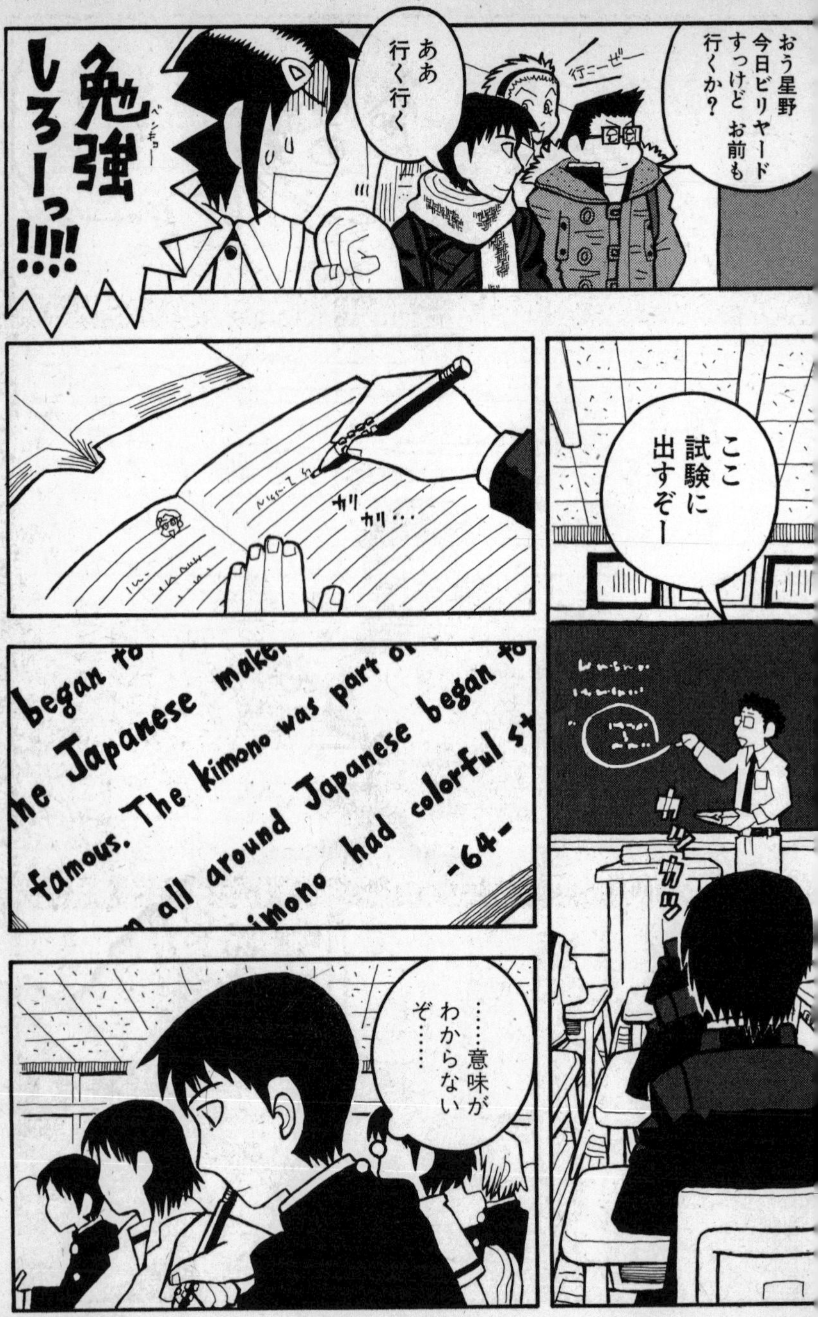
おう星野 今日ビリヤードすっけど お前も行くか？
行こーぜー
ああ 行く行く
勉強(ベンキョー)しろーっ!!!!
ここ試験に出すぞー
カッ カッ
カリ カリ…
began to
the Japanese make
famous. The kimono was part of
all around Japanese began to
kimono had colorful st
-64-
……意味が わからない ぞ……

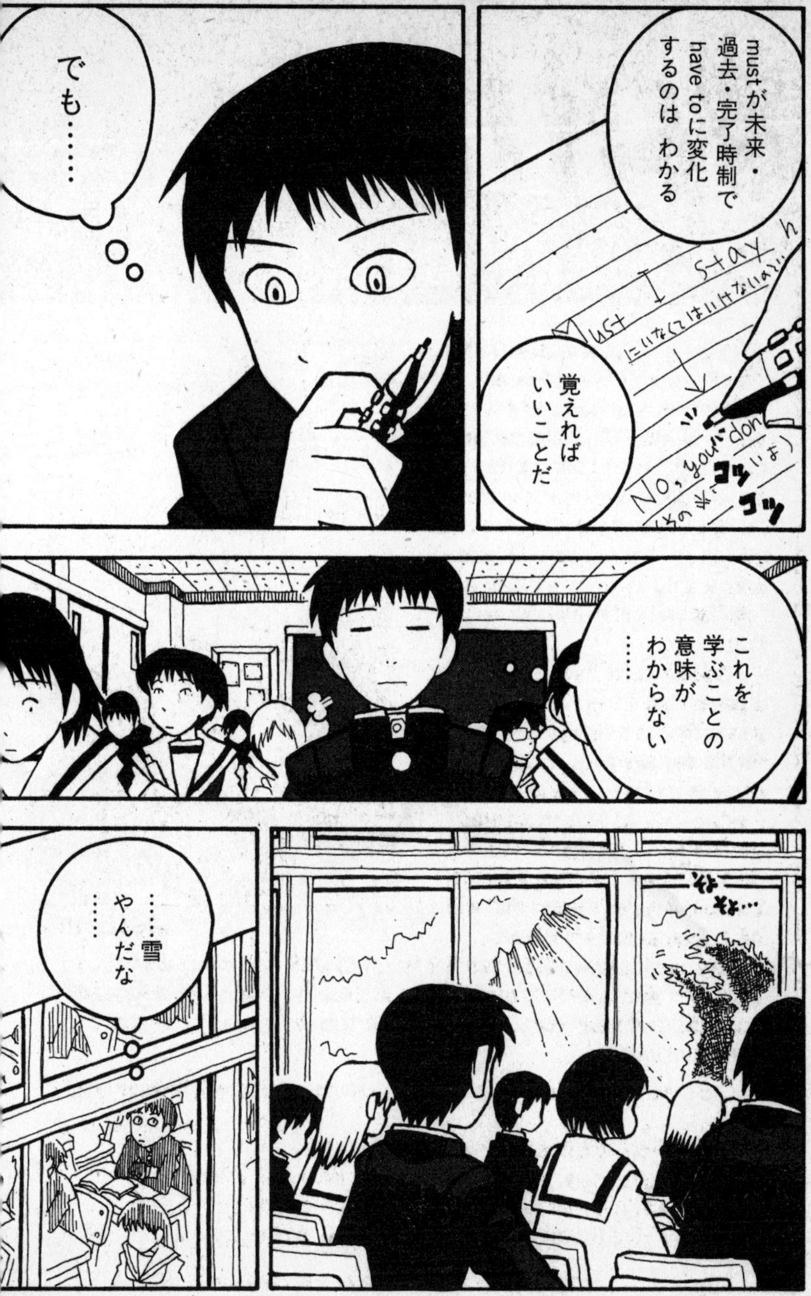
mustが未来・過去・完了時制で have toに変化するのは わかる
覚えれば いいことだ
コツ
コツ
でも……
これを学ぶことの意味がわからない……
そよ そよ…
……雪やんだな……

Gacha Gacha

By Hiroyuki Tamakoshi

Kouhei is your typical Japanese high school student—he's usually late, he loves beef bowls, he pals around with his buddies, and he's got his first-ever crush on his childhood friend Kurara. Before he can express his feelings, however, Kurara heads off to Hawaii with her mother for summer vacation. When she returns, she seems like a totally different person . . . and that's because she is! While she was away, Kurara somehow developed an alternate personality: Arisa! And where Kurara has no time for boys, Arisa isn't interested in much else. Now Kouhei must help protect his friend's secret, and make sure that Arisa doesn't do anything Kurara would regret!

HIROYUKI TAMAKOSHI

Ages: 16+

Special extras in each volume! Read them all!

VISIT WWW.DELREYMANGA.COM TO:
• View release date calendars for upcoming volumes
• Sign up for Del Rey's free manga e-newsletter
• Find out the latest about new Del Rey Manga series

Sugar Sugar Rune

BY MOYOCO ANNO

QUEEN OF HEARTS

Chocolat and Vanilla are young witch princesses from a magical land. They've come to Earth to compete in a contest—whichever girl captures the most hearts will become queen! While living in a boarding school, they must make as many boys fall in love with them as possible if they want to achieve their goal. Standing against them are a pair of rival princes looking to capture their hearts because they want to be king!

There's danger for the witch-girls, though: If they give their hearts to a human, they may never return to the Magical World....

Ages: 10 +

Special extras in each volume! Read them all!

STOP!

YOU'RE GOING THE WRONG WAY!

MANGA IS A COMPLETELY DIFFERENT TYPE OF READING EXPERIENCE.

TO START AT THE BEGINNING, GO TO THE END!

THAT'S RIGHT!

AUTHENTIC MANGA IS READ THE TRADITIONAL JAPANESE WAY—FROM RIGHT TO LEFT. EXACTLY THE OPPOSITE OF HOW AMERICAN BOOKS ARE READ. IT'S EASY TO FOLLOW: ST GO TO THE OTHER END OF THE BOOK, AND READ EACH PAGE —AND EACH PANEL—FROM RIGHT SIDE TO LEFT SIDE, STARTING AT THE TOP RIGHT. NOW YOU'RE EXPERIENCING MANGA AS IT WAS MEANT TO BE.